# Financial Planning Fiduciary Standards

## Under

# Dodd Frank

# Financial Planning Fiduciary Standards

## Under

# Dodd Frank

Mandatory Knowledge and Application of investments, insurance and annuities

Errold F. Moody Jr
PhD, MSFP, MBA, LLB, BSCE

Life and Disability Insurance Analyst

Registered Investment Adviser

ISBN 9780615596532

LCCN

Cover Art- Kartika Aranda

# Acknowledgements

I have read hundreds of text books, hundreds of thousands of articles and various types of research. But there are two individuals who stand out.

**Peter L. Bernstein** provided insight to the investment industry like no other.

**Benoit Mandelbrot's** insight to risk was absolutely illuminating.

They both passed away in 2010 but they left legacies that should never be forgotten. Though I point out their work repeatedly herein, I must reiterate that anyone who even remotely thinks they understand risk MUST review their work.

*

# Contents

FINANCIAL PLANNING
FIDUCIARY STANDARDS UNDER DODD FRANK

# Foreword

About 7 years ago, I wrote No Nonsense Finance (NNF) through McGraw Hill. It referenced all areas of personal finance such as insurance, long term care, ethics, etc., and of course investments. Financial Planning Fiduciary Standards under Dodd Frank (FPFSDF) focuses on the fiduciary elements demanded of financial advisers/planners/consultants et al with specific reference and more detail to the risk and rewards of investing before, during and after the debacles of 2000 and 2008. Of course, such risks easily translate over to insurance and annuities as well since the bulk of products have changed dramatically in the use of guarantees from losses, indexing, guaranteed minimum withdrawals for retirement income and much, much more.

In NNF, Mcgraw Hill wanted to fully eliminate the chapter on Ethics and Fiduciary Duty since 'nobody likes to read that stuff". They probably were right and I had to fight to get some of it in. It is true in this business that most of the effort towards ethics, knowledge etc. has been universally rewarded with.....nothing.

But I am nothing if not stubborn and the current focus on exemplary duty gives me another chance to make a difference. But it still won't be easy. Consumer's hubris in estimating their own capacity for understanding difficult material is only matched by an entire industry of journalists, Congressmen, attorneys, SEC, FINRA, university scholars, consumer unions and more that simply never looked at the bottom line of this business. It is truly amazing how far Dodd Frank has come when nary a one understands the risks of investing. The vast bulk of financial 'whatevers' are no better and have had nil knowledge of what they were/are doing because they have never been trained in the fundamentals of investing or insurance. Licensing knowledge is abysmal. Certainly little to do with real life. And then we can go back to the regulators and the licensing requirements- none have ever required licensees to know the real life application of product to even basic suitability levels. It becomes 'apparent' every time you read a scholarly article such as Financial Advisors: A Case of Babysitters?

http://papers.ssrn.com/sol3/papers.cfm?abstract_id=1360440& To wit, "The Role of Financial Advice- There is a limited but budding theoretical literature on the possible role of financial advisors. Current theoretical work but also policy debate on financial regulation seem to be based on **the idea that financial advisors know what is good for individual customers** but have an incentive to misrepresent this and to take advantage of their customers, who are typically uninformed and cannot figure out the poor quality of advice. Regulation is then needed to make sure that this conflict of incentives is dealt with."

The flaw is that such reviews accept as universal fact that a financial advisor really ***does*** know what to do. The Dodd Frank bill- and I am only dealing with the element of financial advice and the associated fiduciary duty- starts from a 'non factual' and 'non supported' position advocated by the industry and planning organizations galore that their representatives are already extremely knowledgeable and held to the highest standards.

Nope

It is true that certain material can- and is- being misrepresented intentionally. But the problem not addressed by such authors is that very, very few advisors know what they are doing in the first place. Information incorrectly stated by 'financial advisers' (known in the trade as being conveniently stupid or dumb honest) is little different in its ultimate consequences.

Peter Bernstein noted, "Financial planning, like brain surgery, is an extraordinarily precise business. Small mistakes and the wrong tools can just as easily undermine as improve financial health." (For early pundits of this reading, consider the unnecessary losses of 44% and 57% and the consequences to the public.)

These are the fatal flaws in the bill and in those that have attempted to offer their interpretation of what is right without the knowledge of what must be done *first and foremost*. It is absolutely true that a fiduciary standard need be applied- but without the appropriate knowledge, the effort can and will be bastardized by an industry that has money as its pure fiduciary. As an example, have you really seen any of the captains of industry directly involved in causing the meltdown of 2008 go to jail? AIG? Countrywide? Bear Stearns? Mortgage Brokers? Stock brokers? SEC? FINRA? Government?

All culpable.

Adhering to a Fiduciary duty?

I don't think so. You have to know what you are doing.

Has the regulatory effort so far in early 2011 dampened the risk attitude of the giant institutions? From a speech by Financial Services Authority Chairman Adair Turner, "Have we, in the wake of the crisis, patched up the existing system, reformed the technical details, but left our model of capitalism unchanged and existing economic theories largely unchallenged?'

"Have the technicians of financial regulation been radical enough in the reform of capital and liquidity? Have we significantly reduced the probability and severity of future financial crisis?"

Turner gave his answers " no, no and no"

From Federal Reserve Bank of Kansas City President Tom Hoenig

"In spite of all that's been done and debated, the soundness of the largest financial institutions and the systemic risks they continue to pose is no better". "In my view, **it is even worse than before the crisis."**

Why? Because **supervision is ineffective.**

I repeat the focus of my endeavor- to force regulators to educate and legislate financial entities to minimum levels of standards and knowledge. I am addressing the entities that directly deal with individual consumers. But the comment above is absolutely applicable- who will supervise? Supervisors of brokers have the same lackluster education. If there is no knowledge of the fundamentals of investing, the supervision is simply absent. (Recognize I taught most of the securities licenses. No supervisor has been taught the real life application of product. The fundamentals of investing are not tested and, hence, not taught.)

There are two key focuses that are addressed throughout: the first is the risk- more specifically the risk of loss. Another is the fallacy of backtesting/reversion to the mean in selecting potential returns for future projections.

Risk is still bandied about as the simplistic 'the market can go up and down'. Or it is offered as some pretty charts over lengthy periods of time that tend to imply 'great returns are just around the corner'. However, every portfolio allocation has a numerical risk-of-loss reflecting what can go wrong. It is relatively simple to do, but you need to understand the meaning of standard deviation and have the ability to use a personal financial calculator. There is no other way since there are no calculator programs anywhere on the net or in planning software that does it unilaterally. But for good reason- if these numbers got out, there would be an absolute 180 degree shift in how consumers address risk since they would see that the losses sustained in the past (2000 and 2008) were always known (or could be calculated) but never disseminated to them. While it nonetheless requires additional interpretation, such knowledge to consumers would have forever changed the portfolio allocations offered by the bulk of untrained brokers and advisors or merely assumed by naive consumers. And as in NNF, I point to the inverted yield curve as one of the best indicators of extreme economic risk which universally mirrors itself into a market debacle in the near term. The impact of this is described in detail.

There would be a cost to the industry to upgrade since these facts, once known, taught and presented *would* slow sales dramatically. And the instruction *will* cost a lot.

But said advisers WILL remain untrained since the SEC has never required the fundamentals of investing ever be taught in any licensing. Unfortunately I do not see it happening going forward since the current head of the SEC- Schapiro- did whatever she could at FINRA to avoid such knowledge being disseminated. Nothing in the rhetoric has really changed since she switched. In September 2011,SEC Chairman Mary Schapiro testified before Congress and noted that, over the past two decades, "the markets, products, and participants... have undergone a truly sweeping transformation" and that the SEC must carefully examine how it operates to ensure its "effectiveness."

Sure, it is an absolutely accurate statement but it boils down to "why have you just sat there and watched Rome burn?" Think about the Social Security and Medicare deficits that everyone knew about for more than two decades; the sound bites (lies?) from all the politicians about the current deficit- as though it was always someone else's fault that it happened; all ending up in a financial devastation that could and should have been controlled starting a long time ago. The SEC was part of it with its useless words towards consumer education and nil adviser knowledge. Enough words. Time for all to 'put up or shut up.'

But while the Dodd Frank bill does demand massive changes, the huge amount of money and lobbying (and did I say money?) from the industry, the SEC under Schapiro (actually most past heads of the SEC) will probably waste millions of research monies and end up with bowing to the industry that will thwart the necessary fiduciary responsibility to the bulk of consumers. (This text is concerned about the duty to middle class and poorer consumers. I do not address hedge funds, how to do life insurance premium funding and more sophisticated areas that only the more affluent may use. That said, if the affluent don't learn this stuff or use an adviser that does, they may no longer be affluent.) You will read of her rhetoric in 2006 about the absolute necessity of consumer education- yet the knowledge within licensing requirements is a disgrace.

# FINANCIAL PLANNING
# FIDUCIARY STANDARDS UNDER DODD FRANK

At the Fiduciary Forum 2011, "A disclosure-based regime may well have been deemed effective in 1930 when just 1.2% of the population--the wealthier segment of the population--owned stocks. That was then. Today, 80 years later, 50% of the population is invested in the capital markets, and individuals depend hugely on their retirement accounts. Smart regulation is more crucial than ever. As both the SEC and DOL examine what it means for a plan sponsor, advisor or broker to exercise fiduciary duties, it is time to rethink the role of disclosure in fiduciary relationships in securities regulation to ensure that investors' interests always do come first."

The comment is absolutely correct but almost totally worthless at the same time. It *is* mandatory that consumers be advised on what is happening, any conflicts of interest et al. But where is the disclosure that the brokers have never been trained in the fundamentals of investing and cannot even address the issue of suitability and stock purchases (diversification)? Regulation of those who know little by those who know nothing is yet another violation of fiduciary duty to consumers. (Pundits may rail at this, but ever see those politicians and regulators concerned about money with a financial calculator? Not even close. Never pay much attention to those who do not know how money works.)

All told, many/most portfolios violate the basics of suitability, nevermind fiduciary duty. If you do not know diversification, you cannot determine risk. If you cannot determine risk, you cannot determine suitability.

But so what? Our school systems have been engaged in a systematic effort to teach our children to gamble as much as possible to beat the market- which no reliable text even considers. And nobody cares. Ever see comments about the SMG- Stock Market Game- as a precursor to future financial failure? As a result thereof- or for no reason at all- the adults are no better in their understanding of how to invest. The industry in 2011 is still marketing the idea that the purchase of individual stocks through their own effort or that of their broker will still lead to Nirvana. At least, how to beat the market.

Nope

Even given some latitude, the cognitive (in)ability of humans does not lead them into a rational thought process to investing. I do get upset that most consumers do not read, but I also admit some offset since where can they go to get the advice they need even if they did look? Not Kiyosaki. Not Cramer. Not Orman. Those attempting some effort are left with old theories and homilies such as buy and hold, the market always comes back and on and on. History is mandatory to know but it is a poor set of statistics for the future. As Peter Bernstein noted, "The future is unknown".

Returns

But when one looks at projected returns, history is where the bulk of future returns are determined. Using a data set starting 200 years ago, or effectively any subset thereof, has been the holy grail of forecasting returns well into the future. I have had 'heavy hitting' advisers (meaning Assets Under Management- AUM) say that that is the only method of determining what will happen later on. And just about all planning software does the same thing. I disagree vehemently. The idea that the future looks like what happened before or after the market meltdown of the 1970s is just plain ludicrous. Or I could pick 1987. Or after 2000. I am aware that the future is unknown, but if a gauge/estimate/research of returns does not start in the present day first and foremost, I simply do not believe it is inherently trustworthy at all. The cell phone, computer, internet have all altered the financial marketplace forever. We have had two recent recessions and advisers still think tomorrow will be like periods involving 1861, 1889, 1937, 1967, 1994 or .......????

No, and the material identifying how to look forward- even in view of the ambiguity- is explored.

The material herein should be mandatory reading for every first year finance students and all CFPs, ChFCs, CPA PFS etc. and for ALL second year college students regardless of major. The input will be invaluable over their lifetime. That said, it cannot be compulsory mandatory reading for general 401k participants since they do not have the overall background or interest in pursuing such detail. But the real life application must be understood by all presenters of 401k education in a proper fashion. Otherwise, we will end up in a continual morass from which we will never escape. Comments like the following abound (but she is right):

*So what is the meaning of the word retirement, if the only way you can live in retirement is to work? The answer is, there is no meaning to retirement anymore. We're now shifting from lifetime pensions to lifetime work. It's the end of retirement.*

Prof. TERESA GHILARDUCCI, Notre Dame University

Additional mandatory issue includes how budgeting and retirement planning are done by the numbers, why DCA will universally never work, what is this focus on 60/40, does rebalancing work and a host of others.

Specifically for attorneys- I am a financial planner. I do act as an expert in financial matters but not exclusively. The cases and reports are about 50/50 defendants and plaintiffs. I don't take sides though the rhetoric herein suggests a plaintiff's position. No so- it is just real life facts. No matter, both sides need to take a careful look at the reality of the industry regarding training with a specific focus on risk. You may also note I suggest the UPIA needs changing- it's way out of date. Admittedly that can take forever, but current cases will need to be refocused for real life.

The material covers insurance and annuities. While investing does at least have some informational services that provide statistics, effectively the bulk of the insurance is mired in esoteric marketing material, journalistic half-truths and a range of agent knowledge that truly borders on the futile. I will provide some independent insight along with new informational opportunities. But as regards what needs to be done for the consumers, some pundits note that there can really not be a fiduciary duty with insurance agents since the agent, first and foremost, owes a duty to the insurance company. That is true- they must be 'sure' that the client has truthfully answered all the health questions properly, can pay the premiums and so on. But what is not covered under such activity is whether the product should have been used in the first place. The SEC passed on the regulation of indexed products (very difficult material that is universally missold) supposedly leaving the effort to the state insurance departments. A rather absurd dialogue in the first place since neither entity has the knowledge of these products, nevermind the financial or manpower wherewithal to prosecute a breach of duty. Indexing, guaranteed minimum withdrawals and more will be addressed. Not all the answers can be provided since the companies can change internal requirements at a whim, but that will be identified anyway.

There are some studies/research in the appendix I have had to do in the past covering premium financing, variable life insurance and more that hopefully will put some of the commentary into a real life focus.

That is where this book comes in. It is not technical jargon without real life application. It cannot address every blog/article/commentary by the industry but I take umbrage with the bulk of said commentary since they are not generated by 'financial planners' for the most part. The point is that financial planning should really be done by ‘financial planners’. Unfortunately, most are allowed to become one by simply saying 'they is one'. Or by getting some designation. These may have some value in terms of minimum criteria but that is generally it. (The WSJ noted that there are currently over 210 various designations. I just ran into a CPhD. Impressive? It is a Certified Philanthropic Development Officer that was presented to the agent after he got a client to put in over $100,000 into a product) A professional planner is one who has a degree in same. Yet, as I will quickly admit, a degree does not reflect the absolute knowledge base or competency in the field. The material changes every day. But I would much prefer to have surgery by one who has formally studied medicine and is recognized as competent (licensed physician) than from a first year med student. Or a hospital janitor. Or someone that only knows that blood is red.

That extensive level of study and discipline is not mandated to date in this industry. Not even close. Hence the exposure to the problem- those masquerading fiduciary competency without the knowledge or intent by same to attain it. I know that there are those out there that 'care', but without the formal background of the fundamentals, caring just doesn't cut it.

Here are the minimum standards to start with.

Post Script

I am old but I have been 'brought up on the Internet and blogging'. I write linearly- all references are offered directly in the text- no footnotes.

I try to write in a conversational style and get to the point fairly quickly. This is not a text book where I drone on and on about the underlying formulas of certain issues- say standard deviation. It is explained for real life purposes and those wanting more insight will need to do more research. Fact is, one will have to read and re-read some areas several times since there will be material you will be unfamiliar with. Obviously if you just want to know what a fiduciary must consider, an overview may be adequate. But if you want to be a fiduciary, there is a lot of work ahead of you.

This is also the hard copy complement to two video courses approved by the California State Bar- for continuing legal education: one in investments and one in insurance and annuities. , They are applicable under reciprocity for attorneys in other states and for CFP, CPA etc. credit as well. The videos provide visual aspects that help facilitate a grasp of difficult areas or those that are inherently new to the reader. The combination is the start to professionalism and the facts on which to base litigation.

Financial Planning, done correctly, is a multi discipline profession which demands a knowledge base among investments, insurance, human behavior and more. Therefore there are comments addressed in one chapter that need reaffirmation in others. I have tried to limit certain repetition, but specific elements require repeating.

# 1

# Literacy and Aliteracy

Part of this great economic and financial fiasco is the lack of literacy skills by the American public overall. I submit that for the general consumer, it is absolutely getting worse since the Internet, while offering facts, information and knowledge heretofore unheard of, also presents distractions that a society (generally the younger) has been overly eager to embrace-principally swayed by a pretty web site that supposedly projects professionalism. Couple that with the tons of computer software that offer games galore, porn galore and more that distracts from heavy research.

Via an article on illiteracy from the mid 90's, "*over 10%-25+ million Americans- cannot read or write at all.* Another 45 million are functionally illiterate. That's around 28% of U.S. citizens that are devoid of a reasonable thought process. (If you do not read, you simply do not think). 44% of the American adults do not read a book in a year. A publishing industry study showed that from April 1990 to March 1991, 6 out of 10 households did not buy a single book. (Recognize that was well before the Internet.) My difficulty with such studies is that they do not necessarily define ***what*** is read. Even for those that do read books today, they are apt to be Harry Potter rather than some intensive text on finance. Obviously it is better to read something than nothing at all, but if it consists of miscellaneous articles on sports, beauty secrets and other similar "fluff" (except fishing), I find little solace in that. It has been my opinion that there are only about 6% of the populace that does studious research on areas directly impacting their lives- health, investments, marriage, raising kids, etc. Don't agree?? Then you should also read the study, the 1992 Adult Literacy Survey, which shows the lack of competency by the vast U.S. populace in both quantitative and qualitative skills. There was no change as of 2003. http://www.usatoday.com/news/education/2009-01-08-adult-literacy_N.htm A 1999 Gallup poll stated that the only 7 percent of Americans read more than a book a week, while some 59 percent said they had read fewer than 10 books in the previous year. Only 6 percent of those who read belong to a book club. **The number of people who don't read at all has been rising for the past 20 years**

More importantly is this issue: Aliteracy. It reflects people that can read but *don't.* In my circle of contacts, I do not see the reading necessary outside of their own work- assuming that is needed anyway. It is true that the newspaper use has declined precipitously due to the internet. But few use the Internet to its intellectual capacity anyway so a lot has been lost in competent thought process overall.

Jim Trelease, author of *The Read-Aloud Handbook,* has stated that this trend away from the written word is more than worrisome, and that it's tearing apart our culture. People who have stopped reading, he says, "base their future decisions on what they used to know...If you don't read much, you really don't know much...you're dangerous."American historian Daniel Boorstin noted, "In the United States today, aliteracy is widespread."

All in all, the ability to read is paramount. The interest in knowledge is mandatory. Yet the lack of effort is obvious. And as stated, while the Internet offers a vast array of info, most will never make the effort to find it. Just too much work (thinking). What most will desire is short simple directions on what to do or buy. Hence you find Jim Cramer or Robert Kiyosaki. Great marketing and that is about it. There is Suze Orman. Granted some of her material is valid but it is geared to the less astute and financially immature. Ever hear her truly discuss risk and the economics associated with it? And she is now offering CDs that have asset allocations for any financial scenario. Yeah, right.

The other section reflects the misuse of the reams of material by the consumer. There are thousands upon thousands of "professionally" appearing Internet sites offering tips and techniques for beating the market. But the consumer does not possess the background or specific knowledge to recognize the value- or complete lack thereof- of the material being offered. So what do many do? They bite on the bait. No homework in most cases or simply a lackluster one. (That is not to say that the semi literate/knowledgeable agent is any better). Morningstar is a good example. They have used a 5 star rating system for as long as I can remember. Though they have admitted that these simply reflect what happened in the **past**, consumers are still picking funds by such ratings even as the market plunged/plunges. The number of stars may be totally irrelevant as compared to the current risk. It is difficult to find the needed nuggets of gold or simply the facts that provide the truth. But a library is little different and what is there is apt to be so old as to be useless in any case. Those that attempt research via the Internet might/should find articles that have far more insight to any area of investing and insurance than the Wall Street Journal, Barrons and certainly Money magazine, Kiplingers and the like.

*"We are drowning in information but starved for*

*knowledge."*
John Naisbitt

The research is a lot of work and the industry has done its best to present material that is half truth at best. So for those that are literate and do read, they are still mired in confusion- or accepting material that is wrong.

The kicker is, can I provide the sites to look at? Not really. I have accumulated thousands of pages of material at my site as well as hundreds of links that I use in my work. But as many viewers have commented, it can be almost overwhelming in its breadth and depth- certainly for the novice. (Note, it is not just investments- it covers long term care, estate planning, insurance and annuities, ethics in the industry and much more.) The point is that the material for understanding risk and reward is actually there- but it goes back again to the effort by consumers to get their hands dirty (reading). They won't do it. Admittedly some (most?) are not that capable of understanding it. No matter, it is the simplistic, sophomoric and 'pretty' sites that get the exposure. Certainly those that suggest what to do ***now!***

And as much as some entities would like to think that financial planning is simple overall (buy and hold advocates), I submit otherwise. It is hard to comprehend the massive amount of material addressing any of these subject areas that I get or find every day/week/month. It is truly unbelievable. (Consider the guaranteed annuity products now inundating the marketplace with more variations almost every day. The new and 'improved' ETFs. The economic and behavioral studies that no one ever heard about before the internet.)

For the purposes of this work, I have focused on investments and insurance as the key points of interest for readers and present real life theory/application to how it (supposedly) works. There a definite reason why 'supposedly' was put in parentheses. There are vast numbers of how to books on becoming rich overnight, or exactly what historical trends will be repeated that provide great returns, buy and hold as the best strategy, dollar cost averaging and many, many more “perfect”, simple strategies and rules of thumbs that will increase returns and lower risk. Some may have a flavor of truth, most are haggard tripe brought forth by advisers with nil training and even less knowledge.

Our schools are having more and more difficulty teaching their varied students- many of different cultures and languages. Less math, less knowledge, and a precursor to more low and middle income financial devastation, a burgeoning national deficit and a lowered U.S. international stature as the dollar diminishes in value.

The U.S. cultural clash has to be rectified. A civilization rises and falls by the ability and ***willingness*** of its citizenry to converse with each other directly. You will never have full literacy until the populace ***wants*** to understand each other. As far as financial literacy is concerned, that language is King’s English. That is not going to change for decades. It may not be politically correct to state this but it is a real life fact necessary for all to grasp. People will have to 'grow up' or they will forever be financially underserved. Or simply taken advantage of.

Illiteracy impacts the lower income most of all. Aliteracy impacts a much wider section of our society and it is getting worse.

That should be all that is necessary- save for the fact that what is being spoon fed by the government is tripe. See the Stock Market Game. See the financial knowledge base for those advising the literate, illiterate, alliterate. Pretty poor.

If Dodd Frank is not a true upgrade to knowledge, the economics of the country will get worse. The financial capability of the citizenry will continue to further failure. Fiduciary responsibility is paramount. But as referenced time and time again, a fiduciary has to know what they are doing in the first place. That is the weakness of the Dodd Frank effort.

# 2

# Basic Financial Education

This probably says it best- How Ordinary Consumers Make Complex Economic Decisions: Financial Literacy and Retirement Readiness, http://www.nber.org/papers/w15350 National Bureau of Economic Research:

"There can hardly be a better time to make the case for economic and financial literacy... a better-informed citizenry would likely have resulted in more prudent decision making and, consequently, less harm to the economy."

That certainly has been an issue for decades but I am not sure anyone will make the concerted effort. And what effort there is as apt to be a rehash of the same ol', same ol'. A fine example is BetterInvesting.org (formally NAIC- National Association of Investment Clubs) and this comment at their site -***We show you how to beat the market.*** (There are no legitimate texts that suggest than that is nothing more than charlatanism and gambling.) Before 2000, they had a membership north of 570,000 (WSJ February 2007). Then as of 2/2007-and that is after a few good years of returns- the membership was no more than 140,000- dropping lower to 90,000 in 2011. Thousands of "investors" milling around in a non sophisticated environment finding the next best stock or fund that would produce fantastic returns- only to finally recognize they were clueless to the elements of diversification or to economic risk. The idea that a focus is on 'beating the market' is a denial of real life statistics and risk. (Though certainly it conforms to irrationality and cognitive dissonance.).

They also show you how to pick stocks via all sorts of stats from the past. Unfortunately, that is a violation of diversification since one needs far too many stocks that can be picked by an individual (see section herein). From Benoit Mandlebrot and identified as a master mathematician internationally, "to build efficient portfolios, you need good forecasts of earnings, share prices, and volatility for thousands of stock. Otherwise garbage in, garbage out. Finally, for each stock, you must laboriously calculate its covariance with, or how it fluctuates against, every other stock. For a thirty stock portfolio, about the minimum needed to make the numbers work well, that means 495 different calculations of mean variance and covariance. For the entire NY Stock Exchange, 3.9 million calculations. And because prices change, the exercise needs constant repetition."

The ability for consumers to construct a portfolio on simplistic ideology is a waste of effort. Further, no organization goes from 570,000 members to 90,000 if they are doing the right thing. The loss of 80%+ is indicative of the failure to get to the real life application of stocks, diversification, asset allocation or specifically to risk.

From a 2009 article, Financial Literacy Among the Young: Evidence and Implications for Consumer Policy, http://www.nber.org/papers/w15352, National Bureau of Economic Research.

"Previous research has found that financial literacy can have important implications for financial behavior: people with low financial literacy are more likely to have problems with debt less likely to participate in the stock market, less likely to choose mutual funds with lower fees)."

"As the complexity of financial decisions increases and individuals are put in charge of making these decisions even at a young age, it is important to find ways to equip people with adequate financial knowledge. Previous studies have shown that broad groups of the population are not financially literate; these people may be particularly unlikely and unable to manage their finances effectively, and to plan adequately for the future. This paper added to the existing knowledge by exploring what younger adults know and do not know as determined by a set of simple questions that assessed their financial literacy. We found that financial literacy was severely lacking among young adults; only 27% of young adults know about inflation and risk diversification and can do simple interest rate calculations. Moreover, women proved to be the least financially literate. Sex differences between women and men persisted even after accounting for many demographic characteristics, family background characteristics, and peer characteristics. Prior work showed that women tended to display low financial literacy later in life. Thus, lack of financial literacy seems to persist for long periods and sometimes throughout the lifetime. Given the strong link between financial literacy and financial management and retirement planning found in other studies, it may be important to find ways to foster financial knowledge in the population as a whole and among the groups who are more disadvantaged. Similarly, it may be important to develop programs targeted specifically to women, since they display not only much lower financial knowledge but also large differences in investment and saving behavior."

I did respond to the authors with this- 'First a comment to risk diversification- it is effectively a sophomoric commentary overall as is evidenced by the lack of material at the SEC and FINRA level. Diversification is not "don't put all your eggs in one basket" since it has no numerical significance. Just one comment- when you mention risk diversification, there is effectively no one who knows the correct answer. No broker has been taught the fundamentals of investing, nor almost all RIAs, et al. It is one thing to infer the young don't know risk diversification but the adults are using the same sophomoric rationalization. Of course there is some value to the "don't put all your eggs in one basket" but it is statistically useless.

When used with securities, it is how many stock must you have in a portfolio in order to insulate it due to unsystematic risk. More colloquially, how many stocks must you have in a portfolio in order to be properly diversified;

It is a minimum of 50 stocks to the preferable 350. (If one does not know about the 50 stocks- they should simply go to the more conservative 350.) Unless the numbers are presented for real life application, the issue of education for financial literacy and retirement planning is suspect. Those numbers have to be taught.'

Admittedly my note was more than they needed for the report, but their reply was even more overall damaging to financial literacy: "Point well taken, we are aware, but we cannot ask people about the stocks' beta. We got most of the predictive power from the "do not know" answers, **basically respondents do not know what a stock or a stock mutual fund is."**

That says volumes on how bad our educational system is doing. Just terrible. Certain material can be mastered if the instruction of the basics are followed. But there can be nothing to solicit/entice the novice to gambling which has been the presentations to date. Here is an example from the California Financial Literacy Summit sponsored by the California CPA Society. One would assume some mastery of the fundamentals of investing would be evident to provide to an audience of 500 teachers, but the presentation revolved around a PBS fluff video on "gambling". (Never assume PBS knows what they are doing.) It showed a young student about 12 who had decided to buy Nike stock (obviously before the tech meltdown) by just reviewing a couple statistics. And then relying on his mother. That's it. Well, he was successful with just one stock. And then he started to teach other kids what to do. The school he was at was impressed because the other kids were impressed. It was fun. It was easy. And it was profitable. Risk was not even an issue.

That may be 'nice' but the focus on a singular stock defies the first fundamental of investing- diversification-and is the same thing as gambling. No matter, PBS does a 'feel good' piece that was being shown at schools across the country because it got the kids **excited and interested**. Sorry, that is the wrong emotion for investing. And all in defiance with basic diversification. So where was the basic financial literacy? It sure wasn't PBS. It was not the CPA society. And all being delivered in a cutesy sophomoric piece of drivel that will only perpetuate the ignorance and illiteracy of the public.

Here is a far worse- yet more national and institutional-corruption of investing. This one is from the Ohio Centers for Economic Education and Financial Literacy Stock Market Challenge. http://ohiosmc.stocktrak.com There are many others like it.

"This is a web-based educational tool that is used by thousands of elementary, middle, and high students around the state each semester to help teach economics, finance, current events, math, social studies and technology. Each student or team of students receive $100,000 of virtual dollars in an SMC brokerage account and simulates managing a portfolio by buying and selling stocks at real-time prices. Students compete for prizes and/or statewide bragging rights."

Another SMC said this- "Stock Market Challenge brings the **unique *excitement* of live trading** into the classroom. This interactive, experiential learning resource uses the experience of trading to create a competitive and rewarding team activity."

One of their research notes says, "Diversify your investment in at least ***three*** or more different stocks." I suppose one could say that 350 stocks fits in with "more than three", but that is an absurd rationale.

I do not dismiss that there becomes an interest in some element of math, current events and more, but the SMC is a two week challenge to take as much risk as one can possibly imagine to beat another team doing the exactly same thing. This is a ludicrous and dangerous exercise that is designed for a project that totally violates long term planning, diversification, etc., and drives the risk of loss almost to exponential levels.

These are tantamount to new age video games sending the wrong message- TRADE, TRADE, TRADE!!! This challenge is offered in all the states. And even at some universities. It sends the completely wrong message about investing. It is play for money. Such activity has previously devastated retirement assets. As long as this focus on financial illiteracy continues, the school age kids will do no better as they get older. But a current problem is that the teachers believe it also correct. And their state administrators. And our government. And our president(s).

This is the real life financial and investment literacy of our nation. It has to be completely re-engineered. But I do now know who will do it since the government leadership is suspect at its core.

Too strong?

So how'd you like the great professionalism and knowledge as all political parties figured out the debt resolution with calm and dignity?

# 3

# Finance Theory

The United States financial system broke apart in 2008 because of the use of hedging and derivative techniques that had been "guaranteed" to work under any financial stress. But it wasn't simply the likes of institutional hedging that was all the problem for the middle income wage earner- certainly anyone who ever heard a 401k presentation. It was the fact that 99 44/100% of the advisors had never addressed risk in the real world (risk of loss is not taught at all) and were complacent, ignorant- but most of all- inept in figuring out what to do with client portfolios (did they have a financial calculator? If not, why were they used?) So they let them ride down under the well worn decree that one does only a 'buy and hold' and the 'market always comes back'.

These simplistic homilies of reversion to the mean et al, don't have to have any value in today's society. Losses of 44% and 57% clearly demonstrate the unreliability of holding on to severely declining assets. Millions did do this and are now saddled with a retirement that will not last half of their remaining lifetimes. This debacle has changed the economic arena of the world along with a clear reduction in U.S. prominence. There is no reason to think that many old theories or statistics will validate the future- or ever did. The future is simply unknown. One of the greatest minds ever on the issue of investing was Peter Bernstein who noted years ago, "Understanding that we do not know the future is such a simple statement, but it's so important." "............anything can happen. There really is such a thing as a "paradigm shift," when people's view of the future can change very dramatically and very suddenly. That means that there's never a time when you can be sure that today's market is going to be a replay of a familiar past."

"Economics needs to become broader, and less arrogant. It doesn't always have the explanations for human behavior."

Scholars on both sides of the Atlantic have made progress with models that take account of the real-life complexities of financial markets, which are rife with disagreement and diversity, rather than simply explaining away any divergence from so-called rational pricing.

Most major university economics departments are dominated by the mathematical approach, as are the journals in which academics must publish if they want to advance. The problem with economists is they believe the whole world operates according to their models. "We need a bit more variety and a bit more pluralism. Not just there's a problem and we solve the equation and get the answer."

Unfortunately, the admonitions did little good since no one paid much heed. When some decried the lack of oversight, Greenspan said that derivatives were best left alone since the entities were clearly capable of doing the right thing. He "trusted the system" and its captains of industry. So much for blind "trust." The Financial Crisis and the Systemic Failure of Academic Economics, (http://d.repec.org/n?u=RePEc:kud:kuiedp:0903&r=cbe), provides an excellent professional review of the frailty of a system that was sure it knew the Holy Grail of all economics.

"Many of the financial economists who developed the theoretical models upon which the modern financial structure is built were well aware of the strong and highly unrealistic restrictions imposed on their models to assure stability. Yet, financial economists gave little warning to the public about the fragility of their models, even as they saw individuals and businesses build a financial system based on their work. There are a number of possible explanations for this failure to warn the public. One is a "lack of understanding" explanation--the researchers did not know the models were fragile. We find this explanation highly unlikely; financial engineers are extremely bright, and it is almost inconceivable that such bright individuals did not understand the limitations of the models. A second, more likely explanation, is that they did not consider it their job to warn the public. If that is the cause of their failure, we believe that it involves a misunderstanding of the role of the economist, and involves an ethical breakdown. In our view, **economist**s, as with all scientists, **have an ethical responsibility to communicate the limitations of their models and the potential misuses of their research. Currently, there is no ethical code for professional economic scientists. There should be one**.

..........They also presume that there is a single model of the economy, which is odd given that even economists are divided in their views about the correct model of the economy. While other currents of research do exist, economic policy advice, particularly in financial economics, has far too often been based (consciously or not) on a set of axioms and hypotheses derived ultimately from a highly limited dynamic control model, using the Robinson approach with 'rational' expectations.

The major problem is that despite its many refinements, this is not at all an approach based on, and confirmed by, empirical research. In fact, it stands in stark contrast to a broad set of regularities in human behavior discovered both in psychology and what is called behavioral and experimental economics. The corner stones of many models in finance and macroeconomics are rather maintained despite all the contradictory evidence discovered in empirical research. Much of this literature shows **that human subjects act in a way that bears no resemblance to the rational expectations paradigm and also have problems discovering 'rational expectations equilibria' in repeated experimental settings.** Rather, agents display various forms of 'bounded rationality' using heuristic (rule of thumb) decision rules and displaying inertia in their reaction to new information. They have also been shown in financial markets to be strongly influenced by emotional and hormonal reactions. Economic modeling has to take such findings seriously.

In summary, it seems to us that much of contemporary empirical work in macroeconomics and finance is driven by the pre-analytic belief in the validity of a certain model. Rather than (mis)using statistics as a means to illustrate these beliefs, the goal should be to put theoretical models to scientific test (as the naïve believer in positive science would expect).

The systematic analysis of network vulnerability has been undertaken in the computer science and operations research literature. Such aspects have, however, been largely absent from discussions in financial economics. The introduction of new derivatives was rather seen through the lens of general equilibrium models: more contingent claims help to achieve higher efficiency. Unfortunately, the claimed efficiency gains through derivatives are merely a theoretical implication of a highly stylized model and, therefore, have to count as a hypothesis. **Since there is hardly any supporting empirical evidence (or even analysis of this question), the claimed real-world efficiency gains from derivatives are not justified by true science. While the economic argument in favor of**

**ever new derivatives is more one of persuasion rather than evidence, important negative effects have been neglected. The idea that the system was made less risky with the development of more derivatives led to financial actors taking positions with extreme degrees of leverage and the danger of this has not been emphasized enough.**

The current crisis might be characterized as an example of the final stage of a well-known boom-and-bust pattern that has been repeated so many times in the course of economic history. There are, nevertheless, some aspects that make this crisis different from its predecessors: First, the preceding boom had its origin – at least to a large part – in the development of new financial products that opened up new investment possibilities (while most previous crises were the consequence of overinvestment in new physical investment possibilities). Second, the global dimension of the current crisis is due to the increased connectivity of our already highly interconnected financial system. Both aspects have been largely ignored by academic economics."

This comment from Charlie Munger- partner in Berkshire Hathaway with Warren Buffet- may say it best, **"Some of the worst business decisions I've ever seen are those with future projections and discounts back. It seems like the higher mathematics with more false precision should help you, but it doesn't. They teach that in business schools because, well, they've got to do something."**

And from another article, "Although experimental economics has made important inroads into the mainstream of economics and chance, the top journals still publish only a small fraction of experimental papers, the majority consisting of more traditional theoretical and empirical studies. Despite the fact that new theories of economic behavior have been proposed from time to time, most graduate programs in economics and chance teach only one such theory: expected utility theory and rational expectations, and its corresponding extensions, e.g., portfolio optimization, the Capital Asset Pricing Model, and dynamic general equilibrium asset-pricing models.

From Benoit Mandelbrot, "So why does the old order continue? Habit and convention. The math is, at bottom, easy and can be made to look impressive, inscrutable to all but the rocket scientist. Business schools around the world keep teaching it. They have trained thousands of financial officers, thousands of investment advisers. In fact, as most of these graduates learn from subsequent experience, it does not work as advertised and they develop myriad ad hoc improvements, adjustments and accommodations to get their job done. But still, it gives a comforting impressions of precision and competence".

I am not indicating that the teachings may not be reasonably relevant in the overall long term scheme of investing, but they miss the key element- they are not necessarily real life. Theory born in a test tube needs to be tested. Further, human optimism may belie the necessity of addressing the underlying risks. Academia generally does not want to rock the boat and admit their teachings were in error. You therefore have old theories become dogma. And since it is "so easy to understand" (bell shaped Gaussian standard deviation), it can all be measured correctly with just micro seconds of effort. It's wrong, but at least it is quick and supposedly measurable.

The best scenario is this is the complete meltdown of Long Term Capital in 1998. LTC employed two Nobel laureates and 27 PhDs- as much brain power as that building the A Bomb (at least that blew up on purpose). (Read this or go to the bold print) The company used complex mathematical models to take advantage of fixed income arbitrage deals usually with U.S., Japanese and European government bonds At the beginning of 1998, the firm had equity of $4.72 billion and had borrowed over

$124.5 billion with assets of around $129 billion, for a debt to equity ratio of about 25 to 1. It had an off balance derivative positions with a notional value of approximately 1.25 trillion most of which were in interest rate derivatives such as interest rate swaps. But when the Russian Government defaulted on their government bonds, panicked investors sold Japanese and European bonds to buy U.S. treasury bonds. The profits that were supposed to occur as the value of these bonds ***converged*** became huge losses as the value of the bonds ***diverged***. By the end of August, the fund had lost $1.85 billion in capital.

**Understand all that? Well essentially LTC had everything figured out so that no matter what happened in the world economics, the total loss their portfolio could experience would be 35 million in one day. They lost 550 million in ONE day.**

Even Merrill Lynch observed that mathematical risk models "may provide a greater sense of security than warranted; therefore, reliance on these models should be limited." Then again, Merrill screwed up so badly with same that they ended up being sold to BofA (but the departing CEO walked away with a $161.5 million. Just months prior he proclaimed that "We are Merrill Lynch. We know risk.")

As such, stocks may not do well, particularly where the consumer no longer has the income to spend freely. (See SF Fed Warns Baby Boomers May Wound Stock Market, http://blogs.wsj.com/economics/2011/08/22/sf-fed-warns-baby-boomers-may-wound-stock-market/,

The ongoing wave of retirees won't crater the market, but they may well be "a factor holding down equity valuations over the next two decades.)

And many will not partake of more risk in any case which will limit sales the companies depend upon and therefore keep stock values low. It is the simple understanding/statistic that consumer spending drives the

U.S. economy and when that falters- and it has and will continue to do so- what is there to prompt greater stock values? (In a survey in late 2009 by Citigroup, 63 percent of American consumers surveyed said the way they spend and save has been forever changed. Only one-third said spending and saving would go back to the way it was before the recession.) Of course, it might be that we can export to other emerging countries- say China and India- and that is how U.S. companies can continue to grow. Wishful thinking in large part. And in any case, it won't be enough to offset our past spending habits.

I deal with individuals, not institutional clients, and long time readers at my site have known that I have been highly suspect regarding computerized financial plans since they were very limited in almost all aspects. It was apparent to thinking advisers that the theoretical premises regarding risk just did not hold water at any level- if they were offered at all. I have always done my own allocations (generally by hand) since the early 90s and the necessity was even more apparent as the decades passed. Morningstar has put out various statistics since the 80s, but they were all based on the past. Real life is far cry from the past and certainly a far cry from the thunk (not a misprint) tanks in some university. The software programs used by "advisors" are based on past numbers that are rarely evident. I do not feel comfortable in using them- particularly when they do not address the risk of loss. And the algorithms used now are millisecond trading that has to do with an mathematical treatise that has nothing to do with the underlying stock valuation.

At this point, I direct readers to Capital Ideas and Capital Ideas Evolving also by Peter Bernstein. The best critiques ever written on the vast array of economic thinking over generations. One issue notable is the significant disagreement between the theorists on what might be the best way of defining the movements and risks of the market. As you go forward with the critique of each entity, it becomes more difficult to ferret out which one to use and when. Most critically is the fact that almost all the theory, save for a few till most recently, felt that the market was rational and efficient and followed a relatively simple bell shaped curve of standard deviation. And it became belief to almost all.

I still do not see how. One of the key efforts in doing portfolio allocation is determining how one group of investments may work with another over time. Addressed more definitively herein, it is a statistical effort to see how two (or more) investments move when any occurrence happens to one side. Does the other asset move in lockstep and for the same amount in the same manner and at the same time? More importantly, is there some consistency in year after year after year- that is the heart of the matter.

It isn't that hard to do at that level- one merely accumulates data over time on various investments and see how they correspond to each other. But apparently no one bothered to take the time to do it. Because if they had, it would have been perfectly obvious to instructors that the correlations were wildly inconsistent. I started accumulating data on correlations at least from the early 90s. However, as I gathered more and more charts, it was very apparent that the correlations over any given period of time were inconsistent with just about any other period. You could not use statistics from the past since there simply was no validity in doing so. And if you cannot get correlation right to begin with (by not thinking), all other elements of portfolio allocation became an exercise in futility.

*"The correlations between financial quantities are notoriously unstable."*

*"We need to get back to testing models rather than revering them, That's hard work, but this idea that there are these*

*great principles governing finance and that correlations can just be plucked out of the air is totally false."*

Paul Wilmott

(For the uninitiated, Paul is a financial consultant, specializing in derivatives, risk management and quantitative finance.)

Many advisers using such static correlations may have believed what they were doing was right, but a lot never had that much education or knowledge to question the theory. Or gather any evidence to prove what they were doing. As stated numerous times elsewhere, a broker's licensing education is about one college class. A RIA is merely a compliance to offer fee investment advice. A CFP is about one college semester. (A CFA is more demanding but still not necessarily real life). No matter how bright they may believe themselves (and many do), there is very little background on which to base an intellectual scrutiny to risk. (Consumers are out to lunch so let me dismiss that element now). And the risk of investing via current correlations is crucial to the end value you will have. Including the ability to sleep well at night. There is nothing in these backgrounds to real world correlation. Nothing.

It was therefore no surprise that the walls came tumbling down at some point. The theories were simply that theories bred in a lab without input of the real world. The advisers are now seeing the light primarily since they have no choice. A 57% equities loss and a global economy in disarray can make a lot of ignorant and stupid people start to pay attention. They should also have paid more attention to the corruption and moronic incompetency of the "Captains of Industry" that caused a lot of the problem, but the government just bailed out a bunch. It is still waste and ineptness as usual- as evidenced by a governmental morass and the debt crisis. As stated, Dodd-Frank has really gotten nowhere so far at the institutional level and I am suspect of any real improvement at the broker level. The SEC may actually institute some wording for fiduciary responsibility but the powers to be just don't want to recognize that the knowledge has never existed even for the lower suitability standard. How can one be a fiduciary if the definition for diversification is not known?

Here is something more definitive: From The Adaptive Markets Hypothesis: Market Efficiency from an Evolutionary Perspective Andrew Lo, (Harris & Harris Group Professor of Finance at the MIT Sloan School of Management) "The first implication is that to the extent that a relation between risk and reward exists, it is unlikely to be stable over time. Such a relation is determined by the relative sizes and preferences of various populations in the market ecology, as well as institutional aspects such as the regulatory environment and tax laws. As these factors shift over time, any risk/reward relation is likely to be affected. A corollary of this implication is that the equity risk premium is also time-varying and path-dependent. This is not so revolutionary an idea as it might first appear even in the context of a rational expectations equilibrium model, if risk preferences change over time, then the equity risk premium must vary too. The incremental insight of the AMH is that aggregate risk preferences are not immutable constants, but are shaped by the forces of natural selection. For example, until recently, US markets were populated by a significant group of investors who have never experienced a genuine bear market. This fact has undoubtedly shaped the aggregate risk preferences of the US economy, just as the experience of the past four years since the bursting of the technology bubble has affected the risk preferences of the current population of investors. In this context, natural selection determines who participates in market interactions; those investors who experienced substantial losses in the technology bubble are more likely to have exited the market, leaving a markedly different population of investors today than four years ago. Through the forces of natural selection, history matters. Irrespective of whether prices fully reflect all available information, the particular path that market prices have taken over the past few years influences current aggregate risk preferences"

Two more brilliant observations- the first by one of some exceptional talent by researchers at the FED. The internet has provided everyone an opportunity to review papers that heretofore would have languished in a library virtually unread. Here is a decisive article called Failures in Risk Management by Ralph C. Kimball that reflects how bad the arrogance was of the industry: (FED Reserve Board of Boston 2000): "Risk management has received increasing attention in recent years, both from academics and from practitioners. The heightened interest is the result of a number of coincident secular trends, including increased investment in volatile emerging markets and the growing role of capital markets in both developed and emerging economies, as well as the introduction of volatile financial innovations. Risk management has also attracted attention as a result of the repeated and well-publicized failures associated with its implementation. Despite the increased attention paid to risk management, frequent instances still occur when sophisticated investors or firms experience sudden, unexpected, and devastating losses. This article discusses failures in risk management, why they occur, and what can be done to reduce their occurrence. The author discusses the nature of risk and the objectives of risk management. **He argues that intuitively attractive conceptual simplifications often create significant errors in risk measurement. He describes such failures in risk management and goes on to discuss the implications, both for managers and for regulators."**

From Peter Bernstein, 2008, (NY Times) The debacle from which the system is now trying to emerge suggests that prevailing risk-management strategies were managing the wrong risks. Surely, a reversal in home prices was a risk to be reckoned with, but it appears to have played no role, or at least none that mattered.

How will we deal with surprises — outcomes different from what we expect? What are the consequences of being wrong in our expectations? This is the point when risk management begins to live up to its real meaning. Risk means the chance of being wrong— not always in an adverse direction, but always in a direction different from what we expected. Risk management, then, should be a process of dealing with the consequences of being wrong. Sometimes, these consequences are minimal — encountering rain after leaving home without an umbrella, for example. But betting the ranch on the assumption that home prices can only go up should tell you the consequences would be much more than minimal if home prices started to fall.

In this assumption, the word "only" is ridiculous. There are no "onlys" in the future. More things can happen than will happen.

Under those conditions, risk management should concentrate either on limiting the size of the bet or on finding ways to hedge the bet so you are not wiped out if you take the wrong side — if home prices do start to go down, or even stop rising. Risk management is fundamentally different from managing volatility, which is how many investors view it. **Volatility is often a symptom of risk but is not a risk in and of itself. Volatility obscures the future but does not necessarily determine the future.**

Effective risk management starts with the recognition that any forecast can be wrong, then weighs the consequences of being wrong. Only then can we decide whether to make a bet, whether to hedge that bet and how to execute the hedge if needed."

Can the private industry do it? Will they do it? Debatable to both. From the FPA convention in October 2009 this was noted, "They said one question clients are asking is why didn't advisors foresee the apocalyptic ruin that befell the markets in 2008. A member of a panel said that trying to predict what would have happened in the market was almost as good as seeking the truth with Ouija boards and crystal balls. His co-panelist said that economists work in hindsight, so it isn't possible for advisors to predict something like the credit crisis, the housing market collapse and the decimation of institutions that were 100 years old."

**Wrong.**

While true that the extent of the debacle could not be envisioned and that most economists are 'after the fact', a basic understanding of risk clearly indicated a recession in both 2000 and after 2006 and the probability of a 40%+ loss of a portfolio. The inverted yield curve is not a Ouija board or anything of the like. It is a very efficient formal statistic graphed by the FED (and many other institutions) that has been proven to be 100% correct in the direction of the U.S. economy (and elsewhere if you do the homework). (An investigation of inverted yield curve and significant downturns, http://mises.org/etexts/cwik-dissertation.pdf, Treasury spread, inverted yield curve and recessions. http://www.newyorkfed.org/research/capital_markets/Prob_R ec.pdf, The Yield Curve as a Predictor of U.S. Recessions (2007) The yield curve—specifically, the spread between the interest rates on the ten-year Treasury note and the three-month Treasury bill— is a valuable forecasting tool. It is simple to use and significantly outperforms other financial and macroeconomic indicators in predicting recessions two to six quarters ahead.)

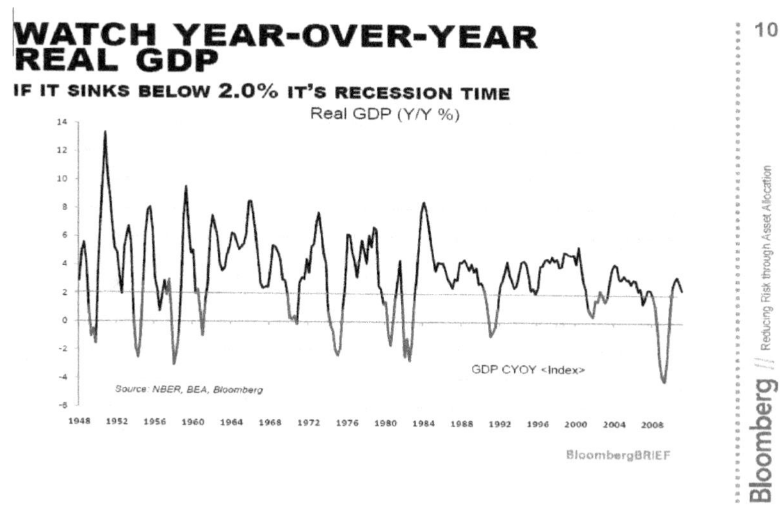


As repeated herein, I cannot guarantee that a recession is always imminent (the future is unknown) but I have no hesitation in stating that a period of high stress will occur which will cause a major disruption to world equity markets. And then there is the also Year over Year Real GDP% (See chapter herein) If it drops below 2%, it's recession time.

Nassim Taleb has reached some prominence regarding the failure of the theories to reflect the risks in the market place. He noted in 10/2010 regarding the Noble prize for past theories,

"People are using Sharpe theory that vastly underestimates the risks they're taking and overexposes them to equities. I'm not blaming them for coming up with the idea, but I'm blaming the Nobel for giving them legitimacy. No one would have taken Markowitz seriously without the Nobel stamp." (That really isn't fair. Their work truly had relevance. It's generally the fact that subsequent users did not/could not apply it to the real world. And a lot of that had to do with using simplistic historical measures and 'plopping' them into a formula that was to solve risk and returns for all mankind. It was the fault of the users who did not put theories into real life.)

**The Sharpe ratio per Wilkipedia-**

"The Sharpe ratio is used to characterize how well the return of an asset compensates the investor for the risk taken, the higher the Sharpe Ratio number the better. When comparing two assets each with the expected return $E[R]$ against the same benchmark with return *Rf*, the asset with the higher Sharpe ratio gives more return for the same risk. Investors are often advised to pick investments with high Sharpe ratios. **However like any mathematical model it relies on the data being correct."**

I cannot say when that last comment was entered, but it begs the issue: can anyone really know if the standard deviation or beta or whatever number is correct when used? No. Further, the SDs are generally based on an fluid Gaussian curve. Looks nice, easy to use for theory. And the SD goes down over time making the ratio look all the better. But that is the reverse to the overall ***risk of loss*** in a portfolio allocation. Are betas really the better way of looking at risk? Fama and French said opposite in 1992. (See also beta chapter herein)

The Markowitz theory per Wikipedia- the capital asset pricing model (CAPM) is used to determine a theoretically appropriate required rate of return added to an already well-diversified portfolio, given that asset's non-diversifiable risk takes into account the asset's sensitivity to non-diversifiable risk (also known as systematic risk or market risk), often represented by the quantity beta (â) in the financial industry, as well as the **expected** return of the market and the **expected** return of a **theoretical** risk-free asset.

Note the term "already well diversified portfolio- and just what is that? Does an algorithm determine that? How does one determine the actual non diversifiable risk? Another algorithm? And the expected market return- so what is it and how is it determined?. Expected return of a theoretical risk free asset- so how is it determined? The words may be 'nice' but unless validated by some method/formula to assure correctness, it is generally left to some theorist/analyst to suggest they have 'the' methods But they don't. They may be close. Maybe they are exceptional for a period of time- Elaine Garzarelli who 'predicted' the crash of 1987 and then????- or maybe lucky. Frankly, how could anyone beat 27 Phds and 2 Nobel laureates. But beat they were.

Of course one uses theories, past history and so on in context. But when the ego resonates more than common sense, real life and the reality of risk, there may simply be a period when the consequences of arrogance materializes.

Many of Taleb's comments are, however, valid. Such theories were taught until they became dogma. For close to two decades I have questioned the Efficient Market Theory. "An investment theory that states it is impossible to "beat the market" because stock market efficiency causes existing share prices to always incorporate and reflect all relevant information. Stocks always trade at their fair value on stock exchanges, making it impossible for investors to either purchase undervalued stocks or sell stocks for inflated prices. As such, it should be impossible to outperform the overall market through expert stock selection or market timing, and that the only way an investor can possibly obtain higher returns is by purchasing riskier investments." http://www.investopedia.com/terms/e/efficientmarkethypothesis.a sp#ixzz1Q0xc6X00.

That said, if all information was provided to all rational analysts at the same time, they all should come up with the same valuations. And they could only change when new information comes into the market. Yet the numbers vary tremendously-certainly when the economy is in strife. And since everything changes so quickly, how does one know that the prices are correct? The daily variations may be 'illogical'- or not. How does one know the 'news' is valid or noise'? No matter, **how can there be bubbles?** Cannot happen because they would quickly disappear as soon as they happened since all other investors could see the erroneous changes and bid it out of existence. Yet we see the dotcom and the real estate mess. The October 1987 black Monday was 23 sigmas from a possibility. See also Predictability of Asset Returns and the Efficient Market Hypothesis. http://d.repec.org/n?u=RePEc:cam:camdae:1033&r=fmk, "This paper is concerned with empirical and theoretical basis of the Efficient Market Hypothesis (EMH). The paper begins with an overview of the statistical properties of asset returns at different frequencies (daily, weekly and monthly), and considers the evidence on return predictability, risk aversion and market efficiency. The paper then focuses on the theoretical foundation of the EMH, and show that market efficiency could co-exist with heterogeneous beliefs and individual irrationality so long as individual errors are cross sectionally weakly dependent in the sense defined by Chudik, Pesaran, and Tosetti (2010). But at times of market euphoria or gloom these individual errors are likely to become cross sectionally strongly dependent and the collective outcome could display significant departures from market efficiency. Market efficiency could be the norm, but it is likely to be punctuated with episodes of bubbles and crashes." That follows a real life pattern of the market- periods of smoothness interspersed with wild periods of 5 or 10 or 20 or even 30 sigma deviations. Which most theory has said is impossible

So where are we today with regulations, oversight, new teachings? Pretty much nowhere. The recession was essentially declared over- or is it starting again? However, we now have trading by computers based on yet another set of algorithms offered by a "bright young men of disheveled appearance [playing out] megalomaniacal fantasies of omnipotence." "...... they have no sense of limits. The assertion that all human knowledge is encodable in streams of zeros and ones--philosophically, that's very hard to swallow. In effect, the whole world is made to seem computable. This generates a kind of tunnel vision, where the only problems that seem legitimate are problems that can be put on a computer. There is a whole world of real problems, of human problems, which is essentially ignored." (M.I.T. Computer Professor Joseph Weizenbaum).

The algorithms now are 'different' in that they have adjusted for risk- so we are told. Well, how can we know? We cannot- there is no way to stress test them- assuming the institutions would provide them for review- which they won't. Some computers time the stock market in milliseconds for the arbitrage that only a super computer can decipher. Admittedly, the computers are oblivious to the underlying stocks- merely looking at statistical 'abnormalities' that might exist. What impact might they have on the market overall-particularly during economic stress? Completely unknown. No one knows what are underlying the theories- if any. Maybe nothing since they are merely exploiting numbers. Maybe everything since they are exploiting numbers. We are told that there is no impact on the market and that they actually help liquidity. Frankly, it sounds like LTC all over again.

In any case, it will take at least a decade before the universities adjust to the real world. Maybe longer. No matter, the impact on the consumer will count little since the instruction has to get to the advisers they work with directly. It won't happen for a very long time. Even if the SEC and FINRA do attempt formal update, they are so far behind the times that they are almost assuredly incapable of providing the insight needed to the vast audience of 650,000 licensees that have never been taught the fundamentals of investing. How are they going to ramp up the instruction? I don't think they have any staff to do it. Certainly the industry would immediately lobby it to death as too expensive (it will cost a lot) and it sure would slow sales, just as I was told before.

Actually, reasonable instruction on risk may not make much difference anyway in the mid America market. Many, if not most consumers do not have the intellect to grasp the information properly (average IQ is 100 and some of this is tough stuff even offered in real life terms); many do not care no matter how material it is to their lives; they would not follow up as necessary; some will just procrastinate to failure; there will still be some who only 'trust' their rabbi or minister or their brother in law or can be marketed successfully with a chicken dinner; many others believe they have the capability of beating the market with a few stocks, and so on. Those reasons are clearly why they had to depend on paternalistic corporations and the defined benefit retirement plans. Except the pensions are almost gone forever. So is the wonderful retirement.

The Dodd Frank bill at the broker level is really a farce since the fiduciary level of responsibility and application cannot happen with the addition of just the word. Massive changes in instruction must include massive changes in the use of old, dying and dead theories.

### Summary

Mandelbrot noted that habit and convention rule. Business schools teach the old theories where the graduating students then have to change most of it to fit in the real world. But who is to say that they are anymore competent nor correct. After all, the teachings were outdated and they are now just making stuff up as they go along. Lots of errors will continue to destroy the financial system of mid America unless proper instruction is instituted.

Another: "Although experimental economics has made important inroads into the mainstream of economics and chance, the top journals still publish only a small fraction of experimental papers, the majority consisting of more traditional theoretical and empirical studies. Despite the fact that new theories of economic behavior have been proposed from time to time, most graduate programs in economics and chance teach only one such theory: expected utility theory and rational expectations, and its corresponding extensions, e.g., portfolio optimization, the Capital Asset Pricing Model, and dynamic general equilibrium asset-pricing models."

I am not indicating that the teachings are not reasonably relevant in the overall long term scheme of investing, but they miss the key element- they are not necessarily real life. Theory born in a test tube needs to be tested. Further, human optimism demands the necessity of addressing the underlying risks. But academia generally does not want to rock the boat and admit their teachings were in error (failure to properly address risk). You therefore had old theories as dogma that are being questioned now- but it is effectively not getting to advisors and certainly not for use by consumers. The focus of this material is towards risk but that will require an effort that I really do not believe will be implemented to a large audience. But fiduciaries must take on the responsibility. Now .

The one very unique current occurrence might change that however. Americans are absolutely fed up with the status quo of arrogance and ineptness by politicians and will vote out many in a wholesale referendum for something better. Maybe they will force many systems to adapt much, much sooner than I anticipated. Perhaps wishful thinking but the polls have never been this low.

# FINANCIAL PLANNING
# FIDUCIARY STANDARDS UNDER DODD FRANK

# 4

# How Statistics Can Lie

This chapter's intent is to orient one to the fact that the statistical numbers offered by literally every site, software program and agent may be "correct" in terms of computations but still have nothing to do with real life. It is so easy to do with a computer particularly when looking at past numbers. And, reinforced throughout, the mantra of the past being the sole or major focus for the future is not only suspect, it is generally a crutch or marketing gimmick to offer very appealing graphs without have to think much at all (see reversion to the mean and more herein). People like to focus/accept what the past has been since that is 'what they know'. (Actually that is really not correct because that tends to be a distortion of what actually happened rather than the true facts. Nothing unique here- it is just human behavior remembering what and how they want to remember something. So reliance on the past may be useless.)

Most everyone is familiar with the term, 'liars can figure and figures can lie'. Here is the perfect example of absolutely true numbers that can be misused to provide whatever support one desires.

Assume we are looking at the number of cell phones

sold from 1959 to 2009. Let's first take 1959 to 1989. I will take a little latitude and say there were none. So if we look at the average number of cell phones sold during those 30 years we get ZERO. A true statistic but with effectively no value.

Now let's take 1989 to 1999- we will use a number of 5,000,000 phones in total for an average of 500,000 per year. Maybe an O.K. statistic but let's also take the full period of 40 years from 1959. That's 125,000 per year. An absolutely true number, but what is the point? The use of the first 30 years of no sales is a useless statistic but it can be used to show a much lower yearly average in case some "adviser" wants to distort reality.

Let's look at 1999 to 2009. I will use another 15,000,000 phones (far too few but remember this is just an example). That's 1,500,000 per year. Looks great- but it actually is a great distortion of reality. Certainly the greatest number of phones were sold between 2004 and 2009- even between 2007 and 2009. An average does not reflect the huge increases that reflect the later years. But unless you thought about this or were aware of the sales, the average is one that a lot of people might accept. And use to support any future projections.

However, if I really wanted to distort reality, I could simply take 20,000,000 phones in total and divide by 50 years for an average of 400,000 per year. Absolutely a mathematically correct number that has little to do with reality.

I submit that when one is given statistics on what has happened for past results in the market, it is necessary to tear apart what is truly taking place with the computations before you commit your funds to an unsupportable position. (See data mining and backtesting herein- it becomes "clear" how AIG could 'validate' a 17.53% return in an insurance policy for the next 50 years.)

That said, this is done all the time since very few

people question the numbers from a computer program. I do not necessarily blame then since it takes some time, effort and experience to know what should have been projected. But to have the major B/D firms do it consistently is a violation of trust and fiduciary duty. (See portion of recent report herein.)

*If you put tomfoolery into a computer, nothing comes out of it but tomfoolery. But this tomfoolery, having passed through a very expensive machine, is somehow enobled and no one dares criticize it.*
Pierre Gallois

As one stats professor noted when giving an exam- "you can use any program you want as long as your wrote it yourself. Otherwise you do not know dirt about the end results." One cannot assume the validity of computer programs. For those with background at this point, consider Long Term Capital. Finest program 'ever' written by 27 Phds and 2 Nobel Laureates, Problem was it blew up and almost took the U.S. banking system with it save for intervention by Greenspan. That is the perfect reason to question everything.

I have found it necessary several times to review software financial plans from major Broker/Dealer firms- Ameriprise and UBS for example- since I could not validate the conclusions they reached for their portfolio/asset allocation selection. Their end results were prepackaged plans that did not have merit- but made all the more difficult to analyze because the firms refused to indicate what they had done in some areas because it was 'privileged'. Such issues were correlation, standard deviation, and, obviously risk. In no cases was the risk of loss for the portfolio identified save for the superficial comments that the market goes up and down. (At least they got that right)

Additionally, and maybe the worst of the inputs, was the fact that the consumer was the one that 'determined ' what risk they were willing or wanted to take. Such interpreted numbers may border on useless since the insight to correct numbers was nebulous at best.

**Fifth grade math**

Here is an absolute gem that I learned from a teacher in around the fifth grade. Take the number .0987327 that is absolutely accurate. Then multiply it by 86,300. However this number is a guesstimate that needs/should be rounded. So I will use 90,000 as 'acceptable'. Crank it out of a computer/calculator and it shows 8,885.943. It appears that that is correct/specific/absolutely accurate since it shows three decimal places.

**Wrong**

It is no more 'accurate' that the number that was rounded. But that is not what the consumer sees or interprets. Nor even what a fiduciary understands. But it becomes acceptable because it "came out of a computer". Caveat emptor

Another example comes from the dotcom. I was approached by several companies to potentially join them since they were poised to make money by gathering a significant portion of the business to business market. I reviewed several privileged proformas. Every number was on a spread sheet, every number matched properly, every number was multiplied correctly- it was a no brainer. Not quite. The problem was that the estimates used had nothing to do with reality. The 50,000 should have been 5,000. The 5,000 should have been 50. The arithmetic was perfect- but the input was either fuzzy or worthless. Did it work for a lot of firms? Of course since venture capitalists put out millions.

Whenever you view financial calculations, you need to be aware of the potential distortions. Few investors think through the material that objectively. Hence they become cannon fodder for the black box calculations. Admittedly, it is just part of human nature. But it cannot be for the fiduciary.

# 5

# Past Success as a Guide to Future Performance

*"If history books were the key to riches, the Forbes 400 would consist of librarians."*

Warren Buffett

One of the key focuses on investing by almost all advisers and the public is looking to the past as a precursor to the future. At this point, I will digress somewhat to this comment on 'backtesting' or "data mining".

Investopedia notes, "Many valuable lessons can be learned from history, but extrapolating historical returns into the future is difficult and complicated. For instance, few investors in 1900 could have predicted the monumental changes that would take place in the world after 1913. The two world wars, profound impact on the global economy and stock markets until the 1970s. The impact of these events suggests that although we can study the past, the social and economic events that might affect the markets in the future are often unpredictable.

In the world of finance, too many quants (those engaged in quantitative finance) see only the numbers before them and forget about the concrete reality the figures are supposed to represent. They think they can model just a few years' worth of data and come up with probabilities for things that may happen only once every 10,000 years. Then people invest on the basis of those probabilities, without stopping to wonder whether the numbers make any sense at all. (Felix Salmon) http://www.wired.com/techbiz/it/magazine/17-03/wp_quant?currentPage=all

Furthermore, despite the clear success of the U.S. markets since 1900 to 2000, investors need to remember that this exceptional performance may be just that: the exception, rather than the rule for the twentieth century. "Triumph Of The Optimists" argues that economic and stock market performance in the U.S. has not been typical of other countries and, therefore, should not necessarily be extrapolated into the future."

Nobel award winner Harry Markowitz does not believe you can use historical returns as inputs in portfolio optimization. He thinks the assumptions underpinning the capital asset pricing model are strange.

More recently, the world has had a revolutionary change matching anything previous- the radio and TV included. The personal computer along with the Internet have altered the world and the investing landscape in a manner heretofore unheard of. It has revolutionalized the dispersion of information beyond anything even remotely comprehended previously. Note however that I am addressing the scope of the change, not necessarily the value. The Internet has flooded the investing landscape with billions of pieces of data that has been misinterpreted by many as being knowledge per se. I repeat- it is information first and foremost that must be formally made sense of. But that is not the interpretation by the majority of consumers and advisors. Even professors. They quickly pick whatever flecks of data they wish to use under the guise of facts and then, more often than not, distort them to their whim.

That is a perfect example of current debacle. The investing arena of the mid 1990s forward was inundated with illogical streams of data on investing- certainly as it applied to the tremendous changes and "absolute" opportunities of the Internet stocks. All sorts of consumers- almost all naive and unsophisticated (no matter what they believed) - begged and borrowed (margin accounts) to be part of the "undeniable" new world order where, per some esoteric commentary by some pretty boys on the nightly news- the international economies had changed and there would be no more downturns- certainly no more recessions. I disagreed with that almost in its entirety (though one can always be wrong) and taught the exposure to risk at classes at UC Berkeley (the losses of 1974/75 in particular). But due to the unbridled marketing of the media, the message never went in one ear and out the other. It never got that far. After all, buying into the Dotcom had been a unparalleled success. Or so they thought. (Never taught another class at UC. Doesn't make a lot of sense to put in that much time and effort if no one wants to pay attention to the real world.)

Per Bill Jahnke, "A lot of the work on formulating return expectations is based on a bad assumption that the underlying population from which returns data is being sampled is stable. If the process is stable, then you can extrapolate. If it is unstable, then extrapolation can be wide off the mark, both in terms of expected return and the distribution of returns. The case against the stable return generating process is that the historical return distributions do not behave in accordance with the belief. The tails of the distribution when you plot them out on a chart are too fat, and they expand at a slower rate than predicted. Also, valuation levels of asset classes in terms of market-to-book ratios, price-earnings ratios, dividend yields and yield curves vary considerably relative to earnings and inflation expectations, which also undermines the notion of a stable return generating system. This is not something that the statisticians and econometricians were concerned about in their analysis of historical returns. For their data to be useful, however, statisticians need it to say something about the future. So they make the assumption that the population they use is stable and unchanging. To do otherwise would invalidate their assumptions about the future. Using historical data always makes that error. If you don't believe the underlying population statistics are stable, however, then there is great uncertainty about the numbers.

So how has that mucked up the work of advisors? What it has boiled down to is that financial advisors were encouraged to plug historical returns into portfolio optimizers, specify the risk tolerance ('determined' by their clients) and come up with an investment policy. Since the historical data just creeps along glacially, once the advisor determines an asset allocation policy, he needs to stick with it. When times get tough, the advisor tells a client to stick with the asset allocation policy because market timing doesn't work. The good news for the advisor is that he doesn't need to really understand very much. How does the bad assumption of a stable return generating system create flaws in portfolios? Portfolios are created with the underlying notion that the longer your holding period, the more likely it is you will get a return close to the expected return, and the less likely it is that stocks are going to under-perform bonds. According to this view, in the long run, stocks are less risky than bonds. The whole focus on managing risk is shifted to managing the short-term variability of returns. This is the central idea behind a doctrine of static asset allocation. But the whole paradigm blows up when the assumption of a stable return generating process is violated. So financial advisors and their clients have to face the prospect that in the long run they won't get returns expected and clients won't get their financial objectives funded. The system is broken."

**The system IS broken**

This quote from Dr. Frederick Mark Gedicks. Professor of Law, BYU, succinctly puts a real life focus on the problem for consumers- "Although the online revolution has indeed afforded individual investors control of their investment portfolios and direct access to market information and services, profits have proven more elusive. Assembling drastically under-diversified portfolios, trading on impulse and rumor, and blithely leveraging their holdings with margin loans, many of these "self-directed" investors incurred substantial losses in self-managed accounts despite the relentless appreciation of equities during the 1990s.

**Others were misled by the initial appreciation of their holdings, misunderstanding this as confirmation that their risky strategies were sound**, when in fact they were not. After the market turned in early 2001, it became clear that **many self-directed investors lacked basic knowledge about securities markets and investing generally, and as a result incurred substantial losses when their under-diversified, speculative, and over-leveraged portfolios evaporated in the bursting of the technology bubble and the general market decline."**

(Confirmation bias. (WSJ) People are twice as likely

to seek information that confirms what they already believe as they are to consider evidence that would challenge those beliefs. A psychologist noted, "We're all mentally lazy." "It's simply easier to focus our attention on data that supports our hypothesis, rather than to seek out evidence that might disprove it." It also is easier for people to rationalize than to be rational. "We're very good at cooking up post-hoc explanations of why our predictions didn't work,")

One of the more compelling validations of the above comes from the number of members of the National Association of Investment Clubs (NAIC)- now BetterInvesting.org- (WSJ February 2007). Repeated again- they went from a peak of 570,000 in 2000 to 90,000 in 2011. Investors, clueless to diversification, and certainly oblivious to the numbers for risk were told that following its advice and formulas, they could beat the market. FINRA, under the guidance of Mary Schapiro, gave a grant of $354,500 to provide investor education (more on government waste later).

Therein is the almost complete fallacy and breakdown of the understanding of risk for all. There is NOT a formal text that even remotely suggests that individuals purchase single stocks for portfolio allocations. While true that texts such as Investments by Bodie, Kane and Marcus fully define effectively most of the elements of corporate stock analysis, they are directly designed for professional CFAs (Chartered Financial Analysts) or university students who deal at a different level than the average consumers. (Though that still does not mean successfully). The point is that any genuine text definitively states the value- actually the necessity- of diversifying a portfolio so that unsystematic risk is effectively eliminated.

The incomparable validation of this significance is the book, Capital Ideas by Peter Bernstein. The text covers every major theorist from Bachelier, Keynes. Fama, Sharpe, Sholes and many more. Not one examination, not one premise, not one advisor even remotely suggests the active involvement with the purchase of stocks by the average consumer (to encompass an allocation). The playing field is not necessarily a zero sum game for all. But it does mean that the average person has probably no hope, save by luck and excess risk- in beating the market. Even the most sophisticated advisers may not do that well- and in time nary but one or two will do better (and we have no idea who they will be beforehand). Think Bill Miller.

There are a number of items on past versus future herein but a couple more come to mind. AIG and the backtesting of three indexes is a perfect example of bad statistics. AIG had shown it was possible to pick numbers from the past and present them for the consumers looking to invest for the future. The consumer buying the insurance never knew what was going on, but the research showed that by finagling numbers and statistics, they were showing that it was possible to get 17.53% each year for the next 50 years. Nobody, even the most lame optimist, believes anything like that, but that is what is out there if no one pays attention. Or if the agent, broker, financial whatever does not have to practice as a fiduciary. (Once again- where is the financial calculator?)

How about some academic studies? A couple come to mind on equity returns-

What Do Past Stock Market Returns Tell Us About the Future? (William Reichenstein):

http://wrfinancialconcepts.com/pdfs/past_stockmarket _returns _future.pdf

"Most scholars believe that the equity risk premium has decreased. A decrease in the equity risk premium decreases the market's expected rate of return and it raises the market's price earnings and price dividends ratios.

The key points are that a decrease in the equity risk

premium first lowers the market's long-run expected return and, second, raises the market's normal price-earnings and price-dividend multiples. Furthermore, because long-horizon stock returns can be explained partially by earnings yield and dividend yield, the stock-predictability literature suggests that the equity risk premium does indeed vary. Everything else the same, today's low earnings yield and dividend yield (or high market multiples) thus imply low future stock returns." Of course there are studies saying the opposite- that returns will be the same. I do not agree since we also have the reduction in dividends

(S&P 500) over the past decades

| Year | Earnings Yield | Dividend Yield | S&P 500 | Earnings | Dividends |
|---|---|---|---|---|---|
| 1960 | 5.34% | 3.41% | 58.11 | 3.10 | 1.98 |
| 1961 | 4.71% | 2.85% | 71.55 | 3.37 | 2.04 |
| 1962 | 5.81% | 3.40% | 63.1 | 3.67 | 2.15 |
| 1963 | 5.51% | 3.13% | 75.02 | 4.13 | 2.35 |
| 1964 | 5.62% | 3.05% | 84.75 | 4.76 | 2.58 |
| 1965 | 5.73% | 3.06% | 92.43 | 5.30 | 2.83 |
| 1966 | 6.74% | 3.59% | 80.33 | 5.41 | 2.88 |
| 1967 | 5.66% | 3.09% | 96.47 | 5.46 | 2.98 |
| 1968 | 5.51% | 2.93% | 103.86 | 5.72 | 3.04 |
| 1969 | 6.63% | 3.52% | 92.06 | 6.10 | 3.24 |
| 1970 | 5.98% | 3.46% | 92.15 | 5.51 | 3.19 |
| 1971 | 5.46% | 3.10% | 102.09 | 5.57 | 3.16 |
| 1972 | 5.23% | 2.70% | 118.05 | 6.17 | 3.19 |
| 1973 | 8.16% | 3.70% | 97.55 | 7.96 | 3.61 |
| 1974 | 13.64% | 5.43% | 68.56 | 9.35 | 3.72 |
| 1975 | 8.55% | 4.14% | 90.19 | 7.71 | 3.73 |
| 1976 | 9.07% | 3.93% | 107.46 | 9.75 | 4.22 |

| 1977 | 11.43% | 5.11% | 95.1 | 10.87 | 4.86 |
|---|---|---|---|---|---|
| 1978 | 12.11% | 5.39% | 96.11 | 11.64 | 5.18 |
| 1979 | 13.48% | 5.53% | 07.94 | 14.55 | 5.97 |
| 1980 | 11.04% | 4.74% | 135.76 | 14.99 | 6.44 |
| 1981 | 12.39% | 5.57% | 122.55 | 15.18 | 6.83 |
| 1982 | 9.83% | 4.93% | 140.64 | 13.82 | 6.93 |
| 1983 | 8.06% | 4.32% | 164.93 | 13.29 | 7.12 |
| 1984 | 10.07% | 4.68% | 167.24 | 16.84 | 7.83 |
| 1985 | 7.42% | 3.88% | 211.28 | 15.68 | 8.20 |
| 1986 | 5.96% | 3.38% | 242.17 | 14.43 | 8.19 |
| 1987 | 6.49% | 3.71% | 247.08 | 16.04 | 9.17 |
| 1988 | 8.69% | 3.68% | 277.72 | 24.12 | 10.22 |
| 1989 | 6.88% | 3.32% | 353.4 | 24.32 | 11.73 |
| 1990 | 6.86% | 3.74% | 330.22 | 22.65 | 12.35 |
| 1991 | 4.63% | 3.11% | 417.09 | 19.30 | 12.97 |
| 1992 | 4.79% | 2.90% | 435.71 | 20.87 | 12.64 |
| 1993 | 5.77% | 2.72% | 466.45 | 26.90 | 12.69 |
| 1994 | 6.91% | 2.91% | 459.27 | 31.75 | 13.36 |
| 1995 | 6.12% | 2.30% | 615.93 | 37.70 | 14.17 |

| 1996 | 5.49% | 2.01% | 740.74 | 40.63 | 14.89 |
|---|---|---|---|---|---|
| 1997 | 4.54% | 1.60% | 970.43 | 44.09 | 15.52 |
| 1998 | 3.60% | 1.32% | 1229.23 | 44.27 | 16.20 |
| 1999 | 3.52% | 1.14% | 1469.25 | 51.68 | 16.71 |
| 2000 | 4.25% | 1.23% | 1320.28 | 56.13 | 16.27 |
| 2001 | 3.38% | 1.37% | 1148.09 | 38.85 | 15.74 |
| 2002 | 5.23% | 1.83% | 879.82 | 46.04 | 16.08 |
| 2003 | 4.92% | 1.61% | 1111.91 | 4.69 | 17.88 |
| 2004 | 5.58% | 1.60% | 1211.92 | 7.68 | 19.407 |
| 2005 | 6.12% | 1.79% | 1248.29 | 6.45 | 22.38 |
| 2006 | 6.18% | 1.77% | 1418.3 | 7.72 | 25.05 |
| 2007 | 5.62% | 1.89% | 1468.36 | 2.54 | 27.73 |
| 2008 | 7.24% | 3.11% | 903.25 | 5.39 | 28.05 |
| 2009 | 5.45% | 2.00% | 1115.1 | 0.8 | 22.31 |
| 2010 | 6.65% | 1.84% | 1257.64 | 3.66 | 23.12 |

You can see how returns are now more heavily focused on appreciation. Since dividends are down, they have a direct and negative impact on total returns. In March 2011, the dividend yield on the S&P 500 was 1.7%.

## Summary

When viewed objectively, and certainly in context with a new world order, huge deficits and more, I am in agreement that returns will be down for the foreseeable future. I do have to estimate returns for the future and there is a formal chapter included that addresses what I review. No matter, investment and bond returns will be lower and this has a most immediate impact on the retired and all the generation y and x that need to determine who much to invest for their future.

# 6

# Cognitive Impairment, Investor Disassociation With Reality and How Marketing Can Misdirect Consumers

**First the basics:**

Daniel Kahneman and Amos Tversky collaborated in the general field of judgment and decision making decades ago (prospect theory). Kahneman won the Nobel prize in Economics for this work. (Tversky would have won as well but they do not award anything for the deceased. Something seems amiss there.) The field really opened up in the mid 90s as more and more researchers worked in the area of the rational/irrational thought process of people in all sorts of situations- noticeably involving investments.

See Behavioral Finance by Albert Phung. Nice concise overview.

http://www.investopedia.com/university/behavioral_finance/behavi oral2.asp

It is not my purpose here to address all the areas of cognitive (process of thought) dissonance (a condition of conflict or anxiety resulting from inconsistency between one's beliefs and one's actions) on the subject but to simply address those specific areas towards investing. Let me give a brief description of the more salient issues. But first, a most important area not generally discussed in any material.

**Unique Circumstances**

I do wish to cover certain issues that distort the thought process that planners- actually anyone- needs to address. If someone has been sick or in pain for a long time, all bets are off in their capability in normal reasoning. Obviously it is possible for them to 'stay alive', but when you are that bad off health wise over time, your brain will seize up at some point. One's life no longer can focus objectively, depression will normally occur and more. There is also the elements of divorce, death, job loss and more and each person is impacted differently, Of course one can throw in all the facets of life that cause problems but the point is to be aware of the times that certain emotional issues can really distort rational thought. If a planner is doing their job, this will become apparent in the questionnaire/discussion phase and the adviser must take special care in whatever they do. However, since it is rarely if ever addressed, perhaps only older planners might recognize how the inherent problems of ill health et al can alter rational thought.

The same can be said about the early stages of senile dementia or Alzheimers. People can try to act normal- and want to- but certain elements will become 'obvious' to a 'seasoned' rep. (Their use of certain words- or lack thereof- are types of tipoffs.) Once again I may mean 'older advisers' since one becomes far more aware of this insidious disease as they see what happens to parents and others. Younger agents may not note such odd behavior as various mental miscues, short term memory lapses, etc. But we are discussing multifaceted issues that need to be known by a fiduciary and caution advised when these scenarios arise. It is therefore mandatory that exceptional notes be taken.

If there is any question, you either do not do anything or you might want to involve a family member, attorney and/or doctor to provide assistance. This is a very delicate area. If there are no relatives to help or they are in denial, the person has refused to get independent help, etc. do not attempt an investment.

**Dissonance Issues**

Recency Bias: People tend to focus too much on what has happened recently. (What goes up will continue to go up. And down to continue down. However consumers tend to 'forget the bad times).

Anchoring: Some investors become "anchored" to certain reference points that influence their decisions. Say an investor buys a stock at $50 and it falls to $40 because the fundamentals have changed or bad news has come to light. The best thing to do might be to sell the stock for $40. But many people are prone to wait for the price to recover to the amount they have become anchored to: $50. And they may wait forever...........

Loss Aversion: Investors are reluctant to realize losses, and conversely, investors are disinclined to sell because they want the positive reinforcement that comes from securing a gain.

Here are two different studies. The first group was asked to choose between a 100% chance of gain of $240 vs. a 25% chance to gain $1,000 coupled with a 75% chance to gain nothing. More than 3/4 went for the sure gain. The second group was a sure loss of $240 vs. a 25% chance to lose $1,000 coupled with a 75% chance to lose nothing. More than 2/3 opted for the latter- the chance to lose nothing. The lesson: **People will avoid a sure loss at all costs because to them, losses loom larger than gains, even if it is not true. It is generally stated that losses have an emotional impact twice as much as a gain.** My experience is that it is true- more so when there is a major loss. But if the market goes up, recency bias is apt to play a part because some investors ‘want’ to forget the bad decisions they might have made and just focus on getting in on the action again. And then continue to buy the wrong things from the wrong people at the wrong time for the wrong reason (or none at all).

I will digress for a moment on the above and how it plays into real life if litigation is involved. I “don’t mind” (latitude taken) that some consumers want to take a flyer with perhaps 5% to 10% of their monies if the rest is allocated properly. What I cannot dismiss is if they take large sections, all or it, or even leverage to use more into an investment that defies common sense. They have to accept some of the responsibility for losses that may very well be sustained. Arbitrators do it; juries do it- there is some personal responsibility that has to be accepted.

Now, within that comment are two distinct issues. The first is if an investment was offered by a brokering entity that has a duty under FINRA to be sure that the risk is appropriate. “It must be suitable”. Therefore there is a much greater exposure for the advisor to do the right thing and such liability should/might result in much greater reward to the litigant. (Unfortunately this may not occur in litigation if none of the parties are versed in what should have happened. There is a big difference in stating something is wrong without indicating what should have been done.)

On the other hand, when there is no direct suitability element- such as buying a house with cheater documents or investing most of their money into affinity scams with no SEC involvement- any returns of funds are apt to be much, much lower because the litigant should have done far more homework of, if nothing else, used common sense.

Mental Accounting: This is the idea that we treat money differently based on where it came from or where we hold it.

Here is a real life example. My brother in law worked for Digital and held lots of its stock (a violation of diversification in itself) as it road up in price to $200 per share. Then the company fell into disfavor and the shares slid down to the mid $50s. Obviously he and my sister felt they should hold on- after all it was 'his' company and the value 'would' go back up. (But losing 75% of value is totally illogical). Unfortunately he died in his mid 40s but she held the stock even though it kept going down to $16 a share. The shares represented her deceased husband. Logical? Not really. Human? Absolutely.

And in another, I was requested to review a stock portfolio that contained inheritances that came from her grandmother. A couple companies had terrible ratings but she would not sell them since they represented her loved relative.

Framing. Two groups were asked the same question in two ways. Roughly 50% said they could **not** when asked "Could you comfortably save 20% of your household's income at this point in your life". But more than 7 in 10 said they **could** when asked "Could you comfortably line on 80% of your household income today."

I offer this in more detail: You go to your doctor and he greets you with a sour/concerned look and says, "I am sorry Mrs., Jones but you have a brain tumor. We can operate but I there is a 10% chance of dying". The next doctor starts with a relatively optimistic tone: "Hello Mrs. Jones. I have some bad new and some good news. The bad news is that you have a brain tumor but the good news is that the operation has a 90% success rate". How do you think one would feel? Same numbers, same risk- just phrased differently. It's obvious.

The lesson: Framing often depends on a person's reference point and what is most likely to influence them

Mental Accounting. The questions related to mental accounting asked a group how they would spend their money in two apparently different retain situations

Would they buy a much needed alarm clock from a local store for $18 or from a store 20 minutes away selling the same clock for $10. And would they buy a new television from a local store for $250 or from a store 20 minutes away for $242. In both cases the savings was $8 (This was well before the cost of gas was a consideration)

Two thirds said they would drive 20 minutes to save the money on the clock but almost 75% would not drive the 20 minutes for the savings on the TV The lesson: We approach decision differently depending on the context in which they are embedded. In this case, people categorize money based on relative, rather than absolute costs. (But even the least astute recognizes the savings is so much less with the TV that I think they just don't want to bother).

And my favorite: Confabulation- "We often engage in something called confabulation, which is basically **making up a story we can believe in to explain away behavior and facts we don't understand, are incapable of understanding or are too lazy to figure out.** . We are very good at pattern recognition, and whether or not we have the story correct as to what is causing the pattern, we naturally learn to associate cause and effect".

This material encompasses a huge amount of variability since the human can "attempt" several rationalizations at the same time. It is very hard to figure out in total and the attempt may take many diversions and interpretations. But the reference for this effort is towards investing.

**RISK**

One very important result of Kahneman and Tversky work is demonstrating that people's attitudes toward risks concerning gains may be quite different from their attitudes toward risks concerning losses. That is a very important distinction. For example, when given a choice between getting $1000 with certainty or having a 50% chance of getting $2500 they may well choose the certain $1000 in preference to the uncertain chance of getting $2500 even though the mathematical expectation of the uncertain option is $1250. This is a perfectly reasonable attitude that is described as risk-aversion. But Kahneman and Tversky found that the same people when confronted with a certain loss of $1000 versus a 50% chance of no loss or a $2500 loss do often choose the risky alternative. This is called risk-seeking behavior. It is generally conceded that the **pain of loss is at least twice the emotion as that of a gain.**

As you have read repeatedly in this material, I make direct reference to the ***risk of loss***. That is what investors want to know, need to know, and are simply not given.

*Risk: Well, it certainly doesn't mean standard deviation. People mainly think of risk in terms of downside risk. They are concerned about the maximum they can lose. So that's what risk means. In contrast, the professional view defines risk in terms of variance, and doesn't discriminate gains from losses. There is a great deal miscommunication and misunderstanding because of these very different views of risk. Beta does not do it for most people, who are more concerned with the possibility of loss*

Daniel Kahneman

There are hundreds of sites that will talk about risk but only in general terms. For example, the legal terminology is apt to be- "Possibility that an investment's actual return will be different than expected; includes the possibility of losing some or all of the original investment. Measured by variability of historical returns or dispersion of historical returns around their average return."

Such definitions however give an indication of the fallacy of the legal system at work because a lot of the above is wrong. While true that owning one or two stocks can show a total loss, a diversified portfolio- say the S&P 500- will never go to zero (assume unleveraged). And the real measurement of risk is an existing standard deviation coupled with a purely statistical loss formula (risk of loss is almost solely computed by a financial calculator). It is absolutely NOT standard deviation with a smooth Gaussian curve as addressed above. But it has been taught that way for decades. And still is.

The use of correlation with standard deviation is an area addressed separately but also makes the measurement extremely laborious. Nonetheless, it is possible to generate a number expressing a range of loss for a particular portfolio allocation and to show what can/will happen when the economy hits a bad patch. Such definitive calculation limits the emotional factors to investing to a more objective one. The investor cannot solely focus on hoping for a high return without recognizing the potential of loss. I submit that such exposure to the real world would have changed the focus of hundreds of thousands of investors during the last decade. And every participant in a 401k plan. I do admit that they may not have paid much attention anyway, but that may more to do with the quality of instruction and material than anything else.

## Marketing

The cognitive instability also can be targeted for marketing and sales. It is possible to sway the reaction of a consumer/investor by asking the questions in a manner that provokes the answer one is looking for. Or, being cynical, getting a nebulous answer that might mean anything. I once again point to the consumer brokerage forms.

The following abstract, How to adapt to changing markets: experience and personality in a repeated **investment game**

(http://ideas.repec.org/p/tse/wpaper/22245.html), Astrid Hopfensitz and Tanja Wranik, is from a series on Cognitive and Behavioral Economics I subscribe to. It is not necessary to read the paper itself to get the gist of the research. It is obvious that there is irrational behavior overall. And such behavior invalidates a lot of prior research of MPT (modern portfolio theory) that people act in a rational process towards investing.

"Investment behavior is traditionally investigated with the assumption that risky investment is on average advantageous. However, this may not always be the case. In this paper, we experimentally studied investment choices made by students and financial professionals under favorable and unfavorable market conditions in a multi-round investment game. In particular, the probability of winning was set so that investment in one condition was advantageous, and in one condition was disadvantageous. To investigate who is more likely to adapt their investment behaviors to the changing market conditions, we also measured personality and self efficacy. We expected that investment behavior in changing markets could be predicted by a combination of experience (students, professionals), personality (anxiety, optimism, impulsivity, and Openness to Experience), and self-efficacy (belief in one's ability to make good decisions in an investment task). Results indicate that professionals do not significantly differ from students in their decisions. Personality and self-efficacy both predicted investment behavior. In particular, we found that optimism and anxiety were a liability in unfavorable markets, leading to unreasonable levels of risk. Impulsivity was a liability in both favorable and unfavorable markets, leading to high risk on unfavorable markets, and low risk in favorable markets. Openness to experience was an asset in unfavorable markets, leading to adjusted risk taking. Finally, self-efficacy (ability to produce a desired result) was generally related to higher levels of risk."

And again: **Something that psychologists certainly know and economists never look at is that people don't learn from their own past mistakes. Economics assumes we learn, and because we are able to learn, we can correct. Cognitive psychologists have done a number of studies that show that *people don't learn from the past.* Because we are not able to learn from the past, we may look at a specific past mistakes and decide if we were only more careful, we could have prevented it. But we don't. We will still get into mania almost the same way the next time and the time after.**

Lifson and Geist, The Psychology of Investing

Such illogical, irrational or subjective positions are endemic/inbred /wired into humans. They are not going to be dismissed into oblivion with the mere architecture of computer software.

**Do we really need the theory?**

Obesity- while some may find this section completely out of context, it is the issue that really focuses on the irrationality of consumers overall. It is not necessary from the 90s forward to address irrational behavior as regards investors/consumers since it was obvious when any person looked at the people on the sidewalk of any city in the U.S. clearly showed a truly pathetic rationalization to their own selves. A huge number of fat people waddling along- into McDonalds, Pizza Hut and every other type of restaurants- all offering meals far beyond the necessary caloric intake. With tons of salt and sugar. Everyone one of these people- with corresponding irresponsibility to their children- consuming gallons of sugary soft drinks every month. The point is that any reasonable person knows full well that eating 22 Deep Fried Twinkies at a sitting is going to add pounds to a waistline. They 'knew' their children's health was being compromised. Didn't they??? Was it that hard to comprehend such actions? We are not talking about some potentially esoteric definition of diversification. We are dealing with a purely visual, purely physical rationalization that defies credulity.

But was all this so new, so impossible to recognize, so hard to put two plus two together when two pounds plus two pounds squared and then squared again equals an absurdity to begin with? In 2009, 23% of the states had an increase in obesity- none going down. If it simply felt good, looked good, tasted good, whatever good, it made no difference in the final tally of silliness. It was already obvious this reflects a populace that is irrational at its core. ***By 2018, 43% of ALL American will be obese***. 103 million people. It never should have taken much for any university researcher to recognize real life- the failure was monumental in its obviousness. Of course people are irrational. Of course they do foolish things. They do not have to be tested in a college setting to show how irrational people can be. Maybe it was not a major issue decades ago, but the expanding waistlines of the last 20 years makes behavioral finance quite conspicuous.

**Affinity Scams**

Real life gets worse. A few years ago I acted as an expert on a $35 million real estate fraud. Some investors had limited education-some had Masters or more. But the first question out of my mouth regardless of background when informed of literally all types of fraud is, "is a church involved" and "was he handsome"? These are called affinity scams. People put down their guard when they are involved with people of similar ideas and beliefs- or possibly projecting an aura of success simply because they looked 'right and said the right words'.

Religion is one of the worst places for affinity scams but it can be PTA, golf buddy, AA, literally anything at all. It is the same with referrals. People assume- or like to assume- that the referred agent has been highly scrutinized by the referee. In the case above, the sons were referred by their mother, a grandson by his grandmother. Irrational, illogical bordering on being insipid. Or greedy and lazy. I know the comments are not nice but losing millions with no thought process at all is far worse.

Think about the Madoff scandal. Those who chose Madoff directly did so because of the exclusivity of the venture- cognitive dissonance at its extreme. The human perception of value was easy to engage because of the proximity of the Palm Beach Tennis and Golf Club or his being Jewish. No homework- just emotion.

Switching to pure marketing, here is an exceptional article on fund marketing by John Haslem, Mutual Funds and Investor Choice, http://www.indexuniverse.com/publications/journalofindex

es/joiarticles/8242-mutual-funds-and-investor-choice.html. The research indicates unsophisticated investor choices are dominated by fund advertising. Fund advertising appeals to investor emotions by resonating with their current beliefs, not by providing direct and objective information that enables more informed fund choices.

Sophisticated investors with self-assessed above-average investment skills view themselves as true "wizards of Oz." They believe their investment skills allow them to select superior-performing actively managed funds. Why should they purchase "boring" index funds that only provide "average returns"? Actually, these "sophisticated investors" should choose index funds because their choices of actively managed funds do not outperform index funds

And, ". . . financial literacy is not related to mutual fund selection abilities. Investors with higher financial literacy scores are not 'smart investors.'" Further, ". . . any fund selection skills among more sophisticated respondents are minor and short-lived at best."

The results also indicate that ". overconfidence is a possible explanation for why even highly sophisticated participants mostly select active funds."

Further comments are already recognized by the bulk of the industry but still should not come as a surprise to the novice- "Ultimately, the purpose of mutual fund advertising is to persuade investors to invest more and to increase fund adviser profits. This is a far cry from advertising that provides investors with full and objective information that enables them to become "smarter investors."

Haslem has done an excellent article on the marketing of product and should be read by anyone focusing on how the individual investor relates to marketing.

But then many people are simply lazy, greedy and just plain stupid (note the repetition). Ponzi scheme after Ponzi scheme offer returns beyond comprehension and people run after the money assured that it will come to pass. There are those that will do some homework, but the bulk of activity is borne out of nonsensical or completely empty thought processes. Unsubstantiated referrals are one of the worst ways.

But considering the thought process of what is being presented to our children at school, it appears that the public enjoy the lack of effort to learn what to do objectify as they focus on the simplistic. As they go have another Big Mac. With fries. And Supersized

**Summary**

It does not require a genius to recognize the illogical activities of consumers at all. Nor the fact that many discordant thoughts can occur at the same time. The point is that the brokerage/planning industry has been able to devise questionnaires upon questionnaires that can point the consumer to what the firms want them to do. Of course the defense might be that the firms themselves do not have the requisite skills to begin with. And the validity of that is what??????

See also, Human (Ir)rationality, Marketing, and Investment Sophistication http://www.efmoody.com/behavior.html

Lastly recognize that brokers, supervisors, CEOs are humans as well and can also be easily 'corrupted' by illogical thought processes. .

# 7

# Ethics, Integrity, Legality, Licensing, More Marketing

**NOTHING IN ALL THE WORLD IS MORE DANGEROUS THAN SINCERE IGNORANCE AND CONSCIENTIOUS STUPIDITY**

**Martin Luther King Jr.**

This is somewhat redundant to the issue of being a fiduciary but demands a separate commentary due a number of inherent problems- why do so many entities feel that they deserve huge commissions and fees irrespective of the duty to reasonable standards. Part of it is due to a lack of civility and integrity in our society that has become pervasive throughout. More so since money is involved. Think of all the firm corruption of the last few(?) years. Think of all the political integrity most recently

The following quote helps to address the

inconsistencies in talking about ethics and duty and actually applying them to oneself.

"Trevyor Sargent noted integrity as being a core value of ethics. Acting with integrity also happens to be the first principle of our ethical code of conduct. If we are really to "walk our talk," it is of fundamental importance that we integrate the ethical principles we have articulated into the operational fabric of our daily professional-and I dare say personal-lives. If we do otherwise, we are simply compartmentalizing ethics into a professional continuing education requirement that we dutifully comply with, and then dispense with thinking about until the next year. Most of us probably believe ourselves to be acting with integrity.

The research on this is an eye opener, but, in some ways, not that surprising. Ann Tenbrunsel, of the University of Notre Dame, cites research showing that the benefits of ethical training are short-lived and that ethical codes of conduct, which are usually part of the ethical training, produce no discernible differences in behavior. She describes the typical ethics training as including "an overview of ethical theory, discussion of ethical principles, and applications of such principles using a case-based approach."

While Tenbrunsel still sees value in such training programs, she attributes their shortcoming to their failure to address some of the more fundamental personal issues such as the capacity for self-deception. In Tenbrunsel's words, **"Self-deception allows one to behave self-interestedly while, at the same time, falsely believing that one's moral principles were upheld."**

Research by Gino and Bazerman of the Harvard Business School presents evidence consistent with the view that many unethical acts occur without the awareness of the person engaging in the unethical conduct. Among their conclusions is that unethical behavior is most likely to follow the path of a slippery slope in which ethical conduct declines in such gradual increments that it goes unnoticed until it is too late. Somehow, well-intentioned people go astray and don't even realize it until it is too late."

I can accept that to a degree. But I am more inclined in this profession to see a conscious denial of what is right since it offers a financial incentive to do so. In a 2009 article by Alice Schroeder, Wall Street Makes It Hard to Earn Legal Living, she noted, "A group of university students I spoke to recently asked if it was possible to make a living on Wall Street without compromising your values. I had to tell them no. Wall Street has many decent, honorable people, but they work in a system that fundamentally compromises people's ethics."

Sargent's article continues, "It is through experience and engagement that moral development and, consequently, expertise in ethical decision-making arise. Our current system of compliance with regulatory requirements, adherence to a well-articulated professional code of ethics, and fulfillment of our continuing education requirement may be a necessary and good starting point.

**They are not sufficient**, however, to facilitate the rise of the financial planning profession as a model of professional excellence earning the highest recognition and esteem of the public. What is needed is a high-profile, pervasive, professional forum of engagement for the ongoing discussion of the relevant and subtle ethical concerns of practitioners. Mere compliance with professional and regulatory ethical requirements is insufficient if we are to fulfill the potential of what our profession can really be."

Unfortunately, there is a critical dichotomy between the taking of the continuing education classes and any belief on what they are truly required to know. And while Tenbrunsel talks about compliance with regulatory requirements, the bulk of fee planners across the United

States are illegal since they refuse to become licensed. That it is too hard to pass the exam or "we're already under a separate fiduciary guideline" (California CPA Society) is some of the recurrent rationalizations (more below). Although the resume is included, it is necessary to note that I have taught most of the securities licensing courses, financial planning courses, insurance continuing education, real estate continuing education, CFP, CPA and attorney continuing education and more. One of the courses was in ethics where, in context with the above commentary, one teaches the fallacies of "moral egoism: and "situational ethics". Moral egoism, as it may imply, is simply doing whatever you want and rationalizing that a long as it is good for you or your family or your business, then it is also morally acceptable. Situational ethics also implies that because of the situation- your wife or husband is out of town- then whatever you do is now OK.

*People cheat. Why? Because they are motivated to hit the goal, and when they come very close to meeting it but don't, it is very tempting to fudge the numbers. In addition, individuals can easily justify their decision to cheat by telling themselves that they deserve to meet the goal, and also deserve the reward that comes with doing so. And how often does this happens? Within the business community, I think it is epidemic.*

Schweitzer

When you start viewing Enron, Worldcom, the current salaries for banking executives with our tax bailout money, etc. it does not take much to show the extent of all the ethical 'lapses' that are justified because they can- or think they can- get away with it.

**Basic licensing**

## FINANCIAL PLANNING
## FIDUCIARY STANDARDS UNDER DODD FRANK

In order to become a series 7 licensee (the basic securities license), one must register with a securities firm first. One usually interviews with a few but the general focus in almost always on the perceived sales that the company will get for sponsoring the new recruit. Though many have heard this, they will be asked who can they bring in as clients- family, friends, business associates, pets and more. Now that is not a bad thing per se since the company will spend some time and effort in developing the recruit after licensing. But what most are unaware of is that the instruction for a class is just on what is tested- nothing extra. And what is tested is a mere superficial offering of stock formulas, economics, options, bonds etc. without effectively any idea of the application in the real world. Bill Jahnke noted that "In focusing on financial services for individual investors, I became convinced that much of the education being given was inaccurate, misleading, and in many cases detrimental to investors' financial well being." Also commented on (very) frequently herein is the fact that diversification (defined as how many stocks must you have in a portfolio in order to insulate it due to unsystematic risk) is not even covered.

The effort to receive a life insurance license is even easier though it depends on the state. California requires mandatory classroom attendance but it basically boils down to checking a pulse to see if the person is simply alive and can pass the exam. Tacky comment aside, in years past the schools that prepared one for the exam already knew what exams were used and already had the answers (same with securities schools). It is better now in terms of formal requirements but the problem is that neither prepared the student for how things really worked and the applications for the products they were to sell. Nothing has really changed.

As an instructor, arbitrator, licensee, etc. I gave

licensees about two years to 'get their act together' since they should have been aware within that time by doing any business at all that they really did not know much of anything. If litigation involved securities, one had to determine if an award was more the responsibility of the agent or the firm supervising them. But after two years, generally more focus was put on the agent. Insurance is a different animal since the companies, save for agents with a captive firm (selling only the products of that one company) had really nowhere to turn once they got licensed. Some of the insurance brokerage firms offered certain seminars in major cities, but they were still the focus to sell. (Now there are tons of on line videos and live internet presentations offered every day). Admittedly it is not all bad but as with any mutual fund wholesalers and insurance brokers, they did not address how they truly worked in the real world. I do not think they knew in any case- but that is not the point to their instruction. It was/is to get people to sell their product. Obviously, they rarely/never indicated how other products might be better, cost less, are less risky etc. Only separate impartial instruction might provide that. But that simply does not happen often.

Both licenses require various hours of continuing education annually but some courses are just to pass the number of hours while others can really get detailed. The issue is how is a licensee know which is which. Or cares. Generally the faster, cheaper and easier course gets the nod.

I know from my experience over two decades ago that it was impossible to know what exactly was the right thing to do since the real life implications were almost nowhere to be found. Insurance was the worst since nary a sole or text gave insight to all the moving parts to what truly was to be expected. The wholesalers for mutual funds provided some insight but it was skewed. Sure, experience does help- but how many funds, policies, application et al that had already been sold were truly the right thing to do. Think about this- a witch doctor having 30 years of experience is worth what???- so nothing is necessarily gained by simply being alive for a long time. One might think they are doing the right thing but without the correct guidance initially, it may be nothing but false rationalization. Are the products offered legal? Yes. But the mere use of something legal does not have to dovetail with ethics, integrity or professionalism. As stated, two years after licensing, agents and brokers must have noted that their background is suspect. But the costs of doing the right thing may be prohibitive- and beyond the industries willingness to offer needed insight and competency since it would slow sales (true).

Here is a real life example that is legal but........... There is a Federated short term bond fund. Current yield of 1.03% with a 2% load and a 1.34% annual fee. Shoot me. It is a legal fund- all charges are identified. Is it ethical for an broker to use? Does it reflect integrity? Is it professional? Does it meet fiduciary standards?

Suitability standards would say that the Federated fund, since legal, was viable to use. Again, I ask you to judge a fiduciary level of such offering to a client where short term bond funds are offered at a .30% fee with no load. Admittedly, many investors have no idea to what is going on and need assistance. And they should be charged something for the effort of a broker in putting them into a fund. But a fund with such fees it is not consistent with a fiduciary duty.

That said, how much should be charged for a short term fund if not on a fee basis? What is fair compensation? I do not have the insight to know what would be adequate compensation via a commission but some integrity is needed. Contrary to some commentary, significant changes due to fiduciary enhancement would result in a vast reduction in the number of funds as some would be found in violation of public policy. The opponents to Dodd Frank are *correct* that the selection of funds would be reduced, some consumers with limited incomes would not be well served, if at all (are they now?), and the costs would ratchet up considerably due to new and increased educational requirements.

Here is another gage of industry 'suitability versus fiduciary standards. In an arbitration, two brokers with Wells Fargo- maybe late 20s, early 30s with about 10 years experience tops had sold an elderly person 7 convertible stocks- two of which were Freddie Mac and Fannie Mae when every newspaper was showing both going down the tubes. The ex SIFMA officer acting as the defense expert said that the only thing a broker had to do was to check the ratings (Freddie Mac and Fannie Mae had yet to be downgraded- a real problem subsequently identified by the misguided(?) rating agencies) and that diversification was not even an issue. That is called suitability within the industry. A patently ludicrous position from a professional level and not even remotely close to acting as a fiduciary. (His presentation did not hold and the arbitrators offered an award based on my position of diversification and that if you call yourself a financial advisor, you will be held to that level of responsibility and liability. But this may only be one case with just these three unique arbitrators so nothing definitive may be judged going forward.)

Some of the ethics and integrity lapses are obvious at the governmental level in continuing the use of outdated and sometimes really useless exam material. But considering the current financial cutbacks EVERYPLACE, and the blinders in the scope of the Dodd Frank bill, I don't think it will get much better. But let's continue with.....

Commissions- these have been around for decades

and are not going away. But they will undergo some massive adjustments under Dodd Frank. They are legal but they have clearly caused anxiety among investors due to the question of whether or not the product was sold primarily for the benefit of the agent than for the client (Federated above).

Well, yes.

Not always of course and there are agents who attempt to do the right thing, but inbred with commissions are always going to be the temptation to sway, cajole, push a client into a product that may only be so- so at best. The industry has 'testified' that many of the less affluent investors will not be able to pay fee advisors and/or that fee advisors would not be interested in them. Probably true to both and therefore commissionable agents will still be around to service them. I just do not know the limitations.

As to securities and mutual funds- here we get to the real problem. Almost all commissionable funds are actively managed with relatively high fees as compared to index funds. See also

http://papers.ssrn.com/sol3/papers.cfm?abstract_id=1532268&.

"We argue that the popularity of active management is not puzzling despite the industry's poor track record. Our model features decreasing returns to scale: as the industry's size increases, every manager's ability to outperform passive benchmarks declines. We find that the active management industry can remain large even after significantly negative underperformance.....and from a great article by John Haslem on the marketing of mutual funds, "Overall, fund advertising promotes speculative rather than contrarian styles of investing. Ultimately, the purpose of mutual fund advertising is to persuade investors to invest more and to increase fund adviser profits. This is a far cry from advertising that provides investors with full and objective information that enables them to become "smarter investors." See:

http://www.indexuniverse.com/publications/journalofindexes/ joi-articles/8242-mutual-funds-and-investor-choice.html.

I am sure you have read this before in some manner- "According to Vanguard, for the 10 years leading up to 2007, the majority of actively-managed U.S. stock funds underperformed the index they were seeking to outperform. For instance, 84% of actively-managed U.S. large blend funds underperformed their index, and 68% of actively-managed U.S. small value funds underperformed, as well. The case is even worse for actively-managed bond funds. In that case, almost 95% of actively-managed bond funds underperformed their indexes for the 10 years leading up to 2007."

The fees for managed funds are about 1% higher. And managed funds have significantly higher turnover resulting in yet another detriment to returns due to increased taxes. So investors are paying loads for funds that rarely, if ever, do better than an index fund.

In fairness, managed funds can outproduce index funds for a period of time. And some managed funds with very low fees can outproduce an index fund. However, it is next to impossible to know which manager/managed funds will exceed the averages beforehand. Think Legg Mason and Bill Miller.

Then also think of the underlying risk and what happened in 2008.

So are managed funds generally a crap shoot with a minimal probability of extra gains.

Well, yes.

Will they also show greater losses overall than index funds when the economy takes a hit by moving into cash? Not necessarily since it is still unknown which managed funds would fare better.

So now we go to the next level. The use of index funds- or perhaps ETFs, another cheap alternative- should be the choice of the professional/fiduciary. It's a pretty simple choice. But not necessarily in real life. Though index funds have taken over a larger share of the overall market, managed offerings still command about 85% of the investor pie. Is it therefore a requirement that brokers now inform clients that their higher fee funds with a commission will not outperform-probably underperform- the index funds? That is not going to happen in real life- but would that not be the function of a fiduciary?

Yes.

And getting to the nitty gritty- is it not the mandatory statement to clients that the use of almost *any* securities portfolio will nonetheless result in losses of 50% in equities once or perhaps even twice a decade? That truly is the responsibility of the fiduciary. Merely indicating/presenting a flat rate of return with either managed or index portfolios is tantamount to a poor retirement if the adviser merely thinks/hopes that a return will merrily come its way based on past history and a smooth Gaussian curve- actually the denial of a curve to begin with. That has been the deception of the untrained adviser and will require- as will be evident- massive reposturing of the entire securities industry whether the orientation is fee or commissions.

It is true that indexed funds will universally outproduce managed funds if essentially nothing ever goes wrong. That however is an absurd statement. The goal of a fiduciary is to plan for real life. Risk is a mandatory subject of investing. Risk of loss must be identified. **It will/may make little difference if the funds are managed or indexed since a 30% to 80% loss won't leave much to crow about either way**.

But the marketing hype of the managed funds will continue relatively unabated since the firms find the hot buttons that sway the public to invest with them (see

Haslem article again). It unquestionably works. Further, being friendly, optimistic, handsome, et al swings a lot of investors/voters/ no matter the underlying issues since the public don't do the homework necessary to figure out what is going on. And they feel/want the ability to be better than the market. To be better than their brother, boss, neighbor, golf buddy and so on. The refusal to view real life led us to a current financial impasse that was well known decades previously. A lower rating of the U.S. debt was accomplished by a lot of friendly, optimistic, handsome dweebs. But the fiduciary effort to an investor must be real life and consider all the options, good and bad. Untrained advisors cannot be fiduciaries. The whole debate between managed and index may be moot after the 44% and 57% losses in equities the past decade and now anticipating roughly the same with this new recession.

Nonetheless, and assuming that nothing goes wrong, indexing will outperform managed funds. So are the agents selling managed funds doing so illegally. Of course not. Are they acting ethically? Perhaps a conundrum when the various commissions in a fund prospectus take up more ink than the type of fund, risk factors (though inherently incomplete or just plain wrong) economic strategies et al. But then everyone knows nobody reads that stuff anyway.

### Insurance

As noted, insurance is not the main focus of the Dodd Frank. It should be and will have to be considering the impact that annuities and life insurance have on any client's life. Note however that I am addressing *financial planners* as fiduciaries since financial "whatevers" mandates that they have a minimal mastery of the subject matter they so indicate. Insurance agents already *do* have a fiduciary duty to their companies but I submit that this has been turned on its head in real life. The agent has a duty to present only those potential insureds who have completely and honestly filled out their applications; that the insured needs the insurance and can pay the premiums. Obviously certain agents also do their 'best' in trying to find the right product. Hence we go back to one of the (supposed) key components marketed by a large group of planners: that they *care*.

Well, at least that sounds good. In truth, caring is valid but it is a catch all crutch to mandatory knowledge base to perform the necessary function. Caring about a family risk begs the issue of why so much permanent life is sold when a term policy was more appropriate. Commissions? Why was so much variable life sold when it was obvious that an underlying risk could decimate the policy. Lack of knowledge? Commissions? Why universal life is sold for permanent positions where a no lapse was preferable. Lack of knowledge? Why were so many indexed annuities sold as 'stock market returns without stock market risk?' Why? Why? Why?

Because the system has failed in its overall knowledge base coupled with the fact that you can get away with most of what you want without recrimination by government, media, organizational affiliation and more. Fact is, one is able to potentially reach a financial pinnacle of AUM (assets under management) or the Million Dollar Club and nary a one might make a peep that some ethical lapse has occurred. Certainly if you are a member of such 'elite' since it is not a good idea to rock the boat.

**Governmental regulators**

This is yet another wholesale lapse of integrity and duty. Admittedly, many of the offices are understaffed but that is really not the problem. It is who they are staffed with. The SEC, FINRA and the Madoff scandal makes the obvious case. It is not possible to take 16 years to ferret out that mess. I have also included herein my biggest failure in a case that took me a year to prove, an arbitration case where the defendant agreed to pay $300,000 in a settlement, didn't, and spent another 6 years through many levels of the Florida insurance and securities staff, CFP Board of Standards, Colorado Supreme Court, two Florida governors, senators, attorneys, journalists and more and on and on only to be met with.....nothing. I honestly thought this would get rectified by one of the entities somewhere along the line. It obviously was not the size of Madoff, but somebody should have stood up to help- but all I was met with was arrogance, ineptness and 'who cares'? And since I have addressed other issues- some described below- I became convinced by real life effort that unless the case is large enough, the small investor can be and will be victimized by just about anyone anywhere. Harry Markopolos was quite correct in his characterization of staff at the SEC- inept and worse than inept. The lack of integrity is monumental. But it gets worse.

**Planning organizations**

My specific focus is on the ethical mandates under the CFP, NAPFA, CPA etc. codes of ethics. The CFP mandates you must be ethical and adhere to all laws required to perform the function of planning. One has to also take a two hour continuing education ethics course every two years. 'Unfortunately as it were', I was familiar with the rules and laws of most states- certainly as they addressed California. The industry preferred that the members lie.

**First the overview to national and state licensing**

As almost all are aware, the entire industry has opted for a strong change over to fee services since many consumers have felt- justifiably in many cases- that the products being offered under a commission distorted the sales process because the broker was looking out for himself first and foremost. Supposedly, the 'remuneration element' is not an issue for fee planners. That is wrong as will be explained shortly. In any case, those wanting to offer fee services on securities have to become Registered Investment Advisers (RIA) which, for the most part, is a form filled out for the SEC or individual state Department of Corporations identifying the person's background, what they will do and how they will charge. If one already had a series 7 license, that was generally adequate for 'acceptance' (which is what I did in 1984 so I am perfectly aware of the requirements). Certain designations were allowed, others could take an exam. This takes some time to do but is generally not that onerous. Once the RIA registration was attained, many then called themselves 'fee only' financial planners or advisors and the bulk of the industry went along with the new criteria. None of these are correct since the only thing they can do is act as fee INVESTMENT advisor. (An 2011 survey of the RIA industry by the Investment Adviser Association and National Regulatory Services shows that 41.4 percent of **RIAs are offering financial planning services)** The term 'financial' incorporates far more than investments and generally requires additional licensing (insurance). No matter, they indicated a wide breadth of capability, licensing and fiduciary duty with the extra terminology. Such identification is illegal in some states but the violation of ethics in attributing far greater comprehensiveness and expertise is unethical no matter how one cuts it. It IS a breach of a fiduciary duty to imply legality and competence where none exists.

Nonetheless, financial journalists, money magazines and all the national planning organizations extol the competency and absolute ethics (via "mandatory" ethical standards and fiduciary obligations) of planners and their organizations. After all, if they declined to interview those who were illegal or simply violating ethical issues, they would hardly have anyone else left to interview. But they generally had lots of Assets under Management and money is what entices readers, so ........

A Registered Investment Adviser per se has no background in insurance of any type and has no requirement to take any education courses in the area at all. (Actually any continuing education courses in anything at all- investments or otherwise). The offering of fee advice on insurance is therefore inherently suspect due to the lack of knowledge. (Insurance and annuities are harder to analyze than securities if for no other reason than the products change daily and there is generally no factual nor impartial description on the product.) The real problem is that in about 30+ states, it is illegal to offer fee advice on insurance unless the agent/broker undertakes another exam and is overseen by the state's Department of Insurance.

California has mandatory licensing requirements in order to offer fee life insurance advice. The law requires years of experience and the ability to pass a special exam to become a Life and Disability Insurance Analyst. As of 2010, there was only ONE CFP out of 8,000 in California who was fully licensed and legal to offer comprehensive fee services. To my knowledge, there are no NAPFA members, CPAs or FPA members who are appropriately licensed. Actually, since there are so few with the Life and Disability Insurance Analyst license in California, there may actually be only one who is fully licensed and legal to offer comprehensive fee services. (I do not know that any of those with this license are also RIAs-hence they cannot deal with investments.)

Are the organizations aware of the law?

Sure are. But you will see the addendum that has the

letter I wrote to the then CFP Board President Dimotroff just two years ago. Absolutely clueless. Was she lying? No. Just grossly incompetent. Same with the CEO Keller. You cannot market the highest honesty and integrity and just sluff off the laws by saying, that as an officer, you were totally ignorant/oblivious of the laws as well as anything that has gone on in the organization for over a decade to demand compliance with the law.

Per discussions I started at least 19 years ago with NAPFA, CFPs et al, they despised insurance agents, commissions were totally in violation of any level of ethics, duty, etc. No way were they going to taint their "high level of responsibility" with the element of insurance. And they could get away with acting illegally since the state had little manpower or money to go after such industry agents. Call it moral egoism or as repeated from above, "**Self-deception allows one to behave self-interestedly while, at the same time, falsely believing that one's moral principles were upheld,**" it is nonetheless illegal and far from providing the honesty and competency expected to a client. NAPFA was quoted in a major planning magazine that they hoped California would not enforce its laws because other states might do so as well.

Oy.

Why won't they comply? Basically, they are not that bright. Basically they cheat. CFPs are notoriously lax in insurance education as part of training and the industry knows it. Same with CPAs who become PFS (Personal Financial Specialists). NAPFA has no accepted training at all- it is merely an association of fee planners(?) who state the highest integrity. But insurance is more mind numbing in its analysis than anything in the industry. In order to pass the exam to become a Life and Disability Insurance Analyst, it takes more effort than any exam in planning. So since they do not know the subject area properly, they will also not bother to expend the effort to pass the exam and simply have decided to lie.

So being the hard nose I am, I worked with the California Department of Insurance in the demand that the planning organizations to attend a formal meeting in 1997 to address the issue.

The letter sent in 1998 can be seen at http://www.efmoody.com/ethics/cdi.html. Per insurance code Section 1844, " **any person who acts, offers to acts, assumes to act, as a life and disability insurance analyst when not licensed by the commissioner per this article...... is guilty of a misdemeanor."** Consistent with current practice, information obtained on individuals in noncompliance will be aggressively pursued."

None of the organizations abided. In fact, the CFP Board allowed directors to subsequently tell members to continue to lie about their illegal activities but just keep quiet about it. I never saw the CPA Society do anything at all.

What's this all mean? Financial Planning requires competency, ethics and a fiduciary obligation not only by its members but its officers and directors as well. And if they lie about licensing, they lie about ethics and it becomes obvious at some point to the members. But if they lie about ethics, it's just a matter of time before they lie about a client's money. Not that they may steal it directly but that their arrogance and lack of competency will effectively do the same thing.

Of course not all planners are bad. But I do demand they uphold the high standards they say they will. I demand they are competent in their work. I have not seen this to date since the organizations allow whatever activity they can effectively get away with. And individual members really won't rock the boat since they will be alienated by the rest. Because the term 'fiduciary' is pretty much a word only, not to be enforced by its officers, none of the planning organizations should be allowed to be the overseeing bodies for any future fiduciary responsibility.

**Insurance Planning**

Of course some of them comment that they only thing they have to do is to tell consumers they need insurance. That's it. Or if there is something more 'difficult', they can refer them over to a licensed agent.

In the first case, most people over age 50 already have a life policy- some an annuity from 403(b) or 501(c)3 plans. So is it realistic, prudent, does it make common sense to have an unlicensed entity review the existing plans? I think not.

As for those approaching retirement, the new annuities may have value. Do you want to use someone who does not keep up on the products? Illogical.

Or you can be referred to a licensed agent who may not be that much better and end up paying a commission plus the planning fee? I want you to pay particular attention to what I just indicated. A fee only advisor says that they get no commissions from their work. No conflicts of interest. (Wrong) But that has nothing to do with the fact that the customer is either getting illegal advice and/or is being moved to an agent where they will get charged a commission. In the latter, what is the point of being charged a commission by someone else as part of the process? Fee planning is NOT that the adviser gets a commission- it is that the consumer is NOT going to be charged one. That is a huge difference that has 'escaped' the industry (and effectively all journalists) in offering full and transparent disclosure.

Another point for those over 50- the use unlicensed and illegal planners. This is a very contentious issue when a number of retirement funds will now lean towards index life insurance or index variable annuities. It seems the height of absurdity to use an unlicensed 'advisor' for such analysis or present in a seminar. It belies any fiduciary status. The annuities *really* require a professional review.

As for conflicts of interest- get real. The fee advisers are universally trying to tie up accounts for 1% or more so there is absolutely a conflict of interest. It is not called a commission but it is remuneration nonetheless that the adviser wants. Of course there is a conflict of interest- but is that so different than an attorney trying to land a case?

Yes

Professionals generally have to have a degree for their business. Attorneys and doctors are universally used by the planning organizations as reference points/comparisons for professional planners. So, how many planners have degrees in planning? Next to none. Further, it is only recently that the CFP Board required college degrees in anything- rubber, glass peeling, etc. (I am perfectly aware of my caustic posture towards the organizations, industry and governmental entities and regulators and pundits can rail at their leisure. But for close to 20 years I have heard essentially nothing but tired words backed up by a conspiracy to defraud the consumer of a fiduciary- even suitable- duty. That it continues today is abominable.)

The 'interesting' philosophy is that the planning industry has generally projected a lot of the 'planners' as being nothing different than gate keeper physicians- they merely need to identify the problem and then refer them to the appropriate professionals. This is either misguided arrogance (is there such a thing?) or a conscious marketing effort by the planning industry to infer, once again, the (supposed) knowledge base of its agents to ferret out what needs/should be done and refer to the competent outside parties. Save it is generally a sham. I have addressed the very limited knowledge- but this is the real problem with the bulk of the industry. You might hear this elsewhere but not often. The general focus of advisors is to offer some sophomoric software plan- where they rarely comprehend the internal machinations- in order to either get commissions or to **gather and retain as much investments under management as possible with a 1%+ annual fee**.

This is the real world of most planning. Not all, but most. Do you see what happened here- financial planners/advisers et al are, for the most part, not really involved with personal planning but with the attempt to gather as much AUM as they can. That is how they make their money. If it was just gatekeeper focus, they would refer clients to asset manager firms as they suggest/infer they do with insurance and other fields. It's a "dirty little secret' that is rarely indicated but true nonetheless

The industry has lorded over those that have accumulated the most AUM- assets under management. It is a badge of honor. It is THE badge of honor. But gathering assets and gathering knowledge are not the same thing. It's more of 'mine is bigger than yours' and smacks of little kids - not professionals- that are marketing an inference to capability while they are far more interested in having the bigger sand pile. I refer again to just how well they did in 2000 and 2008. (Does it also remind you of the politicians recently?) Repeated often herein, a fiduciary has to really offer help on the downside of an economy. If you were paying up to 1% or more, what did you get for the service? If you lost more than 15% in equities, there was a problem with the advice. I repeat- perfection is not possible since investing has risk. But c'mon- a fiduciary is supposed to know something.

While this is a personal item, I have never taken assets under management. That is because I do not do 'asset management' per se. I do financial planning with a form of retainer and where the investments are not under my control (non discretionary account). CDs, real estate, 401ks etc. are included because they are simply part of the entire asset base along with all the elements of insurance, long term care, annuities, pension issues and more. When looking forward, this may/should be the future of financial planning, but until the dust settles with Dodd Frank, it is difficult to know what type of expertise and fees may be applied.

Another key element is the size of the AUM fees. Where is the mandate that AUM fees should be 1% or more. For what? Buy and hold? The worst I have heard of was a RIA charging a full 1% annually on 14,000,000. He did nothing except pay money the beneficiaries requested. That was it. They also lost about $5,000,000 due to 2008. Unusual perhaps but when there are so many investment advisers/planners earning up to 1.5% (and more) on accounts where they merely spew out ol' time homilies such as the 'market will come back', it is difficult to see the all out consternation about commissions. But bad is bad.

And as a fiduciary, is it not incumbent on those offering services (certainly for 1% or more) to indicate that 'better services may be had for less money?' Now I am *really* stepping on toes because you can get the basic service for 0.25% annually (though I still have some disagreement with that avenue as well in terms of the risk scenario). Yet once someone calls themselves financial 'whatevers', they have passed the transparency of being a fiduciary and have the duty to explain that ALL types of services shall/can be had for 'x%'.

But even if relevant material is disclosed, will it make much difference? Yale Management Professor Daylian Cain recently offered a sobering view of what academic research reveals regarding conflicts and disclosure. "Conflicts of interest are a cancer on objectivity. Even well-meaning advisors often cannot overcome a conflict and give objective advice. More worrisome, perhaps, investors usually do not sufficiently heed even the briefest, bluntest and clearest disclosure warnings of conflicts of interest."

**Summary**

If someone even remotely calls themselves a financial 'whatever' they need to be held to that level of competence both in securities and insurance and many other interrelated areas. They must be licensed as required by national and state law- but that level of competency and knowledge is close to a waste. Get a planner with at least 10 years of experience with a degree in planning and all the appropriate licenses. Is this a guarantee of the 'best'? No - but it sure beats the alternatives

# 8

# Governmental (In)Competency, Organizational Lies

Actually, for the most part, I could leave this page blank since that is what I believe is the overall capability of the various government entities that oversee securities and insurance products (the mainstays in financial planning). FINRA oversees nearly 4,800 brokerage firms, about 173,000 branch offices and approximately 650,000 registered securities representatives. But combined with the oversight of the SEC let Bernie Madoff take $50 to $65 billion for 16 years from consumers.

Here's the rub on Madoff. It did not take a Harry Markopolos to bring down Madoff (though he would be necessary to go through the documents.) It is simply the fact that NO ONE can return something like a flat 12% return year after year. It has not been possible (save for the high interest rates in the early 80s with certain bonds) for equities. It was an 'impossible' annuity. Any rational competent regulator should have come in in the early stages and shut it down. That speaks volumes about the competency of regulators in the real world.

Anyway, let's start from the beginning of securities training as an indicator of what the regulators required of brokers. That will be used as an indication of the knowledge and insight of said regulators. As stated on the resume, I have taught literally all the securities classes for licensing as a broker. I had a good pass rate- if you are a good instructor and can take hard material and make relatively "easy" to grasp, the students have a decent chance of passing. That said, I only got paid to teach the material that was tested, not what was needed in real life (and reflected suitability). Any major attempt to offer real world application was, rightfully so, a diversion from the necessity to pass the exam and simply could not be presented.

As such, none of the fundamentals of investing have been taught to the 650,000 agents under the FINRA banner. Diversification, standard deviation, Monte Carlo, unsystematic risk, alpha, Sharpe ratio and more are not addressed. Essentially nothing on risk except the market is risky. None of this was/is tested on the exam and therefore it not taught. Yet, if you do not know diversification, you cannot know risk. If you do not risk, you cannot determine suitability.

Pay attention to the statement about lack of focus towards suitability. It should be obvious to anyone that if suitability is just a word with no application whatsoever, you are leading everyone astray. At least allowing them to. That is endemic in the entire industry, but unless one has spent the time actually deciphering what is inside the series 7 and other licenses, it simply is not known.

Be it Bush, Obama, Republicans, Democrats, Tea Party et al, the government is incapable of providing the knowledge base to the industry- certainly to the consumer. The abdication to private entities with hundreds of thousands of dollars of grant money (Better Investing for example) is not only indicative that the fundamentals will be violated, but that our government can/does pass out another hundred thousand or half a million of deficit spending that does nothing. Unless the consumer can get access to independent objective advice, the current debacle and financial losses will continue to be repeated.

Some of the following may be redundant and pedantic, but it reflects in part just how bad consumers are treated by the various entities you expect to help you. From local agents all the way to the SEC and more, the average American is not treated well at all.

**Government Fraud, Sheer Incompetency and Just Not Caring.**

CFP Board of Standards, Colorado Supreme Court, Florida Department of Insurance, A+ insurance companies, many attorneys. Florida governor, Florida Department of Financial Services, Florida Office of Financial Regulation, SEC Headquarters, Florida Department of Elder Affairs, Senator Bill Nelson, Senator Mel Martinez, Journalists............

There are even more officials than those listed above in one of the most egregious actions that violated the legal, emotional and financial rights of a 77 year old widow and her family. This action started over a decade ago and ceased in 2010 with a curt call by the Florida Department of Financial Services that so much time had elapsed since I had initiated a complaint over 5 years previous, that they would not do anything. I will offer a brief summary of this case via a letter to Florida officials in 2006. If you are part of a large group where, let's say, the state enters the fray to stop improper actions, you might get resolution. Otherwise you can end up like this as the system grinds the bones of a singular entity into the ground. (Some of the other letters to the various entities are included in the addendum. Far too many to include all.) It is also an excellent piece about breach of fiduciary duty, lack of knowledge, affinity scam, greed, elderly abuse, budget, statistics, requests for help from numerous private and governmental agencies, NASD, attorneys and on and on. This is what goes on in real life. And reflects the greatest failure of my career.

March 2006

Florida Department of Financial Services

**Overview of case**

"I was employed by the Smiths almost five years ago to address a purported fraud by CFP Barry, et al. A final report (enclosed) was prepared on January 2002 after almost a year of research and reflects a consistent breach of duty by Barry et al towards an elderly couple for years and even more so after the death of Mrs. Smith's husband in 1999. Due to the Statute of Limitations, a truncated case was filed with the NASD by the law firm Ackerman, Link and Sartory of West Palm Beach, addressing activities of just the last few years of Barry's involvement with the Smiths. It elicited a $300,000 settlement agreement by Barry (remaining unpaid) just before the arbitration was to begin (December 2004). Parts of the case however remain unresolved and were not addressed by Ackerman, Link and Sartory. Barbara Smith (daughter) had, prior to my employment, contacted the CFP Board of Standards and made a formal complaint against Barry for various perceived infractions. The Board sent her a subsequent letter indicating that the matter had been "investigated" and supposedly resolved (though no specifics were identified). Months later, through subpoena of Barry, we received a letter to him from the CFP Board (enclosed) that had officially "exonerated" him of any wrong doing. He was using that statement as major component of his defense. However the Board repeatedly refused to provide to the plaintiff Smith, under subpoena, any of the *documentation* demonstrating that it had reviewed anything at all. Finally, in mid 2004, ***after*** the settlement 'agreement' and pursuant to my continuing demand for the material, the Board released its files. There had been no investigation. The Board had absolved Barry of any wrongdoing without any review whatsoever by their Board of Professional Review or anyone else. There were no memos, no reports, no Emails, no phone calls, no evidence of any communications whatsoever with anyone or any entity- absolutely nothing. Therefore the exoneration was a farce and invalid on its face. Because of this obvious breach of fiduciary duty, I subsequently was able to get the Board to reopen the investigation. But after many months of waiting, not one call to any party, not one report made. Absolutely no further investigation was made by the Board at all. The refusal to pursue an obvious breach by Barry is no longer indicative of just gross incompetency but a direct violation of the Board's mandated fiduciary standards and practices. No matter the breach, it is clear that the Board's involvement in this case is tainted, if not corrupted, and cannot be relied upon when presented as a defense by Barry.

Nothing happened so I wrote this

July 4, 2007 Governor Charlie Crist Tallahassee, FL 32399-0001

RE: Ineffectiveness of Department of Insurance RE: Smiths vs. CFP Barry, NASD Case 03-02522

Enclosed is a letter regarding a complaint filed

against a Florida agent last year. The agent had already signed a settlement agreement of $300,000 pursuant to a report that took me almost a year to prepare. Yet, not one formal reply was ever sent to me regarding the effort that would be undertaken nor the results thereof.

The main point of this commentary is the follow-up I just made. Nobody had a clue to what is going on. No one could find the file, no one could say why the complaint was transferred out of the Insurance Department........ The Bureau of Securities Regulation is now addressing the issue but after a year of fruitless effort, I need to substantiate that this will be handled properly and expeditiously.

As stated in the enclosed, anyone filing a legitimate complaint- certainly where the elderly are involved- should expect a conscious effort to make sure the problems do not happen again. But considering what I have gone through so far, this has been unprofessional at best and a joke at its worst. Barry signed off on a $300,000 settlement on the Smith claim of insurance and investment malfeasance. No one commits that type of money without recognizing the wrongs that have occurred. Surely the Department can also determine that unprofessional, careless and just plain fraudulent sales of unnecessary products is reason for a formal investigation in an expeditious manner.

I would appreciate if you could make sure this is handled correctly this time.

Consumers have a right to expect prompt and efficient review of complaints. Certainly any wrongs done to a consumer.

If this is indicative of what a consumer has to go through (and I have had the same thing with the California Department of Insurance), then there never will be proper coverage for the consumer.

Maybe the Governor of Florida can make a difference."

*Nothing made a difference*. And that includes another request to the CFP Board of Standards to finally step up and do the investigations they never did and said they would.

Absolutely nothing. There are many letters to the CFP president Teslik, then Kevin Keller. A formal complaint to the Colorado Bar regarding their attorney who simply lied and on and on.

The clients got nothing save for untold grief, frustration and additional anxiety. I lost them as clients since they did not want to be reminded that the system failed them (as did I even though I did not charge them for this effort).

The above simply is a real life indication of what lies ahead for many who are wronged and then get ignored by those that are supposed to help. It is not just that the industry that is deficient- look at how many entities I went through over almost a decade to get proper resolution. Perhaps I was being naive in thinking I could make a difference. Maybe it was preordained. Maybe, maybe, maybe. Even in retrospect, I had to try. But to have effectively all the entities who could make a difference simply take a pass was simply a frustration that was difficult to hide. And as a CFP to find out that the bulk of the words from the organization demanding I uphold the highest duty had no meaning to any of the officers and directors...... (I subsequently dropped the CFP designation in 2010- though I had not used it publicly for close to 10 years).

There is more:

As stated in the ethics section, I also had an over 15 year "dialogue" with the planning organizations regarding, simply stated, the requirements for state licensing.

The statement was disregarded by all planning representatives. Subsequently, due to my continued efforts, a letter was sent by the Department of Insurance to national financial planning organizations dated June 18, 1997 wherein it states, "The Department has at all times required anyone offering insurance advice for a fee to comply with California licensing requirements. Such licensing requirements currently include 5 years of experience, passing an examination and continuing education. **Financial planners do not have an exemption from this requirement.'**

The Board replied, in part, that "it is the policy the CFP Board that laws be interpreted and applied by the appropriate authority, not the Board of Professional Review." And that, "until such a time the CFP Board will not be placed in the position of interpreting California insurance laws". Or as I was told by their attorney, "we will not enforce an ethical violation unless preceded by a legal one."

Pursuant to Rule 101, "A CFP designee shall not solicit clients through false or misleading communications or advertisements."

In a meeting in 2009 with Kevin Keller CEO of the Board and Marilyn Dimitroff, President, both were either entirely clueless to California laws, didn't care or were just not that bright. They said they had never heard of the edict from the state nor knew what it really meant. Keller even subsequently attempted a rationalization to the law to allow the illegal activity. Assistant Chief Counsel for the California Department of Insurance Patricia Staggs subsequently confirmed what was already established by her in 1995 and The DOI meeting in 1998- members offering fee planning in California have to have the Life and Disability Insurance License. But then again, they have no money and no interest outside of rhetoric in moving further. As of early 2010, there was only one CFP that was fully licensed and legal and that could offer comprehensive fee planning. There are no NAPFA members, no CPAs, no FPAs. So, is the idea behind a breach of a fiduciary duty or ethics violation to occur if and only if there is a separate state or national case brought to fruition? So what does a fiduciary really mean if there are no repercussions?

How are such breaches allowed in house? I repeat per Schweitzer- **Individuals can easily justify their decision to cheat by telling themselves that they deserve to meet the goal, and also deserve the reward that comes with doing so. And how often does this happens? Within the business community, I think it is epidemic.**

So there is yet another failure within the industry. For the coup de gras comes this spurious and insulting 2006 speech from Mary Schapiro regarding the SEC's "intense focus" on consumer education.

"I'll close with a few words about a different, but related, subject——one that will surely shape the role of regulators well into this century—— investor education as investor protection. I believe very strongly that the people best able to protect investors from mistakes, misunderstandings, deception or outright fraud are the investors themselves——if they are knowledgeable about investing and the markets. I cannot overstate the importance of this, particularly given that we're facing a looming crisis——the impending retirements of millions of baby-boomers, many of whom are financially ill-prepared to stop working."

My reply, **http://efmoody.com/nasd.html** "That is disingenuous as best. Investor education? You will not provide investing fundamentals to brokers. (The fundamentals include alpha, beta, correlation, standard deviation, diversification and more.) You will not provide fundamental education to arbitrators. Actually, I do not believe you have anyone on staff who could provide the fundamentals of investing even if you wanted to. If you could, why haven't you? (The answer was the sophomoric comment from your agent- the "NASD (now FINRA) is a procedural entity not a substantive one".) The NASD statement that attorneys would provide (in whatever manner) the material and facts to a case to arbitrators is laughable. Sorry- attorneys are consumers/investors as well and are clueless to the same issues I state to you: they do not know diversification, they do not know risk. More importantly, the reference you make about mistakes, misunderstanding, deception or outright fraud is what the SEC and NASD have perpetrated for at least the last 15 years. Proof? All one has to do is review the licensing material required for a broker. The fundamentals noted above are not taught for licensing. The idea that you are therefore going to bypass the industry and provide the necessary insight to consumers is absurd, illogical and just plain won't work in the real world. Actually, the idea that a broker does not need to know what diversification is so far removed from a fiduciary responsibility at any level that it is just disgusting. I know this is brusk. But since 15 years has gone by and not one entity has bothered with serious and truthful knowledge and education, I am entitled to berate those who violate their duty. I ask anyone at the NASD to properly define diversification. I ask anyone at the NASD or SEC, to define risk and show that it is being properly defined to any consumer. If I am wrong, it shouldn't be hard, should it? That said, I do not believe you have anyone that can do it. Nor the NASAA, AARP ad infinitum. It is the height of hypocrisy to offer assistance to the least enlightened where you are offering no education- even bothering to recognize the inherent incompetency and fraud- of the very industry you lord over."

The continuation of these entities in extolling their commitment to protecting the consumer is nothing more than flatulent rhetoric. For those that feel this to be a singular diatribe, I stipulate those to pick up any Series 7 and 24 securities licensing manual. Diversification has never been addressed. The fundamentals of investing have NEVER been offered in the past nor now. There are no mandatory continuing education classes that address these either. What is even more comical is that there is no requirement for an adviser to use a financial calculator. If you cannot figure out how money works, you have no business in advising others. PERIOD!

And it gets funnier - "Our foundation issues grants to universities and non-profits for research and programs that help people understand the complexities of investing and the markets. It is particularly concerned with population segments that are underserved, such as minorities, members of the armed forces and senior citizens." Probably the most compelling violation of the above comes from the statistics for the National Association of Investment Clubs (now BetterInvesting) to whom the NASD paid $354,500 in 2006 to provide educational services to the masses (develop and deliver an investment education program to public education employees nationwide"). “The program will be available free of charge to participants. It will include Web-based stock and mutual fund analysis tools, educational resources **and a game** to encourage participants to construct quality portfolios. The program will be grounded in research and designed to serve as a "best practices" model for delivering Web-based investor education to the target audience.”

Now, this is a partial commentary from Mandelbrot indicated previously and is necessary to grasp how involved diversification/risk/correlation is when done at a professional level. ".....Finally, for each stock, you must laboriously calculate its covariance with, or how it fluctuates against, every other stock. For a thirty stock portfolio, about the minimum needed to make the numbers work well, that means 495 different calculations of mean variance and covariance. For the entire NY Stock Exchange, 3.9 million calculations. And because prices change, the exercise needs constant repetition." Try playing that at home.

Not a chance that a consumer has even a clue to the sophistication demanded. It sure isn't even known by the head of the SEC but it probably was fun to give $354,500 away. (Maybe that is why it was so easy for the government to give AIG 150 billion in bailouts later on. Though my favorite was cash for clunkers. )

Actually The Stock Market Game is the worst offering of all because it is directed to the children as part of a **game** they play to see who can earn the most money trading as quickly as possible. That is described in detail herein and is yet another violation of fiduciary duty to citizens in focusing on gambling for their kids. .

Of course you are reading about just MY experiences and may state that they are an anomaly not experienced by others. Probably true but that is due to the fact that I am just about the only one with such background and instruction who can/has pushed the limits of what are words and what are responsible actions. After so many years of teaching and research, you begin to understand that most of the moral conduct expected in this industry does not exist. What may exist lies behind borders of knowledge the industry will not allow its members to cross in any case. Unless and until solid education is provided, fiduciary will be nothing more than a word that only a few people will truly adhere to.

# 9

# The Significance of Being a Fiduciary

This commentary comes directly from the Department of Labor.
(http://www.dol.gov/ebsa/publications/fiduciaryresponsibility.html

(This sounds valid but wait until one tears apart the rhetoric)

"Fiduciaries have important responsibilities and are subject to standards of conduct because they act on behalf of participants in a retirement plan and their beneficiaries. These responsibilities include:

Acting solely in the interest of plan participants and their beneficiaries and with the exclusive purpose of providing benefits to them;

Carrying out their duties prudently;

Following the plan documents (unless inconsistent with ERISA);

Diversifying plan investments; and

Paying only reasonable expenses.

The duty to act prudently is one of a fiduciary's

central responsibilities under ERISA. It requires expertise in a variety of areas, such as investments (not a chance). Lacking that expertise, a fiduciary will want to hire someone with that **professional knowledge** (Will they understand the risk of loss? No.) to carry out the investment and other functions. Prudence focuses on the *process* for making fiduciary decisions. Therefore, it is wise to document decisions and the basis for those decisions. For instance, in hiring any plan service provider, a fiduciary may want to survey a number of potential providers, asking for the same information and providing the same requirements. By doing so, a fiduciary can document the process and make a meaningful comparison and selection." (Not a chance. Simply asking the unknowledgeable by the not knowing does not establish any viability to the results. One has to already know at least some of the answers under this scenario- and neither ERISA nor any other governmental entity has been provided the insight. It is the blind leading the dead. For reference, they should ask what diversification is and how it will be portrayed to employees. ERISA attorneys are clueless so the task is effectively pointless.)

"Following the terms of the plan document is also an important responsibility. The document serves as the foundation for plan operations. Employers will want to be familiar with their plan document, especially when it is drawn up by a third-party service provider, and periodically review the document to make sure it remains current. For example, if a plan official named in the document changes, the plan document must be updated to reflect that change.

Diversification – another key fiduciary duty – helps to **minimize the risk of large investment losses to the plan.** Fiduciaries should consider each plan investment as part of the plan's entire portfolio. Once again, fiduciaries will want to document their evaluation and investment decisions". (No one can really document risk without the ability to do a numerical risk of loss. Certainly they would have recognized that recessions cause major losses, right? Certainly they would have recognized that 44% and 57% losses needed to be minimized, right? Certainly they knew how diversification works under stress, right? Apparently not. Further the above commentary is really about asset allocation, not diversification per se. Semantics perhaps but belies the lack of appropriate terminology.)

## Limiting Liability

With these fiduciary responsibilities, there is also potential liability. Fiduciaries who do not follow the basic standards of conduct may be personally liable to restore any losses to the plan, or to restore any profits made through improper use of the plan's assets resulting from their actions. (Who will figure out the liability? DOL does not have the competency. I find such language and rules to be offensive since they are completely lacking in specificity. But then all presentations about suitability and fiduciary duty do so as well.)

However, fiduciaries can limit their liability in certain situations. One way fiduciaries can demonstrate that they have carried out their responsibilities properly is by documenting the processes used to carry out their fiduciary responsibilities. (Documentation may limit liability but have nothing to do with what should have been done.) There are other ways to reduce possible liability. Some plans, such as most 401(k) and profit-sharing plans, can be set up to give participants control over the investments in their accounts and limit a fiduciary's liability for the investment decisions made by the participants. For participants to have control, they must be given the opportunity to choose from a broad range of investment alternatives. Under Labor Department regulations, there must be at least three different investment options so that employees can diversify investments within an investment category, such as through a mutual fund, and diversify among the investment alternatives offered. (But picking wrongly among three funds or twenty serves no purpose. And the assumption that employees have competency is a breach of any rhetoric. That is a cop out. It is a fraud to even remotely imply consumer sophistication.) In addition, participants must be given sufficient information to make informed decisions about the options offered under the plan (Where is risk?). Participants also must be allowed to give investment instructions at least once a quarter, and more often if the investment option is volatile. (Is that the VIX?) Plans that automatically enroll employees can be set up to limit a fiduciary's liability for any plan losses that are a result of automatically investing participant contributions in certain default investments. (Is a default investment void of the risk of loss? How is someone to know?) There are four types of investment alternatives for default investments as described in Labor Department regulations and an initial notice and annual notice must be provided to participants. Also, participants must have the opportunity to direct their investments to a broad range of other options, and be provided materials on these options to help them do so. (Such as? Yet another cop out to instruction to risk.) However, while a fiduciary may have relief from liability for the specific investment allocations made by participants or automatic investments, the fiduciary retains the responsibility for selecting and monitoring the investment alternatives that are made available under the plan. (How would they know? They won't.) A fiduciary can also hire a service provider or providers to handle fiduciary functions, setting up the agreement so that the person or entity then assumes liability for those functions selected. If an employer appoints an investment manager that is a bank, insurance company, or registered investment adviser, the employer is responsible for the selection of the manager, but is not liable for the individual investment decisions of that manager. However, an employer is required to monitor the manager periodically to assure that it is handling the plan's investments prudently and in accordance with the appointment. (A bank manager has what investment background? Is it Lehman Brothers? Let's try UBS.) Fiduciaries must always act in the best interest of the plan. According to the DOL, ERISA establishes a clear rule that requires fiduciaries to choose investment options based on economic factors (Based on what factors? Obviously they must include risk in the economy and therefore the risk of adjusted allocations.).

*DOL:* Because every investment necessarily causes a plan to forgo other investment opportunities, an investment isn't prudent if it would be expected to provide the plan with a lower rate of return than alternative investments with similar degrees of risk, or is riskier than alternative available investments with similar rates of return. (But that requires an understanding of risk and risk of loss. Risk of loss would be the defining issue but it requires the use of a financial calculator. There is no mandatory instruction for brokers, insurance agents or even RIAs on its use or even what the numbers mean. Further, roughly 90% of the $1.5 trillion in 401(k) and other defined-contribution assets in mutual funds are in actively managed offerings. This is the case despite clear evidence from studies that index funds tend to outperform their actively managed rivals. The point: you must keep fees as low as possible. Does the DOL accept that such excess fees are acceptable and allowed by fiduciaries? There is a risk right there because lower returns over time ARE a risk for retirees. There is a huge dichotomy here with the real life function of investing and the disconnect of advice and the costs.)

**Investment Advice and Education**

More and more employers are offering participants

help so they can make informed investment decisions (No they are not. They are offering simplistic and sophomoric directions from those who know next to none of the fundamentals of investing. And the idea that they offer all sorts of pretty charts on gathering monies for retirement and have no insight on how to hold on to it when the market hits a bad situation (recession). Employers may decide to hire an investment adviser offering specific investment advice to participants (not a broker nor anyone else devoid of knowledge). These advisers are fiduciaries (not if they do not know diversification) and have a responsibility to the plan participants. On the other hand, an employer may hire a service provider to provide general financial and investment education, interactive investment materials, and information based on asset allocation models. As long as the material is general in nature, providers of investment education are not fiduciaries (nor will the education be worth much. General knowledge has to include the specific exposure to risk. Pundits won't like the extra duty nor the cost of retraining instructors. But just look how well the education has done so far: Retirements completely ruined.) However, the decision to select an investment adviser or a provider offering investment education is a fiduciary action and must be carried out in the same manner as hiring any plan service provider." (And just what is that? There is little validity to selecting those that are not trained nor knowledgeable about investing. Great CYA though.)

### Nice thoughts, limited application

Unfortunately, this won't work. It didn't work before and it certainly won't provide the needed financial information now. First of all, who will provide the general advice? A computer software program has been offered at many firms so employees can view their accounts and any specific advice it at any time. But it is universally wrong.

Any attempt to compute solely a flat rate of return has always been wrong. The world of investments does not work like that, has not in the past and will not in the future. A flat rate of return- say 8% year after year after year- has never existed. If it is offered in any format, one has to include a Monte Carlo analysis. And if one includes Monte Carlo, one has to address standard deviation. And if one includes standard deviation- **or simply the term risk**- one has to include the risk of loss. Never has happened before in any of the plans I have seen. I have never heard of an adviser identifying the risk of loss in any but the most generalized terms- the market can go down or how would you feel if you lost 10% of your assets?. (Yet another useless consumer question. It always had to be 'how would you feel about losing 50%?) But the lack of detail is not necessarily farfetched since brokers effectively have learned nothing on standard deviation and most financial planners of any type or designation have had anything more than the most sophomoric of critique on same. What one tends to witness therefore is a simplistic format designed in the 90s formulated by some computer geek sitting in the darkness of theoretical oblivion.

Here is the essence. Almost all plans mention risk. They tend to identify it as standard deviation/volatility. Standard deviation is NOT risk ipso facto. (In November 2011, there is a $1,000 investment seminar in New York where they are addressing standard deviation as risk. Admittedly standard deviation is a form of risk- like many others- but far from the only one nor necessarily the most important at any given point in time. Risk is how much you could lose based on the portfolio allocation you have accepted. Of course, also addressed herein, consumers generally were asked to decide their own risk template (conservative, moderate, aggressive, etc.)- a clearly useless attempt since there are no guidelines instructing anyone as to what level any of the firm boxes on risk actually meant in real terms (see consumer questionnaire chapter herein). The problem was, and continues to be, that the adviser doesn't know either and tends to make up stuff that they think might work- generally for them and the firm.

Actually, does anyone truly think the true exposure to risk and reward will happen with the likes of 401k presentations? No. It can't unless one has the capability to use a financial calculator along with the true understanding of standard deviation, correlation and more. Very, very few do. And you are not going to see them doing a 401k presentation. Too real life.

Overall, the average middle income consumer has not and, almost assuredly, will not get the knowledge they need for at least another decade. Therefore the fiduciary level of competency is more words than application. But it is still worth it to try and make some difference.

**Dodd Frank bill**

This bill was passed after the 2008 debacle to, in part, provide a more transparent opportunity for consumers to judge who is actually working for "them". The point being that Registered Investment Advisers (RIA) must act as fiduciaries (solely for the best interest of the client) while the standard broker selling with a commission must simply provide something for the client that is merely suitable, not necessarily in the best interests of the client.

There are many, many facets to this issue- one being anytime insurance is involved for example. Insurance agents owe a fiduciary duty to their company first so how can they also become a fiduciary to the customer? Of course, that is an extension of the bill per se since a RIA and a broker can, by definition, only include work on investments, not the entire planning gamut. That said, and as referenced herein, the bulk of RIAs and brokers are calling themselves 'wealth managers, financial planners, financial adviser' et al and are obviously delving into areas beyond the immediate scope of the bill. I am stating that once they do that, they 'have' the ability to do it and will be held accountable to a high level of knowledge and expertise. Insurance agents are also doing the same. Hence they will be encompassed by the same definition and fiduciary responsibility.

Pundits note that if a fiduciary status is implemented, it would require far more work, documentation and, obviously, cost. (All true however). Many state that the current 'suitability standard' for brokers is adequate to cover the vast majority of their efforts. That said, and repeated over and over again herein, there are no written suitability standards nor have ever been save, primarily, that a broker has to be sure that the investment is suitable given the facts about the client and that the risk is acceptable. Words with no real life application at all.

There is little question that a fiduciary status is necessary- at least identified by those of integrity and caring. The consumer is supposed to come first but has generally been left with financial crumbs that were quickly whisked away because the advisers- no matter RIA, planner or insurance agent's nil real life financial backgrounds. Sure there are some that have attained education and competence over time. But Dodd Frank is supposed to encompass all who provide advice to consumers, not just the lucky few. The DOL, state regulators, SEC all have to have a hand in the revision to competency but they will have to also reinvent their staffs to the same level to competency. That may take longer than the required education to the advisers.

As such, who will act to investigate, regulate and prosecute? FINRA is saying they can do it. Big joke. CFP Board? Not possible since they have avoided their own ethical mandates. State regulators? NASAA. FINRA wants to take over the effort. No and no and no and....

# 10

# Fiduciary Duty to Seniors

The title begs the question, "is there a special duty that is owed to the elderly?" Not necessarily since fiduciary per se references the highest duty anyway. But the devil is in the details. Due to the decline in mental faculties after age 65 (I am excluding diseases and illnesses at this stage) the elderly are very apt to be confused by the material of risk and reward. Certainly by any of the truly convoluted indexed annuities or anything with a guaranteed payout. Since nil of current investment advisors can actually do an individual risk analysis, just how is it that they will truly be able to express the loss exposure in an understandable format? I simply do not believe that the documents provided by a mutual fund, for example, are adequate for those where there is, statistically, an inability to grasp the significance. Furthermore, anyone who has dealt with clients over a long term knows full well that generally *no one* reads a prospectus. Universally it is the interaction with some adviser that defines what risk is (supposedly) being taken.

It is not my intent of providing reams of documentation to the decline of competency (there are thousands of articles on the Internet to validate) but to simply offer some evidence that demands a level of additional effort with seniors. This extra endeavor will require a separate formal statement outlining to the senior what planning was suggested, why the products were used, what the risk is, what is expected, what monitoring will be done, if any and so on. Frankly, such independent report is necessary each and every time by a fiduciary. The use of a prospectus, as stated, is not adequate nor is the simplistic computerized plan with pretty colored charts. Such review is needed so that the senior is not only fully aware of what is going on initially but this may be used in support of claim in litigation later on. I have been around long enough to see that seniors forget, misinterpret what was being done and expect different results than what was presented. Written formal comments, numbers, etc. can be worth a lot of words in arbitration or court. Miscellaneous notes can also assist- but can also backfire if the planner accepted material that was not corroborated- the computerized financial plan document for example. Or where the definitions are confusing or wrong (standard deviation). Also remember that most states (all?) have statutes regarding elderly abuse for those over age 65.

Actually, considering the almost nonexistent consumer financial literacy to date, effectively any suggestion to anyone requires a separate validation by the advisor as to just what was done and why. This is not an attempt for perfection- one can still be wrong in terms of returns etc. But if a solid effort was made, that is the focus.

**Cognitive Decline in Aging**

http://www.unc.edu/~jdumas/projects/aging.htm

"The decline of cognitive abilities in the aging happens generally after a person has turned sixty-five. However, the decline in a slow process and does not happen strictly on the person's sixty-fifth birthday. Some of the symptoms of this decline effect the person's ability to learn new and complicated material or skills. It is a myth that all older people are cognitively impaired, but there are certain processes, which are affected, mainly but not exclusively physical processes.

There are normal cognitive changes that take place when

a person becomes older. There is a decline in information processing in aging. This means that when an older person is presented with new information, especially of the more complicated sort, it will take them slightly longer to process this information. There is also a need for more repetition when learning this new information. So, if an older person were learning new programming information for a computer, he/she will need more repetition regarding the instructions for that information. Also, since their learning process takes slightly longer, the information should be presented more slowly.

The older population will show a decline in the ability to divide their attention. It is difficult for them to switch quickly from one task to another, in two simultaneous tasks. In regarding "multiple auditory inputs" (Beisgen) there is a decline in being able to switch from one source to another. This means that if the person is doing a task on the computer which an instructor is giving further information simultaneously, it is more difficult for the older person to pay attention to both stimuli simultaneously. It would be better for the instructor to give information, then have the participant follow suit on the computer. However, there is no similar decline for visual input, which means that it would not be difficult for the person to which their attention from one visual aid to another. So, the instructor could be showing some visual aids for the participant and then the person can readily switch their attention on to their computer screen to follow the instructions.

Memory is also affected when a person becomes older. Primary and/or short-term memory is affected, as is long-term or secondary memory. There is greater decline for recall, and less for recognition. This means that it is not as easy for the older learner to recall instructions and directions as for a younger person. But if the instructor keeps repeating the instructions for some computer function, and then says only one part of an instruction, the person can easily recall the rest of the instructions. Also, the older person's performance on tasks is greatly improved by cues, so the instructor could merely use a cue word or a picture and the person would remember the task and the process.

Differentiation of the degree of mental changes in old age can be influenced by the intellectual and educational level. A well educated 70-year-old man, with a wide range of interests, trying to be up-to-date in the fields that attract him most, has much more chance to preserve his mental balance and intellectual elan compared to his uneducated and disinterested peer, in whom passivism and decline of health, physical and spiritual vitality, are much more likely to occur. Therefore, the age of these two is similar only chronologically. Essentially, these are two completely different worlds. It is thus said that every environment, every culture produces its own type of the elderly, making the domain of old age huge and very variable."

Most cognitive processes decline with age

It does appear that most component processes of cognition decline with advanced age if the difficulty level is sufficiently high. For example, the following processes have all shown age effects:

- processes involving attention

working memory capabilities(the amount of information you can work with without losing track of any)

- understanding text making inferences
- encoding(putting information into memory) and
- retrieval (finding information in memory) *end*

The overall problem is that the financial material being/to be discussed is far beyond anything the elderly may have heard before when they were younger- if at all (ETFs for example) Further, much of it might be categorically different than anything they had heard about years or decades previous and on which they felt comfortable- wrong or inadequate no matter. Remember that people tend to forget a lot of the bad things and may rely on that which they think 'worked' years ago. Anyway, the new material may cause them anxiety and concern. Add in math- a difficult subject in itself- along with words such as correlation, diversification and more and the senior may tune it out, simply agree in order not to appear stupid, or become agitated and belligerent to the point of not wanting to do anything. I am well aware that one tries to keep things simple, but too simple means not addressing risk and that is not correct by any means.

Then we have an even more difficult assessment to make regarding dementia, pain and more that will, almost assuredly, taint the entire process:

**Elder health**

Most older adults enjoy good mental health, but nearly 20% of those who are 55 years and older experience mental disorders that are not part of normal aging. The most common disorders, in order of prevalence, are anxiety disorders, such as phobias and obsessive-compulsive, severe cognitive impairment, including Alzheimer's disease; and mood disorders, such as depression.

Ageing persons will experience decline in mental skills almost 15 years prior to their death, even though they may remain free of dementia. Their spatial reasoning, perceptual speed, verbal ability are specific aspects of this cognitive decline, which are not necessarily due to the ageing process according to Swedish researchers. (Males at age 65 have an actuarial lifetime of about 18 years; women close to 21 years.)

The "terminal declining phase" occurring before one's death unfolds many other ailments such as the beginning of heart disease, lack of sufficient mental and physical exercise, or even dementia at a nascent stage, which cannot be detected.

**Dementia**

As stated above, it is very difficult- certainly for younger advisors who have not had extensive dealings with the elderly- to detect certain aspects of early dementia or Alzheimers. (It is not my attempt to suggest in any way that I am an expert in this area. But I did teach Long Term Care for six years for continuing education and have had several relatives and friends suffer the indignities of Alzheimers- including my mother who was institutionalized for over 10 years). Short term memory is one of the first indications of a potential problem. If the client is having problems within the discussion, I'd definitely suggest caution. Of course, that is good advice no matter what age, but is extremely important here. From the Brookdale Center on Aging, If you are 65 years of age, you have a 10% probability of developing Alzheimers with the next year. At 75, the odds go to 40%. In your 80's, the odds increase to 50%.' That is a huge number since the number over age 65 is greater than 35 million. So it is clear that advisors WILL be sitting with those with dementia if they deal with the elderly at all, Be very wary and cautious of any warning signs. Do more homework and read more articles for a better understanding.

**Other fiduciary Reviews:**

When you are dealing with those over age 55, there are two issues that tend to be lost in the planning process. Generally it is not the request to seek an attorney for a will or living trust- that is generally a given for an advisor. The points I am making is for absolutely focusing on what has been identified for long term care. You cannot, as a fiduciary, neglect this issue. The cost is roughly about $80,000+ annually for such care- though that is nursing home care, the most extensive care given. Most do not need that initially (only about 18% need nursing home care) and current policies cover assisted living- generally costing about 1/3 to ½ of a nursing home. The general coverage period for men is about 2.5 years for men and 4+ years for women. (Men either get well and leave or die. Women may die in a nursing home.) How is this going to be paid for- also recognizing that inflation will up the costs greatly over time. (The issue is addressed more definitively herein.)

I suggest that one read: "The Coming Wave: Professional Liability Lawsuits for Failure to Recommend a Plan for Long-Term Care" by Harley Gordon, Attorney at Law (2004). He notes in one area,

"PROFESSIONAL LIABILITY FOR BREACH OF DUE DILIGENCE

Due diligence: "The care that a reasonable person exercises under the circumstances to avoid harm to other persons or their property." Merriam-Webster's Collegiate Dictionary

There are four areas where financial planners face potential liability:

I. Failure to talk about a plan for long-term care as part of a financial retirement plan;

II. Simply selling long-term care insurance (LTCi) disconnected from a plan for long-term care;

III. Selling the wrong type of policy and amount of coverage; Failing to talk about the subject with wealthy clients who think they can self-insure the cost. End

A fiduciary has no choice but to become very conversant on this subject. Merely referring the client over to an insurance agent is not acceptable. How will they incorporate the insurance from the overall planning? Were such costs identified in the formal budget? For that matter, was a budget even done

It is a difficult area to get comfortable with since the subject is almost anathema as death. It is ever-changing with a lot of companies raising premiums or dropping out of the business altogether. Yet anyone stating that they are a financial advisor must cover this competently.

## Life Settlements

Also addressed more fully herein is the simple fact that

most elderly have purchased life insurance decades previously. Can they currently afford it? Is it necessary? Is a termination of the policy being considered? What are the surrender values?

If any of these issues are evident, the advisor must review the potential of a life settlement- the sale of a life insurance policy to a buyer. If the situation is applicable, and one is over 70 (generally) or in ill health (at any age), it is possible to 'shop' the policy in the life settlement market for a value that is potentially much higher than the cash value. Obviously this is not a simple effort but it can provide substantial monies when needed most. But it will require an advisor who has full knowledge of the opportunity. It may have to be referred out to another, but as a fiduciary, the advisor will need to oversee the effort to assure it is properly handled. For those state insurance departments that have demanded special courses on long term care I would definitely suggest they be taken. After all, an advisor has already obtained an insurance license, right?

## Summary

Fiduciary duty is necessary for anyone but seniors do require extra time due to the simple element of aging. Further, the effort is needed because they are apt to misconstrue what was said- or forget it altogether. As such, formal written documentation is necessary to validate what was done and why. One cannot depend on the computerized plan that is far from comprehensive. Certainly the risk questionnaire is so far removed from reality as to be useless anyway. Nary a single consumer knows what their risk level is and to infer a senior (or anyone) can do it with 10 or 15 questions is total folly.

Before any plan is attempted, a budget is almost always required along with individual capability with a financial calculator. This is not idle commentary meant for the future- this is an imperative effort that must be conducted each time by a fiduciary.

Lastly, proper planning by a financial 'whatever' needs to include long term care at a minimum. It definitely demands a good knowledge base by the advisor of this topic since a simple referral to an agent is not going to relieve the responsibility of competence.

# 11

# IRA Fiduciary

I am very familiar with the comments that to require those that deal with small IRAs, agents need to receive adequate compensation for the amount of time to work with such accounts. And that compensation is through commissions. Some would add that the 12b-1 fee is necessary as well for the 'ongoing relationship". But since they are presenting products generally at the highest costs with no real insight to the product and no continuing relationship therefore, how are they to act as fiduciaries? Can't

There is the other side noting that IRA rollovers and such constitute a huge retirement market and that a fiduciary status is necessary to insure that such accounts are handled properly and without such conflict.

I understand both sides with specific emphasis to the compensation for the time for small accounts.

It is true that if these were reverted to fee accounts, nary but a few such IRA accounts would materialize. That is just the way it is. These people are not going to Vanguard or Fidelity to open an account- but that also begs the issue that any of their agents are going to do the right thing either.

No.

And I do not have an answer that will comfort both. I just have the same continuing issue be it suitability or fiduciary requirements- the education levels must be increased so that the products will work in real life.

No need to repeat everything in the material- advisors must understand the full fundamentals of investing and look forward to the future with their recommendations. Returns for equities are not going to follow a reversion to 8% to 10%. Bond funds will be hurt by an increase in inflation. Volatility will stay high overall and there will be more risks since every speck of information and data can/will be magnified by Twitter and the like.

Dodd Frank is not about the word 'fiduciary'- though that is how it is being played out in the press. It is about formal, objective real life competency by the industry to/for any consumer and it cannot exist now under the tutelage of the current system. The financial literacy is dismal be they poor or rich- it is simply the rich that may have more flexibility is accepting the losses of 2000, 2008 and the next ones coming. Or do they? After 2000 and 2008, many are not so rich any more so they need the competency no matter what.

More importantly, and driven home incessantly- the industry does not have the advisers that know risk so IRAs will continue to be decimated that same as other accounts.

### Summary

A fiduciary status should exist for IRAs. Somebody else will have to come up with the particulars to make it work. No matter what, the knowledge base will have to increase substantially for any application.

# 12

# Consumer Risk Questionnaires

This is one of the most ludicrous scenarios that has existed for decades. It is the requirement that the investor indicate what level of risk he/she is willing to take.

Finra notes the following: "Virtually every investor has the same basic goal—to achieve the maximum amount of investment growth at a tolerable level of risk. Accomplishing that balance means knowing yourself as an investor. What level of risk are you comfortable taking? Are you a conservative investor who does not want to risk losing any or most of your principal? Are you a moderate investor who wants to protect your assets while increasing the value of your portfolio? Or, are you an aggressive investor who is willing to take calculated risks with the expectation of achieving greater than average returns?"

The above paragraph is a lot of superficial rubbish. There is not now nor has ever been a definitive statement of what conservative, moderate or whatever risk actually is. Pursuant to the definition FINRA uses for moderate risk, what does "protect your assets mean"? Is it a standard deviation of 10% per year for the portfolio? 20%, 30%.? What correlation? If these items are unclear- and they are- then 99% of investors are clueless to risk. And what is the suggestion of a "tolerable level of risk"? A moderate risk in protecting means what losses does the portfolio have? Is protecting the assets mean that the statistical risk of loss is 30% of all assets? If the risk is aggressive, what is the calculated risk of loss? 60%? (There is no such thing as a calculated risk of loss if no one can use a personal financial calculator.)

It is a waste of words to infer an investor needs to understand loss when the industry has never trained on such. 650,000 brokers and not one had any formal licensing instruction on a financial calculator. You cannot entrust money to those who do not know how it works. Pundits will state that they can use computer software.

No.

I have never seen ANY software that does the risk of loss. That is only done by a personal financial calculator. **If your adviser does not have and can properly use a personal financial calculator, you do not have a fiduciary. Run away.** (Yes, I am fully aware this can get tedious but it is the truth.)

FINRA then notes: "As your goals and priorities change over time, you may find that you need to modify your approach to investing. For instance, if you take on additional financial responsibilities or expect to retire in the near future, you may find it's time to shift to a more conservative investment strategy."

Probably not a bad suggestion overall depending on the numbers developed through a budget. Bonds have been the investment of choice on the conservative side for decades. But what about early 2011 economy and bonds? If one reads the comments from Gross, Buffet and more, there has been a bond bubble for over a decade due to the lowering of overall interest rates. The bubble is now over- though Bernanake says he will keep rates low till at least 2013 and that will temper current losses. But then what happens with total returns on bond funds? Only the yields will prevail- no appreciation. The point here is really focused on bond funds since few consumers have enough monies for a diversified portfolio of singular bonds. The essence is that these funds will almost universally lose in value for a long time when the FED allows inflation to climb. The risk is embedded. Will/does a questionnaire indicate that? (No) Will your adviser indicate that? Think this is being addressed in 401k plans? Get real.

At least a decade ago, I commented on the absurdity of 10 questions that could identify ***your*** risk level: "Here is the issue with literally all the risk profile measures. They are based upon your (limited) knowledge of risk and reward and what you would **LIKE TO DO,** what you **WANT TO DO** or **WHAT YOU HAVE DONE IN THE PAST**. These may be diametrically opposed to what you **NEED TO DO.** Further, that once you got the appropriate knowledge or used a competent adviser, your actual decisions might be radically different than what you had previously assumed. It's just that most of the knowledge necessary to adequately develop the risk scenario is not provided- or not provided in adequate depth- with literally all the profile questionnaires I have seen. The effort universally starts with a very simplistic budget. It also requires a present value analysis which rarely incorporates the areas that are unique to YOU. So, in my opinion, they don't work that well."

I went through at least 20 different analyses that supposedly defined what you wanted to do via the risk 'you decided upon.' (http://efmoody.com/planning/riskprofile.html) The **evident problem (one of many) was that there was no consistency in the questions. Wildly varying- yet all**

**were designed to do the same thing. If it is so simple to designate risk, then there could not be so many deviations. (Yes, I also know the bold print may be overused, but certain issues need highlighting)**

Laurence J. Kotlikoff of Boston University noted that his paper examined "the retirement-spending targeting advice provided by the four web calculators of four major financial institutions – Fidelity, American Funds, Vanguard (which uses Financial Engines), and TIAA-CREF. Their advice is remarkably simple, geared, as it is, to speed households through the planning process in a matter of minutes. But quick and simple doesn't necessarily spell helpful."

This scenario is the same when you go to a financial planner, investment adviser, financial counselor and the like. Simple questionnaires where ***you*** indicate your risk. If you go to a broker, the form may only consist of a couple boxes to check off.

Now think about this. You go to a broker or planner and you tell THEM what risk is suitable for the investments they will offer? That's simply wrong. It is the adviser's responsibility to figure out what you should be doing. After all, they are the ones with the knowledge, right??

Right??

Be it a personal broker, financial planner or an organization like Vanguard, the position of the fiduciary has to be that they figure out what risk is necessary and then explain it in real life application. If they do not figure out the risk via a budget, you do not have a fiduciary.

**Questions**

These are questions from about a decade ago. Notice the similarities as well as why so many people lost money.

As regards loss, the possibility of loss question is something like this- How would you feel if you temporarily lost **10%** of your investment?

I would lose sleep

I would be very worried

I would be sad

The future will be better

That may provide some insight, but it is only addressing a 10% loss. Pretty pathetic given the recent losses of 44% and 57%. And 1973/74 was a 45% loss. And it says temporary. Perhaps so. But when would the loss be made up? One year? Five years? Ten years? After you are dead?

And just what does “the future will be better” actually convey in real terms? It is true that people want to be optimistic and therefore the answer may simply be a marketing gimmick to suggest low returns now WILL become better just around the corner.

And another:

There are four different $10,000 investments over a one year period.

Portfolio A- Best gain= $750. Worst gain= $250

Portfolio B- Best gain = $1,500. Worst loss = $250

Portfolio c- Best gain + $2,250. Worst loss= $750

Portfolio D- Best gain = $3,000. Worst loss $1,250

Which would choose to invest in?

The "worst" loss of $1,250 is a fraud- it actually references little more than a correction in the market (10%15%). History (before 2000) clearly showed that a 25%+ loss as possible in one year (1974). History showed that a 45% loss in two years was possible (1973/74). Yet I do not know of a questionnaire that addressed that type of loss until just recently. None of the questionnaires ever noted that the risk of loss during a recession averaged about 40% to 43%. So much for the insightful questions that would really make a difference. The questionnaire is orienting the investor to a non real life scenario with the proverbial buy and hold and flat rates of return. And they generally succeed with that marketing.

This is another comical question about the breadth of knowledge-

I would describe my knowledge of investments as:

None .. .. .. .. .. 0..

Limited.... .. .. .. 2..

Good.. .... .. .. .. 4..

Extensive.. ...... .6..

This has no bearing on anything, certainly conclusive- even useful. Just what is "good" knowledge? Does it mean they know diversification? Does "extensive" mean they have a financial calculator? No to both. Even if they did, the brokerage community knows nil about either and couldn't put them into the proper focus in any case.

What happens however is that many investors- primarily men- might/would indicate that they have a very good knowledge simply because of ego. They then can be enticed into unacceptable positions because they say they are astute.

It follows the same line of reasoning when a consumer is asked, "How many years of investment experience have you had?"

0 Years

2 Years

5 years

10 or more years.

If one does not know the fundamentals of investing and cannot use a financial calculator, the years of doing something probably wrong in no way merits valid experience. Some advisers with 20 years of "experience' have just taken ones year's worth of activity and repeated it 20 times". It may appear a valid question to many, but when looked at objectively, the legitimacy wanes into oblivion.

And more- A Bank of America question noted, "The overall level of risk you choose is based primarily on your tolerance to assume risk in exchange for potential rewards." I have no idea what that means statistically. What reward against what risk?

For the following, I took two of the leading fund companies questionnaires from 2011 and commented as follows:

1. One asks your age. Obviously that is fine
2. It asks your knowledge of investing
    a. None At least they are honest.
    b. Medium, I have above basic knowledge and understand the importance of diversification and practice it (i.e., I have my money in different types of investments to spread the risks)

    Here we go again- It is the importance of *asset allocation* since diversification refers to individual use of stocks. I am well aware that some say that this is semantics but I disagree. It is true that there is a spreading of risk, but it may not make any difference because all investments can implode together
    c. High, I know how to read a company's financial reports (i.e., profit and loss statements and balance sheet) and understand the factors affecting the prices of stocks and bonds. Get real. Reading a P&L statement demands reading and understanding the footnotes. Extremely difficult. And for proper diversification, the number of companies reviewed would have to be in the hundreds.
    d. Advanced, I am familiar with most financial products (including bonds, stocks, warrants, options, and futures) and understand the various factors that may affect the risk and performance of these financial products. Get real again. No one knows options that well. Futures? If they did, they would not be taking this quiz.
3. What loss is acceptable (Notice how the loss has gone from 10% from old questionnaires to well over 30%)
    a. None Buy a CD
    b. small loss to 5% Reflects a Treasury bill or similar.

Maybe a short term bond fund. But in the last debacle with the rating services so sloppy, there were short term bond funds that dropped as much as 15%.
c. medium to 15% A 10% to 15% drop is a correction IF the economics are relatively stable (no inverted curve). You may have to live with that.
d. Large loss to 30%
e. loss more than 30% is acceptable d./e. When you go to 30% or more, such losses are NOT acceptable. No one should check off those boxes. Use DCAD or another valid method to minimize losses. Or buy an annuity instead. But anything over a 20% loss as acceptable means that the loss *is acceptable to the adviser*. That is not even an issue with a fiduciary.
4. Investment Experience: I have done this before. Just because you bought something you did not understand for the last 15 years does not mean much of anything. Certainly competency. A witch doctor can have 50 years of experience. And you would want to use them because of ????? If you do not know the fundamentals of investing, you are and will continue to be lost.
5. How would you react if you suffered a short term loss of 15% in the last three months and the market is still bearish. This is DCAD (Dollar Cost Averaging Down). A 15% drop can be just a correction but if the risk is still very high and values are still going down, the point of masochism is what? Was there an inverted yield curve previously? How about Year to Year Real GDP%? If you lose 15%, how much do you need to get back to even? About 18%. If you lost 40% and wanted to get back to even, you would have to earn 66%.
6. Household disposable income. Question is fine but requires full budget analysis and income status. Lot more detailed than what it appears.
7. How long is your investment horizon. The longer your horizon, the greater the opportunity to ride out the ups and

downs. The chance to lose money is generally lower when the investment horizon increases but the money needs to be locked in longer. Here is where statistics- or the lack thereof- is a problem. If there are just small losses- a correction- maybe not a problem. But why accept large losses like a dweeb just hoping the values will return in the future? All the people with 401ks in 2000- 2008 were told the same thing. And they may now work until they are dead. Maybe even longer. The question is clearly incomplete.

As for, "The chance to lose money is generally lower when the investment horizon increases"-no! The volatility goes down but *the potential risk of loss goes up.* So after 2000 and 2008, with two major financial losses- certainly in 401ks- how much longer should the consumer wait. Another 20 years? That is generally considered to be the time frame now.

8. What percentage of your assets are you willing to commit to investments. Don't like the question. It is better stated - If you invest in this allocation and the adviser does nothing, your risk of loss is a potential 10% or 20% or 30% or 40% or 50% or 50%+. Now what do you want to do.

9. What is your total net worth Fine

10. Investment Objective

a. preserve capital even if returns are low

b. generate high stable dividends even with some risk

c. balance regular income with stable growth over time

d. stable capital appreciation to grow capital over a long period of time.

e. I will take maximum risk. Unless numbers are put against it, the consumer has no clue. Further, the industry is correct in stating that bonds may lose for a decade or two. So what is preserve capital if bonds may lose?

What is d-"stable capital appreciation?" Stable means what? No volatility? Nice smooth returns? They do not exist.

f. I have no idea what maximum risk could mean to 99 44/100% of investors unless it was close to a total loss. Then therefore 'e'. should simply say that. However, that tends to reflect single issues of securities which means clearly non diversified. How in the world is that suitable? And some more:

1 From 9/2008 to 11/2008, the market lost 31%. If I lost 31%

A. Sell the rest
B. Sell a portion
C. Hold on
D. Buy more
E. Have a hissy fit
F. See a marriage counselor
G. Fire my adviser.
H. Wish I had used DCAD

Just cannot accept that type of loss if one is paying attention. If no one is paying attention, the bottom four are the answers. One would have been doing DCAD well before 9/2008 and the losses would have been not more than 15% in equities. And the rest of the funds would have been in CDs or bonds earning some income.

2. I prefer very little volatility and will accept lower returns Maybe OK but remember that bonds are not generally too volatile but are almost certainly a losing venture for maybe the next decade or two. Also, numbers over time do show that volatility/Standard Deviation goes down. But that is a fraud since the risk of loss go up.

3. I would invest in a mutual friend based on just a conversation with a friend, family member, or the best of all- a fellow church member.

The answer to this is “I am a moron”. There is nothing else to say. (I do admit that it is OK to take a flyer now and then with purely discretionary monies, but the focus on these questions is to formal investing)

5. During market declines, I sell my riskier assets and

invest in safer assets The answer is 'good for you'. That is how it is done. This is the first and only time I have seen anything about selling the riskier assets first. Nice to see it- but about 10+ years too late.

6. My current and future income is stable Good question

7. My previous experience See above. If you do not understand diversification, you cannot understand risk. If do not understand risk, you cannot understand suitability. I have never met a consumer who knew diversification. Actually a broker either. Nor an arbitrator. Nor an attorney. Somebody is out there- just have not met them.

There were 10 questions on each questionnaire on which to base an investment portfolio. Pretty useless as far as I am concerned and would not cover a fiduciary duty. "Accounting professor Shlomo Benartzi of UCLA studied a large sample of investors who filled out a risk-tolerance questionnaire for a major 401(k) provider. Only 7% described themselves as aggressive; yet 33% invest as if they are, putting 80% to 100% of their 401(k) into stocks." They have no idea of their true risk of loss exposure.

**Summary**

In order to figure out any appropriate risk, it is mandatory that at least one of the two entities in the transaction; consumer and/or broker/planner/agent properly figure out what risk NEEDS to be taken. As stated, it is *not* what the investor has done before, wants or likes to do, or is suggesting now. It is incumbent for the professional to figure out just where they are and what they *need* to go to accomplish the goals selected. Or even to determine if the goals are acceptable.

This same examination is required for any 410k participant. Any presentation or seminar offered to company participants must, *absolutely must*, address the amount of a projected risk of loss due to normal volatility. Assume the investor would accept a 30% loss. (In the real world, there would be a wholesale change to investing when one specifies the possible loss. Consumers would really balk. But there is no other number that works, so that is what is used here.) The agent then reverses the formula to determine the standard deviations. Now that there is a single SD, one can then use perceived correlations to make up an asset allocation that fits within the guidelines.

Oh yeah, that'll happen.

Well, that is how it is supposed to work. Admittedly, few in the industry have a clue to just what was stated if for no other reason that they cannot use a personal financial calculator. The investor/client is absolutely clueless.

The point is that the risk of loss for the vast numbers of portfolios- certainly for the 401ks addressed above- is about 40% to 60% of the entire account. Think anyone knows that? A fiduciary has to.

In short, the industry has never provided the basic input for determining risk. It cannot defer the knowledge and fiduciary responsibility about risk over to naive investors who have no idea of the issues at all. And then to unilaterally dismiss the risk of loss.

Risk questionnaires have been a crutch for many agents and firms because if a allocation went bad, they could always point to the fact that the customer chose the level of risk initially. Yet there is nary a customer alive who knows the proper definition to diversification. Repeated ad nauseam- If you do not know diversification, you cannot determine risk. If you cannot determine risk, you cannot determine suitability.

In reality, the questionnaires cannot take too much time. Most people are looking for something quick and simple (you do not need theory for that) and any extended effort or time by the potential consumer would mean they would never finish the questionnaire and move on to some other site where the time constraint would be minimal. Therefore simplicity and marketing prevail. And as long as they do, current financial debacles will continue relatively unabated.

There obviously needs to be wholesale changes to the questionnaires but since the consumers know none of the implications of what they are being requested to answer, it will be up to the industry and the 'fiduciaries' to change the orientation from marketing.

Yea, right.

# 13

# Diversification

The tendency is for most people to use the haggard and generally incomplete and sophomoric definition for diversification: "don't put all your eggs in one basket". I admit that in certain cases this shop worn rule of thumb can work. But when it comes to investing in securities, it is pretty much useless. There are no numbers associated with it at this level. There is no statistical merit to figuring out whether what someone has done is logical, inept, foolish, suitable, stupid or anything else. Probably my biggest gripe is that the numbers are well known, have been around for decades. Yet have never been taught to brokers and only sporadically to those with planning designations. But it is one of the most critical areas of securities investing. Any reasonable instruction to Enron, Worldcom employees, 401ks and the like would have avoided at least 50% of said losses.

In short, there are few individual stock portfolios that are properly diversified and an extended risk is being taken- unquestionably unwittingly in many cases- but nonetheless evident by most consumers.

**Stocks**

Let's get right to it.

Though literally everyone talks about diversification for an investment portfolio, very few understand the true statistical data underlying the issue. In order to properly explain the problem, certain definitions are required: Systematic Risk- this is risk due to the movement of the market itself. The benchmark could be the Dow (normally used by consumers and brokers alike), the S&P 500, Wilshire index, etc., but the index may also be that of select or special uses such as gold, real estate, biotech and other sector funds. If one had one or a few investments in a given area, they could compare its return to that of the benchmark index to determine how well it is doing.

Unsystematic Risk- This is the risk of ONE company experiencing a significant move- either up or down- in a portfolio. This is usually the risk that most consumers would want to eliminate- unless they are TRUE risk takers (few are) and can accept the singular loss even down to zero. It may be tempered- and in fact virtually eliminated- by the purchase of a certain number of stocks or bonds.

In the "old days" before the computer and Internet, a portfolio of 15 to 20 stocks was able to mirror, quite closely, the risk of the entire market (say S&P 500). Of course, that assumes that the correlations were random- the various stocks did not do the same thing at the same time for the same reason. However, if you picked auto, steel, glass, rubber etc., they will do the same thing at the same time since they are all focused to the same thing. In such instances, one would need at least 100 of these stocks to reduce the unsystematic risk.

(There are caveats that even make the "old" theory highly suspect. Ron Surz, CIMA, and Mitchell Price, Roxbury Capital Management state, "we now see that a 15-stock portfolio gets 76% of available diversification versus the Fisher & Lorie 93%; this improves somewhat to 82% if tracking error is used as the diversification measure, but note that the tracking error is still a formidable 8.1% per annum. Even at 60 stocks we still have less than 90% of the available diversification whereas Fisher & Lorie would suggest virtually full diversification at this level.)

Once the Internet gained momentum, it became the center of data dispersal. Millions upon millions of pieces of advice and "information" beamed into personal computers faster than anything seen previously. It was an investors dream to see so much information (notice I did not say knowledge) from so many 'reputable' sources effectively guaranteeing instant wealth. Consumers did bite the bait and tried- as identified with Better Investing previously- to make a killing. As a result of this type of trading, individual stock volatility increased tremendously and it therefore took more stocks to reduce the unsystematic risk down to the market overall (after 2000). (See article by John Y. Campbell, Martin Lettau, Burton G. Malkiel and Yexiao Xu: This paper uses a disaggregated approach to study the volatility of common stocks at the market, industry, and firm levels.) Over the period from 1962 to 1997 there has been a noticeable increase in firm-level volatility relative to market volatility. The minimum number I have seen is now 50 stocks but considering what has happened in the 2000s I am hesitant to suggest a number that low. Other studies suggest from 100 to as many as 350 stocks. No matter the number of 50 or 350, it should be clear that the ability of the consumer to ferret out all material on just a few stocks is mind numbing. To do so on hundreds of stocks is simply beyond their capacity no matter their intelligence. As again noted by Benoit Mandelbrot, "for a thirty stock portfolio, about the minimum needed to make the numbers work well, that means 495 different calculations of mean variance and covariance. For the entire NY Stock Exchange, 3.9 million calculations. And because prices change, the exercise needs constant repetition."

It is simply illogical for consumers to buy individual stocks to properly build a portfolio. While diversification is prudent- actually mandatory for a fiduciary- it is **not** taught to brokers. Once in awhile a CFP, CPA or ChFC might be taught some basics, but it is not required. A CFA is required to know it, but then most of the CFAs go on to do securities analysis of some type- or even make up a fund- but are not generally seen at the individual level. So unless some knowledgeable entity actually offers the facts, most consumers go running off in a blind and irrational attempt to make up something they are sure will work. They may opt for Jim Cramer or Morningstar, Value Line, Money mag and the like.

**Wrong.**

Consumers should not buy stocks to make up their portfolio save for when they have some discretionary funds they want to play with. They neither have the time nor expertise to figure out all the nuances of a company. (Try reading and understanding the footnotes!) Most advisers are effectively as limited.

**Lack of diversification.**

Why Do Individual Investors Hold Under-Diversified Portfolios?: WILLIAM N. GOETZMANN, ALOK KUMAR The definitive article on diversification in the real world. (A little involved but pretty understandable)

Investors' personal characteristics, their stock preferences, and their behavioral biases jointly influence their diversification choices. Younger, lower-income (less wealthy), and relatively less sophisticated investors and those who follow price trends, prefer local (familiar) stocks, and exhibit over-confidence hold relatively less diversified portfolios.

Under-diversified investors exhibit strong style and industry preferences and they also prefer more volatile and positively skewed stocks. Furthermore, we find some evidence to support the asymmetric information hypothesis for under-diversification. In contrast, we find that factors such as small portfolio size, transaction costs, and search costs are unlikely determinants of investors' diversification choices. The unexpectedly high idiosyncratic risk in investors' portfolios results in a welfare loss.

Our results indicate that the majority of individual investors in our sample are underdiversified and the extent of under-diversification is more severe for investors who hold only retirement accounts (IRA or Keogh). Consistent with results from previous studies, we find that more than 25% of investor portfolios in our sample contain only one stock, more than 50% of them contain fewer than three stocks, and **in any given month, only 510% of the portfolios contain more than ten stocks.** Consequently, investor portfolios have extremely high volatility (more than 75% of investor portfolios have higher volatility than the market portfolio) and they have worse risk-return properties than randomly constructed matching portfolios.

**In 1998, roughly 75% of households held five or fewer stocks.**

To gain further insights into the diversification choices of investors, we examine the time variation in the average diversification level of investor portfolios. We find that **during the 1991-96 sample period, the average number of stocks in investor portfolios increases from four to seven.** This results in a decrease in the average normalized portfolio variance. However, the improved diversification over time does not necessarily imply that investors' portfolio composition skills have improved. We do not find any perceptible evidence of diversification improvement by active means. Over time, there is no decrease in either the excess average correlation (relative to benchmark portfolios) or the excess normalized variance of investor portfolios. This suggests that a significant part of diversification improvement results from passive means where investors increase the number of stocks in their portfolios without giving proper consideration to stock correlations.

Diversification level increases with income (wealth) as well as age which reflects an increasing degree of risk aversion with age and income (wealth). We also find that investor sophistication, in particular, their financial sophistication influences their portfolio choices. Relatively more sophisticated investors – investors who hold mutual funds, trade in options and foreign equities, and engage in short-selling – hold relatively more diversified portfolios. The degree of diversification also varies across occupation categories in a manner which further supports the view that investors' diversification decisions depend upon age, income (wealth), and their level of financial sophistication. Investors who belong to the non-professional job category (blue-collar workers, clerical workers, sales and service workers, house-makers, and students) hold the least diversified portfolios in our sample while retired investors are on the other end of the diversification spectrum where they hold the most diversified portfolios. The diversification decisions of investors are also influenced by their preferences for certain stock characteristics and by their behavioral biases. We find that investors with strong style and industry preferences are less diversified. In addition, investors with a preference for volatile and positively skewed stocks hold relatively less diversified portfolios. Examining the influence of investors' behavioral biases on their diversification decisions, we find that investors who are over-confident (i.e., investors who trade excessively and earn lower returns), investors who invest disproportionately in local (familiar) stocks, and those who are sensitive to price trends (i.e., trend-chasers and contrarian investors) exhibit a greater degree of under diversification. The unexpectedly high idiosyncratic risk in investor portfolios results in a welfare loss (Skip next paragraph if desired and go to punch line)

Lack of diversification may also be induced by a variety of psychological factors. For instance, investors may ignore correlations due to their behavioral biases. Unlike stock prices (or returns) and trading volume, stock correlations are not directly available to investors and they must be computed. If investors formulate their investment decisions using information that is easily available, i.e., if they employ the availability heuristic (Tversky and Kahneman (1973)), **they are more likely to ignore correlations** and hold under-diversified portfolios. In addition, investors who rely on past price trends to formulate their trading decisions (e.g., Odean (1999), Dhar and Kumar (2001)) **may ignore stock correlations** (e.g., Kroll, Levy, and Rapoport (1988a, 1988b), Kroll and Levy (1992)). Furthermore, people who frame their investment decisions narrowly (e.g., Kahneman and Lovallo (1993), Barberis, Huang, and Thaler (2003), Kumar and Lim (2004)) may ignore the interactions among their individual stock selection decisions and **they may ignore correlations** among the stocks they hold in their portfolios. It is possible that investors take correlations into account but they mis-estimate the strength of correlations. Experimental research suggests that people misestimate correlations at an intuitive level – they under-estimate small correlations and they are bad at judging correlation differences when the correlations are low (Jennings, Amabile, and Ross (1982)).

**Here is the punch line.** No matter what you read, general consumers are not only incapable of picking stocks, the attempt in doing so has led to grossly undiversified portfolios and huge risk (Enron, Worldcom, Adelphia, Digital). The problem is that the industry- certainly including the effort of the government and its entities (SEC, FINRA, DOL.)- have never been even remotely active in applying the real world element of risk to anyone in the industry. In fact, they have provided grants of millions of dollars to many organizations to promote aggressive stock picking as a major element of investing (Better Investing for example) or suggesting gambling at the most basic level (Stock Market Game). That is Wrong

**Summary**

In short, the essence of seeking greater returns from stock selection is not and can never be an acceptable focus for general consumers. If it was so viable, then everyone should go back to buying individual stocks and forgo mutual funds and ETFs. There simply is an underlying risk that they do not comprehend at all. It may be debatable for institutional investors as well since few have been able to beat the market over time.

If consumers want equities, they can buy cheap index funds. (Though the risk of loss- far less than a small grouping of individual stocks- still exists and must be dealt with.) Again- if you do not understand diversification, you cannot understand risk. If you do not understand risk, you cannot understand suitability.

No investor should be allowed to buy stocks without the recognition of diversification coupled with the separate risk of loss.

I doubt that there is more than 0.005% of consumers who know what the full definition of diversification actually is. It is not much better- if any- for our government entities that oversee the various markets (SEC, FINRA etc) as well as provide the education to the masses. U.S. taxpayers should ask for their money back.

Oh, wait. They gave it away in the bailouts............

# 14

# Beta and a Lot More of Real World Failure

Beta is dead- long live beta.

I don't know who said that but it is one of the most profound statements made about the use of past numbers and projecting forward. Beta is in that realm.

Well, as addressed herein, correlations are a moving target, very hard to figure out, and don't provide hardly any assistance when markets tumbles.

Then there is standard deviation. While heavily promoted as risk per se, it never was. It is just a form of risk like any other. And like many others, has been misused. So that's two down.

Now we have beta. By definition from Wikipedia- the **capital asset pricing model (CAPM)** is used to determine a theoretically appropriate required rate of return of an asset, if that asset is to be added to an already well-diversified portfolio, given that asset's non-diversifiable risk. The model takes into account the asset's sensitivity **to non-diversifiable** risk **(also known as** systematic risk **or**

market risk**), often represented by the quantity beta (β)** in the financial industry, as well as the expected return of the market and the expected return of a theoretical risk-free asset
http://en.wikipedia.org/wiki/Capital_asset_pricing_model

Or I will do it this way (given some latitude). Beta is a reflection of risk as compared to an index- assume the S&P 500. Whatever the index does, it does by a beta factor of 1.0. If a stock or fund has a beta greater than 1.0- say 1.2- it will go up more as the overall market appreciates. In this case, 20% more. If the beta is 1.5, then the inference is that the returns will be 50% higher than the market.

But there is no free lunch with risk. If the market goes down, then a stock or fund with a higher beta goes down more. For example, a beta of 1.2 indicates the investment will go down 20% more than the index.

As is hopefully obvious, if one has a beta less than 1.0, then the investment does not go up as much compared to its index but will also not go down as much in a bad slump (0.8 infers 80% of the movement to its corresponding index). Regular bonds have betas less than 1.0: that's why you see these in more conservative portfolios. And the suggestion to use more of these as you get older. Less risk, less of a potential loss but universally a lower return than stocks (though that depends on the time period reviewed).

There is a lot more to this, quite obviously: betas do not have to be the same up and down. And it is possible that the same betas will not do the same thing at the same time. Here is an example. Assume the S&P 500 index again. Manager 1 picks 100 of index stocks and earns the same as the market. Maybe not a surprise. But manager 2 picked an entirely different 100 stocks from the same selection of 500, has a beta of one as well, but actually returned MORE than the index. How is that possible?

That's because manager 2 was able to select the better

stocks from the same grouping than manager 1. (This is called alpha but is beyond the scope of this material)

So that is how you check out a stock (which I don't think is valid for most people as identified under diversification) or a fund. Everything else being equal, the lower the beta and the greater the return, the better the fund AT LEAST AT THAT POINT IN TIME. It does not mean the returns will stay high, etc. It just means that manager 2 was better than manager 1- and perhaps others- for that period of time. For an idea of what can go both right and wrong, view Bill Miller of Legg Mason. The only manager to beat the S&P 500 for 14 years straight and then went poof.

But this commentary is about the value of beta itself. After all, when you do a formal review of beta with Morningstar or other service and see that it is 0.8, you know that it actually is 0.8, don't you?

No you don't.

Recognize that in almost all issues explained in this text, I might have had serious concerns about various numbers and theories because they 'seemed inadequate' when pushed to real life application. Certain of these issues I could (in)validate myself, certain ones took years of experience to put into focus- but many required the reading and research of hundreds upon hundreds of intensive research papers that the internet has provided. In such regards, I point to two by Pablo Fernandez at the University of Navarra, Madrid, Spain as an example of the expertise that allows this chapter to really identify 'real life'.

Betas used by Professors. A survey with 2,500 answers: http://www.iese.edu/research/pdfs/DI-0822-E.pdf and are calculated betas worth for anything?: *papers.ssrn.com/sol3/Delivery.cfm/ SRN_ID1286436_code12696.pdf?...*

Look at the company betas below on the same date. It

is simply NOT possible to have that much inconsistency between the various rating services. It is impossible. There is simply no way that one can use these numbers on which to base most any calculation or any estimate for the future. Which ones are correct? Which stock s the better?

**Betas of different companies according to different sources**

| | AT&T | Boeing | CocaCola | Date |
|---|---|---|---|---|
| Yahoo | 0.61 | 0.46 | 0.29 | 12-feb-03 |
| Multex | 0.87 | 0.66 | 0.42 | 12-feb-03 |
| Quicken | 1.14 | 0.66 | 0.41 | 12-feb-03 |
| Reuters | 0.87 | 0.68 | 0.42 | 12-feb-03 |
| Bloombrg | 1.00 | 1.07 | 0.64 | 12-feb-03 |
| Datastrm | 1.10 | 1.10 | 0.37 | 12-feb-03 |

Buy&hold 0.84 0.66 0.41 14-feb-03

ATT has a high of 1.14 and a low of 0.61. Boeing has a high and low of 1.10 and 0.46. ATT has a high of 1.14 and a low of 0.61. Boeing has a high and low of 1.10 and 0.46. Coke's high and low are .64 and 0.29. Yahoo has the lowest numbers overall. Will it always be like that?

Here is a larger sample in 2009 for just one day.

Notice that the numbers still vary tremendously. And Yahoo is no longer the lowest. Remember the section on

Betas of three companies according to the most used webs and databases. May 12, 2009

| WEB/Database | COCA-COLA | WALT DISNEY | WAL-MART STORES |
|---|---|---|---|
| Bloomberg | 0.79 | 1.06 | 0.58 |
| Cnbc | 0.60 | 1.00 | 0.30 |
| Damodaran | 0.61 | 0.88 | 0.19 |
| Datastream | 0.31 | 0.72 | 0.13 |
| Ft.Com | 0.80 | 1.06 | 0.57 |
| Google Finance | 0.60 | 1.03 | 0.26 |
| Hoovers | 0.60 | 1.00 | 0.20 |
| Infomercados | 0.33 | 1.39 | 0.31 |
| Msn Moneycentral | 0.54 | 1.03 | 0.16 |
| Quote | 0.54 | 1.13 | 0.19 |
| Reuters | 0.53 | 1.01 | 0.17 |
| Smartmoney | 0.61 | 1.03 | 0.26 |
| Thomson Banker | 0.55 | 1.09 | 0.38 |
| Value Line | 0.55 | 1.00 | 0.60 |
| Vernimmen Website | - | 1.08 | 0.71 |
| Yahoo Finance | 0.63 | 0.99 | 0.28 |
| Max. | 0.80 | 1.39 | 0.71 |
| Min. | 0.31 | 0.72 | 0.13 |

the reliability on numbers. Doesn't the 0.xxx imply some great preciseness (i.e. 1.03). Well, not here in that you have no idea if that is even close to the true values to begin with. The use of beta therefore is highly suspect and makes the formulas containing same highly suspect.

Fernandez offers some great graphs and charts and, for the true researcher, they are invaluable. My effort however is to provide the essence of some exceptional current studies. This is his summary of some betas over just a two month period. Shouldn't vary too much, don't you think?

Historical betas of **AT&T, Boeing and Coca-Cola** in the two-month period of December 2001 and January 2002 with respect to the S&P 500. It may be seen that the beta of **AT&T** varies from **0.32** (January 14, 2002)

**Figure 1. Historical betas of AT&T, Boeing and Coca-Cola.**

Betas calculated during the two-month period of December 2001 and January 2002 with respect to the S&P 500. Each day, betas are calculated using 5 years of monthly data, i.e. on December 18, 2001, the beta is calculated by running a regression of the 60 monthly returns of the company on the 60 monthly returns of the S&P 500. The returns of each month are calculated on the 18th of the month:

$$\text{monthly return of December 18, 2001} = \frac{\text{total return December 18, 2001}}{\text{total return November 18, 2001}} - 1$$

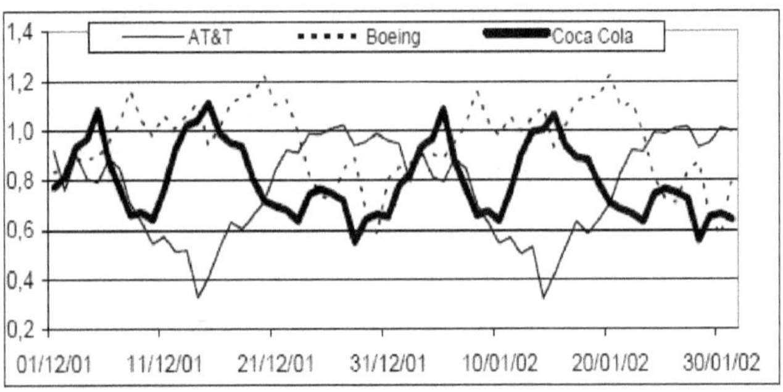


to **1.02** (December 27, 2001), the beta of **Boeing** varies from **0.57** (January 30, 2002) to **1.22** (January 20, 2002), and the beta of **Coca-Cola** varies from **0.55** (December 28, 2001) to **1.11** (January 15, 2002).

Per Fernandez- "We show that, in general, it is an enormous error to use the historical beta as a proxy for the expected beta. First, because it is almost impossible to calculate a meaningful beta because historical betas change dramatically from one day to the next; second, because very often we cannot say with a relevant statistical confidence that the beta of one company is smaller or bigger than the beta of another; third, because historical betas do not make much sense in many cases: high-risk companies very often have smaller historical betas than low-risk companies; fourth, because historical betas depend very much on which index we use to calculate them."

Note again, **High-risk companies very often have smaller historical betas than low-risk companies.**

That cannot be possible, can it? And his reply regarding the status of such numbers-"We do not think that this makes much economic sense."

"Some authors recommend using industry betas, instead of company betas. For example, Copeland, Koller and Murrin (2000) recommend "checking several reliable sources because beta estimates vary considerably… If the betas from several sources vary by more than 0.2 or the beta for a company is more than 0.3 from the industry average, consider using the industry average. An industry average beta is typically more stable and reliable than an individual company beta because measurement errors tend to cancel out". But about the CAPM, they conclude "It takes a better theory to kill an existing theory, and we have not seen the better theory yet. Therefore, we continue to use the CAPM, being wary of all the problems with estimating it."

Fernandez- We rather think that a rejection is enough to beat a model.

**We have shown that industry betas are quite unstable.**

"Fernandez's work shows that betas are all over the place not only for time, but also for the various rating services.

And since I have also viewed them as with the attempts with correlation, standard deviation et al, I simply do not find enough real world application to warrant their use by those who don't even know the fundamentals of investing. It simply cannot work.

So now I have pretty much confirmed that the numbers utilized for many theories may be little more than bad history put through a blender.

What is the fiduciary to do- since this is the focus of the material? There must be a wholesale change in education of advisers before they will even realize the true implications of any of the software programs or the numbers therein.

# 15

# Investment Correlations

Correlation refers to how one investment moves when compared to another. The point being does it move in the same amount at the same time for the same reason in the same direction. If two assets move in tandem, they have a correlation of 1.0. If they move opposite each other, the correlation is -1.0. If they have no specific relationship, the correlation is 0.0.

When involved with the development of a portfolio, correlation becomes one of, if not the most important considerations since the intent is to provide offsetting movements over periods of time. It does not mean that you are looking for -1.0 since a 50/50 allocation means that any gain on one side is being offset by the other. One tends to seek positive correlations that show slightly different movements. Not only are the correlations necessary when the market is moving up, but more important when the market goes down as one investment might offset another's losses. That is the theory anyway- and not a good theory overall as we have seen recently. It is tough stuff that requires a lot of real life experience.

Correlations Rene Stulttz: http://www.cob.ohio-state.edu/fin/dice/papers/2008/2008-18.pdf,When an institution has many positions or projects, the risk of the institution depends on how the risks of the different positions or projects are related. If the correlation between the positions or projects is high, it is more likely that all the firm's activities perform poorly at the same time, which leads to a higher probability of a large loss. **These correlations can be difficult to assess and they change over time, at times abruptly.** A partner of LTCM described the problem they faced in August and September 1998 as being one where correlations that they thought were extremely small suddenly became large. With this perspective, correlations would have been misestimated. **It is well-known in finance that correlations increase in periods of crisis**. Failure to assess correlations correctly would lead to the wrong assessment of the risk of a portfolio or of a firm. The problem of mismeasurement of correlations is more subtle, however, if correlations are **random and sometimes turn out to be unexpectedly large ex post. In this case, risk managers could not be expected to know what correlations will be, but their assessment of the risk of a portfolio or of the firm would depend on their estimates of the distribution of the correlations.**

It might be possible to figure out the correlations between two stocks. But then again, using just two stocks defies all elements of proper diversification and the associated risk. Therefore, if one attempts a diversified portfolio of, say 30 stocks, it is necessary to not only compare the correlations against one security, but also against all the other securities and then tie them all together in the portfolio. Repeated often, per Benoit Mandelbrot, the number of calculations for just 30 stocks requires 495 different calculations of mean variance and covariance. For the entire NY Stock Exchange, 3.9 million calculations.

And because prices change, the exercise needs constant repetition." Not going to happen by consumers.

### False belief

Hence the fallacy again in the selection of individual stocks for a portfolio. A consumer attempting singular securities has no understanding of such calculations for correlations and certainly does not have the computer program capable of the calculations in any case. And it is a moot attempt anyway since they would never select the necessary number of stocks (300+) for a diversified portfolio. So now what?

The consumer needs to select mutual funds (and possible some ETFs) to build a proper portfolio. One looks for the offsetting positions including the S&P 500, emerging countries, bonds, gold, small cap, value, real estate, and many more. Just what are the percentages for each product and why? Are there valuable/valid statistics to use as a guide- and why? How do these products relate to each other when the economy changes? Pay strict attention here to anyone discussing long term correlation trends because therein lies the false belief of correlations over time. Here is a 'fine' example of the distorted rationale by Bill Bernstein, author of The Intelligent Asset Allocator- "In any case, the future for the relationship of stocks and commodities may be changing, but watching correlations is no tipoff about what to do in the here and now. "Changes in correlations over periods of less than 20 or 30 years—or certainly over less than 10 years—are meaningless." Further, "The drop in the 1990s was a **one-time event** tied to the peculiarities of the tech boom. As a result, the bounce-back of recent vintage is a reaction to what he labels a ***"non-recurring event."*** I disagreed fervently. As stated in all my work, the mid 90s has brought about an upheaval in all areas of life with the introduction of the computer and Internet. (If nothing else, consider how the cell phone has forever changed communications.) The old statistics were simply old- actually never did work that well to begin with. Admittedly, they did work at times, but was it sheer coincidence? How can one state that something is non recurring (recessions??) while also using 30+ year old data to make up an allocation? Real life does not stay constant over 30 years- even 10 years. Look at 2011 by itself.

Here is one of the first charts I accumulated. Twenty years of information that is twenty years old. Isn't that good enough for 2011? I doubt anyone would use this, but is this not perfect for those who base the future on the past?

CORRELATION: (Life Insurance Selling) 1970- 1992

| Year | 1 | 2 | 3 | 4 | 5 | 6 | 7 | 8 | 9 | 10 | 11 | 12 |
|---|---|---|---|---|---|---|---|---|---|---|---|---|
| 1 Cash | 1.0 | | | | | | | | | | | |
| 2 Domestic Stock | -0.8 | 1.0 | | | | | | | | | | |
| 3 Intrnat Stock | -0.8 | 0.52 | 1.0 | | | | | | | | | |
| 4 Real Estate | 0.23 | -.05 | -.07 | 1.0 | | | | | | | | |
| 5 Domestic Bond | .05 | 0.4 | .25 | -.24 | 1.0 | | | | | | | |
| 6 NonDollar bonds | -.11 | .13 | .59 | -.09 | .17 | 1.0 | | | | | | |
| 7 Balanced Funds | -.06 | .98 | .51 | -.15 | .53 | 17 | 1.0 | | | | | |
| 8 Managed Futures | .06 | .02 | -.07 | .11 | .04 | -.07 | 0.0 | 1.0 | | | | |
| 9 Venture Capital | -0.8 | .51 | .41 | .09 | .17 | .17 | .50 | .06 | 1.0 | | | |
| 10 Leasing | .64 | .05 | .01 | .08 | .20 | -.01 | .09 | .03 | -.03 | 1.0 | | |
| 11 Gold | -.11 | 0.0 | .26 | .15 | -.08 | .29 | 0.0 | 0.1 | .04 | -.18 | 1.0 | |
| 12 Equity REIT | .11 | .81 | .66 | -.3 | .43 | .28 | .81 | -.14 | .89 | .13 | .01 | 1.0 |

As a further commentary to the drop in the 90s, look at 2008. The changes in the correlations were what broke the market. A severe economic downturn causes correlations to rise and substantially increase risk. You DO have to look at current economic conditions (recession). Staying put means that the lower correlation entities (international) or offsetting (real estate) all start to move to 1.0. Investors lost trillions of dollars that they may never see again. Using correlations established before the Internet and the personal computer reflects outdated statistics and a hope that history will hold. They may work (but why?), and I once again point to 2008. Things change for a lot of reasons.

Peter Bernstein (not a relation to the above) was considered one of the most astute advisers ever and cautioned that "We simply do not know what the future holds" and admonished investors about employing the long run as a benchmark because the long run is not a homogeneous state of the world, a smooth and straight line into the future. A very large portion of the vaunted equity returns over the risk free return, the equity risk premium, is accounted for by just 32 years out of 200 years since 1800, 1950-1981. Bonds outperformed stocks 43% of the time, and stocks were superior over the very long run, but with a high degree of uncertainty during periods of time shorter than 150 years. He concludes that, "...the long run can tell us perilously little about what kinds of environments lie ahead...we have to accept uncertainty."

Pundits of my commentary about the necessity of judging current economics as a guide to investing have been dealt a cruel hand of huge losses- while they sat around hoping that 30 and 40 years old statistics would save the day. Below is excellent commentary by Andrew Lo which puts a focus on past theory:

WHEN THE WISDOM OF CROWDS BECOMES THE MADNESS OF MOBS Andrew W. Lo, October 2009 The financial crisis has challenged virtually every tenet of modern portfolio management. Investors were told to diversify by holding broad-based long-only portfolios of index funds; those who did so by investing in smallcap, large-cap, value, growth, international, emerging- market, balanced and target-date funds all lost money last year.

Investors were told to manage their risk exposures by adjusting their strategic asset allocation between passive stock and bond index funds; last year was a heart-pounding roller- coaster ride regardless of asset allocation.

Investors were told that they would be rewarded for bearing risk; last year risk-taking was routinely punished and the best performers were US government bond funds.

And investors were told to hold stocks for the long run; just how long is the long run, and can we be sure that the short run won't wipe us out first?

These investment principles are not wrong - they are simply incomplete. The world has become more complex over the past 20 years, and we need to update our investment paradigm to incorporate these new complexities.

Diversification is still a good idea, but it has become much harder to achieve. Thanks to the increasing competition for additional yield, every type of investment vehicle and strategy has experienced substantial growth in assets under management.

The influx of significant assets into any given strategy has three effects: 1, it reduces the strategy's expected return owing to competition; 2, if there is any expected return remaining, this portion will be a source of correlation or "beta" among all investors in the strategy; and 3, if enough assets are invested in this strategy over a sufficiently short period of time, the strategy can become a "crowded trade" that is illiquid and subject to large, unpredictable swings in profits and losses.

The most striking example of these effects is the subprime mortgage market, which was the focus of the current crisis, but other examples include the equity market-neutral "quant meltdown" of August 2007 and the unwinding of the carry trade in July 2007.

To achieve true diversification, investors must now have a broader set of asset classes and risk exposures, long and short, in their portfolios. (EFM: But going short with the likes on long/short funds means the manager can not only pick what is going up, but what is going down. They have not worked well at all.) Strategic asset allocation decisions are no longer responsive enough to dynamic changes in risk as competition and financial innovations cause stock and bond volatilities to spike unpredictably.

The VIX index (a forward looking measure of S&P 500 volatility) rocketed from a low of 16 per cent in May 2008 to a high of 80 per cent in October 2008 (400%!!!). (It is was hovering around 23 per cent (2/2010).

But how about the four 400 point swings in August 2011? VIX was around 33% after that.

Such volatility swings are simply unacceptable for most investors. In this environment, managing risk can no longer be easily accomplished via simple buy-and-hold portfolios as before, but requires more frequent rebalancing or "tactical risk management".

This trend is a manifestation of the technological arms race that has given us electronic trading platforms, algorithmic trading, globally integrated markets, narrower bid/offer spreads, higher trading volume and more liquidity, but at the cost of more complex price dynamics. (EFM- the regular consumer trying to capitalize on the inconsistencies in the market just don't have a chance save by luck).

In fact, technology has changed the very definition of passive investing, which used to be synonymous with market capitalisation- weighted portfolios of a fixed set of securities.

Thanks to advances in trading technology, index portfolios no longer need to be static or cap- weighted, and may involve more frequent rebalancings while still being investable, transparent and passive. (EFM- that may be OK if the correlations are correct. Otherwise one could use the simple indexes and adjust for current correlations- though that is a mind numbing exercise beyond almost all investors. They will neither spend the time nor have the acumen.)

The financial system is not an immutable black box; it is a dynamic, evolving ecology in which individuals and institutions compete fiercely for scarce profit opportunities.

In this new investment paradigm, markets are neither always efficient nor always irrational, but are adaptive. During normal times, prices can be trusted to reflect the "wisdom of crowds". During times of distress, investors react instinctively **and emotionally - the wisdom of crowds becomes the "madness of mobs"**

We can protect ourselves from the vicissitudes of these regime shifts only by acknowledging their existence and properly preparing for them in advance. This will require more sophisticated financial technologies that are equally adaptive, and capable of capturing the complexities created by our own innovations.

Fortunately, most of these technologies are within our reach, and the rest we will soon develop in financial markets, as in nature, necessity is the mother of all invention."

I understand his last comment but I do not believe that technology will solve the inherent difficulties of human behavior nor can cover all the elements of a future since they will remain innumerable and mostly unknown. It is certainly being attempted- I just don't think it can work. Which means a lot more effort by a fiduciary.

**Correlation charts**

I have steadfastly argued that outdated correlations were a poor choice to use for the future since they were inherently inconsistent. This was not a theoretical challenge but the gathering of charts from decades prior to present day and **simply comparing them**. There was no correlation within the correlations. (See the multitude of charts at http://efmoody.com/investments/correlation.html and http://www.assetcorrelation.com/user/enter_time_corr to show graphical changes over 3 months to 10 years). I have seen estimates of correlation based on just a few days or weeks but this nothing more than looking at prices of each asset and just seeing how they are moving against or with each other. Sounds reasonable perhaps, but there is so much noise in the market over a short period of time that any serious statistic must be discounted tremendously-possibly excluded depending on the type of news/gossip/terrorism/storm is being 'discussed." Admittedly, the numbers may bear out. But it will generally be by luck.

However, it was a lot worse than just having the wrong numbers overall. What was deceptive and far from reality is that when something falters, it is true that one might get a little offset from varying correlations with a small portfolio decline. But when it all goes really bad, all the products/allocations/portfolios/correlations all go together in the same manner at the same time for the same reason. A recession puts a great risk/high stress on an allocation and, save for cash and perhaps gold, they all suffer the same consequences. This is where the entire industry has faltered. They have been taught that correlations remain constant/acceptable over long periods of time and that is where the focus must be (Bill Bernstein and others).

There have been a few advisers that have recognized the futility of relying on past statistics as the be all and end all of the relationships of risk to the future.

To Paul Wilmott, Gaussian (simple curve statistics-see the bell shaped curve for standard deviation) is an example of how dangerously abstract quant (application of obtuse mathematical techniques to financial investment analysis) finance has become. "We need to get back to testing models rather than revering them," he says. "That's hard work, **but this idea that there are these great principles governing finance and that correlations can just be plucked out of the air is totally false. The correlations between financial quantities are notoriously unstable."**

William Coacker: "The severity of how much correlation changes, even over longer periods of time, has not been adequately understood. His paper analyzed the changing correlation of 15 asset classes measured against the S&P 500 over a 35-year period, and the impact of those changes on asset allocation decisions. It measures the correlations in rolling one-, three-, five-, and ten-year time series, from 1970 to 2004. The article also evaluates whether 15 asset classes have helped or hurt in years the S&P 500 has declined, and whether growth or value styles are more correlated to the index.

Some of the conclusions: The average variance in correlation measured 0.98 over one year and 0.25 over ten years. **In short, the relationship among many of the asset classes appears to be inherently unstable.**

Large value provides more diversification benefits than large growth, and small value provides more diversification than small blend or small growth. Emerging markets may provide higher returns and greater diversification than developed nations. But the low correlations of small value and real estate may not hold up during the next broad market decline.

Correlations exhibit uniqueness, meaning **periods are distinct from previous time periods**. For example, international stocks' correlation to the S&P 500 was 0.48 from 1970 to 1997, but 0.83 from 1998 to 2002.

Lastly, **"Rather than rely on historical correlations,**

**a more comprehensive and dynamic approach is needed in making asset allocation decisions."**

Nassim Nicholas Taleb, hedge fund manager and author of The Black Swan, is particularly harsh when it comes to the copula. (a general way of formulating a multivariate distribution in such a way that various general types of dependence can be represented) People got very excited about the Gaussian copula because of its mathematical elegance, but the thing never worked **Co-association between securities is not measurable using correlation," because past history can never prepare you for that one day when everything goes south.**

**"Anything that relies on correlation is charlatanism."**

From Wharton professors:

"Diebold: I think there are two key issues, or at least two, both of which are very difficult and related. The first is understanding correlations across banks, financial institutions ...

Herring: And understanding how they vary over time.

Diebold: That's number two. And they certainly are different in crises just as volatility is different in crises. And, of course, the way that they're different is often in very adverse ways. **Correlations rise just when you don't want them to rise and you lose, for example, portfolio diversification benefits just when you need them the most.**

**Herring: The dirty little secret of diversification is that it disappears when you need it most. The only thing that rises in falling markets is correlations."**

## Summary

It is true that correlations are a necessary input to allocations. But the wholesale reliance on past numbers to insulate one from most risk was simply a very bad decision that was used as a crutch to defer blame. I did not think it worked that well in the Dotcom mess but most investors are a little too lazy to really think about the ramifications of their actions (or lack thereof) or the lack of competency of their advisors to offer much in assistance. This most recent debacle made the ineptness far more visual. And it is not over yet- far from it. All that said, I refer back to risk overall. Was a recession 100% preordained by the inverted yield curve?

Yes.

What are the losses sustained in equities in a recession?

40%- 43%.

Why did you want to stick around for that? Because of 30 year old correlations?

I don't think so.

How do you do correlations looking forward?

Lots of research and hard work. It's true that you may need to know the past but a fiduciary has to look forward and determine the underlying potential risk of loss of the portfolio initially.

# 16

# Standard Deviation, Volatility

As stated repeatedly, risk is not the simplistic term of "not putting all your eggs in one basket", or volatility or..... But such words are used to supposedly reflect some possibility of loss without ever indicating how extensive it might be. In many/most cases the advisers ask the client what level of risk they are willing to accept. Or they have to answer 10 quick questions which supposedly indicates the same focus (see client questionnaire herein). Yet none of this provides any real statistics to the possibilities of what can happen. In order to address this issue, let me first give you some basics on standard deviation (also called volatility).

**Distribution of sizes for a standard population**

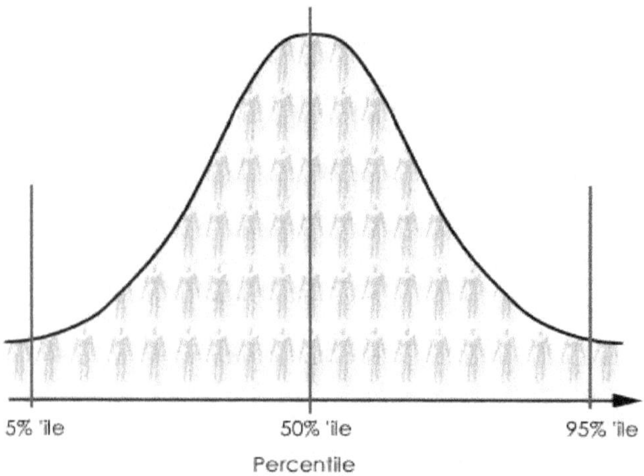


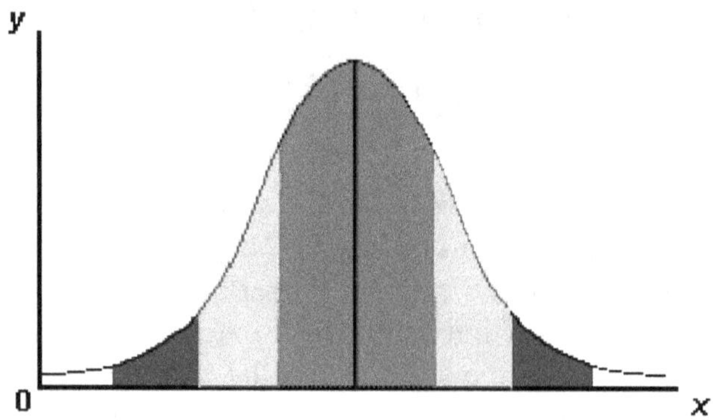


Hopefully all are familiar with the standard bell shaped curve. (They all don't look so neat- they can be skewed left and right- but this is fine for the example.) Literally everything that happens falls into the middle of such a curve with lesser amounts at the edges. Let's take golf for example. Almost all of us have played it at one point in our lives and most people have simply average ability that is best represented by the bars in the middle (see below). We'll say that it represents 68% of all people that play- and that number also represents one standard deviation. The average score might be 100 and the two side bars represent + or -15%. That means in 68% of the time, people score 100 on average with scores of 85 and 115 on each side. If you include the next two bars on each side, it would mean that 95% of all people are covered by the graph. That is the definition for two standard deviations. It would be a score of 100 average but with a + 25 or -25 or scores as low as 75 or as high as 125 for 95% of time. You can keep doing this by adding another two bars that covers 99% of the scores/population. And then finally you get to the extreme left with the likes of Tiger Woods (In his prime- before he was hit by a golf club). Or on the extreme right with scores above, say, 150 or 200. One standard deviation is 68% of occurrences.

Two standard deviations is 95%.

Three standard deviations is 99%.

Notice how symmetrical and smooth it is. Beautiful graph, beautiful theory. And almost a total waste in real life.

Let's take a look at the absolute best of scores. It's 18 holes in one. Absurd. Maybe the best PGA score on a tough course is 62. Therefore the graph on the left takes a different shape since one side is defined by an absolute minimum. What about the other side and let's say I include all people- a blind Eskimo for example. Now I have radically changed the risk side of how bad it can really get. Maybe the number approaches infinity. Some would say that the selection of an Eskimo is simply wrong. What about your 75 year grandfather with glaucoma and a bad back. Can that exist? Sure. So the point is that, as I have previously shown, statistics can be made to cover potentially whatever you want- certainly to describe poor theory.

These simplistic curves are generally what has been taught till most recently but are still universally used in industry software programs. I have seen CFAs still address volatility as risk. Here are some exemplary commentary from Mandelbrot and Taleb regarding the 'standard' standard deviation:

"Then there are those who do warn of risk but package it into a simple numerical measure that seems to put it within manageable limits.

Your mutual fund's annual report, for example, may contain a measure of risk (usually something called beta). It would indeed be useful to know just how risky your fund is, but this number won't tell you. Nor will any of the other quantities spewed out by the pseudoscience of finance: standard deviation, the Sharpe ratio, variance, correlation, alpha, value at risk, even the Black-Scholes option-pricing model.

The problem with all these measures is that they are built upon the statistical device known as the bell curve. This means they disregard big market moves: They focus on the grass and miss out on the (gigantic) trees. Rare and unpredictably large deviations like the collapse of Enron's stock price in 2001 or the spectacular rise of Cisco's in the 1990s have a dramatic impact on long-term returns —but "risk" and "variance" disregard them.

The professors who live by the bell curve adopted it for mathematical convenience, not realism. It asserts that when you measure the world, the numbers that result hover around the mediocre; big departures from the mean are so rare that their effect is negligible. This focus on averages works well with everyday physical variables such as height and weight, but not when it comes to finance. One can disregard the odds of a person's being miles tall or tons heavy, **but similarly excessive observations can never be ruled out in economic life.** The German mark's move from four per dollar to four trillion per dollar after World War I should have taught economists to beware the bell curve.

The economic world is driven primarily by random jumps. Yet the common tools of finance were designed for random walks in which the market always moves in baby steps. Despite increasing empirical evidence that concentration and jumps better characterize market reality, the reliance on the random walk, the bell-shaped curve, and their spawn of alphas and betas is accelerating, widening a tragic gap between reality and the standard tools of financial measurement."

Reality did strike just before printing: the 400 point ups and downs of the Dow in September 2011 are statistically impossible under the smooth curve. And we may see the VIX staying at very high levels for some time.

Warren Buffet noted this- "The measurement of volatility/standard deviation: it's nice, it's mathematical, and wrong. Volatility is not risk. Those who have written about risk don't know how to measure risk. Past volatility does not measure risk. When farm prices crashed, [farm price] volatility went up, but a farm priced at $600 per acre that was formerly $2,000 per acre isn't riskier because it's more volatile. [Measures like] beta let people who teach finance use the math they've learned. That's nonsense. Risk comes from not knowing what you're doing. Dexter Shoes was a terrible mistake—I was wrong about the business, but not because shoe prices were volatile. If you understand the business you own, you're not taking risk. Volatility is useful for people who want a career in teaching. I cannot recall a case where we lost a lot of money due to volatility. The whole concept of volatility as a measure of risk has developed in my lifetime and isn't any use to us."

Ric Kayne notes, "everyone understands the things that happen within two standard deviations, but everything important in financial history takes place outside of two standard deviations." The recent four 400 point movements are far beyond two SDs and should completely validate what can really happen in this new world order.

## Risk of LOSS

I understand what Buffet was saying. But for the average person trying to invest something for the future, they have to have some idea of what risk they are taking. The numbers do have to start with volatility- but that is just the start. Once any firm or agent says 'risk', they have to follow up with the standard deviation as a precursor to determining what their portfolio exposure is. (Where do they get the numbers for a fund? Most likely Morningstar or similar). Then they must show the risk of loss. And no software does it that I have yet seen. So it must be done by hand. (The formula is identified in this paragraph only for validation. You can skip directly to the next paragraph if you want since that contains the 'punch line' of the exercise). I have used this example in my instruction, in my book and anyplace else I can get it out. It is the key to the true definition of risk- how much can you lose given just basic volatility. Let's say you have a moderate risk portfolio (also nebulous since 'moderate' or any standard classification of risk is not definitively offered anyplace) with a one year's standard deviation of 30%. But as time goes on, the standard deviation goes down by dividing the annual SD by the square root of the number of years. If I used 10 years, the SD becomes 9.48%- certainly a much lower number than the 30% and tends to reflect to the unknowledgeable that risk has gone down.

**Wrong.**

The risk we want is risk of LOSS- that is the true concern. That the SD has gone down is almost irrelevant. The formula to next use is 1- SD to the power of the number of years in question- in this case
10. That number is .369. **That means that with a one time standard deviation movement at the end of the 10 years, the investor will have only about 40% of the entire**

**portfolio at that time.** But since most retirees have accumulated monies over long periods already, it does not make any difference if they have just put the money into a new account. The term of years has already been running for a long time. That means that the loss can occur at ANY time- just one day after you put it in.

Here's the bottom line**. If you put money into a investment portfolio that has just regular volatility, if something goes wrong in the economy you should expect to only have about 30% to 80% of what you expected and/or what was projected by your adviser. (I tend to use 40% to 60% but each portfolio must be analyzed.)** If you put money into securities, the firm and agent have a duty to explain the exposure to risk of LOSS. I submit that if any person knew such a risk existed, they rationally and objectively would have completely altered their allocations right from the beginning. Or at a minimum they would have demanded a written document attesting to what the adviser reviewed to mitigate such losses. (Note that I am not suggesting perfection nor that it can be obtained. No matter the yield curve or year to year Real GDP% and all the other factors reviewed, I cannot definitively state what will happen nor when nor even if I will be right since my decisions have to be based on some subjective decisionmaking. However, the difference is that it is based on objective work (economics) that provides a baseline for the analysis.)

## Summary

Theory is great. But it does not have to apply to real life. Nonetheless, the responsibility of advisers is to know the implications of risk. And generally they tend to indicate that the market has risk, blah, blah. Not acceptable since that addresses just that there is A risk. Means very little. It is not an exculpatory clause.

They have to know THE risk of loss. They have to convey it to clients in understandable terms along with what they will do regarding the scenarios where risk raises its ugly head (recession). That is the key. If what they are doing- and will only do- it is just buy and hold and simplistic annual rebalancing based on software correlations that may be 10+ years old, it is illogical to pay a fee for such advice.

Note- an adviser taking on a portfolio with a fee based on a percentage of assets under advisement will lose money if he was to suggest a CD or similar when times are very bad- as the next six months to a year should be as another recession takes hold. If monies are transferred out to a bank CD, they not only lose control of the funds but any fees they 'earn' thereon. Many try to find some offsetting asset to countervail the increasing correlations. That way, they can (supposedly) keep the portfolio from major losses and still earn their fees. It might work in limited economic strife, but not when the economy tips over (as it probably will again shortly). Caution is advised with such advisers- the very bulk of the fee planners.

Currently the only way to do the risk of loss is with a personal financial calculator. If someone is acting as a fiduciary, they have one, can do an asset allocation and then provide the numbers right then and there as to the potential level of risk. If they cannot do that, you do not have a fiduciary. You also do not have a financial planner nor even an investment adviser.

If there is a 401k presentation/education and this is not provided, your employer has not hired a fiduciary. Get one.

# 17

# Risk of Loss

*"The first rule of investing is don't lose money; the second rule is don't forget Rule No.1*

Warren Buffet

The key to all allocations. If you do not know- or have not been advised- as to the potential loss of assets in a recessionary economy, you do not know what you are doing. Nor does your adviser. Very, very simple statement. But it is anathema to the industry. It is not sufficient to say, "well the market can go down". That is true enough, but what is YOUR particular risk if it does. That is what the consumer has to be aware of.

Repeated herein from Jahnke- "Asset allocators view their primarily job as getting a client into an asset allocation solution and advising the client not to abandon the asset allocation solution in volatile markets. But if the fixed asset allocation solution is not right for the client and is inflexible in the face of changing economic opportunities, what is the service worth? Asset allocators claim their advice is designed to benefit the client. But it appears that the advice is really designed to benefit the advisor; the investment process is simplified, and the business risk associated with managing the client's asset allocation is minimized. The asset allocator only needs to provide a package of marketing materials, educate the client on the rewards of diversification, administer the risk tolerance questionnaire, set up a "normal" asset allocation policy, collect the quarterly fee, and advise the client to "stay the course" in volatile markets."

Well, that sucks.

If consumers knew the risk- and all 401k employees must be told- then they clearly would have altered their investment selection. I absolutely admit that the subsequent education would be far different than today and a lot of less educated employees might end up scared stiff. And the problem is???????????? They are already scared of the market or going back in based on some esoteric commentary and pretty charts and graphs from some advisor with a series 7, CFP, ChFC and no formal instruction to the massive economic changes that require wholesale revisions to whatever education they may have had.

As stated, the first issue for consumers is how much risk are they taking.

Almost all employees have seen something akin to a Morningstar report that shows standard deviation.

The effort here is to block out the elements that need to be recognized.

When you see a standard deviation, check the asterisks next to it. Almost universally, they will say that they are 3 year averages. Be sure to check. Sometimes there is nothing to indicate and you might want to check another service to be sure.

The effort here is to block out the elements that need to be recognized.

Assume the S&P 500.

Vanguard shows a SD of 21.79 for the S&P 500

Fidelity shows 21.20

Dreyfus shows 21.78

As with other statistics, the numbers can vary but this seems close enough.

Annual standard deviation is rounded to 21.50

Assume you wanted to look at the standard deviation in 10 years. Divide the above by the square root of 10 which is 3.1622....

And the SD is 6.79%. Now you know how SD goes down over time. And with a nice Gaussian curve, you might feel comfortable.

But once you read Bernstein and Mandelbrot, you must account for when times go bad. Like a recession.

So take 1- SD = .93201

To the $10^{th}$ power= ....4954

. (My HP12c financial calculator keeps 12 spaces for very specific computations. Should I use that? See statistics chapter)

That means you could expect to have only 50% of what was projected.

Of course, one does look at the other investments in a portfolio allocation. Emerging market SD forces the risks up and bonds allows them to go down.

Is this perfect? No. But it is no worse- I submit far less worse- than using future flat rate returns based on past returns from the age of dinosaurs written into a software program by a new age video game Twinkie that thinks the whole world's problems are solved by a new algorithm. Remember Long Term Capital. Two Nobel laureates and 27 PhDs could not be wrong- could they?

Now, is that number a reflection of reality? No it is not. The formula reflects the smooth curve and does not take into account the real world with a risk exposure that can be much greater during any period of time. One should think of it as a baseline risk element that is better defined by the existing economics- certainly not some numbers gleaned from a reversion over decades past.

**Summary**

Consumers must be told of this potential risk exposure. Of course pundits will say that is a deal killer and they need equities for their future. Agreed. But they also need to be told that once, quite probably twice, a decade they will lose about 50% of their equity holdings due to recessions unless the adviser does SOMETHING. If they do not follow current economics, say that they will only do a buy and hold and hope you have a nice retirement as they charge 1% annually, well...........

Or that they will act as a fiduciary and do whatever is possible to help them retain the assets they have grown.

# 18

# Risk, Probability, Timing, Consequences

The basics of risk have been explained but let's put it even more in focus for the consumer by addressing an assumed allocation that is used over time.

As of early 2011, this might have been an 'acceptable' allocation for the middle aged. Yes, there are adjustments for being younger in that (perhaps) all equity could be chosen. The general position for those over age 60 (roughly) is the greater use of bonds. However, the only real way of determining what to do is through a budget. The more equities that are needed- the greater risk to obtain the asset. But, quite obviously, the greater potential of loss.

| | Allocation | Annual SD |
|---|---|---|
| Foreign equity | 30% | SD 19.49 |
| U.S. Total market | 50% | SD 15.68 |
| Intermediate Bonds | 20% | SD 4.89 |

Compute the potential wealth over 15 years with one SD loss

Take the annual SD and divide by the square root of 15 (years). Then that is multiplied by the percentage of the asset held to the entire portfolio.

5.03 x 30% = 1.51

4.04 x 50= 2.02

1.26 x .20= .252

Add together. Subtract 1.0. Take to the 15th power. Final wealth 56% of projected. Potential risk of loss is 44%.

As you can see and has been identified statistically, the longer you hold onto higher standard deviations, the greater the potential of loss should a one standard deviation offset occur.

First of all, is that real life? No. The assumption that one might maintain the same allocation over 5 or 15 years is possible, but, realistically, many personal changes (death, divorce, illness, jobs, children, another divorce, governors having illegitimate children) will occur over time to make the singular risk of loss problematic. But if you did, the pure numbers show the losses that can occur. And this is the issue for fiduciaries.

The formula also references what could happen with just one standard deviation movement- but that is under the smooth Gaussian curve. Now we have to look at the issue that the lack of smoothness- particularly as identified by Mandlebrot- shows an exposure to risk that can be several times that. Recent research suggests that the smooth 3 standard deviations covering 99% of all occurrences is actually something more akin to seven standard deviations. Some suggest even more. In other words, what was thought to be a situation that simply could not exist (Black Monday 1987 for instance) is actually in the realm of probability and ‘bad things’ can happen with far more regularity. It also means the top side can get greater was well, but a review of the national and international economics might/does suggest otherwise.

There is an offset to the above. I did not include any offsetting correlation to the allocation. In other words, as one element (stocks for example) went down, another element (bonds) could offset part of the loss. Quite true. But my point was- and confirmed by 2000 and 2008- when things really go bad, all the correlations go to one and therefore a larger loss- as identified- can occur.

To some, this is a treatise in numbers that may be difficult to grasp. So I will put the probability and 'timing' into perspective. A few months ago the Japanese Earthquake, Tsunami and Nuclear power plant disaster occurred. Libya is having a civil war, Greece should default, Egypt's government has been overthrown and so on. The market has dropped precipitously. Many of these might be referred to as 'black swans' as addressed by Nassim Taleb that signify extreme events (fat tails on the Gaussian curve) that really are so far out that they simply 'cannot exist'.

Even the remote occurrence of a U.S. debt default was a black swan- though considering the ineptness of politics, maybe it's just business as usual.

But the events in the Mid East are known to have happened before and will happen again due to the inherent instability of the entire region. The consequences may vary slightly from Libya to Saudi Arabia to Tunisia, but since the Iraq war et al, there is nothing that says this is so far out it could not statistically exist. The timing may be a unknown per the individual countries- but there will be an unending terrorism and one should expect the expected.

In that context, let's look at something else that most might say is a definite black swan- a dirty bomb in the U.S. Not so. After 9/11- a true black swan- (though I offer this- maybe it wasn't. Remember Pearl Harbor?) - many experts have given it as high as a 100% probability in the next decade And that the target would be New York. I suppose the issue might be if it is something different but just as catastrophic- maybe poison in the water supply. And maybe it will be in the Chicago area instead. But that is basically semantics. Again the specific timing is unknown but not the horrendous consequences. It is not a statistical certainty, true, but it sits within an 'acceptable' standard deviation that it should come as no surprise when it happens. Further, the timing is almost assuredly in our lifetime- which is nothing more than an insignificant blip in all history.

Let's look at the earthquakes. They happen all the time. Many in remote areas where the consequences are limited. But within a reasonable range of statistics, it was perfectly rational to accept that a major calamity would occur at least every decade. Admittedly the Japanese nuclear problem could be considered a black swan as well as the absolute devastation of the tsunami. But a tsunami was certainly not out of a statistical bounds by any means.

What about an earthquake- supposedly well overdue- on the west coast. Here in the San Francisco area, we have expert after expert say a massive earthquake will hit the bay area within 30 years. A black swan as to what will happen? No? A black swan as to the potential consequences? Far from it. We all know the devastation will be of a magnitude greater than Japan. So we know what will happen, how bad it will assuredly be and that it will happen at any time- or not. So what can/will/should be done? Obviously declaring an emergency and have everybody leave the area now is farfetched indeed. The government should make sure the highways and buildings are prepared better and, within financial limits, they have. However, the lot of residents have done little if anything to prepare, so one should nonetheless expect a virtual shutdown of a major financial hub. Maybe a complete loss. Look at the huge number of tornados. That they may not have happened with such frequency and intensity for 50 years is not out of the realm of happening again in our lifetimes. We have seen a marked change in the environment- be it our fault or Mother Nature. It should not come as a great surprise since 50 years of time is nothing at all. That it devastated Joplin is not a black swan. It is within statistical probability. More 'well known' grey swans with better 'forecasts'.

I am going to simply relate to certain periods where the risk and consequences was essentially preordained. The point being that 2000 was not a black swan. Nor was 2008- at least in the initial drop. They both were both inevitable' recessions. That most paid no attention and then were surprised at the results (though 2008 was admittedly extreme) does not make them an occurrence that occurred without warning.

The issue is described more fully elsewhere with the inverted yield curve and the year to year real GDP %. They are 100% indicators of a recession (some latitude taken but not much) so neither 2000 nor 2008 were black swans. That the yield curve inverted is not a black swan, that a general level of consequence (recession) was within a one or two standard deviations is not a black swan, that the timing of the occurrence was relatively well known is not a black swan.

It may simply depend on who is doing the analysis. The illiterate, non thinking consumer can conjure up all sorts of black swans because they have no real grasp of the world and how it works. Most hope/think/pray/believe that an optimistic life should prevail and that the devastations are outside of natural occurrence. But they are not. The lack of preparedness is obvious. The element of human behavior becomes very apparent. But a logical perception of the world finds many of these black swans an occurrence which they have not thought about and are unprepared for- but were always there. However, is all that an excuse for a fiduciary? No. A financial fiduciary acting for the interests of a consumer must research the full gamut of theory and apply it to the real world. Since they do not have knowledge/competency and real world application from mandatory training, the element of being a fiduciary is not only suspect, it is without merit for the bulk of advisors. I am not saying that they will come up with the same risk scenarios for the future, but they must have the insight to these measures before suggesting otherwise.

## Pure black swans

An asteroid hitting the earth within our lifetime.
Aliens landing on earth looking for food (us).
Massive programmed nuclear attacks at numerous U.S. cities this next decade (A single attack will NOT be a black swan- it IS expected)
Another black plague that decimates the earth. (Maybe not a black swan since the addition of two to three billion more humans by 2050 is bound to break the Mother Earth to retaliate.)
Neutrinos faster than the speed of light

In short, there are a few pure black swans. The rest are events within real life probability that have gone unnoticed and unprepared because of the human condition that refuses to do the necessary homework in looking forward.

## Summary

Consumers are not aware of the portfolio risk. They rarely look financially forward and advisors universally look backwards. And what they do see- or are only capable of seeing- is the simplistic flat rates of return and the buy and hold. The continuation of such irrational consequences will be horrendous unless and until the advisors learn how risk works.

# 19

# Inverted Yield Curve

The easiest way to understand this issue is simply to consider what your bank does with a CD. If you get a 3 month CD, I'll say it is for 3% (I am just picking numbers to make the point clear). If you take a 1 year CD, the rate is 4%. If you are willing to commit for a longer period of time- say 10 years- the rate is 5%. Nothing out of kilter here for bonds as well. The longer the time frame, the greater the risk and the higher the return they need to offer to get you to invest.

But economics does not always follow a normal path. There are times when long term rates will actually be LESS than short term rates. It is not necessary to explain all the reasons since politics and economics seldom have to make sense. But suffice to say, once that happens, the economy is in almost complete disarray and must come back to 'normal'. Short term rates must come down or long term rates must risk. As part of that interest rate change process is a 100% guaranteed recession. There you have it. Every time the yield curve inverts, a recession has occurred. It does not state when it will happen (an average of 12 months), nor how bad it will be nor for how long it will last. But it is 100%. (See http://www.ny.frb.org/research/current_issues/ci2-7.pdf) As stated, the average losses are 40%+.

Unlike all the theorists with the fancy computer programs and algorithms, this is a very simple visual graph provided by the FED every day and a dynamic graph over time may be seen at http://stockcharts.com/charts/YieldCurve.html. Take a look at 2006 and you can very easily see the potential recession.

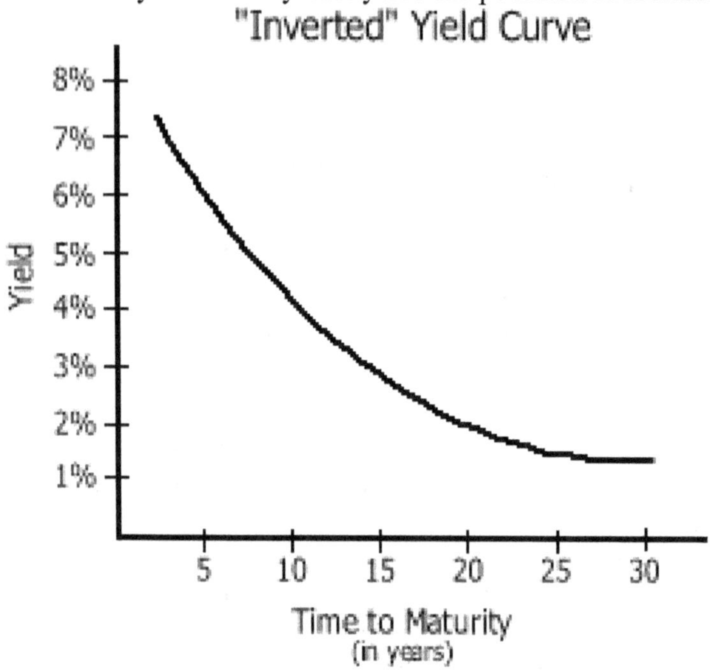


Why has it not been used? I cannot figure it out for many advisers (though most are not that bright, trained, or knowledgeable to begin with so I am not starting from a high point to start with) save for this very important fact. Almost all advisers charge a fee for advice on an ongoing basis. You give them, say $200,000, and they will charge you 1%+ to allocate your funds "properly". Each quarter you are automatically assessed the quarterly fee ($500). But all of a sudden, the economy hits a "bad patch". Then what? My position was to stop putting any more new assets into equities at the sight of an inverted curve but put them into money market funds, CDs and/or bonds. As the economic predicament becomes worse, the current equities were further reduced (DCA Down identified elsewhere) and they went into more CDs and cash type secure positions (some bond funds, but caution advised). It was, and is, the clearly prudent thing to do and does not require and intensive thought process. Now, I don't charge for assets under management- no percentage against asset under control- so I have no difficulty in telling clients to move assets into various banks. But the bulk of advisers don't want to do that because they not only lose control of the funds to an outside entity (banks), they also no longer earn any fees on these assets. It is true that some tried to stem the bleeding but the attempt may have been nothing more than to find another product to put in the mix to offset losses (a fund that sells short for example). But note that it remains a product inside the allocation on which to still charge a fee. And further, most of these other funds did just as badly since, as the market went down so badly, correlations tend to all move to 1.0 which means they all do the same thing at the same time in the same amounts and for the same reason. Further, the adviser may be so late in the game that it was too late for some of these 'found' funds to do any good.

There is a potential caveat to the curve looking forward. With rates so low, the inversion may not be as reliable as an indicator. In that regard, please also see **Year Over Year Real GDP %** herein.

Of course there are other factors in addition- housing, employment, interest rates, political turmoil, FED input, et al- the curve is not used with blinders. But there are so few things that are so direct in a future direction that it cannot be unilaterally dismissed.

# 20

# Year Over Year Real Gdp %

Pundits of the value of the inverted yield have simply been proven wrong. But though none have attacked it as a guide going forward, there is an issue that very well will cause some 'problems'. Simply stated, you have to have interest rates high enough so the long term rates can actually be lower than short term rates. If interest rates are so low- as they are now- any reduction in long term rates may be so minuscule that no real impact is noted. (See how the past was valid- now you cannot even apply it due to very different circumstances.)

Admittedly, the FED has kept rates very low in order for the economy to recover. Any inflationary increases would have, of course, raised rates. But with an economy in such disarray, it just is not going to happen. That is not to say, however, that another recession could not happen. And I think it shall.

My position on the inverted curve developed over a period of 15 years with research of numerous economic factors. Of course it was not the only one that is used since there still must be corroborating indicators to the inverted curve. The unemployment is a major factor but even with some improvement here and there, the jobs being filled were half or a third of what the employee previously earned. The other major one was the number of foreclosed homes that are still waiting to be offered to the public. Is the number several hundred thousand, two million or?? I don't know. Additionally, construction has generally been the lead entity that has led us out of a recession. But with all these homes waiting to go to market, very few new homes will be built. There is also Greece and its meltdown. And it goes on. With such negative news, where does our economy stand for the near term. And so the following:

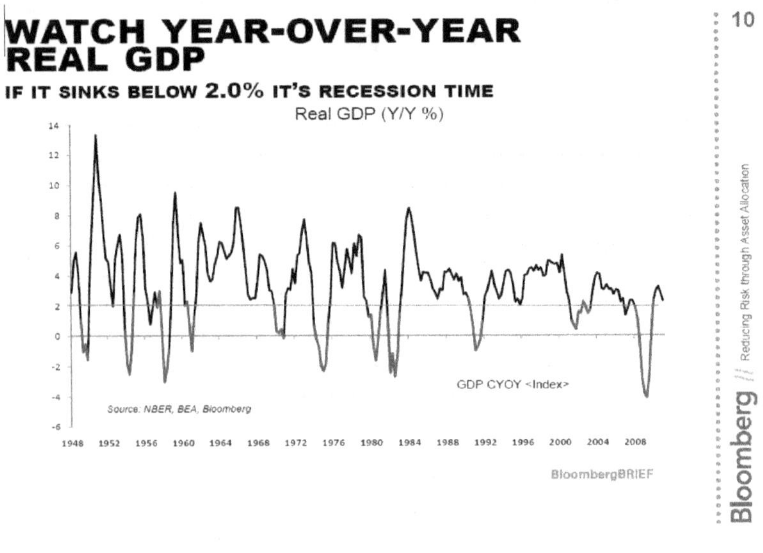


The year to year real gdp% became notable due to Richard Yamarone, vice president and director of economic research at Argus Research Corp. Obviously one follows this number anyway, but he has simply shown that every time the percentage from year to year was 2% or lower, there was a recession. This has stood the test of time since the 1940s.

U.S. Real GDP Growth Forecast-Year over Year Change in U.S. Real GDP. Percent per annum.\
http://www.forecasts.org/gdprealgrowth.htm

| Month | Forecast |
|---|---|
| Oct 2011 | 1.0 |
| Nov | 1.0 |
| Dec | 1.0 |
| Jan 2012 | 0.5 |
| Feb | 0.5 |

Look at the forecast- not even close to 2.0%. Take all the other elements you can think of. Look at the FED beige book, earnings forecast and on and on. That is a recession. A delayed double dip probably geared to late 2011 or by mid 2012 at the very, very latest.

Can the forecasts be wrong? Yes, More importantly perhaps, can I be wrong? Yes in terms of a recession. No in terms of high risk, very slow growth and probable stagnation.

So what is the point? I do know that most planners et al never see this material nor really could understand it without a more enhanced background. No matter, we are now addressing a fiduciary standard to be able to formulate a realistic path to the future. The reliance on some mathematical backtesting is no longer adequate (nor really was it ever). That said, some will take umbrage with the forecast. Fine- but they have to do the necessary homework and provide a reasoned reply and appropriate criticism. They will have to read Yamarone like it or not. That is how it is done. Anything less is a sophomoric and subjective view with no work and less validity. Puerile opinions are not acceptable. (In no way is the consumer capable of addressing this.)

The fiduciary will have to develop a plan that addresses the changes in correlations going forward, the development of a market correction that will continue to "correct" through Dollar Cost Averaging Down to offset what every well could be a lengthy recession and some significant losses.

But as repeatedly stated, on what basis does a broker or 95% of RIAs going to be able to do this? Simply saying that they will do the best for a client means next to nothing if there is no background on which to base competency.

# 21

# Dollar Cost Averaging (DCA)

In the most simplistic format, it means putting money into the market over a period of time instead of all at once. The idea is not to buy potentially at the highest price during that 'period' but to average the price over the highs and low of that 'period'.

For the example, assume you put in $100 per month into Fund X:

| Month | Amount Invested | Share Price | Number Purchased |
|---|---|---|---|
| 1 | $100 | $50 | 2 |
| 2 | 100 | 75 | 1.33 |
| 3 | 100 | 100 | 1 |
| 4 | 100 | 66.66 | 1.5 |
| 5 | 100 | 40 | 2.5 |

| | | | |
|---|---|---|---|
| 6 | 100 | 25 | 4 |
| 7 | 100 | 33.33 | 3 |
| 8 | 100 | 66.66 | 1.5 |
| 9 | 100 | 80 | 1.25 |
| 10 | 100 | 80 | 1.25 |

Total $1,000 and 19.41 Shares

Dollar Cost Average/Monthly Investing = How much the shares cost divided by how many shares purchased = $1,000/19.41= $51.52.

Obviously that is better than buying all shares for $100 and getting only 10.

Except that, for the most part, DCA is nothing more than a manner of reducing risk at the expense of a return. Further, when this fund is viewed objectively, the prices are so volatile that no rational person should have bought it in the first place. The prices went from $100 high to $25 low. That is not an investment- that is gambling. Anyone holding a $100 stock that loses 75% is not an investor.

## MONTHLY INVESTING (MI):

But first is the very simple issue of whether or not you had a lump sum to begin with. If you do NOT have a lump sum, the only thing that you are doing is monthly investing. You CANNOT dollar cost because you have no other alternatives.

So people with 401ks, IRAs and the like are just putting in money when they can (MI). The end result MAY look similar to DCA but is not the same. Unfortunately, nobody really understands or properly addresses the nuance.

# DCA DIFFERS

One main reason that DCA is different with a lump sum over time is that you only put part of your money into the market at a point in time. The rest of the money is in a money market fund earning interest. Of course, with interest rates now so low, any benefit there may be minuscule at best.

## Overall returns:

If you have money to invest as a lump sum, DCA produces a LOWER return than investing the money all at once. Two researchers (Williams and Bacon) have discounted dollar cost averaging by statistically showing **that putting all the funds in at one time (lump sum) outproduces dollar cost averaging by two to one.** They invested a theoretical sum in 90 day T-bills and moved into the S&P 500 over a year's period. They compared these results with investing all the funds at once- starting with different periods from 1926 to 1991.

And another study - (2007)

http://www.uwlax.edu/ba/fin/Research/Dollar%20Cost%20 Edited.pdf. Theoretically, DCA should produce equitable returns. However, the results of this study have shown that, even without dividends, annuity investments into the S&P 500 and other indexes usually fall short of an investment up front. Only the NASDAQ showed contrary results. When the overall dollar value of the investments is considered, DCA falls far short.

And another: Why Dollar-Cost Averaging Does Not Work (2008)

http://habitsforwealth.com/2008/02/10/mathematical-illusion-why-dollar-cost-averaging-does-not-work/

In spite of the weight of evidence provided in academic literature against the strategy of dollar-cost averaging, DCA continues to be practiced by investors and recommended by financial advisors.

* Beyond its psychological appeal, the popularity of the approach can be said to stem from simple illustrations that show DCA resulting in greater stock holdings across a stock market cycle than is achieved by a one-time, lump-sum investment. Alternatively presented, the average cost per share purchased under DCA is demonstrated, by example, to be less than the average price of stock over its cycle.

* This paper challenges that illustration. It shows that variations in stock prices should not follow the mathematical pattern assumed in the examples. In fact, the price movement should follow a particular mathematical form that yields the same number of shares purchased, whether by DCA or lump-sum investing.

* * Absent any benefit from stock price volatility in reducing average cost, the performance of DCA rests on the trend in stock prices, with DCA outperforming in downward markets and lump sum outperforming in upward markets. Since the latter case is the norm over time, customary empirical findings in the finance literature of underperformance by DCA are explained.

* The theory in this paper is confirmed by examining a broad sample of stocks, contrasted over the high-growth trend in the second half of the 1990s against the general market malaise over the following half-decade. In the absence of this trend, DCA and lump sum provide equivalent results.

* A sizeable number of studies have appeared in academic literature pointing to underperformance of dollar-cost averaging (DCA) compared with a simple lump-sum (LS) approach. Other papers finding sub-optimal performance of DCA include Knight and Mandell (1993);

Thorley (1994); Rozeff (1994); Bacon, Williams, and Arinina (1997); Shumway (1997); Bernice (1998); Scherer (1998); Abeysekera and Rosenbloom (2000); Harrington (2001); Leggio and Lien (2001 and 2003); and Bierman and Hass.

Here are some numbers to put the study into perspective. Assuming $25,000 was invested in 1980 and assuming the study showed returns over 15 years to 1995 matched those of 1926 to 1991 (The lump sum approach returned an annualized return of about 12.75% while the dollar cost averaging was just 8.50%- some latitude taken), the lump sum investing would have grown to $151,247 versus the DCA value of $84,993 (annual compounding). That's over $66,000 more using lump sum investing. O.K., you say, the assumptions may not be valid and should have been adjusted downward. O.K. so let's say the difference is not $66,000, but $50,000. Or even half to $33,000. That's still a sizable difference in my book. But whatever you do, you need to recognize the study and its implications before you can dismiss the study.

Here is the same element regarding DCA. Assume I had a client with $1,200,000 in 1984. If I was dumber than a stone, I could have invested $100,000 a year for them for 12 years during one of the greatest bull markets for both stocks and bonds. And I would have/should have been fired years and years ago since the returns would have been terrible. Of course, someone could say that I should have invested $100,000 per month. But DCA doesn't address that aspect. (Though DCA is generally thought of as investing over a 12 month's period of time, it is nothing more than some rule of thumb that became dogma. One can use any period they select.) It is my contention that if you READ and are financially astute by yourself or through an adviser, you could have reasonably determined in that period of time that the market was growing solidly and invested almost all at once. You would have been much further ahead than even the example above.

Thirdly, and perhaps most importantly, many investors using DCA (or monthly investing) don't bother to watch the investments after they start. They may not rebalance the investments- normally a once per year revision. While true that over time stocks have outproduced other investments, you have to pay attention since the managers may have changed, the fund may have changed identity and, most importantly, the economics might have changed. For example, you don't want to end up in another 1970's marketplace where stocks did absolutely terrible for some time- about a 45% loss in 1973-1974. Sure, stocks finally caught back up and outproduced other investments after that, but there is literally no person that can tell me they could stomach a 45% loss without having sleepless nights (even 20%+). That's the absurdity with many magazines saying, "don't worry, just ride it out. It will come back". Well, what happens if the market has been driven down during a period when you weren't paying attention and just when you needed money for your kid's education or some medical emergency or you had just retired? DCA/MI doesn't help you there. Nor does buy and hold.

## BAD LUMP SUM INVESTING

As indicated above, but needing additional commentary, is the fact that if one does lump sum at the wrong time- say the beginning of 2000 or before 2008 or even now in late 2011, the results would/can be absolutely devastating. The funds would have lost significant amounts almost immediately and certainly over just a short time.

But that brings the issue back 360 degrees. Investing at such time was absolutely fraught with risk and only a novice or those less astute (most advisers?) would have done this. In such case perhaps DCA would have worked, but I will not attempt to validate either entity if some type of responsible economic insight was not attempted.

**Summary**

In short, DCA is a marketing tool that reduces risk and hence reduces returns. My point is that if you are unwilling to take such risk, either don't invest at all or utilize less risky investments in your portfolio such as CDs and bonds. However don't just use 60/40 percentages or whatever. A fiduciary has to figure out what to do, when and why. And how to adjust as necessary.

# 22

# Dollar Cost Averaging Down (DCAD)

DCAD is simply a term I coined for situations where the economy/market is in a precipitous decline. It obviously cannot account for major disasters that happen without any type of advanced notice- for example Black Monday 1987 or 9/11..

On the other hand, there are very valid observations of economic events that have foretold risky futures. Note that I cannot state what the returns will actually be since that is not the real concern- it's the potential losses that should/must be avoided. I have found that vigilant oversight of some basic economic developments can provide insight to risk scenarios. Scenarios that most consumers clearly would like to avoid, particularly those above age 55 who cannot afford to have their portfolios decimated by large losses. (Actually, young consumers will be hard pressed to continue investing in a long term strategy where they 'will' lose 50% of their assets maybe two, three or four times during their lifetimes. Think about it - it just does not seem very bright.)

Anyway, I have already fully addressed the inverted yield curve. It cannot be taken as an absolute that a recession will always occur once this happens (though 100% for decades), but the increased risk, at least, is far too great in my mind to maintain.. Recessionary losses average 40%+.

As also stated, a recession does not immediately occur after the inverted curve. But it probably is prudent to reduce future funds into the market. As time progresses and the economy starts to 'wobble', the market will make a correction- or more. A correction, by definition, is a 10% to 15% drop in value in the market as the market tries to reorient itself to 'correct' valuations.

But in a declining economy, the market may continue to tumble. To me, it is that higher risk is truly rearing its head. Therefore, as a 10% correction becomes more definitive, it is realistically prudent to reduce equity exposure by perhaps 15%- 50%. (There are no set numbers- it just depends on how bad the adviser sees the economic circumstances.) The funds can be put into bonds or CDs (normally). As the risk increases/market goes down another 5%, perhaps a reduction of another 15% to 50% of equities. But once you get to a 20% loss in the stock market, most equities are already reduced to minimal amounts. Not everything has to be liquidated (again there are always other extenuating circumstances and client issues to consider.) So in 2000 and 2006, there were both inverted yield curves. Clients were able to avoid the majority of subsequent losses. And with the mess we are now in, the risk is currently very high. (Do you want to buy and hold? Do you want to buy a product that offsets the correlations when they all go to 1.0? Do you know it will do that?)

That is how it can work. It's just that the risk of investing has to be researched at all times. For every dollar expected as appreciation and revenue, there is a current or projected risk associated with it. However, therein is the hard part- the emotionless and lengthy research of the various factors of risk and reward. And once determined, the knowing that the work was extensive and objective. One needs that since 'pulling the trigger' on hundreds of thousands or millions of dollars of allocation does not mean that it will be 'produce the desired results. But if the fiduciary has done the proper homework and communicated it properly to clients, the decision can be accepted as the right thing to do. If it did not turn out as expected- absent pure black swans- the initial decision to adjust was not wrong per se. It is just that other factors have now inserted themselves into the process of research and may need to be addressed. This is NOT reaction to noise- it is serious deliberation of important factors that are gauged to their importunateness and dealt with accordingly.

**DCAD not valid**

There are times when the corrections are simply one of a kind and there is little sense in waiting. For example, when the FED dropped interest rates to essentially nothing in 2011, there was no more appreciation to be forthcoming in bonds. The risk had gone up due to inflationary expectations and are predestined to lose for some time (though the FED has said they will not raise rates till mid 2013). Do you trust the FED? Therefore caution advised.

Of course there are those that say a bond fund is an integral part of a diversified portfolio, and I do agree depending on circumstances. But if the FED had not made that statement, bond funds would have continued to lose.

It's the same with stocks in 2000 etc. Stocks generally do well, but if you are drowning with equities and a recession is effectively preordained, bail out. Lastly, I again recognize that the changes require research, diligence and perhaps nerves of objective steel. But as Peter Bernstein noted, "Many aspects of investing are fun (disagree- I'd rather be fishing), but your future wealth isn't a game. You should manage it in the most coldblooded fashion. Emotion, pride, ego, dreams, and nightmares have nothing to do with the process, although some investors rely on little else."

DCAD is not perfect. But used correctly, it does clearly reduce a significant risk exposure. And investing is first and foremost about risk.

# 23

# 60/40, 70/30, ??/?? Allocation

The industry, as noted, is not very sophisticated. One of the simplistic heuristics (rules of thumbs) that has been used for decades is that some preset percentage of equities and bonds reflect an allocation that covers basic risk scenarios for most consumers. I never could figure out why there was this set percentage of 60/40 or whatever that defined what a client should be doing. If one did a budget and determined what was needed to be done for a client, it was unique to them. Both are identified herein But how do some true professionals view this scenario? Here is more exceptional objective commentary from Peter Bernstein- "For institutional investors, the policy portfolio [a rigid allocation like 60% stocks, 40% bonds] had become a way of passing the buck and avoiding decisions. **The problem was that institutions had settled on a [mostly stock] asset allocation because in the long run, they concluded, that's the only place to be. And I think the long run ain't what it used to be. Stocks don't have to do well in**

**the future because they did well in the past. In fact, the opposite may be more likely.**

This was also noted in an interview with Jeremy Siegel and Zvi Bodie. (It is not my intent to indicate the background of every person herein. If they are listed, readers are supposed to do some of their own Googling to enhance their knowledge and understanding. If you are not going to do that, you missed a good part of what I demand of fiduciaries.) Zvi noted that if you bake a loaf of 'regular' bread, you might need 70% flour and 30% water. But that is simply for that type of cake/bread. If you make a different bread, the mixture is altogether unique. Each person therefore is unique to him/herself and no set percentage is 'acceptable'.

Bill Jahnke many years ago noted "the idea that a pension plan or an individual investor should set long-term fixed asset class weights is flawed. Only if expected returns are fixed should asset allocation weights be fixed. In fact, investment opportunities change over time, both absolutely and relatively. Historically, since 1926, we have witnessed dramatic shifts in stock and bond market valuations."

And, " Consumers want to believe that the professionals can perform the services they are hired to do. Too often in the domain of financial advisors, even those with CFP''s or CPA''s, this is not the case. The consulting communities' **simple asset allocation policy** solution for institutional investors can be challenged on several scores. Why should investors expect that the past relationships between return and short-term volatility are good estimates for the future? Why should institutional investors be overly concerned about market volatility in returns when setting their long-term asset allocation policy? Why shouldn't the asset allocation policy be adjusted if asset class return expectations change?"

That has been the problem within the industry as treating everyone the same- clearly seen in software programs that fits everyone into some type of predetermined allocation. It's a nice simple crutch that got a lot of advisers by for years and years. It may have appeared valid (didn't the dotcom look perfect for years?) but reality has now struck home. Don't be fooled by a set percentage of portfolio allocation. (See retirement planning and budgeting for details.)

Anyway, Let's assume that one actually started with a $100,000 60/40 percentage a year ago- though a longer time for analysis shows the discrepancy in returns even more. I will take the S&P 500 only for the 60% equities and the mid term bond fund for the 40% allocation. So let's say that the equities dropped 15% of value during the year and the bonds went up 20%.

So using the sophomoric rule of thumb (rebalancing herein) to adjust for "risk" at the end of the year, the equity section has dropped to $51,000 and the bonds to $48,000. That is a current 51.5% to 48.5% ratio. In order to get back to 'prescribed' risk, one adds $9,000 to equities (by selling part of the bond fund) which then gets the bond section down to $39,000. Now you are back to 60/40 risk and then everything is fine.

No it isn't.

The assumption is that the risk of equities (and I make specific reference once again to standard deviation and the risk of loss) remains constant.

No it doesn't.

Look at standard deviation of equities: http://schwert.ssb.rochester.edu/sd_day.pdf, Standard Deviation of Monthly Stock Returns from Daily Returns in the Month, 18852010. Do you see consistency in the years over time? No- hence by inference to the formula for risk of loss, merely changing a 'changing' portfolio back to 60% or whatever does NOT indicate that the risk has stayed the same at all. Certainly one can (attempt to) use an average but the folly of past numbers and averages is fraught with error. The use of an average number masks the monthly or annual volatility and is not acceptable.

As regards bonds- I have been unable to secure the annual standard deviation for mid term bonds from any internet search so far. Of course I have averages, but they are just that- reflections that do not relate the true volatility year by year. Admittedly the volatility chart would not be as extreme as that identified above, but such volatility would show that bond standard deviation did vary as well. Sometimes in step with stocks, sometimes opposite.

I did get this-http://www.businessweek.com/1996/28/b348386.htm the standard deviation/volatility of an investment in the long-term Treasury bond was 8.9% from 1991 to 1995. That's below the 12.6% standard deviation in the previous five years. But look further back, and that 8.9% looks awfully high. In the mid-1960s, with inflation at about the same rate as today, the standard deviation was only 2.5%. In fact, in the 14 five-year periods from 1926 to 1995, only four periods displayed higher volatility than the 1991-95 period, mainly because of high inflation. (Is this backtesting?)

Investors have been whipsawed by the bond market's wild swings. In 1994, the market had its worst year ever (think Greenspan and the potential of inflation). In 1995, it had one of its best years. And in 1996, the rise in long-bond yields from 5.95% to 7.04% means that the 30-year bond was on track to have another big year on the downside, measured by total return, (James A. Bianco, director of research for Arbor Trading Group Inc.)

The fickleness of bond investors has added to that market's volatility. Until a few years ago, the flows into mutual funds were almost evenly split between stock and bond funds. But after 1994, when the 30-year Treasury lost 11%, bond funds had outflows of $43.4 billion. Some bond funds holding 30-year Treasuries lost more than 17% of their value.

Fast forward to 2011. Bonds have done well overall for some years as the FED had to reduce rates over and over again to spur an economy due to two recessions. (Remember you get appreciation with higher rate bonds as economic rates go lower). But you can only go so low so many times. Finally the rates went to zero. That simply stopped the appreciation in full. That stopped any excess gains on bonds. So if you look at the charts on bonds to mid 2011, you will see they have dropped quite a bit. And it should resume later as the FED will (probably) have to raise rates after 2013. (See Bill Gross and Warren Buffet). Admittedly it may take awhile due to politics (Bernanke indicating rates will not change till mid 2013). Right now all the bond holders are going to get are the low yields AND the knowing that risk is just ahead.

The point with the above is that every year the 60/40 split attained by simply adding or subtracting funds does not produce the same risk scenario at all.

Next is yet another separate dilemma. Let's assume that the standard deviations did NOT change. Therefore one can be sure that the risks are actually the same with rebalancing

No.

As addressed in the section for correlation, the movement between various investments does not have to move in lockstep at all. Whatever the correlation was in the past year(s) does not reflect what is going on currently. Admittedly, it is difficult to perfectly know what they might be at a specific point in time since it takes a year or so before the correlations could be determined with some(?) accuracy. But a good adviser/fiduciary should be able to realistically adjust the asset mix to reflect what might be happening. Readers obviously note that this is a subjective area as well, but one can only make a valid subjective call with the backing of facts (economics etc.) so the adviser will need to put the reasons in writing in order to avoid misinterpretation then or later on.

So now you understand what needs to be done.

No.

It gets much worse.

The above utilized only a basic S&P index and a mid term bond. Rarely will a consumer use just those two investments in the 60/40% mix. They might have an emerging market, some small cap, total world stock, high dividend, shorter or longer term bonds, municipals and on and on. Now it is possible to determine the overall standard deviation and the accompanying risk of loss. It might be possible to validate annual rebalancing to reflect the same risk of loss. That is good. But how do you do the various correlations one against the other then against the rest of the group?

*It's very difficult to establish underlying models and correlations. And even if you can establish those, it's extremely difficult to treat them with any confidence on a forward-looking basis."*

Kevin Gardner

So if it is that difficult, does it give the fiduciary enough wiggle room to defend an indefensible allocation? Sure it might- but I again point to the requirements that the suggested allocation be validated by a written commentary on what is being selected and why. It may not produce what is the best return/risk for the subsequent year but it defines (or should define) the effort.

Anyone looking at this level of work cannot/should not infer absolute 'correctness'- it is impossible to obtain. And mistakes can be made. I prefer to state 'acceptable and rational errors' if the effort has been put forth. That is simply a part of investing. The issue may fall back on whether the adviser had the rudimentary skills to select any allocation at any time.

**Summary**

In short, 60/40 does not mean much at all. Admittedly the general consumer has no understanding of what Bernanke and the FED is doing. They would not know Zvi Bodie from a bread stick. But the point to the bulk of all this commentary is about your adviser and the fiduciary duty.

# 24

# Rebalancing

Rebalancing has become one of the (supposed) key components of investing as sacrosanct as Dollar Cost Averaging. Its overall intent is to assume that the consumer/adviser has selected a risk scenario that they wish to start at the beginning of the investment process and that it is also the same risk profile that is to be retained throughout the period of retainment.

That is not real world- people change, correlations change, local, national and world economies change, jobs change and more so the overall risk scenario may vary all over the place. By the same token, it is possible to simply change the asset/portfolio mix to reflect the same risk each and every year so the odds of losses remains constant. But advisors do not know how to do that (see risk of loss). Even given that, it is hard to do- but if you don't know the numbers to begin with, it is all guess. You have to have done a retirement analysis first via a budget and then apply the risk of loss. If an adviser cannot do that, then you do not have an adviser.

So how might rebalancing work? In its most simplistic

format- say you owned the S&P 500 and an Intermediate bond fund. One simply makes an adjustment at the end of the year (annual rebalancing is the most common) to reflect changes in declines or appreciation of the assets. Just look at the example in the previous chapter and the

But rebalancing doesn't work if you have a severe bear market and this is where any of the rules of thumb or mathematical historical 'statistics' fall apart in toto. It's not just the fact that money was left to continually lose. It is the fact that, if one rebalanced a portfolio to maintain a specific risk profile, then more and more money is lost.

**2000 Example**

I restate the viability of the inverted yield curve in early 2000 (See chapter herein) and now the Year to Year Real GDP %. Rebalancing under such conditions is absolutely mandatory since the risk scenario would/did unquestionably increase. But when done when a recession is imminent- meaning a simplistic adjustment- it will cause retirees, in particular, financial devastation from which many will never recoup. It happened in 2000 but few did nay homework thereafter (about risk).

Remember this- **rebalancing is based on the continuation of an investment at essentially the risk levels. There are simply times when you do not want to be invested.**

Let me repeat for those that talk about market timing. The essence is that one uses the stock market as the investment du jour. Why? The market is not sacrosanct. There are simply times when no market- or other investments- are valid.

A recession statistically has a 40%+ loss in equities. Is it not better to simply avoid the ruin? Of course, the bulk of planning has rested on the buy and hold- the market will always come back. Quite possibly true even in the future. But that is not real life for many. It may be that the retiree will be dead by the time the market does return. Further, the emotional impact of such losses is extreme and such toil will/can ruin an existing financial life along with the physical and mental.

Assume $1,000,000 in retirement assets where 4% was being taken out annually for living expenses (the fickle use of 4% is addressed herein). They were using a 70/30 split of equities. Also assume that they had $250,000 in a CD that their broker/financial adviser was aware of that was their safe money. They trusted him to do the right thing.

(I will simply use rounded annual numbers. I will show inflation at 0%. CD interest is not included.)

In the first year, $40,000 was used for expenses. But the remaining equities lost 9%. The bonds remained constant. 960,000- (960,000x 70% x 9%)= 899,518.

But the broker suggested it was a great time to buy on the dip. So they took $60,480 from their CD and added it to equities. The next year they still took out $40,000 but the equity section had lost 12%. $920,000 x 70% x 12%= 77,200. But of course statistics had shown that three years of a down market was almost unheard of so they took $77,200 more out their CD and added it to equities. And because we were ‘going to have a strong market’, they still took out $40,000 for expenses. But the market did go down another 22%. $880,000 x 70% x 22%. That is another loss of $135,520.

**They had lost $273,200 over the three years.** The CD was at 112,320 and their retirement assets were at 726,800.

They are not happy campers. How was that money coming back when they are still taking money out each year?

Let’s take something more ‘realistic’. $1,000,000 in a 70/30 split, no extra funds, inflation at 4%, bonds are flat.

40,000 first year payment and 9% loss of equities=

$900,000. Rebalance to maintain 70% equities. $41,600 second year= 858,000. 12% loss (72,000)= 785,000 Rebalance to same split

43,250 third year $742,000. 70% x742,000 x 22%= 114,000= leaves 627,000.

(There are innumerable variations since one can tweak the numbers or situation slightly- decrease the equity side, increase bond returns, etc. But the real culprit is that stock investments have significant downsides. Mandelbrot and Taleb addressed that but it was essentially after the fact (of the 1990s). I did it prior to 2000 in instruction, but it was a worthless gesture to students. They already 'knew' the world had changed to dotcom rules and risk was irrelevant.)

**But rebalancing said to add more to the equities and the end result was an additional unnecessary loss of $186,000** (the first year loss is part of the correction process and should not be included as an unnecessary loss.)

Is that it? Nope. Many consumers were lulled by the Dotcom into putting far more into the higher risk allocations. And many didn't even use bonds. So the losses went far deeper into their financial pocketbook. It was not unusual for me to hear of effectively all IRA investments being lost etc. (Note that a 60/40 split may have helped them keep a portfolio more in line, but human nature being what it is….. )

Next time it will be different is also something that, while I admit the future is unknown, does not necessarily have to apply where risk is concerned.

Obviously after 2003, it was slightly different since equities became a no-no for many crippled by the past losses and people opted into real estate. I have always addressed the issue that real estate is a non liquid asset and that if anything goes wrong, you are stuck. And of course home prices never go down. Sorry, I worked for the Irvine Company in Newport Beach, California in the early 70s and I distinctly remember the gas price and economic fiasco and how developers were trying everything to sell houses. They just were not moving. Free this and free that in an effort to unload the properties. Nobody was buying. Some people got caught holding too many homes and had to liquidate cheaply. Admittedly it was not the same scenario as 2008 but the illiquidity was obvious (addressed by 'formula' herein).

Further, I always taught that a house was a home first and foremost. It was not an investment- it was a place where you raised a family and enjoyed the area- not an esoteric buy that you would sell in 3-5 years at a 'huge' profit. Additionally, the idea that buying a home 25 to 50 to 100 miles from work meant- at least in California- at least a 1.5 to 2 hour drive each way every day. They may have owned a home but they did not have a life. Neither did their spouse or children. I do not remember any commentary on that (though there must have been something) but the focus on buying a home as part of the American dream was killing the inhabitants if they never were there to enjoy it.

Enough said about that right now but it is necessary to see the inevitable recession starting with yet another inverted yield curve (or the year to year real GDP%) in 2006. Pundits of the curve stated it was different this time since the Asians were buying so much of our debt that it had pushed long term rates low. The economy was fine via Bernanke and more, etc. So much for the optimism.

Rebalancing into- or remaining in- equities in view of an economic recession where the losses are 40%+ should not make sense to anyone. Certainly to a fiduciary. The numbers above are clear cut- they follow the same position as the losses sustained in 1973 and 1974- assuming anybody cared. Which they didn't. They didn't for 2000 nor for 2008. Admittedly it is different now since a lot do not have the money to invest in anything. But I am addressing the requirements for a fiduciary.

If a fiduciary is not trained in the fundamentals of investing, they certainly do not grasp the issues of economics and their robotic focus towards rebalancing will exacerbate consumer losses.

Sure some consumers will not imbibe in the market for some time, but those in 401ks will be directed to more equities. All taught by fiduciaries(?).

Something seems amiss.

We are not in Kansas anymore 'Toto".

# 25

# Current and Retirement Budget

Of all the issues impacting retirement, the amount of money you project to spend during retirement has a significantly greater impact on the amount of funds needed than the projected inflation rate, return on investment or anything else. Further, using a rule of thumb- say 60% to 80% of current budget- is invariably a simplistic method designed for very superficial analysis and **should never be used** for any long term planning. If you are off "just a bit", the amount of funds you believe you will need may not remotely match the funds you will spend during retirement. You don't want to find out at 70 years of age that you are going to run out of money in the next five years because you didn't do the number properly when you were 50. It's too late at that point to make adequate adjustments.

(For the purists, I understand that there is a lot of "compromise" and "guesstimates" with some figures and that the projections of inflation and returns in the future are also based on unknown rates. That said, if the budget-which can be determined with some exactness- has no real life element, the whole process can be wasted.. Further, if the retiree/investor refuses to so the necessary homework, the analysis will tend to be valued accordingly.)

The following is the most detailed budget currently in use. It may take quite a bit of time to get all the figures (remember some of your payments may be made only annually and you therefore must track down payments made many months previously).

Now this is how you do retirement budgeting. Look at each one of the line items. See how they might change when you retired. One example is clothes purchases. You obviously are not going to be buying lots of new clothes- certainly business suits- and you should reduce the amount accordingly. Maybe you are going to retire to Florida where you can forget snow removal- by the same token your utilities will be higher in the summer due to air conditioning. The point being is that you simply don't take 65% or 75% of current costs because there are too many factors impacting the decision. So take your time before putting just "any" number in the retirement column. Add up the numbers when through and you should have a pretty good budget on which a good plan may be developed. I also know that the younger you are- certainly age 45 and under- the more difficult to determine valid retirement numbers. But you have to start someplace. For those 45+, the need to focus on retirement numbers is mandatory and you have no choice but to complete carefully.

| **Expense Item** | Current<br>Retirement | During |
|---|---|---|
| **Food** | | |
| Groceries | | |
| Alcohol/Tobacco | | |
| Restaurants | | |

Personal
Work related
Appliances and Cookware/Kitchen

**Entertainment and Recreation**

Vacations
Travel
Recreational Equipment/Activities
Biking/Kayaking/Fishing/Hunting/Hiking
Sporting events
Movies/Theater
Parties Hosted in home
CD's/tapes
Fitness club
Cable TV
Country Club

**Computer**

New computer
Upgrades
Software
Repairs
Supplies
On line services
Miscellaneous Supplies

**Gifts and Contributions**

Religious and Charities
Political causes
Family gifts/birthdays
Non family gifts
Christmas gifts

**Transportation**

Car payments
Auto Maintenance
Auto Insurance

Parking
Parking Tickets
Parking Permits
Public transportation
Carpool costs
Taxes and Fees
Tolls
Gas
Oil
Registration

**Clothing**

Mending/repair
Dry Cleaning/laundry
New purchases
Shoes
Work Clothes

**Childcare/parent/dependent Care**

Daycare
Cleaning
Medical care
Babysitting

**Personal Care**

Hair Care
Toiletries
Personal care appliances
Pocket money allowances
Massages

**Education**

Newspapers
Education/training expenses Books
Magazines
Professional Dues
Personal Tuition

- Personal Room and Board
- Child tuition & Room and Board (Current)
- Child tuition & Room and board (Future)
- Miscellaneous Supplies

**Obligations**

- Income Tax
- Medicare
- Social Security
- State Tax
- Consulting Fees
- Tax preparation
- Other Tax
  - Life Insurance
    - Term
      - Whole Life
      - Universal Life
      - Variable
- Disability Insurance
- Umbrella insurance
- Credit card fees
- Credit Card Payments
  - Interest
  - Principal
  - Finance Fee
  - Cash fee
- Alimony/support
- Child Support
- Child care
- Child Allowances
- Business expenses
- Attorney fees
- Accountant fees
- Other debts/loans
- Union Dues
- Storage Fees

- Postage

**Savings**

- Personal Savings
- Retirement Savings
  - Company stock/options
  - 401(k)
  - TSA's (403(b)/501(c)3))
  - IRA's
  - KEOGH
  - SEP
- Investments
  - Individual Securities
  - Mutual Funds
  - Real Estate
- Annuities
  - Fixed
  - Variable

**Home**

- Home mortgage/rent
  - Interest
  - Principal
- Maintenance
- Furnishings
- Gas
- Oil
- Electricity
- Telephone
- Property Insurance
- Fire insurance
- Earthquake insurance
- Flood Insurance
- Umbrella/liability insurance
- Contents/personal property insurance
- Property tax
- Condominium Fees

Water
Sewer
Well Maintenance
Septic Tank cleaning
Mowing Service
Landscaping Service
Snow Removal
Second Home (repeat above)

**Medical**

Hospital
Physician
Dentist
Prescriptions/Vitamins
Health Insurance
Medigap Insurance

**Pets**

Veterinarian
Food
Board and Care

SUBTOTAL

MISC. 5-10% of subtotal (May seem excessive and will need to be addressed with adviser. However, I think that medical costs and the like might fit in here since they have been escalating beyond all reason. And if not that, why not something else over 20- 30 years? Note that I included parent care along with child care. This is not just a financial burden but a huge emotional and physical burden mostly on women. One might even want to include something for respite care.

Notice pets- we really tend to keep them for a much longer time than in the past and the costs can be substantial.

TOTAL CURRENT YEARLY EXPENSES

Current Yearly Expenses MINUS Federal and State Tax= After Tax Current budget

# 26

# Retirement Analysis

The key to retirement is to figure out if there are enough assets to fund the budget for the actuarial lifetime plus a few more years. It is not simple. Among other things, one views the current health of the retirees, past medical problems, heredity, and more. Medical costs are a dicey issue. Long term care is extremely expensive hovering close to $80,000 annually. Medicare coverage is continually being downgraded. End of life care is very expensive as well. (You are definitely going to find a reallocation of government finances regarding imminent death. Our current society does not have the monies to extend life with no essential value but to make the family feel better.)

Is there a legacy to be left to the kids or a charity? Is there life insurance- what type, in an ILIT, will it last, should it be surrendered, sold, converted. Is it the best time for an annuity, which one, what is the return. How will inflation impact retirement, what return can be projected, what about the underlying risk, do we rebalance, when, why, are bonds better and on and on.

I have included some reports and letters in the appendix and one can understand some of the nuances involved. However you will note the lack of pretty graphs and charts as an inducement to make the process exempt from client discussion. It is *their* retirement, not a software program intended to indicate what product to buy or simplistic allocation to use. (I am well aware of the colored pie charts et al but I think it is more of a marketing effort to see the 'nice stuff' that came out of a computer rather than involving the client in valid discussion.)

Here is the basic formula to determine if the current asset amount might be sufficient. First, you have to identify the inflation factor. You can go back and forth through history but the past is not necessarily a precursor to the future. You will need to do a lot of current reading. Right now I would use two; 3% and 5%.. Some pundits would suggest something significantly higher but if the world goes back to the pre Volcker years of 15%+, we would be in such a financial morass that no budget analysis would accommodate. I have therefore assumed some modicum of reason to international inflation overall in one and two tier countries.

As to returns- certainly equities can go nuts and a retiree will have tons of money. But that is poor planning. I personally have a difficulty in projecting anywhere close to the historical average of about 10%. The political and financial arrogance, gross negligence and outright stupidity in all forms of government has caused a debacle that will continue for decades. Looking backward 200 years- or 75 years- or whatever time frame selected does not have any true significance to looking forward to where the country and the world is headed. I think the U.S. returns may hover around 6%+ and with a lot more volatility than in the last century. I have addressed returns in a separate chapter. I further suggest a review of "The expected real return to equity". http://d.repec.org/n?u=RePEc:fip:fedgfe:2011-

14&r=fmk_and other articles herein. You will find validation of much lower returns. (Of course, one should read the material of Peter Bernstein and Benoit Mandelbrot for a complete analysis of equities.)

But this is how it works. Go through the budget carefully to see if it was filled out correctly and are there any glaring errors. (Obviously for the current budget first and then the retirement next since it works off what is being done now) If the projected budget seems OK, take that amount and put it in PMT in your financial calculator. (Say it is $45,000 annually)

Enter the number of years expected for your lifetime(s). This is NOT taking the expected lifetime of a newborn and subtracting your current age. For example, if a male born today was to live to 79 years of age and you were already 65, there are more than 14 years left to live. The older you get, the longer you have to live. It's just simply that many people have already died before you (hopefully all the bad ones.). A male has roughly 16 more years to live. Obviously if you smoke and are now obese, the statistical odds are against you and you figure accordingly. But still a decent fudge factor is in order to cover for the contingencies.

## COMMISSIONERS 2001 STANDARD ORDINARY MORTALITY TABLE MALE AND FEMALE

| AGE LAST BIRTHDAY | MALE 1000qx | MALE LIFE EXPECTATION | FEMALE 1000qx | FEMALE LIFE |
|---|---|---|---|---|
| 0 | 0.72 | 75.67 | 0.42 | 79.87 |
| 1 | 0.46 | 74.73 | 0.31 | 78.90 |
| 2 | 0.33 | 73.76 | 0.23 | 77.93 |
| 3 | 0.24 | 72.79 | 0.20 | 76.95 |
| 4 | 0.21 | 71.81 | 0.19 | 75.96 |
| 5 | 0.22 | 70.82 | 0.18 | 74.98 |
| 6 | 0.22 | 69.84 | 0.19 | 73.99 |

| AGE LAST BIRTHDAY | MALE 1000qx | MALE LIFE EXPECTATION | FEMALE 1000qx | FEMALE LIFE |
|---|---|---|---|---|
| 7 | 0.22 | 68.85 | 0.21 | 73.00 |
| 8 | 0.22 | 67.87 | 0.21 | 72.02 |
| 9 | 0.23 | 66.88 | 0.21 | 71.03 |
| 10 | 0.24 | 65.90 | 0.22 | 70.05 |
| 11 | 0.28 | 64.91 | 0.25 | 69.06 |
| 12 | 0.34 | 63.93 | 0.27 | 68.08 |
| 13 | 0.40 | 62.95 | 0.31 | 67.10 |
| 14 | 0.52 | 61.98 | 0.34 | 66.12 |
| 15 | 0.66 | 61.01 | 0.36 | 65.14 |
| 16 | 0.78 | 60.05 | 0.39 | 64.17 |
| 17 | 0.89 | 59.10 | 0.41 | 63.19 |
| 18 | 0.95 | 58.15 | 0.44 | 62.22 |
| 19 | 0.98 | 57.21 | 0.46 | 61.25 |
| 20 | 1.00 | 56.26 | 0.47 | 60.27 |
| 21 | 1.01 | 55.32 | 0.49 | 59.30 |
| 22 | 1.02 | 54.37 | 0.50 | 58.33 |
| 23 | 1.04 | 53.43 | 0.51 | 57.36 |
| 24 | 1.06 | 52.48 | 0.53 | 56.39 |
| 25 | 1.09 | 51.54 | 0.55 | 55.42 |
| 26 | 1.14 | 50.60 | 0.58 | 54.45 |
| 27 | 1.17 | 49.65 | 0.61 | 53.48 |
| 28 | 1.16 | 48.71 | 0.64 | 52.51 |
| 29 | 1.15 | 47.77 | 0.67 | 51.55 |
| 30 | 1.14 | 46.82 | 0.70 | 50.58 |
| 31 | 1.13 | 45.88 | 0.75 | 49.62 |
| 32 | 1.14 | 44.93 | 0.79 | 48.65 |
| 33 | 1.16 | 43.98 | 0.85 | 47.69 |
| 34 | 1.19 | 43.03 | 0.92 | 46.73 |
| 35 | 1.24 | 42.08 | 1.00 | 45.78 |
| 36 | 1.31 | 41.14 | 1.07 | 44.82 |
| 37 | 1.39 | 40.19 | 1.14 | 43.87 |

| AGE LAST BIRTHDAY | MALE 1000qx | MALE LIFE EXPECTATION | FEMALE 1000qx | FEMALE LIFE |
|---|---|---|---|---|
| 38 | 1.49 | 39.25 | 1.20 | 42.92 |
| 39 | 1.59 | 38.30 | 1.26 | 41.97 |
| 40 | 1.72 | 37.36 | 1.34 | 41.03 |
| 41 | 1.87 | 36.43 | 1.43 | 40.08 |
| 42 | 2.05 | 35.50 | 1.53 | 39.14 |
| 43 | 2.27 | 34.57 | 1.65 | 38.20 |
| 44 | 2.52 | 33.65 | 1.79 | 37.26 |

| AGE LAST BIRTHDAY | MALE 1000qx | MALE LIFE EXPECTATIO N | FEMALE 1000qx | FEMALE LIFE EXPECTATIO N |
|---|---|---|---|---|
| 45 | 2.77 | 32.73 | 1.96 | 36.33 |
| 46 | 3.03 | 31.82 | 2.16 | 35.40 |
| 47 | 3.25 | 30.92 | 2.38 | 34.48 |
| 48 | 3.42 | 30.02 | 2.64 | 33.56 |
| 49 | 3.64 | 29.13 | 2.93 | 32.65 |
| 50 | 3.91 | 28.23 | 3.24 | 31.74 |
| 51 | 4.26 | 27.34 | 3.60 | 30.85 |
| 52 | 4.70 | 26.46 | 3.99 | 29.96 |
| 53 | 5.21 | 25.58 | 4.41 | 29.08 |
| 54 | 5.83 | 24.72 | 4.86 | 28.21 |
| 55 | 6.52 | 23.86 | 5.36 | 27.34 |
| 56 | 7.26 | 23.02 | 5.91 | 26.49 |
| 57 | 7.95 | 22.19 | 6.49 | 25.65 |
| 58 | 8.63 | 21.37 | 7.09 | 24.82 |
| 59 | 9.42 | 20.55 | 7.70 | 23.99 |
| 60 | 10.40 | 19.75 | 8.34 | 23.18 |
| 61 | 11.59 | 18.96 | 9.03 | 22.37 |
| 62 | 12.98 | 18.18 | 9.76 | 21.58 |
| 63 | 14.47 | 17.42 | 10.55 | 20.79 |
| 64 | 16.04 | 16.67 | 11.40 | 20.01 |
| 65 | 17.65 | 15.94 | 12.33 | 19.24 |

| AGE LAST BIRTHDAY | MALE 1000qx | MALE LIFE EXPECTATIO N | FEMALE 1000qx | FEMALE LIFE EXPECTATIO N |
|---|---|---|---|---|
| 66 | 19.27 | 15.23 | 13.35 | 18.48 |
| 67 | 20.96 | 14.53 | 14.48 | 17.73 |
| 68 | 22.74 | 13.84 | 15.71 | 16.99 |
| 69 | 24.69 | 13.16 | 17.08 | 16.27 |
| 70 | 26.94 | 12.50 | 18.63 | 15.55 |
| 71 | 29.71 | 11.84 | 20.38 | 14.84 |
| 72 | 32.94 | 11.20 | 22.29 | 14.15 |
| 73 | 36.32 | 10.59 | 24.39 | 13.48 |
| 74 | 39.96 | 9.99 | 26.68 | 12.81 |
| 75 | 43.95 | 9.40 | 29.20 | 12.16 |
| 76 | 48.44 | 8.83 | 31.95 | 11.53 |
| 77 | 53.67 | 8.28 | 34.97 | 10.91 |
| 78 | 59.72 | 7.75 | 38.28 | 10.30 |
| 79 | 66.48 | 7.25 | 41.92 | 9.72 |
| 80 | 74.02 | 6.76 | 46.43 | 9.14 |
| 81 | 82.20 | 6.30 | 51.96 | 8.59 |
| 82 | 90.82 | 5.87 | 57.80 | 8.06 |
| 83 | 100.22 | 5.45 | 63.94 | 7.55 |
| 84 | 110.69 | 5.06 | 70.74 | 7.07 |
| 85 | 122.36 | 4.69 | 77.59 | 6.60 |
| 86 | 135.17 | 4.34 | 85.68 | 6.16 |
| 87 | 148.99 | 4.02 | 95.69 | 5.74 |
| 88 | 163.00 | 3.73 | 106.25 | 5.34 |
| 89 | 179.03 | 3.45 | 116.68 | 4.98 |
| 90 | 194.28 | 3.20 | 124.22 | 4.64 |
| 91 | 209.27 | 2.98 | 131.53 | 4.29 |
| 92 | 224.94 | 2.76 | 143.72 | 3.94 |
| 93 | 241.46 | 2.56 | 160.21 | 3.61 |
| 94 | 258.86 | 2.38 | 180.90 | 3.29 |
| 95 | 276.12 | 2.21 | 203.48 | 3.02 |
| 96 | 292.95 | 2.06 | 225.69 | 2.79 |

| AGE LAST BIRTHDAY | MALE 1000qx | MALE LIFE EXPECTATIO N | FEMALE 1000qx | FEMALE LIFE EXPECTATIO N |
|---|---|---|---|---|
| 97 | 310.86 | 1.91 | 240.07 | 2.61 |
| 98 | 329.95 | 1.77 | 247.79 | 2.43 |
| 99 | 350.32 | 1.64 | 263.98 | 2.23 |
| 100 | 369.76 | 1.53 | 285.02 | 2.03 |
| 101 | 386.96 | 1.42 | 307.89 | 1.84 |
| 102 | 405.25 | 1.32 | 333.06 | 1.66 |
| 103 | 424.70 | 1.23 | 360.71 | 1.49 |
| 104 | 445.35 | 1.13 | 390.86 | 1.33 |
| 105 | 467.29 | 1.04 | 422.72 | 1.19 |
| 106 | 490.57 | 0.95 | 455.33 | 1.05 |
| 107 | 515.28 | 0.86 | 488.48 | 0.93 |
| 108 | 541.49 | 0.78 | 522.20 | 0.82 |
| 109 | 569.27 | 0.70 | 557.04 | 0.72 |
| 110 | 598.70 | 0.62 | 591.96 | 0.63 |

This actually goes to age 120 but enough is enough.

As stated, consider a fudge factor of maybe 5 years. (Also note that a man turning 65 now has almost a 20% chance of living to 90, and a woman at this age has nearly a one-third chance.) That number goes in N. (Say 82 -65= 17)

The future value is 0- that means that all the assets are to be used up by death. Obviously this requires an indepth discussion with clients but it is definitely one example to work with. Assume a rate of return and a rate of inflation. Say 7% and 3%.

Take 1- return and divide by 1 - inflation (1-.07/1-.03) That equals 1.03883495

Subtract 1 from above. That equals .03883495

Multiply by 100 3.883495 and put this number into (i) for overall rate of return.

PMT= $45,000

Hit PV- that is the number that reflects how much of a kitty is needed at retirement to fund the budget and with no monies left at the end (assumes a flat rate of return at this point).

What did you get? (If you do not have a financial calculator by this point, pretend you are a U.S. politician guessing how numbers work for our budget deficit. Anyone working with future and present value numbers and absolutely with risk has to be competent with a financial calculator.) For attorneys involved in litigation- anyone addressing risks, returns et al has to have such ability. Never use an expert who does not have and cannot use a financial calculator. I am fully aware that the arbitrators may be clueless to this necessity, but sooner or later it will become clear that if you or the expert does not know how money works… well, I suppose you could become a politician.

Note: all numbers are annual.

The numbers are far more transparent since they really show what is going on. Certainly it is much more transparent than a software programs that merely spits out some arcane number. Further, the above requires a lot more conversation with the clients in judging the value of the numbers rather than taking some sophomoric historical guide.

Example:

Assume male age 65, actuarial lifetime (some fudge) to age 85. He gets 1,500 monthly from social security. He needs 40,000 annually and has saved 200,000. Inflation is at 2.5% and another at 4.5%. Return is chosen at 7% and for this exercise, I have not indicated if it is before or after tax. How much does he need to last his lifetime. So take (1+.07/1.025) -1 x 100, 40,000, no funds left at death and a 20 year remaining lifetime. That equal $525,000 (rounded).

First, what is social security worth? Taking some liberty, I will use an annual amount of $18,000 adjusted for inflation each year. Multiply 18,000 x the number of years (20) equals a “lump sum” of 360,000. Subtract from $525,000 equals $165,000. He has $200,000. Therefore there is an excess of $35,000. Just looking at the pure numbers, he has sufficient funds to cover his retirement- that is assuming flat rates of return, no long term care etc. So he does ***not*** have to take as much risk as the 7% indicates and that therefore ‘determines’ how the risk of an allocation will be based.

(Note: A fiduciary has to do this and I am mentioning this because I am involved in a case where there was an excess, but the CFP had the client change the current allocation to much greater risks which subsequently lost substantial monies in the 2008 debacle. It was unnecessary. But a lot of commissions were involved, so......)

What if I used inflation at 4.5%? That now demands $630,000. Subtract 360,000 equals $270,000. Current assets of $200,000 is subtracted. He is now $70,000 light.

What if the allocations consists totally of bonds earning 3.5%. Or also put inflation at 5%. Or????? There are a myriad of numbers that can be run but the key concern is if there are insufficient funds to sustain a full retirement.

Now what? First thing to do is see if the budget can be reduced. From there one does the formal planning discussion with the client(s) and pulling in all the factors of risk and reward to get the process restarted.

All that said, this is only effectively valid at the time it is prepared. Since everything tends to change, the process will almost undoubtedly require adjustments by a year’s end. When clients are 65 and older, ill health and potential Alzheimers always has me concerned. I have simply seen too many instances of both and am very wary of idyllic retirements.

This is obviously not as ‘simple’ as a software program that might throw out a pretty chart signifying what allocation to pursue. That's because the advisor has to consider a lot of various interrelating issues that will invariably change over time. Probably one of my biggest gripes to the software is that they universally stay the course in a recession letting the assets drop to major lows. Of course that will significantly change the funds available- as it has during all the 2000s. The average consumer with no assistance may have to accept that as fait compli. But the whole point to a fiduciary duty by an adviser is to provide the assistance to narrow huge losses. That is also a necessary education to the masses as well and could have reduced the current need to work till death. The government cannot be absolved of the effort needed for the poor and middle America citizen who has been pretty much shut out with the likes of the Stock Market Game. Dodd Frank should try to get rid of this kind of trash.

Again I stress that this is not perfection. There will always be some lapses and losses but they must be kept to a minimum for any type of retirement planning where there is so little opportunity to make up losses.

# 27

# The Fallacy of Retirement Annual Withdrawal Numbers

This area is truly a distortion of real life and one that the retiree is apt to confront from many planners and software programs. Over the years, advisers- or maybe they were just mathematicians with nothing else to do- wanted to indicate the percentage of assets you could take out each year to fund your retirement. Some would come up with 4%, some 6%- but no matter the number, they would have some validation as to why their statistics were different and better than the other advisor or software program. (Also review again the chapter on Statistics.)

Invariably, the software went back in time and picked up every year from 1880- or maybe 1920- or 1960 or ??? and then put them into thousands of random positions to show how one's retirement would work given the past history of returns (Monte Carlo analysis). Let's say the numbers started from 1900 and, with the ability of a computer, it might show that a retiree would have succeeded 95% of the time in taking out a flat 4% each year. But if the numbers started in 1925, the failure rate might have been 7%. And if the numbers started in 1960 or 1980- you get the point. Anything more to add?

Yes. A June 6, 2011WSJ article noted Fidelity, Financial Engines, Guided Choices and Schwab had retirement calculators. All different and, apparently, all based on past history. And not showing the potential risks of loss. About 2% of those age 65 will reach age 90. Even a 20 year span will present at least two recessions and perhaps four. Each with potential losses up to 50% each in equities. It is absolutely true that one may have millions of dollars in a kitty at death decades hence by using past history as the guide. It is also true that allocations suggest/use more bonds are used as part of the allocation as one gets older. That does reduce the risk exposure to equities but the returns are also down for bonds probably for a decade or two. The risk of bonds is now offered in what 401k presentation? Nowhere since the risk of loss is not identified. If that is not done, how does one figure out proper withdrawals?. Ouija board?

Ed Easterling, in another 2011 WSJ article noted, "Investors had an overall success rate of 95% at a 4% withdrawal rate adjusted ***over time** for **inflation**. But that success rate fell to 76% for those who retired when stocks were in the top 20% of the **historical valuation range**.

The numbers were starker for a 5% withdrawal rate. For retirees starting out when stocks are in the highest 20% of valuations, the probability of success plunged to 41%. Only when stocks were in the bottom 40% of their valuations did retirees stand a better-than-90% chance of not running out of money. (They were at a peak as of the time of his comments.) But again the gauge to success is past history. The future is not going to be that nice.

Historically, it has taken about a 6% or 7% bond yield to be able to withdraw 4% from a portfolio plus an upward adjustment to inflation. U.S. Treasury 10-year notes, meanwhile, are yielding just 3.3%."

* Always think about this- his comment was 'over time'. Sounds OK doesn't it? But the question is "What time?" No idea. Next is, 'what inflation rate". No idea. Historical valuation range? What range? No idea again. Hence, if you look carefully at his quote and similar, as with many statistics, one can make up almost any scenario that is (or at least appears) valid. But the reader has no idea what may be going on and might make assumptions that are just plain defective. Admittedly this is how articles must be written since not every number can be footnoted. And he might be absolutely correct. But it nonetheless reinforces the necessity of caution when reading anything about risk and reward (and I know that I am included).

As stated, a 4% flat withdrawal had been widely used by Wall Street and retirement calculators for some time to show that one will have enough funds for about a 95% acceptance rate. But as the volatility and subsequent losses were escalated in the 2000s, it became very apparent that the bulk of retirees in the past decade found themselves in a financial morass as asset values tumbled once and then twice in 10 years. Some 401k plans note that current balances in such plans are now the same as what they were in 2009- essentially inferring, "see, we told you that the market will come back".

## Wrong.

If one had $100,000 in equities and lost 50% in 2008 (top to bottom losses for the S&P 500 was 57%), there would be $50,000 left. Assuming a return of 6%, it would take 12 years to recoup the 50,000. Obviously therefore, the new balances were due to the continuing employee and employer payments into the accounts. However, if one was already retired, the $50,000 left after 2008 would have been considerably *less* for the majority of retirees since they were taking money OUT of their retirement accounts to live on as the market continued to dive. They were certainly NOT putting anything back in. Vanguard notes "The more investors can tolerate some short-term fluctuations in spending, the more likely they are to achieve their longer-term goals." That simply defies credulity. How in the world can a retiree ever get back to normalcy in that scenario? One can 'accept' that with a 50% loss there would need to be a change in spending. But retirees ended up so far below their needs that a short term spending change turned into a full time asset rout. They are just plain underwater for the rest of their lives. No wonder the emotional and financial devastation of retirees. I do not inherently dismiss Vanguard's suggestion to redo the budget. However the horse, cart, hay and everything else has already left the barn. And the barn is burning. And the ranch has been foreclosed. From Americans Cite Affording Retirement as a Top Financial Concern, Plansponsor.com, "Almost 40% of working Americans say they will never afford retirement, which, for the second year in a row, ranks as the nation's most important financial concern.

http://www.plansponsor.com/Americans_Report_Affording_Retirement_as_Top_Financial_Concern.aspx

That said, such statistics might help a consumer understand where they might stand in some esoteric lifetime, but not necessarily to the real odds of their own retirement. One of the issues in such formulas is that the retiree has a adequate amount of assets to last their actuarial lifetime (plus a fudge) to begin with. In today's society after 2000, the odds were stacked against them. After 2008, that is now rarely the case- at least one that might be proven. Without a formal budget and the numbers in developing the asset base needed, the analysis has limited application. Additionally, the economics of a decade or a century ago are no longer valid- even if they were once. Though some might look that they fit current situations, it could be just plain dumb luck. The point being that 100 years of history from a completely variable local, national and international economies is not reflective of this future by any stretch of the imagination.

## Summary

In short, one can look to the past to get some idea what can happen. But the real world of market swings far greater than the fluid SD curves must be recognized in detail by the industry and absolutely whenever retirees are involved. Buy and hold is a form of investing that can be valid in a flat or growing market. But it is not acceptable for those who can never recover losses from major devastation.

Asset allocation with a major holdings of bonds can temper losses. But such a rule of thumb is just another crutch not to do the necessary numbers to figure out just what *needs* to be done for the client - particularly if the budget is as low as it can get.

Obviously it is incumbent to get working consumers to save more well before retirement. It looks like the savings rate may be increasing, but until another decade goes by, no one will know for sure. In the interim, it will be a lot of hard work to figure out how to adjust, when and by how much. It is immense amount of reading coupled with specific fundamentals that heretofore are not required of financial counselors. Until that happens- and it will take a decade to get up to speed considering the capability and competency of government- more and more older workers may have to work until they die.

I do not see how any retirement payout can be utilized without a careful analysis and monitoring of the assets throughout retirement. I know consumers cannot or will not do it. I know that the current activities of advisors does not have either the interest, willingness or competency.

The only way that one might get a potentially decent return is through the use of some type of indexed annuity. The principal is guaranteed but the industry's excessive fees keeps returns low. Even then with stock and bond returns so low, the "safe" return may not do much good.

But the use of any type formula that states there is some method to use that will allow "$X" per year based on past history is tantamount to a breach of fiduciary duty.

# 28

# Reversion to the Mean

This is a short chapter on one of the most detailed theories that almost every planner/adviser uses in one form or another. There are hundreds upon hundreds of articles I have read on the subject over the last 30 years and it was next to impossible to figure out what author, what research, what time frame was valid in picking out the returns that should be used in the future while taking effectively all the data from the past. Essentially it means that if current returns are higher than normal, they will revert to the lower mean that has been identified from year ?????

Or if current returns are too low, they will go higher because of the statistical mean starting from year????

Now, if returns are really too low or too high, I have no difficulty to say that they should/will adjust to something more meaningful over time. The amount of time? Unknown? Why? Because it depends on the current economics both nationally and internationally. And because of the real estate debacle, it can include statewide and local economics.

As to what they should return to? Unknown since, as Peter Bernstein noted, the future is unknown. True, it is necessary to recognize the past. But it is far more preferable to view current conditions and- admittedly this is hard- to research what might work to the future. Of course if the fiduciary is merely using the standard preprogrammed software package, why is that adviser in use? Computers are mandatory, but investors and advisers have abrogated the necessity of hard work (reading and thinking) over to programs they know very little about.

Now this may sound out of context but fits perfectly with how the past does NOT work for me on a most 'simplistic' level. I belong to a bass club in Sacramento CA. It is a working cattle ranch where they built some irrigation ponds more than a century ago. I enjoy the fishing and am pretty good overall (is that the male ego talking?). Anyway, I am not trying to catch an Einstein with scales. It's a bass. It's a fish in water. How hard can this be? Yet every year has been hardly anything like the year before. The amount of rain during the winter, temperature all year round, wind, type and number of weeds, depth of water, pelican predation, number of fish overall and on and on. I am not talking about billions of people internationally impacted by politics and economics. Therefore, with the 'limited' changes at a bass pond, I should be able to do a reversion to something that happened in the past and plan my fishing trips accordingly. After all, it's just a *fish.* Unfortunately, for 15 years at a minimum, I have had to restart the process of how to fish these ponds over and over again. Everything has changed so much during the winter months that if I was to do the same thing- or expect the same thing- as what happened one, five, ten years ago, I would be wasting my time. I might have to wait 20 years or 30 years or ???? years before the current year fit a pattern from the past. I will be dead by then and have proved nothing. Not that I won't catch something in the interim but as they say 'attempting the same thing again and again and expecting a different result is a sign of madness.' Actually, it should be 'attempting the same thing over and over again *in a completely different (economic) situation* and expecting the same results is madness'. Well it's not madness when talking about a fish (or is it?) but it is stupid. On the other hand, maybe I will try to figure out what exists currently and then attempt to make adjustments to the future over the next few months. Based on experience and research with a water quality manager, I try different times, lures, depths, whatever. Am I going to be successful? I don't know. But the effort of doing something different in recognition of new events is going to almost assuredly mean that I will be more successful than doing something over and over again that doesn't fit the conditions. I won't be "great" since that is not a reasonable position at all. But at least I will fish in water where there was none the past five years due to a drought. Or in massive weeds. Therefore if a prudent fisherman/woman would definitely look forward, is it not a reasonable expectation that a fiduciary handling a consumer's future should not do the same?

What about medications? Does one ignore current drugs and the potential innovations that are currently being tested? Or does one opt for the research applications from the past when dysentery was the problem? Or polio? Of course not (or at least very rarely). We look to the practitioners to do the right thing for our health with the best medicine that exists now or that will/may become available later. We pay profit and non profit institutions to figure out what might work as time goes on- not to do the same thing the same way with the same equipment and same knowledge that has existed in the past. There are tons of other similarities, but looking to the past while living in a world so advanced and advancing is ludicrous in the extreme.

So we must demand that fiduciaries in the planning, investment and insurance industries do the same in updating their knowledge base and using forward looking thinking in figuring out what to do- certainly what is the best interests of the consumer.

# FINANCIAL PLANNING
# FIDUCIARY STANDARDS UNDER DODD FRANK

This is really going to require a revamping of the knowledge base and competency of hundreds of thousands of planners, investment advisers and insurance agents. We cannot keep doing the same thing as existed 10, 20, xxx odd years ago. Will these changes take place under current guidelines?

No. They were developed in the past and are way outdated. The licenses have effectively nothing to do with real life. None are required to have any financial background before or after licensing. The point about the licensing is there is nothing on the table with Dodd Frank that will make it any better. I know this gets tedious, but calling someone a fiduciary to help the consumers where they have no clue to risk of loss is indicative of the SEC, FINRA, NASAA, DOL and more living in the past when they used rocks as currency. If anyone is in disagreement, go to http://www.regulations.gov/#!documentDetail;D=EBSA-2010-0050-0001. There are 300 replies and only one- mine- gets to the heart of 'fiduciary'. How can so many entities assume that everyone calling themselves a fiduciary actually has the competency in doing so. (Maybe they just live in the past.)

Therefore I refer readers to the section on returns. It is my position that returns over the past 100 and 200 years are not reflective of where we are today. The projected returns will be lower than the past averages and somewhere around 6%. Reversion to a mean 30 or so years past with a now declining United States economy is illogical.

I know that the vast numbers of advisers will say this is heresy blah, blah. And of course I can be wrong.

But I don't think so

# 29

# Securities Arbitration

The first question by most consumers who have had investment problems is, "Are arbitrations fair?" Perhaps better expressed as, 'do they really cover the mandatory issues for a claim?'

*The quick answer is no.*

*They have never been, are not now, and probably will not do so in the foreseeable future.*

For pundits those who think otherwise- certainly attorneys- I point to this material offered at
http://www.finrafoundation.org/web/groups/foundation/@foundation/documents/foundation/p119054.pdf

INVESTOR'S GUIDE TO SECURITIES INDUSTRY DISPUTES How to Prevent and Resolve Disputes with Your Broker

PUBLISHED BY THE PACE LAW SCHOOL INVESTOR RIGHTS CLINIC EDITORS:

Professor Jill Gross, Director and Supervising **Attorney,** Pace Investor Rights Clinic Alice Oshins, Esq., Staff **Attorney**, Pace Investor Rights Clinic

(It was funded by a 'generous' grant from the FINRA Investor Education Foundation)

It notes, "For legal advice, please consult a licensed attorney in your area or call your local bar association for a referral to an attorney. For more information on finding an attorney experienced in securities mediation or arbitration, please read the section of this booklet on "How to Find an Attorney."

Take a look at the above first and tell me who are the authors/publishers? Attorneys. Lots and lots of attorneys. Therein is the first clue to the limited fairness of securities arbitrations. Not a one trained in the real life application of investments. Sure there may be one or two with personal experience with investing but invariably no training in any of the *fundamentals* of investing. It is not offered as part of any legal classes. An attorney simply does not possess the requisite skills in understanding investments nor, certainly, the associated risks. Additionally, I have scoured all the national bar associations. My two California Bar Association approved continuing legal education courses have no comparable offerings anywhere. In fact, over months and months of reviewing bar offerings, I found nothing on the subjects at all. I know there was nothing in my law degree- though that was about 35 years ago. But there is nothing now either- though the financial sophistication of products has risen a 100 fold. That should not be the case.

The reference above is to attorneys already dealing in arbitrations and litigation involving investments- those attorneys with no background at all are out to lunch from the get go and should be avoided at all costs. That said, the inference reflects a cautionary element towards 'somewhat' experienced plaintiffs' attorneys since they may not be dealing in the subject matter all the time and are rarely well versed on the subject matter certainly the practical application. (Obviously defendant attorneys may do a lot of this type of practice and are more versed in securities laws. But they are nowhere close to knowledgeable about what 'should have been done nor have an understanding of product application". That said, if you do not have someone on your side who does know, you are apt to lose on a complaint reasonably filed. Personally, I think that aspect is why so many claims are denied or awards limited. It is not just that something maybe wrong, it is necessary to prove what should have been done given the circumstances at the time of the problem..

And more, "Pace Investor Rights Clinic (PIRC), a legal services organization affiliated with Pace University School of Law. PIRC offers free legal services to eligible individual investors who have disputes with their securities brokers and brokerage firms. PIRC aims to protect the rights of individual investors, particularly investors of modest means who traditionally have been underrepresented in the legal system."

I do not dismiss the largess with Pace's offering of free services but their comment misses the key element to why those of modest means have been underrepresented. It is because those of literally ***any*** means have been misled by the very foundation that is offering the grant (FINRA). FINRA has never undertaken the instruction of the fundamentals on investing (yes I am aware that this can get tedious repeated over and over, but the comment is not just for a singular governmental entity- it is effectively all governmental entities that have gone adrift in the real world of investments for decades.) Nothing is more definitive on the lack of competency then this following scathing rebuke of the SEC:

http://www.sec.gov/spotlight/secpostmadoffreforms/oig-509-exec-summary.pdf

## Report of Investigation

United States Securities and Exchange Commission Office of the Inspector General Case OIG-509

Investigation of the Failure of the SEC to uncover Bernie Madoff's Ponzi Scheme

(This is covered in more detail in the governmental oversight section but gives an excellent idea of the insufferable competency overall);

"The OIG investigation did find that the SEC received more than ample information in the form of detailed and substantive complaints over the years to warrant a thorough and comprehensive examination and/or investigation of Bernard Madoff and BMIS for operating a Ponzi scheme, and that despite three examinations and two investigations being conducted, a thorough and competent investigation or examination was never performed."

**And**

"The OIG found that between June 1992 and December 2008 when Madoff confessed, the SEC received six substantive complaints that raised significant red flags concerning Madoffs hedge fund operations and should have led to questions about whether Madoff was actually engaged in trading. Finally, the SEC was also aware of two articles regarding Madoff's investment operations that appeared in reputable publications in 2001 and questioned Madoff's *unusually consistent* returns"

There are two specific issues that may not be readily apparent. First look at the dates. Over 16 years of ineptness that allowed a $50 to $65 billion Ponzi scheme to run amok. A couple of years, maybe. But 16!!!!

Secondly, and what should have been the true tipoff, was the consistent returns. You CANNOT have consistent returns in a volatile market- certainly when you were yielding 12% each and every year to participants. Investigators did not need a major reinvention of option strategies to recognize the real world of investing. And therein is the problem. They simply do not have the skills to understand what a basic finance major could have told them and secondly, they have no education/experience on real world investments. The SEC does not know real world risk. FINRA does not know real world risk. NASAA does not know risk. Brokers do not know risk. Attorneys do not know risk. Consumers do not know risk. (So why is the Dodd Frank assumption that merely calling a RIA a fiduciary supposed to bestow same with knowledge never before presented?)

It therefore should be obvious that in arbitrations that you have few entities, certainly including the arbitrators, who have much of an understanding of risk at all. It is not taught at effectively all levels. If the knowledge was evident at the top, perhaps some latitude would be available. There isn't. So there isn't.

One of the major complaints to arbitrations generally focuses on the fact that the investment must be suitable (others include negligence, breach of fiduciary duty, failure to supervise- though these can be dovetailed into suitability).

See http://www.finra.org/ArbitrationMediation/AboutFINRADR/Statistics/index.htm for current statistics on issues and products in arbitrations.

But what happens in arbitration is the defendant B/D universally states that the plaintiff is sophisticated, knew the risk and was fully cognizant of the suitability of the products and its applications in the real world. This is way out of context since the broker clearly is untrained and unknowledgeable in the fundamentals and applications of securities. And no instruction on risk. It therefore begs the issue why the focus is put on investor sophistication and not on broker and supervisor sophistication. (Of course that is easily understood. Since none of the players- including the arbitrators generally have a clue to what the licensing instruction entails- they assume that such sophistication must already exist at the industry level of a broker.

Also, the panel of three includes a industry arbitrator who may infer that the industry is trained. (I heard that in an arbitration. Totally wrong but not unexpected.)

The Pace study reflects just three risks- market, liquidity and inflation risk. The description is so sophomoric and superficial it borders on uselessness. Certainly the risks are identified in words- but to merely indicate that there is "A" risk without identifying "THE" risk is disingenuous at best. Where are the numbers for market risk? Where is the ***risk of loss?*** The study goes further and says that the investor should know how much risk they are taking. Another truly ridiculous statement. None of the brokers know risk. None of the attorneys. So how is the consumer to know what their risk is? This issue is more formally flushed out in a separate section but suffice to say that the simplistic questionnaires where the consumer is almost solely responsible for picking risk limits of conservative, moderate, aggressive et al is ludicrous in the extreme. Such lack of specificity has been on purpose by FINRA since it is beholden to the industry. (It could be due to incompetence as well- take your pick. Both?) But it nonetheless is a violation of the rules of suitability since the investor has been effectively misled into securities investments that will lose 40% to 60% at any given point in the economy (risk of loss). Pursuant to new legislation demanding a fiduciary duty, it would appear mandatory that the entire industry would have to be retrained to address the fundamentals. They will have to include the potential risks of loss (required by a personal financial calculator) for any allocation- as well as give a formal position to how they calculated an allocation of a certain risk with inconsistent correlations. Frankly, even with suitability guidelines, this has to be identified in any case. Otherwise, how can one determine the suitability of the investment? Read that again. Even if Dodd Frank is a complete loser. The bulk of material herein is valid in almost all cases regarding suitability. Recognize that I am NOT giving consumers a free ride when they lie or distort the truth. Just stating facts for many arbitrations.

Of course, this reeducation demands that the arbitrators also have at least some current understanding of real world application. Nope. Here is the rub. Back in the mid 90s- since I taught the securities classes and acted as an arbitrator, planner, etc., I was fully aware of the lack of knowledge and 'suggested' to the NASD (now FINRA) that I teach some classes in the fundamentals of investing because it was obvious they had little idea of what risk was and tended to address the proceedings on the peripheral areas of the actual claim (old age being the most notable). Rarely would either attorney offer much regarding the fundamentals that were violated since they did not know them, they didn't care and/or it was beyond their capability to learn (one would need to use a financial calculator- ever seen an attorney with one??)

So what did the NASD/FINRA say regarding education? In the mid 90s it was that the brokerage firms would never allow it (education/knowledge) since it would slow sales (absolutely true). That settled that. In the mid 2000s, they noted that FINRA was a procedural entity not a substantiative one (They would not/do not offer education). That came directly from the then FINRA president, Mary Schapiro, who now heads up the SEC (should give one a clue about the direction of knowledge.) Those comments directly reflect why the securities exams are so outdated and will remain effectively unchanged. The industry wouldn't have it any other way. A true insight to risk would clearly reduce sales of almost any product.

I can also give a real life expose if an arbitrator is too knowledgeable. I was a industry arbitrator in the San Francisco area during the 90s. I was called on to review a lot of cases because of my background- maybe 75. Of course, most of these were settled,, withdrawn, etc. But when I did serve, it was readily apparent that the cases were rarely addressed on the fundamentals of investing. Here is one example: A merchant seaman had retired with $150,000 in assets and social security. He supplemented his income by working with a Merrill Lynch broker where he bought some high yield bonds. The purchase of singular bonds with low ratings was problematic at best. In any case, he ended up later buying a $60,000+ junk bond that had a very low rating (maybe a 14% overall return). It went under in about six months. He sued the broker saying the broker came to him with the offering and should have known better. The broker said the seaman had come to him wanting to buy the bond. The two arbitrators said this was a 'he said, she said' dispute and that was the end of it. (One was a practicing attorney, the other a practicing CPA, both with a number of cases under their belt). I looked at them in disbelief because the sale of this issue to this individual was classically unsuitable- even if the seaman brought the issue to the broker directly (which I was hard pressed to believe anyway). The purchase of this bond would have violated every tenet of diversification and could never be allowed. More so since it was so lowly rated anyway. An award was justifiably made. What bothered me was that had I not been there, the plaintiff would have inexcusably lost. (That's not ego- just an observation that such situations are not unusual. The whole point with education and fiduciary standard is that they should be.)

In another case, an inexperienced attorney had filed a claim for a woman that bought a limited partnership. The sides went back and forth for quite a while. But I stopped the proceedings and issued a statement that the claim at hand had not addressed the fact that the sale to this person was simply ***illegal***. Only accredited investors could have purchased an interest and she was far from that. So we have the plaintiff attorney that didn't do his homework and the defense attorney who (apparently?) thought the issue would never come up. I also forced the issue 'upstairs' to the DBCC (district business conduct committee) but neither the arbitrators nor the NASD liked it. (I don't think it went anywhere.)

But one should not rock the boat- at least in this industry- and I was subsequently the arbitrator who was given the preemptory challenge (the ability for either side to select another arbitrator) and that was that. Once you decide cases on the facts because you happen to know more than the system- certainly the attorneys-you are out.

As a result, you are apt to see arbitrators who may allow awards, but do so in such a limited manner for most cases that the industry firms will accept their decisions without too much animosity

Of course, all this begs the issue “is a court system better”? Yes and no. The ability of an attorney to provide experts to a ‘blank slate’ so to speak to a jury instead of ‘professional’ arbitrators who are not that astute, seems to me a better choice to address the facts and the truth to a case. That said, and while arbitration is now taking longer and costing more than before, they still take less time and less money to utilize. Further, an arbitration award is effectively final whereas a court case with its many appeals can go on forever. And then who is to say that the courts are perfect in their awards anyway.

In short, arbitrations use arbitrators over and over again who do not know the fundamentals of investing and may not want to. The attorneys are pretty much out to lunch and the NASD/FINRA doesn’t really care. The requirement of one industry arbitrator is also problematic but it was clear in my case that an understanding of real life application and risk of a product was not wanted.

This is just the tip of some of the issues involved. I have written a 50 page white paper on the topic and certain items were simply picked for this text.

# 30

# Real Estate

Here is the 'best' way to compare the returns of real estate versus stocks or many other investment It's not perfect, but, done objectively, it is possible to objectively compare returns of each and see which way you'd like to invest.

It requires the form below, some basic calculations and an understanding of risk overall. It can be used for any property considered. It will give a total equity rate which you can then compare to other types of investments and is an excellent tool for initial evaluation. But, I repeat, you have to put in real life numbers. After you are through, I will provide the real risk that makes singular ownership of real estate so highly risky. It is the reason for the bulk of the losses from 2008- and always will be.

**Comparative Investment Analysis**

1. Sales Price- non expendable transaction costs

   **This is the total price that the property cost.**

2. Less Total Loans

**equals**

3. Equity

**1 minus 2**

**PROPERTY INCOME ANALYSIS**

4. Gross Scheduled Income

Make sure the rent is reflective of the neighborhood.

5. Less Vacancy and Credit Losses

   Always add in 5% to 10% unless there is absolute evidence of something different. But don't use 0% even with an exuberant economy. Perchance you have single rental such as an office or industrial building, be careful in that the vacancy rate can reflect 100% if you lose that tenant.

6. Gross Operating Income

**4 minus 5**

7. Operating Expenses

   Careful if you take it from a Realtor sales form since the amount is apt to be less than actual. Owners are notorious for showing less than spent. And/or there may be deferred maintenance. There are several services, some of the Internet, that can give you realistic estimates on how much you should anticipate.

8. NET OPERATING INCOME

**TAXABLE INCOME**

9. Net Operating Income
10. Less Interest Payments

    If you are taking out a new loan, recognize that almost all your initial payments will be interest and (normally) deductible.

11. Less Depreciation

12. Taxable Income (If negative, can be offset by passive income (where you are not actively engaged in the management of the property. See http://www.irs.gov/publications/p17/ch09.html#en_US_2010_publink1000171747). If owner has 10% or more interest and income is under $100,000, $25,000 of loss may be offset against regular income. Otherwise passive loss may not be used and must be carried forward)

**SPENDABLE INCOME**

13. Net Operating Income
14. Less Principal and Interest Payments
15. GROSS SPENDABLE
16. Less Income Tax (Subject to qualifications above) (If a negative number, remember that minus a negative number becomes a PLUS)
17. Less Capital Improvements
18. NET SPENDABLE ANNUALLY
19. Per Month

**EQUITY INCOME**

20. Net Operating Income
21. Less Interest on Loans
22. Less Income Tax (Subject to qualifications above)
23. NET EQUITY INCOME
24. Net Equity Income Rate
25. Plus Equity Growth Rate (What is expected appreciation? Keep realistic)
26. Total Equity Rate

At this point, it is possible to start comparing real estate to equities save for a couple specific issues with real estate. The first is liquidity. But to put it into perspective, I need to define the difference between marketability and liquidity. Marketability refers to the 'value' of the asset. Liquidity refers to the ability to be able to easily dispose of the asset for the market value. Traded securities are both marketable and liquid. You can simply call up a broker and immediately sell the securities for the value at the time of trade (some caveats obviously apply but the generalism is valid). On the other hand, while a real estate property may be marketable for, say, $500,000, the ability to immediately liquidate the property is remote. The average time to list, sell and close a property may be several months. As such, it is necessary to offset the return by the amount of risk that is taken with a non liquid property. Yes, it is true that you might not need the money that quickly, but that's not the point. It is the essential requirement to try and compare apples to apples. Hence, the return for a non liquid asset of any type must be reduced. Can I select what discount to use? No. Each state, county, neighborhood or block will have its own characteristics so you will need to make an educated "guess". That said, be realistic. Don't get caught in the euphoria of recent real estate returns- that's nothing different than using the 20% returns that many 1990's investors thought was going to exist forever with securities.

Here is a relatively simple example for the analysis of a $1,000,000 property. Rounded numbers

1. Sales Price- non expendable transaction costs $1,000,000
2. Less Total Loans $750,000 @ 8% for 30 years ($5,467 monthly or $66,000 annually rounded)
3. Equity 250,000

**PROPERTY INCOME ANALYSIS**

4. Gross Scheduled Income 125,000
5. Less Vacancy and Credit Losses 10,000
6. Gross Operating Income 115,000
7. Less Operating Expenses 30% 35,000

8. NET OPERATING INCOME 80,000 (Cap rate of 8%)

**TAXABLE INCOME**

9. Net Operating Income 80,000
10. Less Interest Payments (Assume $60,000 of $66,600) 60,000
11. Less Depreciation (Land at $300,000; Improvements at 39 years) 18,000
12. Taxable Income 2,000 ($80,000- $60,000- $18,000)

**SPENDABLE INCOME**

13. Net Operating Income 80,000
14. Less Principal and Interest Payments 66,000
15. GROSS SPENDABLE 14,000
16. Less Income Tax (Use 30% (Fed & State) x $2,000 Taxable Income) 600
17. Less Capital Improvements (None used)
18. NET SPENDABLE ANNUALLY 13,400
19. Per Month 1,120 (Rounded)

**EQUITY INCOME**

20. Net Operating Income 80,000
21. Less Interest on Loans 60,000
22. Less Income Tax 600
23. NET EQUITY INCOME 19,400
24. Net Equity Income Rate ($19,400/$250,000) 7.8% (Rounded)
25. Plus Equity Growth Rate 4.0 (Estimated)
26. Total Equity Rate 11.8%

Pretty straight forward, eh? Of course that begs the issue that you have been done your homework and are reasonably accurate with net income.

The "fun" part is the equity growth rate. I know that real estate has once again surfaced as a great investment, but I caution you not to get overly aggressive with the appreciation. Further, real estate also suffers significant cycles and a high rate of return is not suggested. (I wrote that after 2000 and it is obvious that no one bothered to use caution. Sticking in 20% annual appreciation can make anything look great.)

So, is that it? Can you take the 11.8% and compare it against the stock market and make your decision. Nope. As stated above, real estate is an illiquid asset whereas stock can be liquidated with a phone call. There is therefore a significant risk due to illiquidity that must be adjusted into the equation for total equity rate. The problem is that there is no universal number that one would use to delineate such risk. In my experience with clients in all areas of the nation, getting stuck with a piece of real estate at the wrong economic times is worth at least a 3% to 6% reduction. Let's assume I use 4% so that the return is now 7.8%. Does that compare favorably to the stock market's return over the last 50 years which has been about 10%. But let's not forget that the future returns, according to many analysts, may be no greater than 6% to 8%.

By the time you enter all this in to the computations, the equity growth rate is zero at best and the liquidity factor is 10% or more and therefore makes the ownership of just a simple piece of real estate very problematic. But my point was that this analysis was not done by consumers prior to the huge run up in prices. If so a lot of problems could have been avoided. However, it is always easier to look in hindsight.

Unfortunately that's not all. I have not addressed the emotional strain of dealing with tenants. Some people can handle it. I could not. I had no interest in deadbeat tenants- and no matter how careful you are, you are apt to run into these. Secondly, if you tried to do your own management, you must make the time and commitment. If you can handle a call at 9pm on a Saturday night that someone's kid had just flushed their pet moose down the toilet, go for it.

In short, real estate ownership has been a major fixture of wealth in the United States. However I am addressing ownership of properties for the middle class consumer that entails more personal involvement and emotion than the institutional properties with professional management. Sure it can work, but do the numbers above for comparison and then include the various risk factors I identified.

Given all that, you simply do not put that much in illiquid investments to begin with. Probably no more than 20% in a proper allocation.

# 31

# Men Versus Women

There have been a number of studies regarding the difference in the ability of investing between men and women. Here is one from 2011:

Twenty-five percent of women reported feeling confident with how their investments were allocated compared with 42% of men. Significant here is a huge difference in women's and men's general knowledge of stocks, bonds and mutual funds: 64% and 84%, respectively.

Sixty-three percent of women said they had a handle on their cash flow versus 80% of men.

The smallest gap appeared in retirement preparedness, but both women and men are woefully unprepared, the report said. Only 12% of women and 19% of men were confident they would be able to replace 80% of their income in retirement.

Even so, women may be investing too conservatively to meet their income needs in retirement, according to the report.

So there you have it statistically. Women are poor investors as compared to men, are too emotional, don't know what they are doing and cannot do math very good at all. They need additional help with investing versus men and should turn over a lot of their funds to their husbands

What a crock!

I told you statistics can be deceiving. And you can make up any insight with numbers. The difference in my focus is that I have dealt with, obviously, both men and women in all areas of planning. If I had my druthers, I would always pick an intelligent woman over an intelligent man. Why? Some will know this- more will now.

It is the male ego. Far too many men effectively state they "read a magazine once and they know where a book is". They know all about investing and will say as much on a survey. They are far too quick in making assumptions based on limited knowledge and do not ask the probing and necessary questions about an adviser and what they are doing and why. (Men are more aggressive however and will pick more aggressive strategies- hence greater returns overall in most situations. But they also face the greatest losses as well since to sell losing positions clearly impacts their ego.)

I am not saying that women are inherently more knowledgeable to begin with with investing since they are not taught anything more useful than men during their lifetime (stock market game for instance). But given the opportunity with a good adviser, they will more readily admit to their lack of understanding about a subject matter so that the adviser need take more time to explain what is going on. Men brokers don't necessarily like that and may/do short shrift to women in the process. (To be fair, neither a male nor female adviser has been taught the fundamentals so a lot of gibberish is spewed out by both.)

When you look at the numbers above, the number of women feeling comfortable would be less than men because simple experience with both clearly shows that men have a superior attitude to their competency and would invariably note a higher confidence. The idea that 64% or 85% or whatever % stated has a decent knowledge base on stocks and mutual funds is belied by the formal professional studies which show the true lack of knowledge. No matter, nary anyone has a clue to the correct definition of diversification so that pretty much ends the discussion.

It is true, and should be obvious from my comments, that women will take more time to work with because they do ask the necessary questions (when given the chance and they feel comfortable. Admittedly society has 'trained' them to be subservient and quiet in many situations.) But why is asking lots of questions a problem? That is what is supposed to happen- lots of questions about the entire process. If the adviser is explaining the risk and return elements properly, there should always be many questions and the necessity to fill in the blanks.

There are more women getting college degrees then men now. They are the ones that will be making the money. They are the ones, that at some point in time, will be the decisionmakers in our society (unless men blow up the world in the interim). They will be asking more and more questions that require more and more insight from responders- and far less ego.

It will not happen overnight. But in the meantime, recognize that women will end up with most of the wealth anyway since the bulk of men will die before they do. (Married men live longer than single men. But married men are more willing to die.) And once the women wake up to the fact that they can demand background and competency, the financial industry *as fiduciaries* will have to do a lot more homework with them than merely presenting superficial commentary.

# 32

# Uniform Prudent Investor Act

It was not my intent in writing this text to address the shortcomings of the UPIA but real lie displays itself once again.

Over the quarter century from the late **1960's** the investment practices of fiduciaries experienced significant change. **The Uniform Prudent Investor Act (UPIA) undertakes to update trust investment law in recognition of the alterations that have occurred in investment practice.** These changes have occurred under the influence of a large and broadly accepted body of empirical and theoretical knowledge about the behavior of capital markets, often described as "**modern portfolio theory.**"

This Act draws upon the revised standards for prudent trust investment promulgated by the American Law Institute in its Restatement (Third) of Trusts: Prudent Investor Rule (**1992**) [hereinafter Restatement of Trusts 3d: Prudent Investor Rule; also referred to as **1992**

Restatement].

EFM- It is interesting to note in the first sentence that it refers to the late 1960's and the need to update the UPIA. The need is even more necessary now due to the massive changes since 1995 that have obliterated or extensively revised the basis on which the UPIA was formed. For example, MPT refers to a mathematical formula of using asset allocation in selecting combined assets that have a overall lower risk than any individual asset. It also assumes that investors are rational and efficient. And it assumes a nice smooth risk scenario blah, blah. Since that does not exist, the UPIA needs an update. But more necessary is not simply the words, but the people that can act on it. Whether a trustee, broker or otherwise, the mere reflection on MPT in no way demonstrates that a practitioner would have been able to understand the nuances of the original MPT nor certainly any of the necessary changes after 1992. Not if they do not understand diversification (and they don't).

Case law does not define suitability, prudent or fiduciary. The industry does not define suitability. The government does not define suitability. They/it cannot simply because the participants do not know and have not bothered to learn the fundamentals of investing. A very harsh statement- but then no one has effectively ever critically examined the Stock Market Game, so..............

**Literature**. These changes in trust investment law have been presaged in an extensive body of practical and scholarly writing. See especially the discussion and reporter's notes by Edward C. Halbach, Jr., in Restatement of Trusts 3d: Prudent Investor Rule (**1992**); see also Edward C. Halbach, Jr., Trust Investment Law in the Third Restatement, 27 Real Property, Probate & Trust J. 407 (**1992**); Bevis Longstreth, Modern Investment Management and the Prudent Man Rule (**1986**); Jeffrey N. Gordon, The Puzzling Persistence of the Constrained Prudent Man Rule, 62 N.Y.U.L. Rev. 52 (**1987**); John H. Langbein & Richard

A. Posner, The Revolution in Trust Investment Law, 62 A.B.A.J. 887 (**1976**); Note, The Regulation of Risky Investments, 83 Harvard L. Rev. 603 (**1970**). A succinct account of the main findings of modern portfolio theory, written for lawyers, is Jonathan R. Macey, An Introduction to Modern Financial Theory (**1991**) (American College of Trust & Estate Counsel Foundation). A leading introductory text on modern portfolio theory is R.A. Brealey, An Introduction to Risk and Return from Common Stocks (2d ed. **1983**).

EFM- The reason I included the above paragraph- look at the dates. Up to 40 years old. The regulation of risky investments was written for lawyers starting in 1970. The latest is 1992. No one or litigation trying to relate 2011 to 1992 or earlier is living in the real world.

**Objectives of the Act.** UPIA makes five fundamental alterations in the former criteria for prudent investing. All are to be found in the Restatement of Trusts 3d: Prudent Investor Rule.

(1) The standard of prudence is applied to any investment as part of the total portfolio, rather than to individual investments. In the trust setting the term "portfolio" embraces all the trust's assets. UPIA §
2(b).

EFM- the words are nice but how is this supposed to be done. You cannot do it without an understanding of correlation and standard deviation et al.

(2) The tradeoff in all investing between risk and return is identified as the fiduciary's central consideration. UPIA § 2(b).

EFM- Define risk.

(3) All categoric restrictions on types of investments have been abrogated; the trustee can invest in anything that plays an appropriate role in achieving the risk/return objectives of the trust and that meets the other requirements of prudent investing. UPIA § 2(e).

(4) EFM- I repeat- define risk. If that cannot be defined by a number- and a trustee is universally clueless- then this is just another bunch of words. Also, what are the other requirements? I need to know what they are in order to comment. If they are not defined- and they are not- then just how are cases litigated?

(5) The long familiar requirement that fiduciaries diversify their investments has been integrated into the definition of prudent investing. UPIA § 3.

EFM- Define diversification. It first has to be done by the numbers for singular securities. Asset Allocation is what is used for a integrated portfolio. One has to know the difference between diversification and asset allocation in order to get this right.

Diversification is defined by how many stocks must you have in a portfolio in order to insulate it due to unsystematic risk.

6. The much criticized former rule of trust law forbidding the trustee to delegate investment and management functions has been reversed. Delegation is now permitted, subject to safeguards. UPIA § 9.-

EFM: Delegate to whom and how? This is all left up to esoteric rulings by litigants with nil knowledge to either application.

A comment from an adviser notes that " Basically, the Uniform Prudent Investor Act stipulates that your investment activities follow the Modern Portfolio Theory five step process in which procedurally prudent judgments replace intuition and/or emotional decisions influenced by market noise, press appointed investment gurus, or product peddlers. Here is a five-step outline that you can follow to make certain that you are on the right side of the law and prudence:"

1. ANALYZE THE CURRENT SITUATION through a documentable, due diligence process.

Identify specific investment objectives, such as

producing a specified monthly income, producing a total rate of return that exceeds taxes and inflation by a specified amount, or constraining downside risk to a certain level, etc. Then, measure the probability of their achievement, given current circumstances (assets held, strategy being employed, taxes, inflation, disbursements, etc.)

EFM- obviously a due diligence process is correct. But how one can pick a flat total rate of return is bothersome (though constant monitoring is recognized below). I absolutely have a problem with 'risk' however. No fiduciary can pick a number for return without also identifying a number for risk- which is the risk of loss. The real problem is that the entity doing this is almost assuredly clueless to how to constrain downside risk (where is that taught?) or probability of achievement? Where in the world will that come from? A Ouija board? An algorithm by a Nobel Laureate from Long Term Capital?

2. DESIGN AN OPTIMAL PORTFOLIO through a documentable, due diligence process. Consider appropriate risk parameters, the types of investments already owned or available, the time horizon of the portfolio, and income or return objectives. Given all of these factors, determine the asset mix (combination of investments) which will either minimize risk at the desired rate of return, or maximize return at the desired level of risk.

EFM- Once again I address risk. If one uses past history, the longer the horizon the greater the odds of having stocks outperform bonds and provide an acceptable return. Current philosophy points to about a 20 year period will be necessary to provide that possibility. I have no way of knowing whether that is true or not. But relying on past numbers from an economy while I am currently looking at a bunch of stupid politicians playing games with the deficit increase leads me to believe that the future may be mired in colossal arrogance, higher volatility and more recessions. Certainly lower returns overall.

More importantly, the longer the time horizon, the greater the risk of loss. No matter, a substantial loss is possible right now. Is it the inference that it is possible to design a portfolio that can anticipate that loss and offset it? Nice words with no application at all.

Correlation is the major focus you look to to determine probability allocations. But there is no way that you can really know if they are true. Worse yet, they can all change at a whim. And even worse than that, correlations all move to one when a dire economic period exists. It is absolutely fluid. You do not start with return first- you start with the risk exposure you can deal with for two methods- no one watching (so why bother hiring them?) and with an experienced and knowledgeable adviser with the insight towards real life economics.

3. DRAFT A BLUEPRINT which will enable you and your team to "stay the course," amidst the financial ups and downs that constantly surround us. A simple statement of objectives, desired investment mix, procedure for rebalancing the assets, and the delegation of duties among consultants, money managers, custodians and other parties to the process will also serve to promote continuity when overall responsibility passes to a new trustee, or to the next generation. Such a document is referred to as an "Investment Policy Statement." Along with minutes or memoranda of meetings and discussions, it forms the basis for any defense of your investment decisions in court.

EFM- Staying the course, the market always comes back, simplistic rebalancing et al are the reasons trillions of dollars have been lost this past decade and will be the reason for even more losses as this type of hackneyed tripe is heaved onto more unsuspecting investors- certainly those with 401ks. The Investment Policy Statement might still work in court- probably for many years- until the industry ramps up its real life knowledge. I’d like to think the Dodd Frank bill can make a difference but since none of the entities involved have even addressed knowledge, the UPIA may allow decades more absurdity.

4. HIRE PROFESSIONALS to help you design, implement, and monitor this process. Find investment counsel who specializes in prudent investing. Favor money managers and mutual funds who specialize in one particular asset class and style of investing. You will have greater flexibility and control; and evaluating their performance will be easier and more accurate. It is also advisable to separate service providers into distinct functions. Rather than simply hiring one firm to hold the assets, advise you on how to invest them, and execute the necessary transactions, try to hire the best firm to perform each of these functions independently. In this way, you can document that you have performed your due diligence, which includes avoiding unnecessarily high management, custodial, and brokerage expenses, as well as unwarranted taxes.

EFM- Sounds nice in many parts. But I am still not sure the fiduciary has the insight to do much of relevance while touting the absolutes of MPT, staying the course and not addressing the risk of loss. Finding 'investment counsel that specialize in prudent investing' is terribly absent in specifics. Hiring those that lost their clients hundreds of thousands of retirement dollars seems a folly indeed. Yet what can one do? No new knowledge is being provided and none is on the books.

True that the documentation may indicate an effort was made. But since the term "professional" is not defined (monikers, Assets Under Management, best golf score?) I have no idea how this could be corroborated in court properly.

5. MONITOR AND SUPERVISE all components of the process on an ongoing basis. A thorough evaluation generally requires skills and resources beyond the means of

the layperson. It must address not only performance, but precisely how that performance was achieved, i.e. good/bad management, luck, or exposure to appropriate/inappropriate risk. Periodically (generally quarterly), you will need to rebalance the portfolio to compensate for disparate rates of return among different investments. At least annually, you should analyze your progress to make certain the portfolio is still on target toward its stated objectives.

EFM- Nice words once again. The review is beyond the layperson. Problem is, it is beyond most fiduciaries as well- certainly those living with the past as their main- if not only- guide to the future. And while I understand that the attitude regarding returns prevails in the industry, it is the risk first and foremost that determines what is adjusted.

This is going to be most interesting in the court system since none of anyone will have a clue to what is necessary to be changed. Probably most will be very, very resistant to change.

# 33

# Insurance and Annuity Overview

According to the NAIC, 62% of life insurance policyholders don't know what they own or how it works. Personally, I think the percentage is low.

From “Life Insurance”, by Black and Skipper, "Despite the widespread belief in the need for life and health insurance, and its vital importance to those who purchase it, few persons attempt to become familiar with the management, business policy and practices of the insurers backing their contracts. Even assuming that a considerable portion of policyowners could be induced to take an interest in the condition of their insurers, few would be sufficiently knowledgeable about insurance matters to ascertain intelligently the true state of affairs" and, "A competent, informed, trust worthy insurance adviser is perhaps the consumers best insurance against making and unwise purchase decision. Regrettably, some agents and other insurance advisers, although well-intentioned, simply are not well-informed. Too often, a state agent's licensing examination is not sufficiently rigorous to disqualify those with the inadequate knowledge. Additionally, in most states, many persons who give advice about life insurance are not required by the state to demonstrate any level of professional competence in life insurance matters. The use of an unqualified adviser can result in any inadequate, poorly designed, or unnecessarily costly insurance program."

And also from the National Underwriter, Blazzard, JD, Hasenauer JD 2002, "Given that the subject of life insurance is rarely taught in law schools or accounting courses, most lawyers and accountants know little more about insurance than does the general public. When asked by their clients to advice on insurance, then, it is often easier to discourage their purchase than to expose the fact that they are truly ignorant about life insurance and how it works. Even the training that is available on these subjects may be inadequate to provide a level of comfort that lawyers or accountants need in order to recommend a purchase. As things now stand, we know of no reference material that is currently available that would enable an insurance professional or lawyer or accountant to access the technical information that applies to these new insurance products."

Though these comments may be from over a decade ago, the situation is now even worse with all the new product types. This is a 8/2011 commentary from a survey by Saybrus Partners, “The survey affirmed statistically what we have heard anecdotally for years -- financial advisors often do not discuss life insurance during the financial planning process. They are missing an opportunity to fill a critical gap in some existing financial plans while at the same time differentiating themselves and expanding their practices. Additionally, there are benefits to including assets such as life insurance that are not tied to the financial markets and therefore not subject to the same volatility we are currently seeing.

"According to the study, **47%** of U.S. adults who have a financial advisor and have life insurance said their **advisors have never reviewed their existing life insurance policy** with them. In addition, 34% of U.S. adults who have a financial advisor and a financial plan said that over the last two years, their advisor has recommended that they add some form of insurance to their financial plan. But only 24% were advised to include life insurance specifically, while **just 10% said their advisor had recommended long-term care insurance.**

"Life insurance can be complex, and many advisors are reluctant to introduce it into the financial planning conversation. However, some of these financial professionals are finding that they can use outside specialists to help them advise their clients on the most effective and efficient life insurance uses for each unique portfolio."

(One can now introduce annuities into the paragraph as well. They are at least as difficult to understand.)

However, I do disagree with 'outside specialists' as used in their comments. Specialists like Maczuga and Flagg are not doing planning per se. They do a specific job for life insurance. But they cannot do the planning for long term care, annuities and more- that is the job of the financial planner/consultant/adviser or whatever. Pundits and the industry will continue to rail at this requirement by maintaining that the job of a planner is to simply refer to others with more expertise- they are the finance gatekeepers and that is all.

**Wrong**

A planner cannot refer a client in need to an investment hack that is 20 years behind the time and uses a $500 or $5,000 piece of software that treats everyone the same. And they certainly cannot refer insurance and annuities over to licensees who are focused on commissions. Remember, I am talking about a fiduciary level of knowledge and competency. And I will repeat again- literally anyone dealing with a fiduciary level of money for middle Americans must have the capability of a personal financial calculator. I will never accept anything to the contrary. Insurance and annuities absolutely demand that capability. Being a realist, I know it won't happen. Such requirement would deaden the industry, sales of 'stuff' would plummet and a lot of people would leave the business. Maybe just like we will finally do to a lot of politicians. Sometimes you just have suck it up and start over.

## Insurance Overview

Let me address some legal elements first: insurance should generally only be placed on an individual where the beneficiaries are financially dependent on them. Some of these are identified in the individual sections but the obvious should be the coverage for a family breadwinner. He/she is responsible for the family's financial lifetime in case of death. The financial responsibility is the key.

There are other valid uses for businesses with key man insurance, gifting for charities, estate purposes and more.

But here is one where I have changed my focus over time. That is putting insurance on children. The parents are not financially dependent on them, so what is the need? There are some agents that say some coverage is necessary for a funeral in case the child dies. I do not find that valid, but this is: due to the continuing poor health, diabetes or other afflictions of parents potentially being transferred to the children, life insurance might be valid so that, should such illness occur, the now older children will have coverage on their lives. Otherwise they might not be able to get anything- or at an extreme price. Not the norm I admit and it is certainly not to suggest something unneeded, but the more I read about full diabetes showing up on young people, well……

The necessary point here is to state that putting insurance on just 'anyone' is not allowed. It would be against public policy. Imagine putting $5,000,000 of insurance on a stranger and then arranging his termination. There has to be a legitimate reason for coverage- though certain activities in the last few years has lowered the level of care. (see life settlements and STOLI- stranger owned life insurance.) Unfortunately, though not necessarily unexpected- regulators were slow to step in and a lot of damage was done to buyers and sellers of policies. If Dodd Frank is to do any good, it has to find entities that can react much faster to blatant violations of ethics and legal maneuverings. Once again, probably wishful thinking but is that not what the bill is about- to demand a high level of expertise and knowledge to consumers?

Most of all, insurance is a useable tool ideally suited for risk reduction. Unfortunately, in my opinion, it has become bastardized into all sorts of concoctions designed more for the sale of a product with 'multiple purposes' that may stretch tax laws until they break. Prior to 1985, it was the norm to put in huge sums into insurance policies so they could grow tax deferred. Insurance coverage was, at least, secondary. Then there were lots of split dollar mixtures for (supposedly) charitable purposes that would allow fully tax deductible premium contributions. Many backed by some esoteric legal validation by an attorney located in Botswana.. Then when investments were added for variable products and indexing for guarantees, it is no wonder that the public is confused as to what will work, when and why. And whether the product offered pays the maximum amount of commission to an agent who is equally confused.

Anyway, in its most simplistic terms, life insurance is leverage. You pay a 'small' premium for a large payoff (though one you do not want anyone to generally claim for a long time.) The pooling of large numbers of people paying into an insurance company kitty allows them to reasonably determine the risks and timing of the death benefits and, after costs, what they can make as a profit. The death benefit paid on early deaths is offset by those that continue to pay into the policy for a very long time and those that terminate (lapse) a policy prior to death. (It is key to remember this term in insurance. Many policies are priced based on an assumed lapse rate the company anticipates. This means that the policyholder terminated the policy prematurely and the company will never be required to pay out the death benefit. Further, the company has received payments for perhaps many years, some of which will remain in the company's coffers as part of their overall profits. But what happens when the lapse rate does not materialize? The best example is long term care policies as defined in the chapter herein. Huge increases in premiums and cessation of business because the anticipated extra dollars would never materialize.)

You only want to buy the highest rated companies from the likes of AM Best and S&P. Nothing less than an A rating. If there are some problems/confusion with one rating, combine with others. But remember that these are financial ratings only and have nothing to do with the real use and application of their various policies/products. The price competitiveness and options/riders vary all over the place and, heretofore, it has been impossible for an agent (or anyone else for that matter) to compare policies side by side. Policy illustrations are not an effective method to do so unless one is viewing only the guaranteed amounts only. Even then there are issues.

Basically the information to do a comparison has never been available save for in the direct filings the companies might make with the state. But nobody compiled them, nevermind had the ability to compare one policy to another. Finally one has with the likes of Barry Flagg (Confidential Policy Evaluator (CPE) Research Reports, http://www.theinsuranceadvisor.com/Confidential-Policy-Evaluator/How-CPE-Works) and Joe Maczuga (Life 180, http://feeadvisorsnetwork.com/p-2438-our-mission-and-overview.html) were capable of getting the information and devising methods of comparing what the policies might do over time (there are others now on the internet as well). That has made the tasks much easier for financial advisers and agents searching for an independent analysis of what the policy may actually do- though it also assumes they will buy these services. With the impetus of some type of fiduciary status, such services should have more of an impact in choosing the right policy.

I have had an insurance license since 1983 and have been a Life and Disability Insurance Analyst for over a decade and can state without hesitation that as an individual I could never accumulate the info nor have the competency to devise the software programs that evaluate the internal machinations. They are not perfect (neither am I) since I have disagreements with how they analyze variable policies. But that aside, they have committed to something that does have direct value to the consumers/agents who need or wish to use certain types of policies.

The focus for these services is primarily with universal policies. Term insurance is pure insurance and effectively nothing else. Whole life is designed with set premiums for life and certain types may come under scrutiny (generally how the interest rates are determined). But the guarantees are in place for a lifetime. Universal life is the question for many agents and consumers. There are a lot of moving parts in such policies and it is necessary to review what the company has done in the past along with current statistics to figure out what might happen in the future. (Is it realistic to assume that cash value policies might average 5% over the next 30 years? 6%, 7%)

Universal variable policies are difficult to decipher since returns are 'controlled' by the owner who can select from a group of mutual funds. Further, the internal expense costs can materially impact the ultimate returns.

Universal index life insurance is the newest of many hybrids and becomes an extremely hard animal to figure out. Some of those issues will be expanded upon in some detail.

No lapse policies are a unique policy in that the internal cash growth is irrelevant. It is guaranteed insurance up to as high as 130.

All these will be addressed in varying detail.

There are two other areas that require separate emphasis. First are the policies that are already in force. Many of these have never been reviewed since inception (note the Saybrus report above. But the statistic of 47% of consumer saying their policies have not been reviewed is not necessarily the defining number. It is whether the other policies that were reviewed were done competently or were an exercise to sell other insurance outright or do a 1035 exchange of the existing one. And were surrender charges involved? (Those numbers are not going to be obtained independently by a service.)

Trust owned policies inside an Irrevocable Life Insurance definitely demand annual review since most have been funded with non guaranteed universal life. But per an article by Mark Teitelbaum, "among professional trustees, fully 83.5% indicated they had no guidelines and procedures for handling trust owned life insurance. For non-professional trustees, 71.2% indicated they had not reviewed their trusts' life insurance policies in the last 5 years. Both groups did not focus closely on handling the subaccounts for variable life. Among professional trustees, 95.3%, had no guidelines for handling the asset allocation components of VL. Among non-professionals, 94.7% indicated they had no procedures in place for the allocation component of VL. Another pair of surveys indicated that anywhere from 70%-95% of all trust owned policies do not have a life insurance agent servicing the contracts.

Secondly, my work is to decipher if the policies- or any policy- should have been utilized in the first place. Even if one used the best policy of its type, it does not mean that a policy should have been sold in the amount, type or circumstance indicated. (There are a few reports I have done that are included in the appendix along with other comments from some arbitrations and law suits where I have acted as an expert.)

**Annuity Overview**

In past decades, annuities were considered to be simple 'investments' for the most conservative. Yes, they were conservative as compared to the volatility of the stock market and real estate. But they were not simple then and they sure aren't now. Two tier annuities were the norm in the 80's' and few consumers had a clue. (The annuity offers one rate that one could get in cash later on and another higher rate where the account can only be annuitized.) They certainly were missold. As we entered the 2000s, there was a proliferation of indexed annuities, guaranteed payouts, bonuses, long surrender charges, minimum returns and many levels of two tier offerings that are next to impossible to keep track of. There is NO service that provides insight (Flagg and Maczuga deal with insurance only). Unless one is a licensed insurance agent who does a lot of research, there is no way to figure out what is going on. Obviously there is some material from the company, but it reflects mostly marketing (what else is new). Further material from the contract provides certain insight, but there is also no way that a life insurance agent per se has the background or training to determine when and how they should be used.

Any fiduciary in this area will have to have many years of experience plus the ability to do a separate critique of each for use.

Those are going to be few and far between.

What is unique in this discussion is that an insurance agent already DOES have a fiduciary duty- but it is to the company, not the consumer. They are required to only submit true applications of the medical conditions of the insured, that there is an insurable interest and the owner can pay the premiums Certainly agents may attempt the reflect upon the right product for the individual/family/business, but the interceding focus on commissions makes the decision suspect. The marketing of annuities strains credulity.

The industry attempts to project and instill a sense of professionalism around the marketing, Nope. Here are a couple instances I ran into. A major insurance firm in San Francisco used captive agents- those that could only use the products of that one company. An agent had a client that had been in Alcoholics Anonymous for several years. She wanted to get him insurance but the odds of going through her company was about very limited. They simply did not have the actuarial background to view this health condition. But the manager demanded she go through the hoops of this firm before he would allow another firm with solid history of underwriting to take this type of risk. The denial was preordained- he was not approved. It took over two months and I am not sure she held the guy as a client. Certainly it was not fair to the client but since some sales quota had to be attempted……….

Here is another one that requires note that very few people have heard of. There are some companies that offer different commissions and interest rates on the same product at the same time. The agent can pick which one he/she likes. Just as an example, assume a 4% annuity with 4% commission. Or the agent could choose a 3% rate and a

5 % commission. Or a 2% rate and a 6% commission. Perfectly. Legal. The client does not have to be informed- it just is the agent's choice. Any statistics on what actually happens? No. Want to guess?. Is it perfectly ethical since it is perfectly legal? Does it fit within fiduciary requirements?

Here is another: Some of the caustic view is from a report that I did where the major insurance company has indicated that they and their agent should be absolved from responsibility for allowing the purchase of a policy where the premium was 75% of the owner's income, fraudulent signatures occurred on at least four occasions, the 30 year 'experienced' agent said he didn't really know how a universal life policy really worked and so on. That simply validates why so many people are uncomfortable with insurance overall.

As a licensee, I am inundated with countless ads via email every single day (hour) with new products (generally annuities) from brokerage firm all offering something with a bonus or whatever coupled around the commissions I can earn. Always the commission. Or how to prospect clients and get $4,000 to $10,000 a month from the comfort of my home. The prospect listing business assures me that they can get seminars filled with 25 of their hot contacts eager to buy and I should be able to close so many and get an average $15,000 of commissions. Maybe more if I can combine an annuity with life insurance that has long term care options or…..

## Knowledge and Regulation

I am primarily familiar with California licensing and it requires classroom instruction. It is far more demanding than other states but the info is past due and there is essentially nothing on real life application to consumers. Policy illustrations are not addressed so the industry takes over in most cases and the agents run rampant with a limited understanding of the potential repercussions. Not all. But far too many. The AIG report enclosed is a fine example of running numbers to entice the commission. Further, if licensees are not well versed in economics, mortality and more (and they are not), even those who try to do the right thing may be clueless to the end result. Insurance agents (and brokers) are not required to use a financial calculator. I see no way one can act as a fiduciary with insurance, annuities, securities and more without being totally conversant with how money works.

Note- I do wish to point out the fallacy of agents never having to review a mortality table in licensing instruction- or generally thereafter. It was amazing that so many people that had been in the business for years had effectively no idea how long someone might live.

And policy illustrations: I know I already addressed this but it is impossible for an agent to sell a policy without a definitive instruction on what they can and cannot with these. It still amazes me after all these years that the primary tool for agents is left untouched in training. And for consumers with non guaranteed insurance- you should get an in force illustration probably every year. It is used to determine how the policy is working, how long it will stay in force under current conditions or under alterations, etc. Great tool for anyone with whole or universal life coverage.

But where does one get info on split dollar and the tax implication thereof? What about charitable gifting? No Lapse insurance is not taught so who is going to inform the consumer? Certainly a solid agent might, but on what basis is that knowledge assumed? Not from a license. Not from general courses. I have seen far too many scenarios where the agents remain in a mindset of the wrong policy for the wrong situation. And it happens since there is little insight to what is supposed to work where and why. Then we have the commissions………..

As far as regulation goes, unless there is a claim of the most egregious nature or the wrong is committed against large numbers where the regulators can hit a home run, don't expect much. Admittedly there is money and staff problems at all state levels. But having dealt extensively with California and Florida regulators, I am left with a bunch of attorneys that just don't understand how life insurance and annuities are supposed to work. Even when presented with the whole case.... Nothing. Or maybe they don't care.

Enough. The knowledge of the proper real life application is truly abysmal. Insurance agents need to become full fiduciaries. Period. Dodd Frank does not state that but any agent remotely referring that they are financial or retirement 'whatevers' will be held to the higher level of expertise and responsibility. If they wish the lower level of responsibility, then merely indicate they are a life insurance agent ONLY. No monikers implying anything else.

Consumers really do not know how much they are being taken advantage of but they do have a reason for contempt.

# 34

# Term Insurance

This should be a relatively short discussion. But lost in the general identification of this insurance are a few items that are not readily apparent.

Term insurance is chosen for a set period of time. Once that period of time elapses, there is no more coverage. It is, obviously, not designed for any cash buildup or to do anything beyond what is necessary and called for- pure risk coverage.

## Cost

Term is the cheapest policy you can buy (I am not going to do a PV of whole life etc.- just addressing out of pocket). Admittedly there are differences between carriers but you only use companies with the highest financial ratings. That may eliminate the cheapest overall but anything under an AM Best rating of A is simply not worth consideration.

For this exercise, assume you went on the internet and chose one of the firms displayed both for 'ease' and to avoid an agent. Can you get the best price? Possibly if you are of the best of health and usually young- I will say under 30. But if you have had a problem- diabetes, obesity, high blood pressure, etc.- be aware that the internet service you are using may initially look easy and cheap, but the service could backfire.

Once you need more specialized coverage, other than the cheapest company almost assuredly will need to be contacted. Will the internet agents do this for you? Debatable- and that assumes that you would know anyway. My point is that if you were denied by such companies, you may have wasted time to get coverage no matter the price.

On the other hand, an 'experienced' agent would know what companies offer the specialized coverage for the condition acknowledged. In other words, the underwriters for certain companies are very experienced in certain conditions- ex alcoholics, heart bypass for example- and can not only hurry the process along, but offer better rates than other non specified companies that might actually decline the risk.

The problem for most consumers is 'who is a good experienced agent'. The second question- tacky though it may be- is will they attempt to continue to get the term insurance or will they possibly steer a consumer over to the more expensive policies. I wish I knew the answer but this is always in the back of the agent's mind. Term insurance is going to be "cheap' and the commissions 'cheap' as well. If a policy cost $800, that might be the size of the commission. And that might translate into 5 to 15 hours of agent time depending on what is needed to be done. And that is only if the transaction actually goes through. In fairness to the agent, it might simply not be worthwhile to spend that many hours on a potentially fruitless endeavor. Personally I won't do it unless it is part of other work under contract with a client. I did it when I was younger and needed experience but the value per hour spent makes it unrealistic later on.

I have had a man not provide info about a malady and I went and spent the time to get him a policy. He was declined because he lied about his past history. The odds of getting coverage at that point was limited and frankly I did not want to bother spending any more time with him. Another young woman was obese and said she was 270 pounds. When the paramed weighed her later for the physical, she was 320 pounds and put her far above the limits for the company's ratings. (I think she ate the paramed.) And so on. Agents do spend a lot of time on accounts that never pan out and while a new client could care less, it simply is part of the insurance business. You ARE apt to get steered to a higher price policy because ‘that is where the money is’. No matter how the industry may rationalize life insurance transactions, the commissions will remain in the backs of the minds of both parties. Let’s face it, a $10,000 commission with universal life is a far better steak than $800 for Term.

**Annual Renewal Term (ART)**

Assume you wanted the very cheapest insurance for a one year period. That is ART. Very simple to understand. However, were you to attempt to extend this insurance, the prices keep going up and up and UP each year due to the older age. It can start to get very expensive over a relatively short period of time. Some consumers and agents have tried to ‘play a game’ in getting brand new coverage each year to keep prices at the very minimum. That type of activity is not only frowned upon, it violates the duty owed by an agent to provide a policy the company can rely upon for the future to recoup its costs (mainly the commissions) and to make a profit. Further, it can backfire to the point of absurdity. If risk coverage at an acceptable rate is desired, consider that if the insured should become incapacitated due to disease or injury, they could be denied coverage altogether thereby ruining any attempt at longer coverage. And they will be stuck with a policy that really becomes very expensive after just a few years. ART is cheap and can provide acceptable coverage for generally only the shortest periods of time.

## Extended Term coverage/Level term

This type of policy covers a myriad of risk exposures for set periods of time. It is simple and direct (some commentaries later) but involves the ability to get flat rates on insurance over periods of 5, 10, 20, 30 years or even longer. You pay the same amount each and every year. At the end of the period, there is no more coverage. Certainly one can extend term coverage at that time but the age and health condition may invalidate continuance because of the very high costs. But with proper planning, they can cover risks at a very acceptable rate for a set period of time.

## Need for coverage:

The most obvious need is a young married couple raising a family. The breadwinner should cover for at least 18 years of age for the children. One can also add in college costs- which is a healthy addition of coverage- mortgage costs and more.

Insurance maybe/is viable for the non working spouse since the costs of rearing the children would increase upon death for the survivor.

Others may want coverage till retirement when there will be, supposedly, enough funds to cover all contingencies thereafter till death of a surviving spouse.

A term policy may fit certain business needs due to limited cash flow now but with greater funds for more permanent coverage later (caveats apply).

There are lots of scenarios for consideration but the main point with pure insurance is that there are no extra funds going into the policy for anything but coverage. And once the term is over, supposedly the risk is over as well and nothing more need be done. Pundits will note that you never get back anything for the years you paid. And the point is what? Pure insurance is something you do NOT want to use. You do not want a fire, you do not want to be in the hospital, you do not want an auto accident, you do not want to die. Hence it is simply a 'cost of living' that provides a lot of emotional comfort should a problem befall them.

**Term with return of premium**

There are term policies that will return your premium at the end of the period. Worthwhile? Generally a rider where one pays extra into the policy over time with the funds earning an interest rate that accrues to provide the necessary monies later on. It may be viable for some situations but if the essence is to buy cheap insurance, then just buy straight term and avoid the extra costs.

**Term with a conversion**

Term policies do have riders where one can convert to a permanent type of insurance later on without evidence of insurability. While I might have dismissed this in the past, there is a definite reason for its use. Assume you had a 15 year level term. During the last years, you become ill and have a much shorter life span. The convertability can allow you to 'upgrade' to a universal life policy without any issue of insurability (Not all policies allow conversion for the entire period- some only allow it within the first year. Convertability may be allowed after that but require new insurability. Don't bother with those.) Now you have insurance coverage that can provide additional coverage as needed. Here is a key element however- you do not get to choose which policy within the company you may want to convert to. They generally have only certain policies where they will allow conversion so you need to review to see if you can afford the policy first and foremost. If too expensive, try to lower the coverage if you need to keep something going (lower coverage, lower price).

There is another reason for convertability- one that has only really developed in the last decade. In this case, we will assume that a company had purchased a 5,000,000 term policy that was to terminate at the officer's age 65. The company got what they wanted- cheap insurance- and that is the end of that. However, and as addressed later- there are life settlements- the purchase of a policy from the owner for cash and where they buyers get the proceeds upon death. Admittedly at age 65, the insured is considered too young for a settlement since there is too many actuarial years before the insured may die (see chapter 26 for male age 65 and note there is approximately 18 years to live. Add a 5 year fudge factor and it means 23 years before the "average" 65 year old may die). But assume the officer has become quite ill- or the age is 75 or............ The point being that instead of terminating the policy and walking away, it may be possible to convert the policy and sell it for a life settlement.. But when you read the Saybus report in chapter 32 where only 47% clients had had their current life policy reviewed, it suggests a real breach of duty for many older insureds. Never terminate a life insurance policy for either the elderly or the infirmed without full consideration of the alternatives.

Never.

# 35

# Whole life and No Lapse Insurance

Whole life insurance is viable where one 'intends' or needs such insurance for their entire lives. It has no time limit per se for premium payments though most older policies will endow at age 100 (depends on company, how old the policy is, etc.) which means they will pay off the full value at that time. Newer whole life policies may continue till age 130 though most premiums would cease by at least age 100.

The purchaser pays a (generally) set premium each and every year for life and is guaranteed by the insurance company that the policy will not lapse (terminate).

But the real issue with whole life is that one pays 'extra' into the policy so that the excess in early years not only covers the higher actuarial insurance costs as one gets older, but there is extra cash in the policy that can grow at 'some' rate. It is not the intent to provide details of the various types but to establish whether the cash value buildup is a viable way of saving money. (For some independent commentary on whole life types, see this link to New York State Insurance Department- http://www.ins.state.ny.us/que top10/que_life_who.htm )

Policy Needs

Let's address what the policy is needed for. Well, it says for your whole life. If you do not need a policy for your whole life, don't buy this- buy level term. Much cheaper and you can purchase it, at least in your early years, for coverage lasting 30 years. Sometimes more.

If you need insurance for your whole life- notice I just said *insurance*- buy a no lapse policy (described later). It is just insurance- like term. There is a cash value but it is effectively irrelevant to the purchase. However, the cash value is a major issue with standard whole life.

In the earlier years of insurance, the cash value was instituted to at least give something back to owners if they canceled or lapsed their policies. Then it became a fait compli to build up cash for some other purpose- retirement, college expenses vacations, etc. Prior to the 1980's the return was 'acceptable' given the yields of that period. But once interest rates went through the roof in the early 80s (Volcker), the lackluster returns on insurance was no match for rates above 10%. So there was disintermediation- funds coming out of one area with low rates and going into another at much higher rates. It happened to banks and it happened to life insurance products. As a result, insurance companies had to come up with something (supposedly) better. That was universal life to be discussed subsequently.

But once rates came down (1990/2000) the magic of universal life waned and whole life came back into use. Universal life required additional payments if it did not work as expected as illustrated (notice again the focus on illustrations.). Whole life just demands that you pay the insurance premiums. As long as you do, you have insurance .

The main reason that whole life is sold is, tacky though it may be, the commissions. They can be as much as the first year's premium- which obviously is a lot more than that for term and universal policies. The reason presented to the public is generally the internal buildup of cash value for use later on. There are times when extra cash may be needed and you can borrow from the policy. But if you borrow a too much, there will potentially not be enough funds in the policy left to maintain the policy since the company is charging you interest on the loan you took out. So if you do not have extra money to put back into the policy (and you apparently don't since that is why you took out a loan), then the policy might lapse/terminate. Now you have some of your cash back and you have no insurance (and may no longer be able to qualify for term). Is that what you wanted to do?

(This discussion can include dividends, graduated premiums, paid up insurance and a host of other interweaving issues. But I am trying to keep this review directed at the salient points).

I will repeat the statement. Why are you buying the insurance? Whole life is not pure insurance- though never addressed that way. It is a mixture of insurance plus extra 'unneeded' cash that grows with the idea there will be a internal cash kitty available at a later date.

It is true that if the interest grows at a good rate and dividends are high, the cash value *might* become fairly large later on. If the kitty is large enough, perhaps the interest earned is enough to make the next premium payment and the next and the next.... This tends to be called 'vanishing premium'- but it is a misnomer. The premium payments never cease- they are either paid by the owner of the policy or the cash inside the policy. The difficulty is that interest rates have gone down and insurance companies are not paying the dividends as they had in the past (dividends are not guaranteed.) However, whole life and universal life have certain guarantees- such as the lowest interest rates they will pay irrespective of what happens in the marketplace later on. Those purchasing policies many years ago may/will find these returns much higher than those offered on current policies.

A lot of people do not understand what insurance they are really buying until later on when they may do a little investigation. Generally, that involves noticing that they may not be able to afford the premiums. Certainly if they find out how low a term policy could have cost. Or they needed the cash in the policy *now even though they had to pay a surrender charge.* About half of the people who purchase these policies cash them in within five years. That says volumes about the understanding of what they bought by agents who probably just sold them something for the commission.

Illustrations and Policy illustrations are tables of numbers showing how your policy can act under various conditions going forward. That's the thought anyway. You can look at the non guaranteed elements of an illustration (and most consumer eyes are directed to it) but it is the guaranteed portion that people should tend to focus on- assuming they have a clue to what is contained in the numbers.

Actually, hardly anyone does- hence the material by the likes of Maczuga or Flagg that become important. But the bottom line is even if you did find a good policy- what are you trying to accomplish? And here is a perfect example of the defects of state departments of insurance, internet sites ad infinitum, agents and more. If you did look at the New York insurance department's commentary, they note that whole life is a fine policy to use for estate purposes. Maybe- but that was a long time ago. Maybe 15 years ago. Kind of out of date, don't you think? And therein is an easy comment on why insurance is so mind numbing. Regulators are out of date and out of knowledge. (See no lapse herein)

Insurance is really leverage

The true idea behind insurance is that you are putting in, say, $1.00 into a life policy and perhaps gets 10 times that amount in insurance coverage. Or $10,000 gets a $100,000 policy (numbers are just as an example). That is why it can be great for estate tax purposes since the taxes are not being paid $1 for $1 but perhaps $.25 on the dollar (but the longer one pays into a policy, the lower the ultimate return/leverage.)

But since estate taxes are not being levied on the average citizen, here is how it can be used for 'general' purposes. Assume an elderly person in decent health wants to leave monies to someone. The amount is currently $10,000. He has no need for the money at all to fund any of his retirement. He can use a CD or annuity. He dies in 15 years. At a 3% return, the value is now is $23,370. The beneficiaries will get the annuity but any amount above the initial $10,000 is *taxable*. On the other hand, he buys a paid up policy that might have a death benefit of $50,000- even $35,000. When he dies the beneficiaries get it all *without* tax.

If a planner or insurance agent is confronted with this scenario, the fiduciary duty would be to use the life insurance. Admittedly some seniors dislike the idea since an annuity keeps on growing while they are ALIVE while life insurance refers to DYING. Some do not want to go through more testing and all the forms. Two issues come to mind. First it is possible to get insurance without a formal underwriting. The benefits are limited but it bears looking into. The second issue is if the elderly refuses to hear anything about life insurance, just document as possible the conversation you have had with them and maintain any correspondence. There may never be a problem with the insured, but depending on the circumstances, there could be a problem with the beneficiaries if they perceive that poor planning was done. Actually that they may have lost out on tens of thousands of dollars.

Let's take a different focus on the wealthy that will have estate taxes to pay. (I have absolutely no idea what Congress will ultimately do regarding the lifetime exemption for estates. I had expected something like $2,500,000 to $3,000,000 this past year but the politics over all financial items has become excruciatingly perverse. Sorry- I meant stupid.) Anyway, assume a family will have a 10,000,000 of estimated estate taxes to pay. It can be paid with cash- obviously no leverage. It can be paid with a $10,000,000 life insurance policy. But if that policy is not initially put into an Irrevocable Life Insurance Trust, the $10,000,000 death benefit will be added to the insured assets and be taxed along with everything else. I will round this tax to another $5,000,000. It is illogical to do that since now the tax now owed is $15,000,000. In the alternative, one would establish an Irrevocable Life Insurance trust that would end up purchasing the $10,000,000. Upon death, it remains outside of the estate.

This technique is not unique or untested. But the problem that I found for well over a decade is that none of the legal texts mentioned anything about the type of insurance to use- or the ones to avoid. They did mention life insurance inside of an ILIT, but that was the extent. Without a definitive direction, all sorts of stuff was put in- primarily cash value insurance. (It simply reinforces the issue that attorneys may know the legal ramifications of estate taxes and trusts but are simply not conversant with insurance. That is not meant as a derogatory statement- just a fact. But since the agents used are not very astute either, you have an open door to a mess.) I do have a comment that attorneys, judges et al will not like. That's if they refer clients to insurance agents or securities brokers without determining the viability of the referred. Simply because they know someone at church or the golf course doesn't cut it. Such referrals could come back to haunt them. And it does not adhere to a fiduciary duty.

Accepting the original premise of just buying 'insurance' therefore, the use of cash value policies is not necessarily prudent. There were some low cost whole life policies in the past but they depended heavily on increasing dividends that did not materialize into the 2000s.

So the bulk of policies ended up in universal life. Can these work? Yes if one simply pays the premiums sufficient to keep in it afloat. But that may not happen since, whether the insured or a trust starts or ends up with the policy, it invariably was based on non guaranteed elements that require review every year. Certainly in view of the way interest rates had dropped early 2011. It is estimated that up to 80% of policies have not been reviewed in the last 4 years.

They are in serious jeopardy of lapsing unless substantial monies are reintroduced. The real problem is no one is doing the review and even if they tried, I am not sure they would understand the implications. (Do they even know of in force illustrations)? There are times when a trustee may find it necessary to add funds, but he could be liable for not addressing the problem earlier as a fiduciary. On the other side, some older policies could/should be exchanged into newer policies that are cheaper and better even though the insured is older.

No Lapse

This is slowly getting known in the industry and has limited use till after 2000. But it is THE policy that is the defacto choice whenever a permanent insurance is required. Generally when it looks like a duck, quacks like a duck, it is a duck. Not so here. No lapse insurance does have a cash value buildup but it is totally irrelevant. All one does is simply pays the premium as due and the policy stays intact till 100 up to 130. It is not whole life. It is not universal life. There are no loans considered, no interest rate concern if it goes up or down. Just pay the premiums. That's it. There are some insurance companies that have no lapse riders and may call them GUL policies- guaranteed universal life. Again, the cash value is nil and I therefore refer to them as no lapse because of this issue. I did a report suggesting a no lapse several years ago but the agent who had sold him a variable life policy kept pointing out to the client that "look how lousy the cash buildup is" in the no lapse. Don't bother with interest rates! The cash value is not an issue. You do not use this policy for a loan.

So what is the catch? You need to be sure to have used a highly rated company. That's where the risk is. A poorly run and financed company may not end up with the assets to pay off a large policy in later years. But only using the highly rated companies is always suggested no matter the type. There were some concerns years ago that the companies were not setting aside enough reserves for the no lapse contingencies (called shadow account) It bears investigation but very few in the business probably even heard of the issue. However my point is that a highly rated company will back these policies or end up with a terrible reputation so my position to the purchaser is still positive...

# 36

# Universal Life

Universal life came about due to the changes in interest rates in the 80s'. Companies needed a type of policy where the rates were greater than the traditional whole life and also where the consumer could have more control over the premium payments. Then as the stock market went wild in the 90s, there emerged all types of variable products moving further into index life when the risk of loss became painfully evident in 2000 forward.

These basic universal policies allow one to view the independent aspects of a policy- how much insurance is being charged, what the interest rates are and the costs charged by the company for maintaining the policy (and premium taxes as applicable). The policies allow you to stop and start premiums (assuming there is still enough cash in the account to keep it afloat), increase or decrease the face amount and a host of other flexibilities.

But, once again, I ask 'why are you buying insurance? Do you need long term permanent insurance? Can you not save independently? Is it to take out loans later?' I submit that universal life insurance- and more- are really not insurance in the strictest sense. When you combine cash growth as a major emphasis (for middle America), you are combining two different elements that may be counterproductive. If you need insurance, just buy insurance. But then that begs the issue that you were informed by a fiduciary as to the correct options available. Probably not since the industry is not set up that way.

Of course, one can upgrade the issue over to another hybrid of universal life- that of the variable policy. (This requires an agent licensed in both insurance and securities.) The idea is to make as much money as possible inside of the policy tax deferred through the use of various mutual funds. Great idea- if you know the risk of loss.

**Vanishing Premium**

One of the major problems is that the illustrations (and agents as well) will show/inform you that as the cash value increases via the interest rates presented or, more obviously, with the higher returns of mutual funds, that one would not have to pay premiums anymore because there is more than enough cash in the policy to pay the needed payments. Obviously, the premiums do not vanish- the idea is that the internal returns in the policy will pay them.

Oh really?

Consider the economic returns/interest rates in the 1980s. They were very high and policy returns were illustrated far into the future at the same rates. Dividends for participating policies were also estimated to be high and even increasing. But once inflation's back was broken via Volcker, along came Greenspan and continued the FED attempt to drop interest rates. Hence, the returns/dividends on universal policies subsequently dropped as well- precipitously as it were. The cash values for the vanishing premiums did not materialize and hence the law suits in the 1990s and early 2000s where the vanishing premiums 'didn't' (as many agents had 'promised') and caused a lot of demands for extra cash infusions or the policies would lapse.

No agent was immune from the falling rates- it is just that if they did suggest/pursue/state that to the owners they not only would not have to pay any more into the policy but would have extra money to take out as a loan, they overstepped the element of 'puffing'. Many courts also felt that way as it levied penalties against major firms.

See THE LAW AND ECONOMICS OF VANISHING PREMIUM LIFE INSURANCE, 1997 Delaware Law School of Widener University, https://litigation-essentials.lexisnexis.com/webcd/app?action=DocumentDisplay&crawlid=1&doctype=cite&docid=22+Del.+J.+Corp.+L.+1&srctype=smi&srcid=3B15&key=140bcbbfcd84171d9e433adb2ad955c8

**Universal Variable**

In an effort to avoid the low interest rates and dividends, the insurance companies offered universal policies that utilized mutual funds in an attempt to increase returns. Anyone in the 90's could (supposedly) see the value of this since returns were so high and effectively stated to stay that way by 30 year old pretty boys on CNN and FNN that told us the entire world order had changed and everything was now dotcom or nothing. Then came 2000 and 44% losses in stocks (which is where the bulk of the monies would be invested). Actually, the tax deferred element of a variable policy infers the use of the most risky of funds (does tech ring a bell?) and losses would have been closer to 60%+. With such losses, there were a lot of policy owners that now had to put in more monies to keep the policy afloat if they had been depending on the internal appreciation to fund premiums. Others certainly had far less for loans for retirement or other reasons they had anticipated. But it got worse. Along comes 2008 with a 57% loss in the S&P 500 and greater with the more volatile funds. Then think about this. If returns are now far less than historical averages (and they will be) will a variable policy might/still be illustrated with a 10% flat rate of return. Sure, why not? The regulatory bodies won't do anything The more 'experienced' purchasers might/would say that was too high, but I am addressing the least sophisticated lulled by marketing and reversion to some unsupported mean. I submit that returns greater than 6% in the overall market are about the tops for some time (and there are a lot of extra costs in these types of policies so the net return compared to an outside fund should always be less). Even if policyholders put in large amounts of money into the policies to start with (remember, universal allows lots of flexibility in what to put in and when) losses of the type seen recently and/or returns that low could pretty much decimate the policy since it would take a LOT of money to keep it funded.

It should be obvious that the risk of loss scenario needed to be identified to such owners since they were in even more jeopardy in losing assets. On one hand, some might say that the insurance agent has only a fiduciary duty to the insurance company. But as soon as the securities license takes hold, the minimum duty was under the suitability limits as prescribed under the old law. No matter, once one defines themselves as a financial ‘whatever’, they have upped the ante under Dodd Frank to that of a fiduciary and now are held to very highest standards to the consumer.

So what are the problems therein? Well, most is obvious. Even those agents attempting to do the right thing rarely/did not have the background to interpret the facts (economics mostly) and separate from the noise about variable insurance policies. They therefore may make presentations that cannot hold up except in the most optimistic scenarios. Suffice to say, prior to 2000, the projection of returns might have *felt* valid given the huge returns almost year after year in almost all types of funds. But as developed by Mandelbrot, Bernstein and a host of others, risk is a nasty surprise that does not fall into convenient graphs and charts. And as pointed out continuously, the ability of an insurance agent per se to gauge the potential risk is essentially nil and brokers are little better.

An offering of a variable product must include the risk of loss and all the ramifications within an insurance product. However a partner in this mess is the SEC since it requires the illustrations use only flat rates of returns-which were as high as 12%. Flat rates of returns do not exist, have not existed in the past and will not exist in the future. But the SEC is pretty much out to lunch in its real life application of statistics (see Madoff) so what can one expect.

Lastly, as evidenced in every page of this book (ad nauseam), is the fact that brokers and agents have never been taught the fundamentals of investing. Losses have to be expected though they should be limited to about 15% to 20% no matter how bad the economy becomes (DCAD). But most policies of any type are sold and rarely monitored and when you have universal life policies, you really need to keep on top of them because there are a lot of moving parts that ARE moving.

Then there are the commissions.

Lastly, as one looks to the massive changes in international economics, a huge budget deficit, incompetent politicians and more, one should probably anticipate a 75% to 90% chance of one debacle in a decade that will cause around a 50% loss in equities. And a 50% chance that there could be *two* scenarios in a singular decade that would do the same.

Let's be fair however. It is true that first year commissions can be as high as the total first year's premium- sometimes higher. If the agent has truly researched and found the best policy and monitors it over time, maybe OK. But that is highly debatable with minimal training. Yet if one gets a low load policy from an unlicensed fee planner where the planner doesn't know what they are doing and cannot monitor the policy- or farms it out to someone at his church to sell where a commission is generated in any case- nothing else has been accomplished either.

It should be clear that the fiduciary concept has been somewhat lost in the element of insurance. The ability to upgrade to a fiduciary level is highly suspect. Can I therefore provide the organizations and entities that will do the job correctly?

No.

I have been around too long and seen too much incompetency via lack of knowledge by those who (supposedly) had experience and knowledge. I recently had a VALIC officer ask me why universal life policies charged more as he got older. And as an expert against a State Farm agent with 30 years of experience- the defendant stated in a depo that he did not know how universal life really worked. I did a report for a wealthy person who had been sold a $30,000,000 variable policy where there were too many risks and that he ought to check out no lapse. The licensee who had sold the three brothers $90,000,000+ in life insurance (million dollar club obviously) said that the cash value returns in the first years did not match those of the variable policy he held???? (Cash value in a no lapse is essentially useless.)

There must be major changes in the educational criteria for insurance agents since it still is the wild west in many cases. Policyholders seeking cash value, free premiums and insurance till death will be sorely disappointed- probably already so during the last debacle. Or I suppose they all could go to AIG that showed that a 17. 53% annual return is possible. After all, they must know what they are doing to get $150+ billion bailout. Right???

Our government knows what is best.

Right?

Then there is the lobbying.

**Summary**

If a consumer wants to overfund a policy in the early years to possibly avoid a call for extra funds in later years, that might work. But if the intent is to pull out a loan later on, then it is back to the detailed monitoring of the policy at least on an annual basis to determine if the current and projected economics can still keep it afloat.

If a universal policy of any type- and absolutely one with a loan- is not actively monitored, there are no fiduciaries in the system. If the agent does not have a financial calculator- particularly with a variable product- there is no reason at all to use them. They are incapable of establishing a proper allocation of funds and doing a risk of loss.

As always, there is the underlying question. Why are you buying insurance? It is possible to get the highest financial ratings and do a separate policy analysis with Flagg, Maczuga and others, but the real focus to a purchase is to determine if a policy should have been purchased in the first place.

Whenever more than pure insurance is involved, the fiduciary has to clearly indicate the risks. Ain't happening.

Then there are the ........................

More: The discussion above does not address the use of insurance to shield monies inside a life policy from creditors. I am simply focusing on mid America.

Many universal policies allow access to face value if one becomes disabled, enters a nursing home, death is expected in a short time and more. If a policy purchase is valid, then these riders may have added value. However, this discussion focuses on the basic requirement for insurance and any 'extras' may be/tend to be superfluous to the underlying need.

Current policies tend to have a LOT of moving parts that require examination- certainly where there is probable cause for termination, sale, or exchange. It is part of a planning process that cannot take place via a software program. And the process cannot be conducted by life agent per se. It's even tough for me.

# 37

# Annuities

As I reviewed what to include in this section, some material was essentially known by all. They are tax deferred, essentially all have surrender charges, etc. But having seen the industry put out material that tends to be effusive optimism, I opted for some detail on various points.

Annuities are useful for those people concerned about payments while they are still alive rather than the focus of life insurance which is to pay a benefit to beneficiaries when they die. The individual pays the insurance company a set amount of money during the accumulation stage (when putting money in) either as a lump sum (single premium deferred annuity) or on an annual or monthly basis.

The main issue has been the annuitization phase (taking the money out through the company) since almost all investors have taken out the accumulations as a lump sum rather than annuitize over a period of time. The problem recognized by most annuity purchasers was, for most part. they lost control of the monies during annuitization- they just got their monthly payment. They did not have the right to get a hold of their principal once the contract was signed (small caveats apply). I tended to agree that way in many cases since as you get older, a lot more stuff can go wrong and the need for immediate assets becomes absolute (ill health and long term care for example).

(Though if you compare this to a defined benefit pension fund, it is pretty much the same thing as an annuity payment. The difference being there was no ability to get the discounted cash flow (monthly payments) as a lump sum. It appears that if this was possible, retirees would also take the money and run. And then trip into a quicksand of incompetence. Why the cynical attitude? One, because that is what they do. Two, because many are bombarded by financial 'whatevers' extolling the virtues of how to make a lot more money with their products with no risk. And they also get a seminar with a free chicken dinner. And as we all know, retirees love 'free anything'. Marketing is extremely effective on humans.)

## Fixed Annuity Lump Sum

A deferred fixed annuity is one where the company provides one set rate for a period of years- one, five or perhaps 10. You invest a lump sum and you know exactly what you will get and when (3% for three years). The surrender period lasts for the period under contract. Once the period is ended, the money is yours to do with whatever you wish. They are great ‘investments’ when economic rates are declining since you can tie up ‘guaranteed’ higher rates for years. It is also one reason why these types of annuities can be used in non taxable accounts such as IRAs. They are not used for tax deferral- they are primarily for higher returns. They universally pay more than CDs. Once the 3, 5 or ‘x’ years is up, the money is completely liquid with no interference at all. Admittedly if you cash out, you have to pay income tax PLUS a penalty before age 59.5 so some caution is advised.

On the other hand, tying up funds in an annuity for any significant period when economic rates are going down is guaranteed underperformance. Better to use shorter term CDs until rates stabilize. (And though I am loathe to suggest specific investments since things "change", take a look at GNMA funds. The volatility during all these recent messes is fairly smooth. They will go down once economic interest rates go up, but if Bernanke stays true to his 'promise', no higher rates are expected till mid 2013.)

## Fixed Annuity Monthly/Annual Payments

This is different from lump sum annuities since monthly or annual premiums are paid in over a period of time. These are used a lot by teachers and non profits under codes 403(b) or 501(c)3). The company may guarantee a rate for one year only and then subsequent interest rates are based on economic conditions and 'whatever they want to offer'. Will they be really be reflective of the times or will the company just keep its rates low since ‘it has already captured the client’? Therefore, at inception, the owner may/will have a real tough time trying to figure which company might be better.

For example, a company may take all the funds after one year (the general one year guaranteed period) and put it in a "pot" with all the other funds it has collected throughout the years. Or it stays with all monies collected just that year. There are several variations of this "pot" and are known as weighted average, portfolio and modified portfolio rate. Unless you are very familiar with the formulas used, it is very difficult to determine what final return could be forthcoming. Sometimes a system will be better if interest rates in the economy are rising. Other times a different formula is better for the client when rates drop. I do not know of a service that can help here- perhaps a very experienced agent might help. However, as just addressed, the comparison of which formula will produce more may be nothing more than chance - assuming you got all the info to do so. Which I doubt is possible to get.

In the 1980s, almost the entire focus of annuity returns was based on the investments of the insurance company known as their general account. Since all companies tend to use bonds in such accounts, the companies were limited in their ability to offer special enticements in marketing to consumers since, to do so would impact their bottom line of profits. (Exceptions did apply. Executive Life and a few others used mortgages and junk bonds to boost yields that were unsustainable. Then they blew up and took a lot of consumer with them. Other companies bought out the book of such defaulting companies, but the damage to the industry's image was severe.) However I am addressing how the standard conservative firms could 'appear better' compared to another?'

## Bonus Interest

These are the teaser rates that a company would guarantee for one year. It doesn't take a brain surgeon to know what happens next. The company then drops the rates after one year to something lower- perhaps much lower than those companies not offering teasers. After so many years, the (potentially) higher annual rates from the non teaser company will/may outweigh the initial surge of value by the teaser company. While it should be obvious what is going on, it is nothing different than marketing of almost anything. People love deals and it did not take much to get one to switch accounts by simply dangling the higher rate in front of them.

However, there are situations where the bonus rates are perfectly valid. Companies would offer higher rates if the teacher/nurse stayed with the company for, say, 10 years. It was generally a win win for both sides. The company 'knew' it could depend on certain monies to stay put for a decade and therefore it would have lower costs overall and determine its future with more precision. The teacher also avoided the temptation to jump from one company to another trying to find the Holy Grail of returns. Of course with the teacher and agent incapable of using a financial calculator, it is debatable that a lot of true insight was available.

## One and Two Tier Annuities

Two tier annuities were the norm in 403b accounts for years and not really beneficial to almost all purchasers. They offered two different rates of growth for the same contributions. The higher rate was available upon retirement with the condition that you would annuitize the contract WITH THEM. There was no lump sum withdrawal of *this* account. The lower rate was for accounts where the lump sum could be withdrawn. It hopefully is obvious what was going on. The higher initial rate could not really be justified unless the company offered less returns during the payout period. Putting monies into an annuity for 20 years at age 45 allowed the company to use low payout rates (annuitization) for the 25 years that the annuitant may live till death. As it ended up, few people annuitize anyway so it may have been a moot point for the company. People took their monies out at the lower rate and the company saved a bundle.

But along came one tier annuities. WYSIWYG. (What you see is what you get). No teaser rates, no one or two tier games. Just one single rate all the time. Admittedly, the rates did change after a year like all other companies- but the rates universally stayed above the lower rates of the two tier product.

Assume deposits of $400 monthly for 20 years. (Round numbers chosen for table)

| | |
|---|---|
| Two tier 5% | $158,716 |
| 4% | $142,934 |
| One tier 4.5% | $150,582 |

Obviously the $158,716 was attractive but only was available if the teacher annuitized and then at unknown rates (one needs a financial calculator). Having seen the offerings of some companies, the rates were 'lousy'. Some were zero. But most people ultimately wanted their lump sums so the company sent out checks far less ($142,934) than that of the one tier ($150,582).

A lot of the two tier companies lost favor but the two tier concept has come back in a different form with the indexed annuities explained later. Further, due to the massive stock losses of 2000 and 2008, there has been a lot more interest in using annuities that can fund a retirement no matter how long one lives. And without the fluctuation of the stock market.

## Variable annuities

Variable annuities require an agent to have not only a life insurance license, but a securities license as well. The securities license, either a series 6 or series 7, allows an agent to sell mutual funds. A variable annuity is essentially a tax deferred mutual fund account- but with extra fees and restrictions. Remember that the bull market of stocks started around the mid 1980s to 2000. A number of companies started promoting the use of mutual funds as a way of making the owners far more money than offered under the fixed rates. Teachers were offered 403(b)7 accounts- for the use of mutual funds- and, assuming a decent portfolio allocation, they might have done very well indeed.. However, as with effectively all equities, participants were clueless to inherent risks and once they-

and 401k accounts- took a tumble twice in just a few years with 2000 and 2008, their mindset to risk has changed dramatically. The impact on these investors was the same as many 401ks that had invested in stocks for so long: they may have been very close to retirement and then seen their assets decimated.

It is true that large returns can grow tax deferred in a variable annuity account. Some may have done exceptionally well in the past *if* they got their money out in time. But the growth was generally by luck since the major use of equities in an account pushes the potential risk of loss well above 60%.

As a result of the stock returns in the 90s and the losses in the 2000s, the industry masterfully built new products to entice the conservative investor. They really were unique. But a lot were missold and a number of the rest were completely misunderstood. That said, there are guarantees that were added to variable policies allowing the annuitant to receive at least the amount of their contributions back and sometimes more. But recognize that each of these guarantees comes with a price and it is necessary to review what the end results might be. In any case, according to a Milliman survey involving 19 insurance carriers whose variable annuity sales represent approximately 57 percent of the VA market, guaranteed living benefits figured prominently in variable annuity sales.

Ninety-five percent of variable annuity sales in the first six months of 2007 occurred in variable annuity contracts under which a guaranteed living benefit was available.

In new variable annuity sales of contracts offering a guaranteed living benefit in the first half of 2007, such benefits were elected in cases involving 74 percent of sales premium.

Guaranteed Minimum Accumulation Benefit

The guaranteed living benefit also known as the guaranteed minimum accumulation benefit (GMAB) allows a variable annuity contract owner's principal by permitting them to surrender the contract after a specified number of years and receive a lump-sum surrender amount equal to first-year net premiums, regardless of the contract's actual surrender value. Costs can be as high as 1%

The Guaranteed Minimum Income Benefit (GMIB), permits the contract owner to access the benefit of a life annuity for one or two lives based on

- a hypothetical benefit base comprised of net premiums paid for the annuity, accumulated at a specified interest rate; and
- conservative life annuity rates contained in the GMIB benefit provision

(For your reading pleasure, here is the info regarding how to annuitize and GMIB- (Paul Winn, webce.com) an insurer's current annuity purchase rate for a life and ten-year certain settlement option for a male age 65 may be $6.20, whereas its purchase rate for the same settlement option under a GMIB, also for a male age 65, may be $4.73. Annuitizing outside the GMIB would generate monthly payments of $6.20 for every $1,000 of the contract's accumulated value. Electing to annuitize under a GMIB would produce monthly payments of $4.73 for every $1,000 of the benefit base.

In light of the very conservative annuity rates used with the GMIB, a contract owner may find that annuitizing a smaller accumulated value amount under the insurer's current annuity rates will produce a larger annuity income than annuitizing the higher amount represented by the benefit base under the GMIB guarantee. In such a case, the contract owner may elect to annuitize the variable annuity contract's accumulated value under the insurer's current annuity rates.

Let's say, for example, that a contract's actual accumulated values were $90,000, and its GMIB benefit base was $115,000, and the just-stated annuity rates applied. The owner would receive $558 a month if he annuitized the contract's accumulated value outside of the GMIB ($6.20 *x* 90) and $544 a month if he annuitized under the GMIB ($4.73 *x* 115). Alternatively, he could elect to annuitize, say, $75,000 of the annuity's accumulated value, receive a monthly income of $465 ($6.20 *x* 75) and keep the remaining $15,000 of the values in the contract for continued growth. Annuitizing under a GMIB usually requires the owner to annuitize the entire benefit amount."

As much as I may indicate how tough these annuities are to figure out, multiply the above description by about 5 to 10. One needs a financial calculator, a lot of time and a table full of numbers to compare these internally and externally. If litigation is involved, it will take an expert a lot of time to do the analytical work.

The most popular is the Guaranteed Withdrawal Benefit and allows the variable annuity contract owner the opportunity to access the living benefit and receive an income without being required to annuitize the contract. This GLB consists of two options:

- guaranteed minimum withdrawal benefit (GMWB)
- guaranteed lifetime withdrawal benefit (GLWB)

(Once again I offer a small description of the product (Winn): "If the variable annuity contract's accumulated value was less than the GMWB benefit base at the time of the withdrawal, the excess withdrawal will (1) cause the remaining benefit base to be reduced by the amount of the withdrawal and (2) be further reduced to the contract's accumulated value immediately following the withdrawal. Not only is the benefit base substantially reduced by an excess withdrawal (if the accumulated value is less than the benefit base at the time), but the maximum annual withdrawal amount permitted under the GMWB is recalculated when an excess withdrawal is made. For this reason, the annual maximum withdrawal amount may also be reduced. In the case of an excess withdrawal, the new annual withdrawal amount is equal to the *lesser* of the annual withdrawal amount immediately before the excess withdrawal or the accumulated value immediately after the excess withdrawal multiplied by the annual withdrawal percentage.")

Wasn't that fun? Very, very few people can read these contracts and decipher which might work, when and where. The material cannot be taught to an agent. It is so far beyond their capacity to learn it would not even make any sense to try. Further, only but a few might take the continuing education course and Winn notes that these agents end up stating it was 'too dense'. (It is a tough course but it is also the reason that pundits of insurance knowledge overall simply take the easiest courses available.) Perhaps one out of 10,000 might be able to grasp the pertinent issues and be able to compare products. And that person would probably be an old engineer (with an insurance license and background) used to deciphering complicated problems. That said, I am not attempting to scare anyone per se with the sophistication/moving parts. But nary a sole can ever infer that client understands what they are purchasing and how it might work nor, certainly, how the product compares to other simpler products (though for those seeking such expertise, I point one back to Paul Winn and his course at webce. Best I have seen.) . But a fiduciary must- that is what this focus represents. It may not be that the fiduciary would sell one but they must be able to analyze when called upon. If they do not want to deal with the issue at all- particularly where guaranteed benefits are being extolled at all levels- then you do not have a financial adviser.

Sure that is harsh- but it is real life and factual. And isn't Dodd Frank demanding knowledge to protect and assets the average consumer?

Old Age Annuities

These are brand new. One can now buy an annuity that is conditioned on if you happen to reach, say, age 85. Then this annuity would start to pay for the contingency that you were going to live a long, long time. Admittedly, if you died before then, your account went in to others. And so on.

Worthwhile? Possible for those with families with long lifetimes. I also believe the companies will provide other policies also conditioned on unique circumstances. Maybe Alzheimers. It will be interesting.

## Summary

Annuities have and will continue command a definite share of the market for retirees. But the devil is in the details and a lot are misunderstood and missold.

Caveat Emptor to any that suggest these are simple products overall. This is mind numbing material.

# 38

# Indexing

The concept behind indexing is using an investment in bonds with a little bit of cash that can be used to buy options. It is absolutely valid, can work and actually could provide a lot of nonprofit entities a way of achieving decent returns with limited risk. Notice I said 'non profits' since when you turn the idea into a product for consumers, the insurance companies have made it so difficult to understand and have so many layers of costs that, while they can still work at certain limits, it is debatable that anyone can really comprehend what is going to happen. Further, the returns have to be lowered due to such heavy fees.

It is estimated that $33 billion of indexed annuities would be sold by the end of 2010, up from $29 billion in 2009. Forty-one percent of fixed annuities sold in 2010 were deferred annuities linked to the market.

First the basics as to how they system work (forget annuities for the moment and just concentrate on the example.) Assume you have $100,000 to invest. You could buy straight into the market- say the S&P 500- but the risks are pretty high. A one year's standard deviation is close to

40%. Or put another way, the losses sustained in the 2008 drop for the market was 57% top to bottom. Are you willing to accept that type of loss? Probably over and over again during your lifetime? Want something more secure?

What you can do instead is put about 90% into bonds. Take the other 10% and buy options on the, say, S&P 500. You make a relatively steady and low risk income stream on 90% of your money. On the options- if they go up in value, you buy the underlying stock and make extra profit. If there is no upside in the value, you do nothing. If the underlying value goes down- well, it should be obvious- you also do nothing.

It is that simple. Not quite foolproof but close. The issue is possibly adjusting the types of indexes etc. but not a huge amount of thought is necessary. Not an awful lot of people in the mix either so not too many ways to screw it up. Costs could be kept to a minimum if the government decided to use these for pension accounts. They could use this for Social Security to bulk up returns without much of a concern about a 2000 or 2008. But due to its size in buying billions in options, it would become the controlling entity in the market and that would be illegal at best. A state could do it but is probably a little too large. A large city might try it. Corporations might use it in context with a 401k as long as the costs were kept low (though the details of use start to get foggy when so many entities get a piece of the premium pie.)

Certainly some upside is lost in an up market since you are not getting full appreciation, but it is the downside that has forced consumers and many other entities to reconsider the risks of equity investing.

Here is some commentary from an article titled, Real World Index Annuity Returns by Jack Marrion, George VanderPal and David Babbel: "A study by Eric Crittenden and Cole Wilcox (2008) at Black star Funds was conducted using Russell 3000 data from 1983 through 2006. The findings were that "about 40% of the stocks had negative returns over their lifetime, and about 20% of stocks lost nearly all of their value. A little more than 10% of stocks recorded huge wins over 500%" (Richardson, 2009). These data indicate that most of the positive market return over time comes from relatively few performers, which lends support to the use of stock index strategies as part of an overall portfolio. Furthermore it supports the notion that there is significant risk in the stock market and thus, for moderately to highly risk-averse clients, the need for principal protection programs such as fixed indexed annuities (FIA's). Nearly 96% of FIA's possess reset (or ratchet) features that allow for locking in positive returns each annual or biannual period. By eliminating the prejudicial effects occasioned by significant stock market declines, and locking in returns annually or biannually, there is less of a need to try and capture large upside market swings to recover from the declines."

## Options

Of course certain readers are somewhat lost once the term 'options' is used. Here is what we are looking at. You could buy 100 shares of the S&P 500 for a hypothetical value of $100/share ($10,000). If it goes up, to 110/share, you now have 11,000 and you go out to dinner more often. If it goes down 50%, you have $5,000 left- and your dog leaves you.

On the other hand, you buy an option on 100 shares. What this means is that you now have the **right** to buy 100 shares of the S&P 500 for, say, $102/share (liberties taken but necessary to make the essence clear) over a period of a year for a cost of $500. If the share value goes up to $115, you buy the 100 shares for $10,200 (what the seller agreed to) sell them for $11,500 (current value) and make the difference as profit minus what you paid ($500) or $800.

If the stock value stayed at $100, you obviously would not buy and would have lost the $500 as a 'gamble'. On the other side, if the stock went down to $50, did you lose that much? No- only the $500.

$500 cost to buy option, current prices $10,000

| Current value | Contract to buy at (Strike Price) | Value at 1 year | Decision/profit/loss |
|---|---|---|---|
| $10,000 | 10,200 | 11,500 | Buy Profit $11,500-10,200- 500= $800 |
| | | 10,700 | Buy Break even $10,700-10,200- 500= $0 |
| | | 10,200 | Don't buy Loss $500 |
| | | 5,000 | Don't buy Loss $500 |

For the uninitiated, this is what you need to know about a very limited risk scenario that allows one to get a piece of the stock market appreciation if it goes up, limiting losses on the downside to almost nil and while also getting an income stream at the same time.

Does this work the same for consumers via insurance offerings?

No.

## Index Annuities

These are pretty much a black plague in the industry. Not that they may not work. I indicated they can. But they are very hard to understand for the agent, harder to grasp for the consumer, are therefore sold incorrectly, if not fraudulently, and are **nothing more than bond funds.**

Probably that last little quip is the most telling tale of indexed annuities. This is a bond fund. While the index is tied to an equity (S&P, NASDAQ, STOXX, Hang Seng and many more), and while it is possible that the returns can provide some nice upside, by the time all the fees and associated costs (commissions) are taken away, and the company takes a piece of the returns for its profits and other costs, a consumer is never going to get the high returns they either have been told or are apt to assume/misconstrue from the literature.

In the late 1990s when these first came out, I went through a number of seminars to find out not only what they really were but how they were being presented to agents. Well, the instructors danced around what was actually going to occur by providing all sorts of market speak on the sizzle the agents could introduce to clients. They may not have said "get stock market returns without the risk" but they came close. When all is said and done, this is what I felt:

In 60% to 80% of the time, you should get returns greater than bond funds; in 20% to 30% of the time, you will get returns the same as bond funds; in 5% to 10% of the time, you will get less than returns of bond funds. (Bond funds would generally be mid term investment grade with low fees.)

Of course that was a time of higher interest rates and stock returns and before the debacle of 2000 and 2008. Where am I today? I will stay about the same since the economy and markets are so volatile. And because overall returns are down so much in both stocks and bonds, the insurance companies are not going to give away the store at the risk of their profits. So, effectively no change. I repeat these are bond funds.

Per Advantage Compendium, over the past five years ending in November 2010, the average index annuity credited a 3.9% annualized interest rate. By contrast, one-year CDs yielded 2.8% annually and five-year CDs yielded 3.8%. By contrast, the S&P 500 index grew at just a 0.65% annual rate. (These figures are not verified but seem reflective of what this product is capable of. Admittedly 3.9% is not huge by any means but it beats no or negative returns from directly using stocks.)

Why are the returns what they are?

### CAPS

The market may actually provide a substantial return- assume it is 20% for the past year. And when you look at that you think you are a 'winner'. Not so fast. The company may have already stated that the greatest amount of gain is 'capped' at 10%. Is that what you will get? Not even close

### Participation rate

Of the gain that is mentioned, it still does not mean you will 'participate' in all of the gain. Maybe the contract says 60%. Your returns have dropped even lower. You now are at 6%.

### Spread

This is a cost or charge by the insurance company against the consumer returns. If there was a 3% spread on the above returns, the consumer would net 3%.

## Why it may not mean much

Even if the initial elements look good, here is the crux to all policies (at least as far as I can determine with current policies)- the companies can change the spreads, caps, participation rates at their whim. You have no idea how to gauge most anything because you have no idea what will happen later on. No idea at all. Older policies had fixed caps, etc. but not now. All three items above do not have to move but no matter. The movement of one can substantially alter the end result. I repeat you have no idea the end result other than the possible ranges I listed above. But you sure are not going to get stock market returns.

## Guarantees

Yes, many companies will guarantee a minimum amount of a return on what is invested - though it has now dropped to around 1%. It may be on the entire 100% of your contribution, but not necessarily. It may only be on 85% or 90%.

More importantly, they do not guarantee the 1% on a year where the market returned nothing- it is 1% if the entire period did not return that amount. The entire period is generally going to be a standard 7 to 10 years that represents the surrender period (though you will find all sorts of time frames).

Here is what I mean. Assume in years 1,2,3,4 the stock market went down 25% each year. Because only the options monies were lost and not the entire contribution, the companies will show that you had no loss for each one of those years. That is the real benefit to indexed product. You do not suffer horrendous losses when the market takes a momentous tumble. At least you can earn something. But in the case at hand, you did not earn 1% for each of those years. If year's 5,6,7,8,9,10 all showed a profit and the average of the entire 10 years was 5% due to just the last 6, that is what you earned. But zero was entered for the first four.

On the other hand, assume that the average return for all 10 years was 0.5%. You are guaranteed a return of 1% on your investment (or perhaps 85%+ if the contract so states).

## Which index to use

Actually there may not be a choice- a product may only allow one generally the S&P 500. If there are a few, I do not have a suggestion as to an allocation absent that I would do a formal analysis of previous returns and current economics to see what I would start with. Then adjust as necessary or allowed later on. But that may not be the real concern anyway.

The companies have various methods to determine how the returns are formulated. There can be high and low points for the entire term, start and end points only, averages and many more. I did review the statistics in a 2010 book, Index Annuities- A Suitable Approach by Jack Marion and John Olsen (a must read) on which method might be better overall. There isn't one. There are those that have a pattern of returns based on what the economy has done over a period of very few years. Since these products have been around for such a very short period of time, there is very little that can determine what the best method is. It might be possible to 'estimate' where the economy is going and to match it up with a formula that best exploits that pattern, but one must recognize that these policies are generally set up for long periods of time and the volatility of the economy cannot be determined that far out save by luck.

## Bonus

Many of the firms offer nice bonuses as a further inducement. These are persistency bonuses only. You will have to be in the account generally to the end of the contract term before the bonus is applied. Nothing really unique here- just good marketing. Also note that the company does not lose anything by this inducement. All they have to do is change the cap, spread or participation rate and get it all back anyway. You'd have to look at the activity of the company for, perhaps, 10 years to see what rates they did offer consumers in similar products as compared to economic rates. Good luck in getting the information. Better luck in determining if the rates they offered were good or bad. It is not an easy process to begin with and the new economy does not necessarily lend itself to estimating that far out.

**Summary**

You certainly do look for a company with a high financial rating. From there it is tough. The book mentioned above, Index Annuities- A Suitable Approach, can help but I can tell you that the product maze has changed so dramatically that whatever was, no longer is. It really is amazing just how many offerings I see each week with every type of incentive or 'uniqueness'. (And commissions. It is really annoying when the ads keep pushing these. But it simply is the way these are sold. By the same token, is it so terribly different when fee planners just do minimal work to try and get as much money under managements for 1%? Again, that is just how the industry works.) You can try to see if there is a pattern in the way the company has or has not made adjustments over time- though once again there has been a very short period to work with. It will be a very frustrating experience to get the info, I can assure you. Not necessarily impossible, but definitely difficult.

I do unequivocally state that these are solely bond funds- they cannot be anything else. They are not investments in the stock market. If anyone says otherwise, they are frauds. And a lot of agents have been doing exactly that. Or that the bonuses are available immediately for withdrawal. (I reported one agent but it was a waste of effort.)

I do state that if someone does not have and cannot use a financial calculator, do not buy from them. I cannot guarantee that if one has such a calculator that they are sophisticated, but the lack thereof is almost a given that they are clueless to the underpinnings of a difficult contract. You have to know how money works.

## Summary

You have a decent chance of bettering a bond fund of similar time frame but that is the best you can get. They can be used in certain scenarios since getting a nice bond return may not be bad. But the fees, moving parts and more make it problematic that the agents are selling them appropriately to clueless consumers. But at least they got a free chicken dinner

# 39

# Long Term Care Insurance

## Overview

The insurance industry has attempted- with varying degrees of success- to provide multifaceted policies to cover the costs of long term care since many elderly will be impacted by the illnesses of age. Such infirmities now may not end in early death since the elderly are living much longer (see below) no matter the sickness. Those leading unhealthy lives tend to die “soon”- it is those that had been previously healthy that tend to live the longest. They simply tend to linger quite a while even with major illnesses- though the inception of illness occurs generally is later in life. Cost of care can be greater than $80,000 annually and last for a decade or more, certainly if senile dementia/Alzheimers is apparent. But it is not simply the patient that needs care- caregivers (mostly women) are using up their physical, emotional and financial existence in an effort to keep a loved one from a nursing home. In essence, though the patient may have received care for a decade or so before entering a facility or by dying, the caregiver is both physically and emotionally exhausted leading to yet another patient to a nursing home or assisted living facility. There are currently more than seven million long term care policyholders in the United States (though the types vary tremendously. But the sales have not been without controversy due to the inconsistent and unclear coverages as well as the more recent escalating premiums for those already covered.

The situation appears to be becoming more tenuous.

## Author experience

I was an instructor in many areas of insurance, securities and financial planning from about 1979 forward. I was very attuned to the issue of baby boomers and the impact of various health issues during retirement not only because of the pure statistics of aging, but because I was in the same loop and had a number of friends with major infirmities. I taught the mandatory 8 hour long term care continuing education course for California insurance agents for over 6 years due to what I perceived as a major issue and cost to society and the consumers alike.

I generally opened up a class dialogue with students on Alzheimers particularly since my mother had it for about 10 years before her death, two uncles, a friend's wife got early onset and had it about 8 years before her death, other friends, etc. It is insidious and nothing really stops the toll once it has started. A recent study indicated that effectively all the attempts of curing or reversing the problems have not had success. Caring for such individuals is extremely difficult. The point was to bring home the reality that who will provide the care necessary to such individuals- and all the others impacted by the Activities of Daily Living (ADLs- bathing, continence, mobility, eating, dressing, toileting) as well as the increasing elements of senile dementia?

Prior to the use of insurance policies, it is quite obvious that the universal caregiver was the spouse in a marriage- most likely the woman due to the man being older and in poorer health. Some of the children might pitch in, but it was very clear that the wives were the main caregiver. However, as bad as it was, it may not have lasted that long since people did not live much past 70 in the 1950s and 1960s. Men certainly died the soonest with the wives not that far thereafter. We must also note that it is the women who universally care for parents needing various levels of care.

## Aging

There is extensive material on my site at http://efmoody.com/estate/lifeexpectancy.html. As everyone knows, Americans are now living longer- those reaching age 65 can expect from 18 to 20 years more lifetime.
Of men who are now 65,

28% will live to 90,
11% will live to 95;
2% to 100.
Of women who are now 65,
40% will live to 90;
19% to 95;
5% to 100.

As the actuarial lifetime increased, so did the manifestation of more and more diseases that required care. For example, was Alzheimers a major concern decades ago? No- it did not usually occur till after age 70 and in the 1950s or so, most of the elderly were already dead. (Of course Alzheimers was improperly diagnosed as part of the 'obvious' senile dementia which most old people would (supposedly) acquire sooner than later.)

As another insight- what was called the "old person's friend "decades ago? Pneumonia. Not a very nice way to die overall but it did stop the continuing onslaught of other diseases. Now it is way down the list of reason why people die (CDC Mortality at various ages http://205.207.175.93/HDI/TableViewer/tableView.aspx?ReportId=673)

However, the statistic can be misleading in terms of the condition and the quality of life. There were 16,100 nursing homes in 2004 with an average of 107.6 beds and a occupancy factor of 86.3% and covering 1,492,000 patients. It is estimated that over (cdc Website- http://www.cdc.gov/nchs/data/hus/hus09.pdf#105) 1,300,00 over age 65 were in nursing homes as of 2004.

Nursing Home patients

| Year<br>Age | 1977 | 1985 | 1995 | 1997 | 1999 | 2004 |
|---|---|---|---|---|---|---|
| Less than 65 | 117,100 | 172,700 | 124,000 | 143,700 | 158,700 | 175,000 |
| 65+ | 1,126,000 | 1,316,800 | 1,406,300 | 1,465,000 | 1,469.500 | 1,317.200 |
| 65-74 | 211,400 | 212,100 | 189,000 | 198,400 | 194,300 | 174,100 |
| 75-84 | 464,700 | 507,800 | 506,500 | 528,300 | 517,600 | 468,900 |
| 85 | 449,900 | 596,900 | 710,800 | 738,300 | 757,100 | 674,200 |

When you compare the numbers of 2004 to 1995, you would logically assume that people were getting healthier since the numbers of the elderly in nursing homes had actually dropped. Not really. Read on.

## Nursing Homes

Per the CDC- There were 17,000 nursing homes in the United States, providing service to 1.6 million current residents and 2.4 million residents were discharged in the year prior to the survey, according to the 1997 survey of nursing home facilities.

Of the 17,000 nursing homes in the United States, 67 percent are proprietary, just over a quarter are voluntary nonprofit, and the government operates about 7 percent of the homes. Almost 80 percent of nursing homes are certified by both Medicare and Medicaid, only 4 percent are not certified, and the remainder are certified by either Medicare or Medicaid. There are nearly twice as many nursing homes and nursing home beds in the Midwest and south as in the northeast and west. Over 60 percent of nursing homes are located in metropolitan areas and over half are affiliated with a nursing home chain.

Nursing home costs - The average basic daily charge of private-pay nursing home residents varies by the level of care of the facility as well as certification status. The highest per diem cost is the $217 reported in Medicare-certified homes compared to $98 in Medicaid-certified facilities. Costs also vary by ownership with voluntary nonprofit homes averaging the highest per diem rate of $147, compared to the $132 charged in the propriety homes and $129 homes operated by the government. (Remember this is a 1997 survey but does give some idea of the difference in overall costs).

For the record, the statistics are fine but the emphasis focuses on what *used to be.* Initially, all policies offered just nursing home care. During the late 90s and thereafter, assisted living facilities- where patients did not extensive skilled care, took over the mass market of those impacted by two of the six ADLs.

Nursing home services and staff - Certified nurse aides provide the majority of care to residents of nursing homes. Nurses' aides and orderlies account for nearly two-thirds of the nursing staff, while registered nurses make up only 15 percent of the staff involved in direct patient care. On average, nursing homes employ about one staff member to provide nursing care for every two residents. Counting administrative, medical, and therapeutic staff the ratio jumps to about 90 full-time equivalent employees per 100 residents. Just over 70 percent of homes provide hospice services.

**Nursing home residents** - The overall occupancy rate in nursing homes in 1997 was 88 percent, with little or no variation in occupancy rate across facility characteristics. Women accounted for 72 percent of nursing home residents, continuing a long-standing pattern where about three-fourths of nursing home residents are women. On average, women residents are older than their male counterparts. The majority (87 percent) of nursing home residents are white.

To meet the needs of a growing elderly population, nursing home care is an increasingly important component of health care. More than 90 percent of current residents are 65 years of age and over and almost half are 85 years or over. With the 85-and-older population expected to double in the next several decades, data on nursing home availability, utilization, services, and cost will be essential to plan for and monitor this facet of health care

In 2008, there were 16,000 nursing homes covering 1,700,000 beds. Between 1995 and 2008, the occupancy factor ranged from 82 to 85%; That is roughly an average of 1,420,000 patients.

Another study indicates there were about 1,500,000 patients in 1985.

There is a potential inconsistency in the statements above. Exactly what is a nursing home? The point is that a nursing home, by definition, can cover the most detailed care- skilled nursing care for example- and were not designed solely for ancillary care of just bathing and eating. They were primarily a sterile environment with too many stories of bad care and simply a place to die.

That attitude has declined somewhat as governmental overseers of homes have tried to enforce more rules for the patients. Well, no matter the reality or perception, nursing homes are not desired by the public and really were not designed for general care.

It takes no insight to know that people do not want to die in a nursing home. That is why the statistics through the mid 90s - http://www.cdc.gov/nchs/pressroom/00facts/nurshome.htm - don't really increase even in spite of the increase of the elderly population. What is the implication?

## NURSING HOME POLICIES

In the late 1980s and early 1990s, the insurance companies focused on the statistics of nursing home care and presented consumers various policies that would help to reduce or even eliminate the costs of nursing home care if it might befall them. The pricing became very competitive in an attempt to gather as many under contract as possible. They needed economy of scale for the numbers to work. Nothing unusual here save for the fact that there was very little historical numbers on which to truly base the number of consumers who would purchase a policy, how long they would use etc. They really didn't know how much to really charge. The actuaries viewing each potential policyholder were not that skilled- it was estimated in the mid 90s that there might be 50 actuaries in the entire U.S. who had any real experience with the elderly or nursing home statistics. While the inexperience certainly was a cause for mispricing, it was not the main culprit that caused the ultimate- and continuing- problems with the policies. It was the lapse rates.

Simply stated, whenever a life insurance policy is sold, the company expects- by its past history- that so many of the policy holders will terminate their policies before they ever use them. Hence there are not only no payments ultimately made by the company, but they have, in most cases made some profit on the time that the consumer has paid.

As a result of inaccurate estimates and an attempt to garner business, the lower prices (Penn Treaty for example) initially offered new entrants were unsustainable. And the mispricing resulted in huge increases in subsequent years when the premiums were found to be insufficient. A lot of the elderly had to cancel their policies because they could not afford the significant increases. Certain companies were more 'professional' in their approach and even noted that, in subsequent years, they had not raised prices. I am just not sure they can maintain a status quo.

Assisted Living POLICIES

But the above reflects the 'pure' nursing home policies. Few elderly want to go to a nursing home no matter how sick since it represented a 'death sentence' in a cold environment without their loved ones- certainly the sociable element with friends that they enjoyed in their own home.

So there was some statistical evidence that while someone did become sick enough for a nursing home, they- or their spouse- kept them out of a facility for as long as possible. Maybe they died without using a facility- or perhaps were so sick once they entered that they did not live in a nursing home that long. The statistics in years past showed that men entering a nursing home either got well or died in two years or less. Women did stay alive in a nursing home. So when presenting numbers on what to do, one would suggest a policy length of about 2.5 years for men. Women should be covered for an extended period of, say, 4 years or more.

But then everything changed. Mostly for the better in terms of facilities assisting the elderly.

## Assisted Living.

For the uninitiated, nursing home care is high maintenance, high intensity nursing care designed for the very sick. It is not for those needing general care consisting of 'simple' bathing, continence, mobility, eating, dressing, toileting and early stage senile dementia and Alzheimers (later stages are very intensive). In any case, nursing home care is not really necessary for those needing basic assistance of two of the ADLs. The industry recognized this and started building less intrusive units for such care-known as assisted living. And they caught on. Here were units that offered the necessary care for, say, bathing and dressing in an aesthetic environment that offered social mingling and activities far more extensive than had nursing home facilities. And they cost far less due to the unnecessary effort to cover the very sick. Overall, costs could be 35% to 50% of a nursing home.

And, as might be expected, the insurance industry noted this great opportunity to provide care that started at the assisted living level. So there was a radical change from pure nursing home care to the new offering consisting of assisted living first that could escalate over to nursing home as needed if conditions got worse. This, I thought, was an excellent vehicle that could fit in many more budgets and realistic in their thinking since a review of such facilities (where activities were the focus) was far more 'enticing' than that of a nursing home (where people went to die). All the major companies revised such policies though there were always just a few that dominated the market.

This is where the statistics changed. There were fewer people in a nursing home since far more elderly were entering assisted living where they might stay until death.

## Pricing

I had also assumed that these companies had now enough experience to correctly price their products. That said, the escalating costs of medical care kept the policies 'expensive' for many budgets and it was obvious that there was less and less of an effort by agents to get involved with what was a complex policy.

The death knell by the insurance companies was, once again, the inability to actuarially quantify what the purchasers would do- generally meaning lapse rates. Once a contract was made, most of the policyholders held on. They apparently recognized- perhaps in taking care of their own parents- that the ability to get the necessary care was truly a value that they did not wish to exclude.

The insurance companies, once again, recognized that their capital base was not going to be sufficient to cover the projected costs in the future. So they petitioned the states to increase premiums on policies already written (almost all policies are guaranteed renewable but NOT at a fixed price over time. The company is allowed to increase premiums to an entire group in a state if the proposal to the state is accepted).But these were not simply incidental increases. They were substantial and impacted current policyholders who were, after 2003 through 2008, really having to watch all the expenditures they made. That said, statistics seem to indicate that they were still holding on to their polices no matter the impact. That was one of the major problems addressed by the companies- the lapse rate was far lower than projected which meant that far more policies would be subject to claims.

Other problems reflected the increasing life expectancy of the elderly- though that was known by all entities for some time. There was also the expected returns by the insurance companies- which, similar to most corporations and analysts- never included the stock market fall as badly as it had nor recognized the precipitous drop in interest rates on which they projected internal returns for the company.

There are more than 28,000 assisted living residences in the U.S., housing more than one million people, according to the National Center for Assisted Living (NCAL). The "typical" assisted living resident is an 83-year-old woman and the average age of all assisted living residents is 83. The average male/female ratio in assisted living residences is 74% women and 26% men. According to NCAL, the average size of an assisted living residence is 43 units and ranges from three units to 200 units. The average number of residents in a facility is 40, with a range of one to 175.

NIC Research & Data

Key Financial Indicators - Occupancy Rates - Quarter Ending 3/31/10

*For stabilized properties (those open 24 months or longer) of major providers*

| Property Type | Mean Occupancy (%) | Number of Properties | Number of Units (*Beds) |
|---|---|---|---|
| Independent Living | 85.5 | 531 | 74,827 |
| Assisted Living | 88 | 1,391 | 101,994 |
| Nursing Homes | 83 | 889 | 112,159 |
| CCRCs | 88.5 | 142 | 53,435 |
| Independent Units in CCRCs | 87.5 | 137 | 36,639 |
| Assisted Living Units in CCRCs | 91 | 116 | 7,515 |
| Skilled Nursing Beds in CCRCs | 88 | 125 | 9,281 |

Occupancy is defined as: number of occupied units or beds divided by number of total available units or beds "set up".

**MEDICARE COVERAGE**

According to a 2009 Prudential survey, 37 percent of people think that Medicare will cover their long-term care costs.

This number is down from a decade ago but still reflects a poor understanding of Medicare overall. Medicare will cover for some skilled care but that is about it. Only about 1% will use that so the onus is upon them to provide for their own care. The same thing is true with at-home care.

## ODDS OF NEEDING CARE

Journalists focus on the odds of using this insurance. Some statistics note that for people age 65 and older who have long-term care insurance, there is a 45 percent chance of making a claim, though it ranges from 30 to 56 percent depending on gender and marital status.

Once a claim is made, there is about a 14% chance you will need care for three years and a 4%+ chance of needing it for five years. So the essence is to suggest that the odds are so limited that 'why bother'.

Well, the chances of using your homeowners insurance are about 1 in 88. The odds of using your auto insurance at about 1 in 47. The odds of a house fire is about 1 out of 1200 though having a house completely burn down is minuscule. However, the chances of using your LTC insurance is about 2 in 5. One out of two women and one out of three men will spend some time in a nursing home. The journalists et al have got the numbers skewed about most insurance. You never hope to use them. You may simply get the most worthwhile element- the emotional security that there is something backing up the risk. Considering what I have seen Alzheimers do, a policy can be very comforting to a family.

## SELF-FUNDING

The issue of course is how much is the cost of the risk. A Metlife survey indicated that the average cost of a private room in a nursing home was over $83,000 annually. (Once again I will point to statistics that can be deceiving. The charge is correct- though varies dramatically by location- but few may really need a formal nursing home. Most retirees experiencing 2 of the 6 ADLs can use assisted living which is a third to half the cost.)

Considering the costs of care and the odds, it is a very valid policy- certainly if there has been a history of Alzheimers in the family. But the real world of finances precludes the ability of a lot of families to purchase. I do not see how the situation will get better.

### MEDICAID

Long Term Care is available under Medicaid and covers the bulk of individual care. The number of long-term care enrollees went up by 80% between 1990 and 1998. Actual spending on long-term care increased 3 times faster than enrollment. From 1990 to 1998, Medicaid spending for long-term care skyrocketed 225%. Medicaid nursing home care is for that only- it does not cover assisted living. And it is only for the 'poor.- those with less than $2000 in assets (spousal offsets apply). The problem is that with so many more elderly living so much longer and with severely depleted funds, the deficit spending is going to get worse and worse as they seek coverage in the late stages of their lives. I have no idea how this will play out over time but with less governmental funds available.................

If there are sufficient assets, a LTC policy of some type must be presented to retiree. A fiduciary has a duty to do this. And the duty to tell them to avoid Medicaid care is preferable since, no matter the comments to the contrary, there is a stigma to the quality of care that can manifest itself

**Policies**

Due to the massive changes the companies- mergers, going out of the business- there is no specific list for me to offer as to which company to use. I will note this- if your employer offers a policy as part of your company benefits package, do look at that first. The options are generally more limited than a private policy but not so much as to cause a 'problem' with overall coverage. The main point is that they may be significantly cheaper than a private policy.

And I can only cover generalities here- the policies change so much that they only way to deal with them is to get three or four different company programs and try to analyze them. Even here it gets difficult since the terms they may use- such as mild or severe- have different meanings by different companies.

Elimination period- this is the amount of time that you will pay for benefits yourself. The longer this time frame, the lower the premiums.

Coverage period- Many companies offer discounts if two people are covered. Sometimes one can use part of the other's benefits if one policy is used up. As stated, these are not cheap and the premiums are not guaranteed unless the company has a special policy where you pay an upfront cost to (supposedly) absorb future costs.

If you can afford it and your family has a history of Alzheimers, try for a longer coverage. Alzheimers can take up to 10 years and the costs are greater the worse it gets.

Daily costs- check out your area first to see what the costs are in a facility you might use. Remember, almost all policies now cover for assisted living AND nursing home so pick your costs accordingly

Inflation rider: If you are (roughly) age 70 and younger, buy enough to fund current costs. Then also use the standard compounded inflation rider. If you are over 70, it is generally preferable to purchase a higher amount initially (compounding takes a few years before it makes a difference).

Also make sure how often the company has raised rates.

These are not simple contracts so be sure you do your homework- or try to find someone that has a good history with long term care.

# 40

# Life and Viatical Settlements

Viatical settlements allow a terminally ill person (one with a life expectancy of two years or less) to sell his/her life insurance policy to collect cash while he/she is alive. The Viatical settlement market emerged in the 1980s as a way to give terminally ill AIDS patients access to their life insurance death benefits. Once protease inhibitors came on the market, the patient's lives were extended far into the future and the Viatical industry had to change focus. The sale of insurance for terminal patients is still a valid opportunity for many owners but with the Viatical marketplace now limited, the industry looked to other alternatives. And the life settlement industry evolved.

A life settlement transaction is similar to a Viatical settlement except the insured's life expectancy is generally between two and ten to fifteen years. The viator (known as the "insured" in a life settlement), sells his/her life insurance policy for more than the cash surrender value but less than its net death benefit to a "Viatical" or "life" settlement provider. In return, the settlement provider pays the future premiums to keep the policy in force and receives the face amount of the life insurance policy when the viator/insured dies.

The unfortunate element in such sales- certainly in the initial stages for both Viatical and life settlements - was that the insured got a relatively paltry sum. And/or the purchaser received a policy that was not as expected. Generally the actuarial lifetime was 'misrepresented'- meaning it was far longer that the contractual lifetime indicated. And the commissions were very large. Lots of fraud. It was an industry out of control for many years.

One of the worst violations was STOLI- stranger owned life insurance. Agents would engage the elderly- say over age 70- who could still get insurance. Many would hold seminars at retiree communities assuring them of large rewards. The agent would give the insured a cash payment for agreeing to the policy. The agents would pay the premiums for the two year incontestability period (where the insurance company can challenge a policy) and then sell the policy in a life settlement after that time. Obviously the policy size had to be large enough to go through the effort, so agents tampered with the income and assets of the insureds to validate the large size policy. Of course some insureds getting these upfront payments would rationalize that what they were doing wasn't bad since no one would get hurt- or that the insurance companies were bad anyway (see moral egoism). No matter, the policies violated many issues not the least of which is the insurable interest. There had to be a true reason for the insured to provide a benefit to another. Well, there *was* a 'legal' beneficiary but just for the two years to run (and that is what some attorneys rationalized). No matter, these were sham transactions to begin with so a lot of these contracts are in dispute- and justifiably so. But the money looked good to many and a lot of controversy will exist for years. Unethical (and really stupid) licensees are still trying these.

Finally a little commons sense- and many lawsuits and some state regulation- controlled the excesses. Commissions dropped, actuarial lifetimes were now more precise and buyers are finding legitimate contracts to purchase.

## General provisions

A life settlement is valid for an unneeded or unwanted policy for insureds over, generally, age 70 and/or in ill health. If an individual was age 55, far too much time, risk and premium payments would have to be made to justify a purchase. (Actually had a 55 year old physician call me a few years ago that had seen my website. He was approached to put up two rental properties to purchase a $20,000,000 policy which, he was told, would be sold after two years. I asked him if he was almost dead since no one would bother to buy a policy from a healthy 55 year old. But a lot of people did do things like that and it will cost them dearly as they may have to pay the premiums for decades or simply let them lapse and be out thousands of dollars. But the agents already got a huge commission from the first policy so they did pretty good.

'An unneeded policy might be when an officer retired from a company and the policy is, obviously, no longer needed. Given the health circumstances and age, the company could receive a lump sum far greater than any surrender value. Even if it was a term policy, perhaps it could be converted without evidence of insurability to a permanent policy which could then be sold. These transactions are not against public policy. Perhaps the most obvious lack of need comes from a retiree who held a policy until retirement and insurance is no longer in the picture.

There are those where the policy is too costly. Here is one I did for a client years ago and a summary of the case is provided herein. (Agent would carry a bible into the first meeting showing how honest and reliable he was. Just a big jerk. See also affinity scams.) An elderly woman had been sold a $5,000,000 policy by an agent where the premiums were larger than her income. There was no cash value. She was absolutely distraught. Everyone told her to simply terminate the policy. Her daughter contacted me and after careful analysis, the policy was sold netting the family $677,000.)

A most important item however- NEVER assume one life settlement company will provide the highest value. These must be shopped around to find the best price I know some say that a single company is adequate to get prices all over the U.S., but I am leery.

Here is a scenario where a policy that should not be converted. Assume an elderly man with a $1,000,000 policy and $75,000 in cash value. He is very sick, cannot afford the policy and seems prime for a life settlement. Not so fast. Maybe he can get $400,000 in a settlement. But if he keeps the policy and lets the $75,000 pay the premiums, he might die soon and his beneficiaries would get $1,000,000. If he does live five years and the cash is now depleted, he will be all the sicker and older and then may get $700,000 in a settlement (numbers are just for the example).

Lastly, make an assumption that there is a $1,000,000 policy but the insured needs money for medical emergencies. Not just money for whatever- but a valid medical need. Many policies now are designed to provide payments for just that purpose- even term policies have now added such riders. So the life settlement might not be necessary. Older policies may not have these features but just call them up anyway. They might just be able to help.

Also assume any of the scenarios above. Remember that the beneficiaries will lose their benefits if a life settlement is conducted. Maybe they can pay the premiums- or friends, or...........

## Summary

If someone is old and/or sick, do NOT unilaterally surrender a life policy. Check first with the insurance company on what might be paid out without a sale. But if the options are weak, a life settlement is a fiduciary requirement. And always be sure to shop the policy.

Can your agent act as the rep to sell the policy? Maybe, but this issue is also not addressed in formal training and they would not have the requisite knowledge or expertise. You will probably have to shop around to find one that is familiar with these- though the planner bringing this to your attention should also have a life license and be able to guide the process.

No life license?- then you do not have a financial planner/advisor so the point of having all this done correctly is moot. I am not saying a life license may do much good, but not having one breaches the fiduciary duty.

# 41

# 401ks

**"People spend more time choosing a TV than choosing their 401(k) investments,"**

**Jeffrey Miller**

This general section covers a myriad of issues impacting the average middle class employee with a 401k plan who hopes to earn enough money for retirement. Unfortunately, the bulk of education provided to participants has been woefully inadequate and the results manifested themselves most recently with devastating losses that could have been avoided in good part. However, the Department of Labor is effectively clueless to the real world application of securities and the risk of loss. A continuation of current policy and instruction is inadequate at almost all levels in predicting a viable retirement. Those doing the instruction are generally focused on outdated homilies and theories that did not work in the real world of risk.

The commentary below capsulizes some of the issues

of this book, However, it does not cover the actual personal planning for an individual. That is far too involved as described later.

## Diversification

Enron and Worldcom losses in 401k plans should never have happened. In part it was due to the irrational activities of the employees heavily focusing on a single stock that effectively mirrored their entire retirement asset base. Investors may want to pick individual securities but only AFTER they have been properly informed that they will need from 50 up to 350 stocks to reduce the excess (unsystematic) risk in order to get to some semblance of a diversified portfolio. The 'simple' question is 'how many stocks must you have in a portfolio in order for it to be properly diversified? I doubt that is in any 401k presentation anyplace. But since the employer is acting as a fiduciary, they now will have to be sure it is.

No matter, rarely has any required seminar simply and directly offered the knowledge and real life fundamentals on investing and put a stop to the bulk of poor competency coupled with irrational behavior. The Department of Labor- overseeing the dissemination of seminars and info to 401k participants- does not have employees on staff who understand risk. I contacted the DOL in 1994 regarding the elements of diversification and no one had a hint to much of anything. Considering their activity since then with the continuing lack of required instruction on the fundamentals of risk for employees, it is no wonder company employees lost so much money over the past decades and certainly most recently.

For the real world of investing under a 410k, no presentation EVER can be found acceptable without an absolute statement that the lack of diversification is tantamount to a fraud upon the employee. Such instruction was mandatory for any investor before Enron and is even more necessary now due to the higher volatility overall. No presentation on investing can focus on the purchase of single issues of stocks without a direct and definitive statement on the huge outright risk of the use of individual securities.

This is nothing unique at all. It is basic research and basic instruction. It is what a prudent man would be expected to do. Obviously an adviser should be held to higher standards- that of a fiduciary who, by definition, has the position of only doing what is right for the client. Of course the employer is the one actually signing the contract to the point of fiduciary reference but he can sign off to others so it may be difficult to figure out "who's on first". There are a lot of levels of service- still the employee should come first.

## Fiduciary Standards

This is flushed out further in chapter 9, but suffice to say that the problem I have with 401ks is that an employer may release their fiduciary responsibility by utilizing an outside service.
(http://www.dol.gov/ebsa/publications/fiduciaryresponsibility.htm)
"What Is The Significance Of Being A Fiduciary?

Fiduciaries have important responsibilities and are subject to standards of conduct because they act on behalf of participants in a retirement plan and their beneficiaries. These responsibilities include:

Acting solely in the interest of plan participants and their beneficiaries and with the exclusive purpose of providing benefits to them;

Carrying out their duties prudently;

Following the plan documents (unless inconsistent with ERISA);

Diversifying plan investments; and

Paying only reasonable plan expenses.

"The duty to act prudently is one of a fiduciary's central responsibilities under ERISA. It requires expertise in a variety of areas, such as investments."

That does not exist except in the ego of the company. No one has even bothered to understand diversification so the issue of a fiduciary is moot.

"Lacking that expertise, a fiduciary will want to hire someone with that professional knowledge to carry out the investment and other functions."

That does not exist except in the ego of the investment company. No one has even bothered to understand diversification so the issue of a fiduciary is moot.

O.K., I realize that was repetitive and that an investment company has greater skills. But if no one has bothered to address risk other than the market goes up and down along with buy and hold as the mantra of investing, then what could be expected? A greater skill in doing things wrong provides nothing.

But the employer can be off the hook because ERISA notes that "Prudence focuses on the *process* for making fiduciary decisions."

The process is corrupted since the process must address the risk of any type of investment for the employee. Is that not the bottom line of the ERISA?. Apparently not since the losses sustained in 2000 and 2008 have destroyed financial lives irreparably

"There are other ways to reduce possible liability. Some plans, such as most 401(k) and profit-sharing plans, can be set up to give participants control over the investments in their accounts and limit a fiduciary's liability for the investment decisions made by the participants"

Nice words but essentially moronic. Government officials have known for years and years that the focus of the industry was essentially the Stock Market Game. It certainly could not have been the education for licensing since they knew it was set up for gambling as well. Didn't they?

Well, didn't they????

ERISA continues- For participants to have control, they must be given the opportunity to choose from a broad range of investment alternatives. "....**participants must be given sufficient information to make informed decisions about the options offered under the plan"**

This entire text addresses the fallacy of 'sufficient information". The use of sufficient information is a non sequitur for all intents and purposes.

Of course, everything is made whole because, "..... while a fiduciary may have relief from liability for the specific investment allocations made by participants or automatic investments, the fiduciary retains the responsibility for selecting and monitoring the investment alternatives that are made available under the plan."

Get real.

The material from the Department of Labor's legalese is a smokescreen for real life application of what should be done. That said, it probably takes its cue from the incompetency of SEC and FINRA- as identified by their incapability for over 16 years with the Madoff Ponzi scheme.

I submit that responsible instruction to employees would have averted most of the Enron and Worldcom losses since the bulk of 401k employees- when read the riot act about the lack of diversification- would have severely limited their exposure to company stock. From a Morningstar Journalist about my Fundamentals of Investing Instruction- "You could have saved Enron employees nearly $1 billion!". A real life understanding of risk can avoid a lot of heartache.

Look at the past two debacles and the losses sustained

on 401k plans. Such losses are emotionally devastating to the point of paralysis- or overreaction. Maybe all of this would have happened the same no matter the education. Nonetheless, the real life education was mandatory. It has never/rarely occurred. It cannot under current regulatory guidelines and officers and directors.

I repeat that FINRA (NASD) has never required the fundamentals of investing ever be taught to brokers. Even with all the huge losses sustained most recently, I do not believe that FINRA has staff that can adequately address many of the types of risk. They do not have anyone capable of calculating the risk of loss in various allocations. Until that is corrected, the investor will remain at risk for more financial debacles. So what is going on as of mid September 2011.

Rick Ketchum, CEO of the Financial Industry Regulatory Authority (FINRA), told lawmakers that FINRA stands ready to take on that role. He noted, "experience in operating a nationwide program for examinations and our ability to leverage existing technology and staff resources to support a similar program for investment advisers, we believe we are uniquely positioned to serve as at least part of the solution to this pressing problem."

That is a travesty. Period. C'mon- operating a licensing program and knowing what to put in it are entirely two different animals. Also recognize that the SEC is now headed up by the same person that refused to consider broker education (Mary Schapiro) so don't expect much save for useless rhetoric.

I know these comments will never endear me to the governmental agencies, planning organizations et al, but somewhere along the line, they have to acquire the knowledge to guide the advisors. They have to retrain the adviser. Without that, employees are forever lost.

## 401k Funds

Do not bother with high fee funds with high turnover (High turnover and possible taxation of gains is not an issue in a tax deferred account, but tends to be mirrored into a lot of brokerage costs.) You can use some actively managed funds (low expenses) but the major focus still must be towards index funds- such as Vanguard- which have extremely low management fees. Further, the basic index funds have low turnovers since they are not actively buying and selling securities. If you violate this tenet- along with that of diversification- you almost assuredly will have a bad retirement. That's not to say that some actively managed funds have not done well, but they are few and almost impossible to know beforehand. It's tough to successfully compete against a index funds due to the higher internal fees of managed accounts.

Per Ranking Mutual Fund Families: Minimum Expenses and Maximum Loads as Markers for Moral Turpitude;

Edward Tower and Wei Zheng, 2008 (http://www.econ.duke.edu/Papers/PDF/Ranking_Mutual_ Fund_F amilies.pdf) "We find that mutual fund families which charge loads, high expenses to their most favored investors and have high turnover tend to perform badly, even gross of these fees. However, gross of published expenses, managed mutual fund portfolios of those families without loads, with low expenses in their least expensive class, and with low average turnover beat the corresponding indexes." This quote was notable: **"It may be that families that charge high minimum expenses do not cater to sophisticated investors'** and clearly identifies why so many managed funds are sold. The least suspecting, least knowledgeable or those putting in the least amount of effort are effectively going to be cannon fodder for brokers who are selling product for a commission.

“.... a one percent increase in the expense ratio of a fund to reduce net return by 1.54% age points, per year, and a large cost of turnover: “a 21.5 basis point cost for (one-way) buy trades and a 63 basis point cost for sell trades.”

Of course, that still does in no way dismiss the fees charged by “fee” advisers. (Though commissioned brokers have been known to charge ongoing fees as well) since a 1% additional charge for allocation will absolutely cause a reduction in returns. That may be a moot issue for 401k plans since outside advisers would generally not be involved but it is a necessary issue for many other situations.

Unfortunately, 401k plans are riddled with excess fees anyway. Per David Loeper, “of the 600,000 401(k) plans in the United States, many, if not most, have hidden fees that are ripping off the participants and the advisors who administer the plans.”

"Advisors are used to defending the need for all fees but they can help themselves and plan participants by finding out what the fees are." For example, a 401(k) participant whose plan had a $120,000 balance cost 1.3 % or $1,566 per year in fees. Only $384 of that went to the advisor. The rest went to the product vendor, whose administration cost was just $246, while its profit was $936.

"The advisor and participant were both getting ripped off. The same rip-offs are occurring in 403(b) and 457 plans, he says. "Nothing is being done because plan participants do not know they are getting ripped off so no one is complaining."

That is pretty much true. However, the employ*er* may not care since he ‘did his best in finding a reputable firm and that was all that was asked of him.’

Actually I do know of employees that complained bitterly not only of the fees but the funds utilized. They got nowhere. But they might try this- Advisors can find out their clients' or potential clients' retirement plan fees by filing a U.S. Department of Labor form requesting the information. (If the advisor will not file the request, you got the wrong advisor). What I find interesting is that if the new fiduciary requirement is imposed on advisers and firms, what changes will occur? The transparency should be immediate and substantial and the fees should be known upfront. But a lot of inequities go unpunished due to the lack of funds, manpower- and outright incompetence of governmental entities. No matter the expensive or inexpensive funds, the allocation education has been- and will almost assuredly continue to be- lacking in an understanding of the risks being taken. Very few presentations have addressed risk save for some that might have mentioned volatility/standard deviation in some sophomoric content. But in doing so, they had to clearly mention the ***risk of loss*** (see herein). You absolutely must inform investors what their exposure is during times of stress. It is not enough to cavalierly mention that the “market has ups and downs” That is merely mentioning that there is A risk, not THE risk. Big difference. No 410k presentation is valid for any investment offered by a securities representative or firm that does not adequately the potential risk of loss.

## Portfolio Allocation

In any case, the whole point to investing is to adjust a portfolio according to economics reflecting existing CORRELATION- how one investment may act to another investment or a host of investments. I have hit upon this as much as possible but that is one of the most critical elements in defining an allocation. The world economy, the national economy- and certainly politics- all change at a whim. Which means that any given point in time, the allocations are different. That is real world. Whenever I have taken on a client and needed to arrange an allocation, old statistics were simply not adequate, reliable or true to the times. It was necessary to analyze all sorts of data reflecting current economics and projected/perceived returns from various areas. The plan always indicated that the allocation was only valid at the time of inception and would change some time thereafter possibly making the current selections slightly 'off' and, at other times, totally incorrect, given the new information.

The reference was to, prior to 2000, 1973 and 1974, since losses sustained in a buy and hold were about 45%. The economy had changed, the correlations changed and therefore the allocations needed to change as well. A static position was not acceptable since such losses devastate a lifetime of savings and assuredly the participants retirement. That it may be hard for the worker to make such adjustments even given the warnings, it is a breach of a fiduciary duty not to state problem, potential scale of loss and the overall necessity of avoiding same.

Risk is also a far greater enemy to investing than the simplified old allocations consumers were told to use or that comes out of the sophomoric software of most 401k presentations. The bulk of the theories on investing were never that valid since they failed to take into account the radical changes by governments, institutions, and the vast audience of people who are emotional beings who are swayed by marketing, herd behavior and more. They certainly were incorrect in their interpretation of risk as is clear by those truly skilled in the analysis (Mandelbrot). I am talking again about the adjustment to risk via correlations.

The whole key to proper/adequate investing is the selection of cheap index funds coupled with a correlation that closely dovetails with current economics. The first part is easy, the second takes a lot more effort. The effort requires input from outside sources/services. Even then, most are suspect.

While it is obvious that the industry is now going to have to reinvent itself to the real world, it will takes years if not a decade or more before the knowledge base is disseminated to employees. In the interim, those who have been most vulnerable to bad advice will continue to lose.

I have reviewed a number of 401k commentary from the 'industry'. In the past, they simply used the MPT (modern portfolio theory- a mathematical concept of selecting a collection of investment assets that has collectively lower risk than any individual asset) as a guide to investing and the element of buy and hold. Didn't work then unless there was effectively no stress on the market. If there was, all the assets tend to fall together- hence lose even more. No idea how industry education can straighten out. I just don't see the competency.

**Market timing**

Market timing- hoping to buy low and sell high- has been considered an absolute no no by effectively all articles. Some will attempt to move in and out- though most will stay with stagnation of poor allocations or singular stocks. In any case, it has effectively been proven that active management via market timing does not work overall. That does not mean it cannot work for a period of time. Sure it can, but by the same token, you are apt to lose, lose and lose. Probably one of the best indicators of what can go wgron is Bill Miller of the Legg Mason Value Trust. He was the only fund manger that had beaten the S&P 500 for 14 years straight- only to lose all the excess gains in the recent debacle. Think about that- a superlative record based on Value stocks that plummets further than the S&P 500 and loses all its excess value of 14 years. Admittedly the fund is back up more than the S&P as of this commentary, but the future is completely unknown so don't hold your breath with any managed fund.

*"We are going to have an extremely risk-averse economy*

*for a long time....The people who think we will have turned [the corner economically] in 2009 are wrong."*

*"When you invest, the consequences may be a lot more crucial to your decisionmaking that the probabilities."*

*"You cannot manage returns but you can manage risk"*

Peter L. Bernstein

The last statement by Bernstein is the key to adjustments in an allocation. I do not do planning for returns per se. I start and always focus on risk. For every dollar expected, there is an element of risk of loss involved. If that can be kept in focus, the investor should receive an appropriate return for the risk exposure to loss. It is not perfect since there are thousands upon thousands of intersecting issues in the economy at any point in time. And some losses must be expected from market corrections. But the definition of market timing clearly infers the **buy low** and sell high expectation. I submit that there are simply times when there are NO investments that may be valid at all. Moving out of an investment does not mean you are going to go back in. Maybe it is simply cash for a year or more to keep additional losses beyond a correction to nil. Investing in 'something' is not mandated anywhere.

From Mandelbrot- "Brokers often advice their clients to buy and hold, focus on the average annual increases for the ideal moment to buy or sell. But this is wishful thinking. What matters is the particular, not the average."

I repeat from Bernstein **"You cannot manage returns but you can manage risk".** I believe that a fiduciary must examine closely the risks being taken-economics obviously- and do what is necessary to manage the risk/losses. If they cannot do that, why were they hired?

**Buy and Hold or "How long is long?**

"The long run can turn out to be extraordinarily long, far longer than an investor's investment horizon." (Peter Bernstein) If an investor entered the market last century when the Dow was one-standard deviation above its long-term trend line, an exuberant bull market top, how long did they have to wait? Leuthold (InvestmentNews, 5/21/2001) notes that an investor at the peak in 1929 took until August, 1998, almost 69 years, to reach a nominal return of 10% on their money, including dividends. This is an after inflation yearly return of about 7%. Thus, it took 69 years for an investor to reach the long-term average return for stocks, and had an investor in 1929 relied upon long-term stock returns data to calculate their future net worth or retirement income, they would have been sorely disappointed.

In 1997, Bernstein cautioned investors about employing the long run as a benchmark because the long run is not a homogeneous state of the world, a smooth and straight line into the future. A very large portion of the vaunted equity returns over the riskfree return, the equity risk premium, is accounted for by just 32 years out of 200 years since 1800, 1950-1981. Bonds outperformed stocks 43% of the time, and stocks were superior over the very long run, but with a high degree of uncertainty during periods of time shorter than 150 years. He concludes that, "...the long run can tell us perilously little about what kinds of environments lie ahead...we have to accept uncertainty."

I cannot completely dismiss the buy and hold rule of thumb because anything can work at some/any point. But real life does not have to conform to the past and the idea of holding on to terrible investments in the hopes of returning to normalcy (whatever that may be) is an unacceptable tenet by a fiduciary.

## Summary

Bernstein noted, "Although mathematicians, economists, and engineers are well versed in dynamic programming, the architects of traditional financial planning software are not. Or, if they are, they are constrained by their superiors to keep things simple, which, in this context, means failing to elicit much of the information, such as the path of future labor earnings, prospective changes in housing, and plans for retirement account withdrawals, needed to generate an accurate dynamic program. Let me make a medical analogy. None of us would go to a doctor for a 60 second checkup. Nor would we elect surgery by meat cleaver over surgery with a scalpel. And any doctor who provided such services would be quickly drummed out of the medical profession. Financial planning, like brain surgery, is an extraordinarily precise business. Small mistakes and the wrong tools can just as easily undermine as improve financial health."

The unknowledgeable 401k industry, along with inept governmental oversight, has failed to address the real world of investing. Having some simplistic employee presentation of empty homilies has caused massive harm. Though the market will improve, it does not mean by any stretch of the imagination that the future will be significantly brighter nor that it will help current employees offset the massive losses already sustained. Employees need to demand a concise real life presentation. They must be instructed on the true risks of investing as well as a mandatory number on their own portfolio of the risk of loss. I do not see that any of these issues will be forthcoming for some time. Therefore the bulk of 401k employees will continue to lose confidence in their retirements. Certainly when losses of 50% of an equities allocation should be expected at least once every decade.

# 42

# Conclusion

Dodd Frank is a necessity but if it ends up in effectively name only, as I suspect, nothing really will be accomplished. None of the regulators (that includes Congress, SEC, DOL, State insurance and securities regulators, NASAA, AARP, (did I miss anyone?) know what is going on in the real world and I was surprised-even with the financial debacle- that something was passed. But as Charlie Munger might say- 'well, they had to do something'. As to the current success- at the top end, Dodd Frank has not accomplished anything- too big to fail is just bigger no matter the contrary statements of Bernanke.

The attempt for higher responsibility by retail advisors for their customers has been pushed by several organizations pursuing one element of fiduciary standard on investments while obscuring the fact that most of they and their members are violating laws and ethics with impunity (and have been for decades). This is not some blasphemous sophomoric NOR unnecessary comment meant to demean the (supposed) intent of getting more quality advice. It is meant as a factual statement to force regulators, journalists, consumers, RIAs et al to recognize that those demanding higher standards must prove that they are worthy of the loftiness.

Admittedly I am also looking at more than just investments since there are very few entities that state/infer that investment advice is all they do. The monikers they use demand *financial planning* fiduciary duty so they shall be held to that level of expertise.

Unfortunately few can meet the qualifications. The bulk of brokers and RIAs coming from the industry have never been taught the fundamentals of investing. It's not required for licensing. As for financial planners, advisors, et al, they must have the necessary knowledge base to insurance and annuities and that is simply not happening.

As such, be careful of all monikers and designations. They tend to be just that- nothing more than monikers and designations. I will tell you straight up that if you want a planner, get one with at least degree in planning- not some CFP, ChFC or CPA with a just one college semester for their planning designation. It may be 'nice' that they might also have a degree in Soap Monitoring- but it has nothing to do with the intensive review needed in all areas of personal planning. The bulk have not even had formal education on risk so caveat emptor.

That said, I do have a MSFP and while the knowledge base was far more extensive than any designation, the real life application of products remained seriously remiss- and remains so today. Coursework would cover trust applications but there was effectively nothing on what insurance to use and why. Investments would cover the theoretical elements of MPT, standard deviation, efficient market et al but only as it pertained to 'theory'. The world has radically changed in a way few could have envisioned and historical guidelines are not the precursors to success- if they ever really were. Risk will now dominate, returns will be lower, volatility greater. Dodd Frank must move beyond some cursory effort and train/retrain hundreds of thousands of advisors if anything truly useful will transpire. The essence of the issues are described here. But I am nothing if not a realist. It's not going to happen. Probably the best I can hope for is a change in licensing to update to some minuscule level of competence. Even then, the average series 7 licensee is not going to have the background or intellect to grasp the fundamentals and move forward with them. That's just the way it is. And unless and until the universities adjust their old focus of relying on formulas and software to solve all issues of mankind- absent the human factor- nothing much will filter down either.

I have addressed some of the most obvious problems- though the list is massive. From misapplied statistics and fluid correlations and betas, improper client questionnaires, standard deviation treated as "risk" and on and on- yet all pretty much used by the industry to sway the public to invest into something where the advisor thinks (hopes?) that the marketing hype might just work. Dollar cost averaging, annual rebalancing, the proverbial flat rates of return and buy and hold all have to be, if not thrown away, at least revisited with proper clarification to consumers. Sure, they might/can work given an up, or even flat, market but that is not the essence of truly helping the client.

As is evidenced by the minimal financial literacy rate (actually all literacy), the consumer is bereft of the skills to understand what must be done. Add in human behavior to all functions and it becomes clear that they may not/do not act rationally in many endeavors- absolutely including money. The duty of a fiduciary is to help them grow assets but said duty escalates/solidifies with the critical responsibility to help them keep what has been earned. That sure did not happen with 44% losses in the 2000 debacle and 57% in 2008. Advisors have lived in the past (buy and hold again) since it is much easier than trying to do the hard work to look to the future. Bill Jahnke said it correctly years ago- “Asset allocators view their primarily job as getting a client into an asset allocation solution and advising the client not to abandon the asset allocation solution in volatile markets. But if the fixed asset allocation solution is not right for the client and is inflexible in the face of changing economic opportunities, what is the service worth?” Not much. Why the problem? Very inadequate, old, not well thought out, intransigent instruction by very mediocre, sometimes old, definitely little thinking instructors with not well thought out real world understanding of how the products were to work. That probably is the real culprit to the bulk of the problems regarding not only the losses sustained by consumers and businesses but by our country as well- old theories that were not tested for real life offered by old fogies who still can’t use a computer. Yet accepted by the masses, politicians and advisors et al since they neither had the curiosity to question the results nor the intellectual capability to do much with it in any case. The real problem now is unless someone gets a real grasp of what to do now, the failure of our economic system will escalate beyond our grasp.

That has been the flaw of the top rung of governmental economists and advisors who have burdened out country with insurmountable debt. This irresponsibility and general outright stupidity has also run rampant with the SEC, FINRA, DOL and more. Of course the greatest reflection of a breach of duty is the failure of the SEC to a gather in Madoff. This general ineptness by these entities is the reason for the bulk of losses sustained by consumers in the last decade since there has never been an attempt to demand that brokers and RIAs know the fundamentals of investing. What did one expect to happen? Schapiro’s flatulent commentary about increasing consumer literacy is truly laughable. The DOL allows computerized 401k data- that is merely a cop out to not even addressing the fundamentals as well. That software is easy to do and the masses love it is a sad reflection that no one at the DOL bothered to do much more than give a clean bill of health to stuff that had long past its value. Or that they could even figure out. (Note: I am not asking for perfection. But when you look at Enron and Worldcom et al, it's obvious that the organization is an empty shell of incompetent attorneys and bureaucrats. At a minimum, diversification MUST be taught.) ERISA rules are necessary but they miss the salient point of being a fiduciary- do you know anything?

Not really.

It's the same as Congress and more- the assumption that a current fiduciary is actually someone who can address the real world. That is not necessarily done at the university level, nevermind simplistic licensing. Licensing does not address standard deviation; universities still tend to call Standard Deviation/volatility as risk, ipso facto.

The focus should have always been risk- specifically the risk of loss. It's not a perfect measurement of the losses that might be sustained- actually it is on the light side. The point may be, 'so what?' since if you cannot spot a soft patch, it is effectively useless.

Well, this is one area where the advisors really need to grow up. They have not been provided much of an insight to real world economics and activities but there is some excellent material coming forth that must be addressed and passed on to licensees. In essence it is a new world order and a lot of updated education is mandatory.

But Dodd Frank is demanding a fiduciary competency. You cannot say that "I will provide the best service to my customer" if you do not even know what diversification is. Dodd Frank obviously did not remotely think of new education for hundreds of thousands of advisors, but that is what will be necessary. It is going to cost a lot of money contrary to a lot of current comments.

Education at this level will not be cheap but it is clear that the lack of it got us to where we are today.

And somehow the essence of fiduciary duty has got to get rid of the offensive Stock Market Game directed to the most naive. Getting "high grades" and your name in the paper for gambling is not something our generation should be noted for. Past and current generations have been arrogant bordering on just plain stupid by allowing this trash into our school systems. Let's not let our children share in this blame.

As for insurance- I know Dodd Frank has not directly addressed the need to bring these agents into the fiduciary fold, but if the intent of all legislation is to help the consumer make better decisions, it will need to include this element. The education on insurance is unquestionably outdated and, save for a few services now offering some insight on universal life, there still is nothing on life insurance product application nor effectively anything on annuities. But since insurance agents are stating they are advisors, they are stuck with the higher standards.

Since so many monikers include the activity as acting as a formal planner, let's include everything at once. An attempt to do this piecemeal- well, that is really kicking the can down the road. And finally one that will be covered with so many cans, no one will be able to traverse. (Of course maybe we can turn them all in for the deposit and make so much that California will become solvent.)

It will be a vast undertaking taking time and money. But if no one does anything, the following ERBI (Employee Benefit Retirement Institute) ***2011 Retirement Confidence Survey*** probably will get worse: http://www.ebri.org/pdf/surveys/rcs/2011/PR914_15Mar11_RCS.pdf

"In a sign that Americans are recognizing the realities they face about their chances for a comfortable retirement, the 2011 Retirement Confidence Survey (RCS) finds workers are more pessimistic than at any time in the two decades the RCS has been conducted: More than a quarter (27 percent) of workers now say they are "not at all confident" about retirement, up 5 percentage points from the level measured just one year ago.

Reinforcing that trend, the percentage of workers saying they are "very confident" of a comfortable retirement ties with 2009 at 13 percent—the lowest rate ever measured by the RCS.

The survey also found that roughly a third of both workers and retirees said they had to dip into their savings last year to pay for basic expenses." and

From Americans Cite Affording Retirement as Top Financial Concern, Plansponsor.com, "Almost 40% of working Americans say they will never afford retirement, which, for the second year in a row, ranks as the nation's most important financial concern.

Lastly,

"Baby Boomers will be facing a very different kind of retirement life than their parents. The research shows that they might be able to keep the same amount of income, you know, relative to what they earned, so the middle class Baby Boomer may also maintain their middle class lifestyle into retirement. But there's one big difference. The only way they can do it is if they work. The only source of income to retirees - and I understand the irony in what I'm just going to say. The only increasing source of income to retirees is from work.

So what is the meaning of the word retirement, if the only way you can live in retirement is to work? The answer is, there is no meaning to retirement anymore. We're now shifting from lifetime pensions to lifetime work. It's the end of retirement."

Prof. TERESA GHILARDUCCI, Notre Dame University

# FINANCIAL PLANNING
# FIDUCIARY STANDARDS UNDER DODD FRANK

The term fiduciary is just a term used loosely to authenticate the (deficient) knowledge base and competency of advisors. Little may occur under Dodd Frank without a massive overhaul of licensing and very strong mandatory continuing education.

I do not have a clue who can make it work. But since the current system is so useless, hopefully some entity will take on the responsibility to readjust a broken system. Only then will a fiduciary be able to do the best for the consumer.

# Appendix

This appendix includes a compilation of private reports, studies, letters, and other commentary from the mid 1990s forward that validates more of the issues that have been addressed herein.

On July 27, 1995, Patricia Staggs, Assistant General Counsel and Chief, Compliance Bureau of the Legal Division, Compliance Bureau of the California Department of Insurance, wrote regarding Investment Advisers:

"That exemption appears at Insurance Code Section 1831(e) and provides an exemption to the chapter regarding life and disability analysts for "an investment adviser as defined in section 25009 of the Corporations Code, when acting in that capacity." Section 25009 of the Corporations Code provides as follows:

"Investment adviser means any person who, for compensation, engages in the business of advising others, either directly or through publications or writings, as to the value of securities or as to the advisability of investing in, purchasing or selling securities, or who, for compensation and as part of regular business, publishes analyzes or reports concerning securities. "Investment Adviser" does not include (a) a bank, trust company or savings and loan association; (b) an attorney law, accountant, engineer or teacher whose performance of these services is solely incidental to the practice of his profession; (c) a broker-dealer whose performance of the services is solely incidental to the conduct of his business as a broker-dealer and who receives no special compensation for them; or (d) a publisher of any bona fide newspaper, news magazine or business or financial publication of general, regular and paid circulation and the agents and servants thereof, but this clause (d) does not exclude any person who engages in any other which would constitute him as an investment adviser within meaning of this section.

A life and disability insurance analyst is defined in insurance code 32.5 as follows:

"Life and disability insurance analyst" means a person who, for a fee or compensation, paid by or derived from any person or source other than an insurer, advises, purports to advise, or offers to advise any person insured under, named as a beneficiary of, or having any interest in, a life or disability insurance contract, in any manner concerning that contract or his or her rights in respect thereto."

The Department's view to that exemption set forth in insurance code 1831(e) is that an investment adviser need not submit to regulation by the Department of Insurance so long as the activities engaged in by the investment adviser fall within the defined activities of an investment advisor as set forth in Corporations Code section 25009. It is noteworthy that the definition of an investment adviser contains no reference to insurance related activities (emphasis mine). Therefore, any activities included within the definition of life and disability analyst, such as advising as to life insurance products, are clearly outside the "capacity" of an investment adviser, and would subject the person to the provisions of law relating to life and disability insurance analysts.

Patricia Staggs

**ERROLD F. MOODY JR.**

August 7, 1995

Certified Financial Planner Board of Standards, Inc.
1660 Lincoln St., Ste 3050
Denver, CO 80264-3001

I contacted the Board in October, 1994 and about March, 1995 to request that the Board review the illegal activities of California fee CFP's acting without an insurance license or unregistered as Insurance Analysts. I was told that the Board did not have the ability or resources to proceed and that I would need to file against individuals separately. I indicated I would.

This issue is not taken lightly. I have discussed this issue/requested input not only with the California Department of Insurance but with other life licensees, CFP's, NAPFA, Insurance Commissioner Chuck Quackenbush, Governor Pete Wilson, Senator Lockyer, Assemblyman Byron Sher, an Adjunct Professor of Ethics, California Broker, among others. The result of this review has led me to no different position than that established many years ago when I first identified the illegal activity. In fact, considering the ever-changing product development as well as the volatile economic and financial environment, proper licensing- coupled with continuing education- is mandatory to protect consumers.

Further, as addressed in countless articles- including CFP Today- the intent of the Institute is to make sure any individual acting in a planning capacity, even incidentally, must conform to proper licensing, governmental oversight and regulatory control. While addressed almost exclusively to SEC registration, the essence is no different here for the demands of the California Department of Insurance. Further, it ALREADY is the law.

I will make note of three issues that several CFP's state is the reason they do not have to comply with the law. The first two are clearly and definitively addressed by the letter from Chief, Compliance Bureau which is and HAS BEEN the position by the California Department of Insurance (Department) at all times. And since I initiated discussion with them for four+ years, I can confirm this unwavering position.

The first comment some attempt is that the California code provides an exemption for "Investment adviser... when acting in that capacity". Since almost all fee planners are registered as advisers with both the state and SEC, they are all absolutely aware that there is NO insurance competency nor background necessary or required for registration. The California Corporations code section enclosed in Ms. Staggs letter clearly addresses what a registered investment adviser does-investments. Any attempt to try to apply the exemption to insurance is an obfuscation of the issue that any individual-even an attorney- would readily recognize. The attempt in itself violates the basic tenets of the Institute and is unethical. Any attempt to include a comprehensive insurance review demands licensing by the Department. I will note that not one of these individuals has provided any proof whatsoever that anyone has ever even talked to anyone at the Department in an attempt to discuss the issue.

The second comment that more seem to attempt is the fact that they really don't do <u>anything</u> in insurance as *comprehensive* planners but simply refer the client over to someone else. Or that they might ONLY run some numbers to determine how much insurance a client might need and, again, then refer over to a commissionable agent. Nothing else. This "incidental" work- as many call- it is clearly a violation of their position as a *comprehensive* planner- someone having the <u>capability and the willingness</u> to do reasonable research in risk management-addressing the types of insurance, needs analysis, etc. *Comprehensive* CFP's dealing with business planning must have some competence in split dollar insurance, deferred comp through annuities, cross purchase agreements, etc. Estate planning requires an understanding of 1st and 2nd to die life insurance policies and irrevocable life insurance trusts. Of particular note is the fact that anyone addressing retirement planning must at least have a reasonable understanding of long term care. Yet the California continuing education requirements specifically require an agent take a minimum eight hour continuing course in long term care. All that work is NOT incidental. NAPFA members, and, I submit, *comprehensive* financial planners, identify themselves in their marketing with clients as having the capability and willingness to work on estate planning, retirement planning and risk management. NAPFA membership defines *comprehensive* advice (a definition that will be used to describe all *comprehensive* planners) to incorporate the considerations of income tax, cash flow, retirement planning, estate planning, investments, risk management and special needs. Further, NAPFA members are REQUIRED to offer comprehensive advice. You can't say you'll do it and not do it. You can't say you'll do it and then offer purely sophomoric commentary. Either of those "rationalizations" is unethical in their own right.

Third on the list is their statement that the Department had not pursued the issue of non licensed representatives. True, because in my direct telephone conversations with the investigative arm, they indicate that their resources are extremely limited and the cases they do investigate are of "little old ladies" and those consumers who have been subject to egregious behavior by a licensee. However, are we to say that **as long as you don't get caught violating a law, then it's O.K. to continue the illegal act?** Surely, ethics demands more than that.

Lastly, I will address California Assembly Bill 1485, introduced on February 24, 1995 which, until my notice of such bill, was in the position of being passed by the legislature (irresponsibly I submit). The bill, sponsored by Assembly member Byron Sher of Palo alto, was to give Certified Financial Planners acting on a fee basis an exemption from the licensing requirements as Insurance Analysts in California. The bill makes specific reference that **"existing law provides that a person who acts as a life and disability insurance analyst when not licensed by the Insurance Commissioner is guilty of a misdemeanor"** and that "Certified financial planner means a person who has been conferred the Certified Financial Planner designation by the Certified Financial Board of the Standards and whose designation is current and in good standing." So, the legislature clearly recognized that prior to the assumed date of passage, any CFP charging a fee for insurance advice without licensing as an Insurance Analyst WAS GUILTY OF A MISDEMEANOR.

I pursued the amendment through my assemblywoman, Assemblyman Sher and the California Department of Insurance since, in my opinion, the passage of the bill would violate the intent of the Institute- and certainly my moral and ethical guidelines- to make sure all representatives are licensed and under regulatory control for the benefit of consumers. The partial commentary below is taken directly from the letter to Assembly Sher.

"Continuing education is required for CFP's and while it is true that some may take a course or two in insurance, the bulk of the additional courses (and attendance) has almost been solely directed to investments NOT insurance. And as a member of the Northern California Association of Fee Planners, I can assure you that I continually hear of the tremendous disdain for the insurance industry so that many simply avoid any involvement in this difficult area. (I have some letters on file that can be used to support this statement.) My point is that insurance licensees are required to take continuing education (25 hours EACH year for the first four years for a new licensee and 30 hours of credit every two years thereafter with an additional requirement that eight hours must be in long term care) is a major positive element in increasing professionalism and skills in an industry that is trying to improve objectivity and competency. To allow ANY group to avoid mandatory continuing education is a dishonor to the Department of Insurance and consumers alike. The current requirements of being licensed for five years before taking the Insurance

Analysts exam is completely appropriate considering the difficulty and importance of the underlying issues. The enclosed copy of the extensive list of areas tested on for the analysts license is MANY MANY MANY times more encompassing than the material addressed in the CFP initial designation. And while some areas may be touched upon in CFP continuing education, it is only viable if the CFP takes it. The current mandatory provisions are essential to maintain and INCREASE skills.

Mr. Peterson of your office indicated that CFP's might find that objectivity is an issue. I have a difficulty with that since licensing does not require that insurance be sold. There are a number of insurance companies that offer fee products (no commissions) and they will **sponsor** CFP's for a license. However, since some CFP's may have a difficulty with even this, I suggest that they be required to register with the Department of Insurance without the licensing exam (BUT THAT ChFC'S BE ALSO ALLOWED THE EXEMPTION) but be required to maintain the same continuing education courses that are mandated for life insurance agents throughout the state. At the end of five years, per the current law, they would be allowed to take the Analysts exam. Let them prove their capability rather than through a simple exemption. That's what the consumers need and should expect- knowledge and competency. The current bill does not demand that and should be revised.

Recognize that I have no ulterior motive for this effort. As an Registered Investment Adviser and a CFP, one might say that I would like the exemption since I could reduce my continuing education requirements. However, I believe that fee planners, such as myself, should adhere to and be forced to participate in continuing education as least to the same level of life agents. If "regular agents" are forced to learn, so should CFP's. It is literally the ONLY way that the industry can reach higher levels.

I will also note that prior to my learning about the bill last week, I had been in communication with the Department of Insurance regarding this same matter. My continuing concern is simply the significant lack of insurance knowledge that financial "professionals" commit to and their almost absolute reluctance to do continuing education in this area. That does not conform to the essence of your bill.

I understand that your office will contact me regarding this issue and I am willing to meet you at your office to discuss further. However, I feel so strongly about this that I wish to be heard by any committee reviewing this bill if a revision is not made. I cannot in good conscience watch as more consumers receive information that is inadequate and that could lead to serious financial disaster." The bill was "killed" shortly thereafter.

The NAPFA code of ethics, and, which I again submit is consistent with *comprehensive* planners, espouses the requirements of Objectivity, Full Disclosure, Integrity and Honesty, Competence, Fairness and Suitability, Confidentiality, Professionalism and **Regulatory Compliance**. Paragraph B of the NAPFA membership questionnaire requires the candidate to "agree to comply with all federal and state laws, rules and regulations applicable to the practice of financial planning". I have no compunction in stating that this continued irresponsible rationalization to avoid licensing as required by law repudiates many of the ethical guidelines *comprehensive* planners are required to submit to. If you don't want to be licensed, then don't hold yourself out to the higher standards of competence as a *comprehensive* planner. Don't say regulatory compliance and then try to hide behind some insupportable and unsubstantiated blather.

In summary, I will comment on a question recently asked me about "how do I feel about sending CFP's to the Board of Standards". My reply was that I am fully aware of the personal and professional repercussions that I have had and will assuredly bear in the future due to these actions. But the Standards clearly indicate that I have no choice but to follow the law and to require others to do the same. I do not like this nor certainly want the aggravation, but since no other entity will take on the responsibility, then I have no choice. The law requires *comprehensive* fee financial planners to be licensed by the State of California or they are guilty of a misdemeanor. Any individual that presents his/herself as having the competency and willingness to provide information on the critical areas of a consumer's financial well being- which includes insurance- must clearly be licensed. You cannot back track later and say you really didn't mean it or only do superficial work. That is a fraud upon the public and a violation of the Code of Ethics. This is the first of many submissions. Each will also be submitted to the California Department of Insurance for investigation.

Errold F. Moody Jr.

## CALIFORNIA DEPARTMENT OF INSURANCE

February 3, 1998

On July 30, 1997, a discussion concerning the life and disability insurance analyst license was held between the California Department of Insurance (CDI) and members of the financial planning industry. As you participated in this dialog, I am writing to communicate CDI's policy on this matter.

The focal point for this issue is consumer protection, not the interests of the individual factions. With all parties based in customer service, it is sad that this detail has been lost in much of the discussion. As defined by insurance code Section 32.5, a life and disability insurance analyst is

"... a person who, for a fee or compensation of any kind, paid by or derived from any person or source other than the insurer, advises, purports to advise, or offers to advise any person insured under, named as beneficiary of, or have any interest in, a life or disability insurance contract, in any manner concerning that contract or his or her rights in respect thereto."

The fact that there are only 46 life and disability analyst in California is not a valid argument for repealing this code. In fact, the limited number of licensees and population in noncompliance begs for increased education and enforcement. While the easy solution for those in noncompliance may be to repeal this law, consumers who pay for fee advise on insurance matters deserve an analyst educated in insurance per CDI standards. The current licensing requirements ensure that relationship. Any legislative effort to repeal this law will likely be opposed, on the basis that such action is harmful to consumers, by consumer groups, insurers, agents and brokers, and the California Department of Insurance.

At the July 30, 1997 meeting, representatives from the financial planning industry raised two additional suggestions concerning CDI's examination requirement. The first seeks to allow issuance of a Life and Disability Analyst license to Certified Financial Planners and Certified Public Accountants following the successful completion of their own professional examinations. Again, this is an idea that requires legislation and will certainly face opposition. CDI's position remains at only those individuals who pass CDI's exam are to be issued a life and disability analyst license. CDI is the agency charged with enforcing this license and will remain, via its examination and related or regulatory functions, the authorizing agency for this license.

The final suggestion request a waiver of the requirement than an examinee must have five (5) years experience as a life licensee, or employment experience under said licensee, to sit for CDI's examination. Again, this is an idea that requires legislation. CDI will reserve judgment until the full breadth of this proposal has been introduced to the state legislature.

Despite some groups interest in changing current law, there is an existing law which is, and has always been, quite clear. While a financial planner may be illegally engaging in insurance analyst activities and may not be aware of their violation, it is my hope that this explanation of policy will provide them with the impetus to come into compliance or cease the illegal activity immediately. Per insurance code Section 1844, " any person who acts, offers to acts, assumes to act, as a life and disability insurance analyst when not licensed by the commissioner per this article...... is guilty of a misdemeanor." Consistent with current practice, information obtained on individuals in noncompliance will be aggressively pursued.

Jeffrey Kenny, Assistant Ombudsman and Legislative Liaison

**ERROLD F. MOODY JR.**

January 22, 2006
Ms. Sarah Ball Teslik
CEO
CFP Board of Standards
1670 Broadway, Suite 600
Denver, CO 80202-4809

RE: Constance P. Smith and Cynthia M. Smith, individually and on behalf of various family trusts v. The Johnson Financial Group, Inc., Asset Management Securities Corp., James Johnson. and William Johnson (Johnson) NASD Case No. 03-02522

Dear Ms. Teslik,

I have waited for some time to determine if the Board actually would re-review the above file as it had indicated. I had hoped to see a formal reprimand against Johnson because the breaches of duty were so open and obvious- further, no one is willing to pay $300,000 if they did nothing wrong. But when the Board's recent newsletter arrived and addressed those who had been reprimanded, nothing was noted. I was not surprised- no one contacted the Smith's, no one (according to Johnson's attorney) had contacted he or Johnson and certainly no one had contacted me. What was the point of reopening an investigation if the Board was not going to do anything? The entire fiasco by the Board is almost laughable were it not for the transgressions by Johnson and the emotional and financial suffering by the Smith's. The Board has continually violated literally every level of integrity and competence. You demand the utmost of CFPs- integrity, honesty, competence, fairness and all the rest of the issues made mandatory by the ethics course but which you and the Board flatly have decided you do not have to adhere to.

I will be filing my (expanded) report with the Florida Department of Insurance, the Florida Office of Financial

Regulation, Florida Department of Elder Affairs and the SEC. No one, specifically a CFP effectively absolved of all wrong by the Board, will be allowed to practice purposeless and fraudulent planning on the least suspecting of the public. I am fully aware of the 'rules' about indiscriminately harassing another CFP- actually anyone for that matter- but my report speaks for itself and the settlement by Johnson confirms the violations. I will also be submitting to these entities some of the letters I have submitted to you addressing the inadequate/barren analysis by the Board so that Johnson cannot use the previous exoneration as a defense.

As stated, all of you should be ashamed. I would have fired each and every one of you for your obvious incompetence and fraud. Even just for a lack of caring. Consumers- particularly the elderly- deserve better.

Very Truly,

Errold F. Moody Jr.

**ERROLD F. MOODY JR**

March 6, 2006

Florida Department of Financial Services
Department of Insurance
200 East Gaines Street
Tallahassee, FL 32399

Florida Office of Financial Regulation
Division of Securities and Finance
200 East Gaines Street
Tallahassee, FL 32399

SEC Headquarters
100 F Street NE
Washington, DC 20549

Florida Department of Elder Affairs
4040 Esplanade Way
Tallahassee, FL 32399-7000

RE: Betty P. Smith and Ellen M. Smith, individually and on behalf of various family trusts v. The Johnson Financial Group, Inc., Asset Management Securities Corp., James Johnson. and James Johnson Jr. Betty (Johnson) NASD Case No. 03-02522

Gentlemen,

The following report is a synopsis of a case against Florida resident and insurance and securities licensee James Johnson, Certified Financial Planner (CFP), James Johnson Jr.; CFP, et al. It is my assertion that after formal review of this case, the various Departments and organizations will see fit to examine in detail the files of other clients at Johnson Financial because identical violations of suitability and the law have occurred throughout its activities for years. Such activities include the sale of variable annuities into IRAs, sale of unnecessary life insurance policies, flipping of policies with needless surrender charges, use of a variable life product for the elderly, inadequate planning budget where the life insurance premiums were bankrupting the client, and much, much more.

Be advised that I receive no remuneration for this work I am now presenting. It is being processed as part of an ethical duty to rid the system of planners who have violated basic planning procedures, integrity and fiduciary duty. Additionally, they have no business dealing with the elderly. This scenario is a travesty that must be stopped.

## Overview of case

I was employed by the Smiths almost five years ago to address a purported fraud by James Johnson and James Johnson Jr., et al. A final report (enclosed) was prepared on January 2002 after almost a year of research and reflects a consistent breach of duty by Johnson et al towards an elderly couple for years and even more so after the death of Mrs. Smith's husband in 1999. Due to the Statute of Limitations, a truncated case was filed with the NASD by the law firm Ackerman, Link and Sartory of West Palm Beach, addressing activities of just the last few years of Johnson's involvement with the Smiths. It elicited a $300,000 settlement agreement by Johnson (remaining unpaid) just before the arbitration was to begin (December 2004).

Parts of the case however remain unresolved and were not addressed by Ackerman, Link and Sartory. Ellen Smith (daughter) had, prior to my employment, contacted the CFP Board of Standards and made a formal complaint against Johnson for various perceived infractions. The Board sent her a subsequent letter indicating that the matter had been "investigated" and supposedly resolved (though no specifics were identified). Months later, through subpoena of Johnson, we received a letter to him from the CFP Board (enclosed) that had officially "exonerated" him of any wrong doing. He was using that statement as major component of his defense. However the

Board repeatedly refused to provide to the plaintiff Smith, under subpoena, any of the *documentation* demonstrating that it had reviewed anything at all. Finally, in mid 2004, ***after*** the settlement 'agreement' and pursuant to my continuing demand for the material, the Board released its files. There had been no investigation. The Board had absolved Johnson of any wrongdoing without any review whatsoever by their Board of Professional Review or anyone else. There were no memos, no reports, no Emails, no phone calls, no evidence of any communications whatsoever with anyone or any entity- absolutely nothing. Therefore the exoneration was a farce and invalid on its face. Because of this obvious breach of fiduciary duty, I subsequently was able to get the Board to reopen the investigation. But after many months of waiting, not one call to any party, not one report made. Absolutely no further investigation was made by the Board at all. The refusal to pursue an obvious breach by Johnson is no longer indicative of just gross incompetency but a direct violation of the Board's mandated fiduciary standards and practices.

No matter the breach, it is clear that the Board's involvement in this case is tainted, if not corrupted, and cannot be relied upon when presented as a defense by Johnson. Johnson's second insupportable defense involves calculations that have no real life application to the Smiths. Here is the scenario: If one had $5,000,000 of assets, then the amount of value would increase over 10 years to $6,000,000 (rounded) at a 2% return and to $13,000,000 at a 10% return. With such supposed appreciation, various estate tax offset planning via life insurance is potentially viable. Unfortunately, while the computations are correct, the real life application is totally without merit. **The Smith couple had $5,000,000 in 1991- but it never changed over 10+ years. Up until Mr. Smith's death in 1999- and supported by audit in 2001- the asset based remained at $5,000,000.** Johnson indicates that the Smith's estate was between $10,000,000 and $12,000,000 in early 1997 (increasing to $20,000,000 by 2007) but did not/could not provide validation- nor has been able to subsequently. Therefore, in 1999, without any idea of the true value of their assets, Johnson now takes the existing policies in the Smith trust (over $3,000,000) and flips and increases them to a $5,000,000 face value to cover for estate tax on an asset base that he declares is substantial and growing rapidly. It should be clear that you do not increase the size of a policy for an obviously non growing asset- though anything is possible if you simply project unsubstantiated numbers.

The existing policies in trust were already more than adequate. Further, the increase in the premiums were such that the payments would reduce the Smith's assets down to zero before the actuarial lifetime of the insured. **The premiums were more than Mrs. Smith's income!** He had previously stated in 1997 that they were living comfortably on income without depleting their current estate. He had no idea the validity of the statement since no budget or income flow was identified. He sold excessive policies that were without merit at all times.

Next is Johnson's failed defense for the sale of Ellen's two $2,000,000 policies: Her 1997 inheritance ($750,000) was projected to grow to huge sums over her lifetime ($2,300,000 in 10 years). The computations are correct- but once again the logic and real life applications are without merit. There was no budget; the premiums were greater than her income had ever been. Further, Ellen's daughter was going to college and this would take considerable funds. Johnson's neglect of basic planning- a personal budget- produced the sales of excessive policies. Pacific Life Insurance Company would not cover for $4,000,000 of life insurance as originally submitted by Johnson since it was "not willing to underwrite a future need of this magnitude". Outside of my report, you cannot ask for a much more independent validation of a planner gone awry. They did place $2,000,000 but Johnson had to go elsewhere for the other $2,000,000. The premiums would need to come from her parents since Ellen was unable to pay for them. But said annual payments of $66,000 only reduced Smith's estate even faster. **The end result was that Mrs. Smith was paying premiums on her own $5,000,000 variable life policy; then had to pay gift**

**taxes for the premium into her irrevocable trust; then had to gift the premium of $66,000 to Ellen; then had to pay the gift tax on that amount; lastly Ellen then had to file a gift tax report in order to put the $66,000 of premium for her own universal life policy inside her irrevocable trust.** Anyone can manufacture numbers to support whatever they wish to sell- and therein is the problem. If you have not done either a formal budget or net worth, you can present any erroneous future value position. It is "easy" to document an enormous estate tax values well into the future. It is "easy" to sell a policy to cover such contingencies. But it makes no real life sense. The fallacy of unsubstantiated numbers is clearly represented by the Smith's situation. The report I completed documented the error of his plan. There was no plan.

An additional item that was not addressed in my initial report (I was still awaiting the subpoenaed material from the Board prior to the arbitration in December 2004) that is an absolute breach by Johnson- Johnson flipped the universal life policies into a variable life policy that was in an irrevocable trust. That is inconceivable. **The purpose of a variable life policy is NOT for insurance but for the inside buildup of money**. These policies are far more expensive than pure guaranteed insurance (no lapse policies). Estate taxes are to be paid from pure insurance- you use the leverage of the insurance rather than cash. A dollar of cash only pays a dollar of estate tax- an irresponsible focus in an irrevocable trust. The intent to the inside mutual fund buildup within a variable policy is to take the money OUT of the policy to be used for other purposes. The problem is how are you going to take money out of a variable life policy that is in an **irrevocable trust**? If the money is taken out (loans), there is an incidence of ownership that draws the entire insurance proceeds back INTO the estate for tax purposes. An expensive variable policy for a 77 year old put into an irrevocable trust where no one has a clue to asset allocation is beyond credulity. An internal cash buildup that would cause less insurance at a higher cost that was also not needed is completely irrational.

Yes, it is true that the Smiths never should have bought the policies, they should have been aware of their financial condition and more. But they are not sophisticated in finances- far from it. Further, they trusted Johnson and assumed he was running the proper numbers and knew what was best for them. The planning was inherently flawed primarily because it was nonexistent. Only during Mr. Smith's illness did Ellen realize their desperate financial condition and subsequently question Johnson's tactics.

A case was filed to the NASD which culminated in an incomplete settlement. Johnson stipulated a payment of $300,000 to Mrs. Smith but the payments were distributed over such a long period of time as to make the payments worth far less. The Smiths did not sign. Further, once the CFP Board defense was found to be false, Johnson refused to complete the negotiations. Mrs. Smith has subsequently been quite ill and under a doctor's care. Ellen Smith has fared little better. They do not have the physical strength nor the financial resolve to start all over again with another NASD arbitration. The NASD will not impose any restrictions unilaterally. The Smiths were informed six months ago that I would independently be pursing this issue. Johnson's attorney, Alan Lerner, was also informed that I would submitting a formal complaint to governmental officials.

So in addition to the flipping, surrender charges, costs beyond the ability of the Smiths to pay, we have excess gift taxes and a wrong policy that was NEVER acceptable in an irrevocable trust and even more so for an elderly client. No matter the attempt by Johnson to rationalize the sale of these policies- or other actions as identified- the attempt fails miserably. Johnson cajoled, impressed, etc., the Smiths into continuing policies and practices that violate not only fundamental planning concepts but also all common sense. Only because Ellen felt something was very wrong and contacted me for an independent analysis has this farcical scenario been identified.

I contend that most of his other clients have been faced with similar situations but have had no one capable of pursuing the issues knowledgeably. However, as stated in the initial premise, it is imperative that not only are his activities ceased, but state and federal agencies need to put out clear directives to all planners that this type of activity will never be condoned. There must be far more specific education and enforcement. But no matter the future adjustments, **current planners and firms already accept the fiduciary responsibility to know what to do and *to do it.***

As such, this material is submitted in order to put a stop to what were unconscionable acts by Johnson- and what I believe is indicative of many other similar acts upon others who do not have the understanding of what was happening to them. The scenario of the CFP Board's fraudulent release of liability was presented in order to invalidate any attempt by Johnson to subsequently utilize the previous "exoneration" as a defense. And the fallacy of computing specious numbers that have no relevance to real life. I repeat, you do sell a policy that costs more than the income of the client. And for a non growing asset. Under any independent and knowledgeably review, Johnson's actions are unconscionable and blatantly wrong. They were physically, emotionally and financially devastating to the Smiths. Neither he nor anyone like him should be able to practice- at least to the elderly. The legal and system failed the Smiths. The system is responsible for correcting this debacle.

This formal complaint incorporates all the issues in my report plus the additional comment regarding the invalid use of a variable life policy inside an irrevocable trust. Such issues include the sale of variable annuities into IRAs in the mid 90's (when there was no insurance guarantee upon the death of the annuitant. It was just greed). They include the flipping of whole life policies into universal life policies into variable life policies for a widow who was over 75 years old. The flipping caused significant surrender charges. What is the most egregious was that the Mrs. Smith **never had enough money to pay for the policies.** Johnson never did any formal planning for Mr. And Mrs. Smith, nor for the widow Smith, nor for the daughter Ellen. Formal planning is not "nice" and "sophomoric" words meant to sway a sale of a product or a spurious procedure. It is intensive planning of all areas of and for the client. Such a plan **must** include a complete and specific budget and its current and future implications. A new plan is mandatory after Mr. Smith's death. There was none. The result of Johnson's ineptness was financial deterioration and emotional devastation.

In short, these are egregious actions by a Certified Financial Planner that never should have occurred. The CFP Board of Standards should have acknowledged what was obvious and revoked his designation. (See letters to Board attached). The Board's marketed position to protect consumers from illegal and irresponsible activities and/or to investigate same are a fraud and their exoneration should be given no value. The financial planning was inherently defective since Johnson had little interest in computing a mandatory budget at any time. You cannot address risk nor reward without concrete numbers regarding a client's income and out flow. The rationales presented by Johnson are totally flawed. The Smiths are incapable of proceeding further. Therefore, of my own volition, I have decided enough is enough. Johnson et al has gotten a free ride for years and now is the time to put a stop to these offensive activities.

Johnson et al is a securities agent- the activities identified in the report are clearly a violation of many securities laws- suitability most obvious. The switch of IRA assets into a variable annuity is unconscionable. Further, in the 90's, there were no "death" guarantees that could be used as a rationalization for the sales. It is my contention, after additional review and questioning of his activities, that this was a standard practice with other clients.

Johnson et al is an insurance licensee- the activities of the sale of unnecessary policies, flipping; sale beyond capability of purchase- the list is extensive. The licenses for Johnson Sr. and Jr. should be revoked.

The enclosed report and accompanying letters provide proof of the actionable claims against Johnson. He effectively admits to same for $300,000- and that is just for the abbreviated claims submitted to NASD. But my comments are beyond that-regulatory departments need to investigate Johnson et al fully for what I believe are acts that clearly breach the fiduciary duties to his other clients. The various Florida departments and the SEC must initiate an immediate investigation of the Johnson's activities going back to at least the mid 90's. Further, all departments need to step up reviews and prosecution not only for Johnson, but for a large segment of the planning firms that deal with the elderly. The Smiths were not an isolated case.

I am aware of the supposed liability of this action. But I have no personal, financial or business gain in this endeavor. This is an activity that has decimated an elderly client and that I am confident exists at various levels with Johnson's other clients.

I will testify as required.

Errold F. Moody Jr.

cc: Senator Bill Nelson
716 Hart
Senate Office Building
Washington, DC 20510

Senator Mel Martinez

**ERROLD F. MOODY JR**

July 4, 2007

Florida Department of Financial Services
Department of Insurance
200 East Gaines St.
Tallahassee, FL 32399-0319

Florida Office of Financial Regulation
Division of Securities and Finance
200 East Gaines St.
Tallahassee, FL 32399-0319

RE: Constance P Smith and Cynthia M Smith NASD Case 03-02522

Gentlemen,

There is something seriously wrong with your divisions. Very wrong. I have enclosed a copy of a letter over a year ago. I have tried- generally without success- to find out some idea of what is happening with this complaint. While I do understand the confidentiality, there has to be some formal communication to me at some point regarding the status. One could at least tell me whether the complaint was being reviewed or simply dustbinned. I repeat, I receive nothing for this effort. I am committed to this effort simply because Barry committed egregious acts that no planner, insurance salesperson or securities agent should be allowed to do. My report is as complete as anything you can get. It identifies the losses sustained by the Smiths and the subsequent signed $300,000 settlement by Barry. I will also repeat- no one commits $300,000 for an invalid or frivolous claim.

Anyway, I tried to follow up again about two weeks ago by calling the Insurance consumer help line. The individual had problems finding the complaint. Finally, he did find a computer file by referencing my name, Smith and Barry but indicated that the complaint had been turned over to the Securities division and an individual, Tobi Pam in the legal section in West Palm Beach. I left her two voice messages inquiring about the status of her effort. What I got in reply was a telephone call from Robert Kynoch, Financial Administrator, Bureau of Securities Regulation who indicated that neither he nor Ms Pam had a clue to what I was referencing. In the discussion, we also 'agreed' that the matter was an insurance claim primarily, not securities related (though there were some mutual funds and stocks involved and an insurance policy was a variable life). He requested I send him documents which I did by pdf. His reply- "It appears we have not reviewed this material. I have started a background check on the agent and will determine how to proceed next week. Thank you for providing the material to me. "

It is nice he followed up so quickly. But after a year plus in trying to do something for the public, and providing a complete report that took me almost a year to complete, I find Florida's response to this effort to be absurd- certainly unprofessional. Yes, I know that the Department has lots of issues, lack of funds and manpower- but no professional organization can be this slipshod. If nothing else, you have to communicate. Formal written documentation is a mainstay to such complaints but the dearth of this effort is sad indeed. Consumers submitting valid causes of action will never bother if the effort is so wasted.

I feel, under the circumstances, that someone do what was called for initially. Respond to me professionally. Then do the investigation. And please do not tell me months and months are needed. I already did the work. I will testify to any of it. And Barry signed a $300,000 settlement to avoid more problems.

Enough is enough. Get your act together and somebody do some work.

Very Truly,

Errold F. Moody Jr.

P.S. I know the comments are harsh but considering over a year of time, I am entitled. Further, if I conducted any business (or lack thereof) such as has been communicated (or lack thereof) to me, I would be fired in a heartbeat. If you want to protect the elderly from fraud, etc. you have to do better than what has been offered.

**ERROLD F. MOODY JR**

June 2, 2007

Mr. Joe Borg
Alabama Securities Commission
770 Washington Ave. Suite 570
Montgomery, Al 36102

RE: Financial Advisers, OWS article

Dear Mr. Borg

I read an article that had this: Q: What's your feeling about the state of investment expertise for the average registered representative at the major full-service firms?

A: **There is a good level of expertise among most financial professionals.** Yet the average Main Street investor does not know that in one part of the conversation, he can count on the representative for the fiduciary standard for advice--but not when he's being recommended a stock. The "Merrill Lynch rule" was very confusing. There should be just one standard: the highest standard. It can be done by the SEC or NASD rules, in conjunction with state regulators, without congressional action. **The SEC should do a study and have a frank discussion on how the public makes investment choices in the real world.** [It should] recognize that the average investor is not going to differentiate between an investment advisor and a broker-dealer.

**You are just plain wrong about expertise.** I know I have said it before but I need to do it again just for the record. Until such time as the powers to be- yourself included- demand knowledge of brokers, the expertise is almost forfeit. I had to review several securities licensing manuals again (Series 7 and 24) for an upcoming case. There is not a person alive that can state that a broker has ever been taught the fundamentals of investing- simply because they are not requirements of the test. Not a person alive. All anyone has to do is simply go to

Dearborn or STC and look at the manuals from 1, 5, 10, 15 years ago. No diversification, beta, alpha, standard deviation, correlation and so on. And look at the NASD glossary. A short little blurb on beta- but no alpha. You cannot do one without the other. No correlation- that is mandatory. No diversification. No standard deviation. So how can you determine risk? How can you determine suitability? You cannot.

Admittedly it is true that continuing education is required of brokers. But nothing mandatory toward the above subjects.

I do not dismiss the confusion about who could do what. But you cannot request/state a fiduciary standard for advice when either or both of the broker or firm are ignorant of the fundamentals of investing. If you do not know diversification, you cannot determine risk. If you cannot determine risk, you cannot determine suitability. It doesn't make any difference if it is for stock or mutual funds in regards to investing, retirement, estate planning or just about anything else. There has to be a fundamental knowledge. It does not exist. What I am stating is not a slanderous tirade. It is a simple statement based on what any fiduciary- yourself, any NASAA agent, Mary Schapiro et al can validate by just looking at the requirements of the exam.

Therefore, how can you, the NASAA, NASD, SEC et al defend the expertise of the adviser/registered rep at any firm when you know- or should know- that they are delinquent in the fundamentals of investing? How can you do this?

No person alive can say that a broker has been mandated knowledge of a fiduciary either through initial licensing or continuing education. Any statement suggesting that is a fraud.

If the NASAA wishes to really help the consumer, every state securities agent, every NASAA attorney, **every member of NASAA** MUST become familiar with the basic concepts of investing and how they are to be applied. You have no choice. It is real world. It is the "fiduciary" thing to do. Only then can you relate to the expertise and the fiduciary standards owed to the consumer.

Very Truly,

Errold F. Moody Jr.

PS- The enclosed is what people do in selecting advisers/investments. This will save the SEC in spending thousands and getting it wrong anyway.

**ERROLD F. MOODY JR**

February 12, 1996

Mr. David Ruder
Arbitration Policy Task Force
C/O NASD
1735 K Street NW
Washington, DC 20006-1500

RE: Securities Arbitration Reform

Dear Mr. Ruder,

I am in receipt of the Report and must state that I find it incredulous that the powers to be have yet to acknowledge the significant lack of broker, attorney and arbitrator knowledge of security application.

A mere statement that arbitrator training requires improvement with almost sole emphasis on the law misses (as the panel saw in my correspondence to Ms. Mascussi) the major reason for arbitrations- suitability. There is NO training at the broker level regarding security application for a client profile nor is there anything at the basic level for attorneys. Actually, there is patently little training on securities anyway in the licensing training requirements.

It is clearly evident that the emphasis for the report came from attorneys- where probably but a mere handful could definitively state the proper definition for diversification. Can you? Could any member of that panel? Having done arbitrations in the past, it is obvious that arbitrators, NASD personnel and, equally, attorneys and expert witnesses had- and have- negligible understanding of basic investment application. True, many had a reasonable- if not excellent- understanding of the law but were, for the most part, incapable of applying it appropriately because they did not know what should have been done.

Perhaps the task force, as attorneys and industry personnel, felt the deciding issue was that attorneys simply have the responsibility to present their perceived facts of the case to the panel- irrespective of proper application. Fine, but then don't bother with training. But if the NASD accepts training, why the continued focus on Motion Practice, Evidentiary Issues in Arbitration, Managing Multi Party Complex Arbitrations but yet NEVER requiring a review, for example, of step up in basis? If you don't know the application of step up in basis- applicable to many senior consumers- then you can do as much motion practice as you want and never decide the case properly. Since I have done classes for attorneys, insurance agents, security agents and consumers, I can assure you they do NOT understand that major element to investing- assuming they ever heard about basis to begin with. And, as stated in previous correspondence, other elements of investing such as correlation, beta, asset allocation, etc., are left untouched in training at all levels.

This is not to indicate in toto that the recommendations did not have merit. But the commentary regarding arbitrator recruitment and training was sophomoric and a sham on the consumer. Some of you should be ashamed.

I fully recognize that my comments, before and now, will have a negligible impact on the knowledge and integrity of the industry. But at least someone told the truth.

Errold F. Moody Jr.

CC: John Hardiman

Worth, Kiplinger's, Smart Money, Money, Mutual Funds Magazine
Wall Street Journal

# FINANCIAL PLANNING
# FIDUCIARY STANDARDS UNDER DODD FRANK

**ERROLD F. MOODY JR**

August 25, 2010

RE: SEC File 4-606

I have enclosed a resume to indicate more background than anyone responding. In short, I have taught the bulk of securities licensing instruction, insurance and real estate continuing education, wrote two courses approved for continuing education by the California Bar, Practical Investment Theory and Application and Practical Life Insurance and Annuities Analysis and Application. Taught CFP courses, wrote two books on planning, act as a financial planner, provide expert testimony............

What is so patently laughable in this observation is that there are effectively no "retail brokers" nor "registered representatives" left in the United States that deal with consumers. Ever see any cards with those simple words identifying who they are? No. They have all changed to various monikers describing levels of competency and knowledge far exceeding that of a broker- "financial counselor, financial consultant, wealth manager, financial planner" and on and on. In recent testimony, I stated that a prudent reasonable person hearing such potential capability would clearly assume independent analysis of all areas financial- including insurance, budgeting, analysis of standard deviation (recognize that most use Morningstar), risk of loss and more.

The defense argued that there are no laws denying that right of use. True. But if one even remotely wants some suitable", those titles have to go since they deceive the public.

But you want to know the real problem? The NASD, FINRA, SEC et al have never required its 650,000+ licensees to know the fundamentals of investing to begin with. Licensing requires nothing on alpha, correlation, diversification, standard deviation, risk of loss, or how to use a financial calculator. If you do not know how money works, you have no idea what you are doing.

The SEC currently has over 650,000 agents who are clueless how to properly allocate a portfolio. If you do not know diversification, you cannot determine risk. If you cannot determine risk, you cannot determine suitability.

It is entirely disingenuous to attempt- under current regs of suitability- almost any level or review since a rep doesn't know what suitability is to begin with. Neither do the compliance officers et al. There is no mandatory continuing education to same and Schapiro's comments that the attorneys in a claim will provide the insight is ludicrous in the extreme. As an arbitrator, I never met an attorney that knew the correct definition of diversification (nor will only 0.5% of readers), no judges nor any expert from the industry (though there must be some). Arbitrations are judged on a lot of superficial elements of investor (supposed) sophistication while there is no sophistication at the broker level. Interesting reversal of defense but quite valid when the plaintiff's counsel is ignorant of the basics of investing.

So, go ahead and apply a fiduciary standard. All you will do is line the coffers of attorneys who might learn what suitability was meant to be and then try to apply some fiduciary standard on top of that. Unless and until the SEC and FINRA step up to the plate with real life application of product via mandatory licensing requirements, all the organizations will remain in a limbo of useless words.

Actually, when looking at RIAs, you can dress up a broker with some type of oversight via the SEC or state, but let's get real. You do not have anyone at the SEC or FINRA that has much of a clue to the fundamentals of investing in any case so the fiduciary level of competency will always be suspect at its core. The Madoff oversight was not a fluke and considering the refusal by Schapiro to demand broker competency (see my letters to NASD starting in 1995) and I think this is a parade of political tomfoolery.

Let's take a look at some of the organizations behind this- CFP Board, NAPFA, FPA. Think they are competent? Why? The CFP is one semester in planning. NAPFA is fee only but what is the point if there is no fundamentals of investing that they truly may have learned. Beyond that are the ethical mandates. Are these organizations adhering to the same standards they demand of their members? Nope. Out of 8,000 CFPs in California, not one is fully licensed and legal to offer comprehensive fee services. No NAPFA. No CPAs either. See Section 1848 of the California Insurance Code. See also http://www.efmoody.com/ethics/cdi.html. Check another 30+ states and you will find the same thing. Irresponsible and illegal behavior in willful violation of the laws and ethics but with effective impunity due to unavailable and inadequate investigations by any state organization (that makes it right?).

So now we have the ethical entities acting illegally telling clueless Senators (and their staff) that a fiduciary level of review is needed.

http://efmoody.com/nasd.htmlTaking some liberty with one of your responses with no direct offense intended:

1. We feel the effectiveness of existing legal and regulatory standard of care for brokers, dealers, investment advisors and associated persons for providing personalized investment advice and recommendations is adequate.

EFM- As stated, there are no brokers. Investment Advisers are not required to know the fundamentals of investing- where does it come from?? They cannot offer personalized investment advice even under suitability standards (which are unknown).

2) We feel there are no shortcomings with the current standards in the protection of retail customers relating to the standards of care.

EFM- how would they know? They are not taught either. The current standards allow deceit directly to customers.

3) Retail customers may not fully understand that there are different standards of care applicable to brokers, dealers,

investment advisors and associated persons of each. This could be explained with increased disclosure to retail customers.

EFM- Not really. Retail consumers are clueless. And it would have to be phrased correctly in writing. But they wouldn't read it anyway. Verbal is useless.

4) We feel the differing standard of care is not a significant source of confusion for retail customers regarding the quality of personalized investment advice that retail customers receive. The quality is not affected by any confusion they may have.

EFM- Retail consumers are clueless to what is offered. Always will be. Legalese in imperfect language will never work. Attorneys don't have the skill to write the material effectively.

5) We feel the current system of examinations of brokers, dealers, and investment advisers is adequate. The frequency of examinations of investment advisers could be shortened so that misappropriation of funds could be found more easily and the volume of data examined is not so extensive. The length of time of the examinations is reasonable in most cases.

EFM- the current examinations in no way address the competency of the plans and probably never will since the examiners have never been taught anything about suitability. Misappropriation of funds does not occur that frequently.

6) We feel the regulation differences between brokers, dealers and investment advisers when providing personalized investment advice is appropriate because the type of advice given is different. Typically, registered representatives are typically giving advice surrounding a single investment within a portfolio, while investment advisers are advising based on a full portfolio or financial plan.

EFM- disagree. If a rep is describing a single security, it may be unsuitable since it must mesh with the other investments. If you do not know diversification, you cannot determine risk. If you cannot determine risk, you cannot determine suitability.

Standard deviation, correlation, diversification, risk of loss etc. are not taught.

7) The current regulation and oversight of investment advisers provides adequate protection to retail customers in the instance of disclosure, however, the regulation and oversight of brokers and dealers is stronger overall because more rules and regulations exist, and there is more oversight at both the firm level and the SRO level.

EFM- the oversight of brokers may be more but the point may be moot since who is overseeing the incomplete knowledge base for the products? Not Series 24- they have not been taught the fundamentals either.

8) The existing legal and regulatory standards of State regulators is adequate. The powers given the State regulators should not be decreased, or increased.

EFM- Even given that, there is no money, staff or, more specifically, knowledge of what should have been done. The planning organizations are actively violating state laws for well over a decade. That is the level of actual enforcement.

9) The potential impact on retail customers of applying the fiduciary care standard to the range of products and services offered by brokers and dealers would be detrimental. Retail customers with accounts under $100,000 would no longer be profitable for firms or their associated persons to service. The costs of the additional liability of a fiduciary standard and the required insurance coverage, would outweigh the fees earned for many advisers. A large portion of the investing public would be without adequate service if requirements of the Investment Advisers Act of 1940 were applied to all brokers, dealers and associated persons.

EFM- perhaps true. But if all have no idea what is a suitability standard, what is the fiduciary level of care. The exposure to liability is now high but nobody does much since the consumer is unaware of the lack of competency of their "financial consultants".

But it is generally true that many smaller accounts may not be handled that well under the new standards. But they are not that good now.

10) If the broker-dealer exclusion were to be eliminated, the impact and harm to retail customers would be wide-spread. Each recommendation could be viewed as personalized investment advice and such recommendations would no longer be available to small investors, as outlined in number 9. The additional litigation, insurance and oversight costs would require significantly higher levels of fees to be passed on to the lower net worth customers. The resources are not in place to regulate the hundreds of additional firms, and thousands of additional associated persons.

EFM- small investors are already hurt. But it is true that litigation costs will go up. But consider this. With proper knowledge, hundreds of thousands of consumers might have avoided the 44% losses of 2000 and 57% losses of 2008. The Enron disaster to its employees could have been mitigated by 90%. But not if you do not know diversification or correlation.

11) Since investment advisory accounts typically have higher minimum fees and account size, the lower net worth customers would not have access to the same level of service or care as higher net worth retail investors.

EFM- true in part except it the level of service is NOT the same.

12) Changing the standard of care would not benefit retail customers in the protection from fraud, as the largest fraud cases in our recent history have stemmed from advisory activities. It would also reduce the access and availability to personalized investment advice for all but the high net worth customers, as explained above.

EFM- direct fraud is not that common, Inadequate, erroneous and unknowledgeable advice is. But it will make little difference since the examiners (attorneys) don't know either.

13) We feel that changing the standard of care guidelines could impact customers in many unintended ways, such as having to pay ongoing management or advisory fees instead of a one-time commission. The cost for brokers, dealers and their associated persons could be immense because of the requirement of maintaining dual registrations, and dealing with dual examination and bookkeeping requirements.

EFM- tough one since ongoing advice can stop with commissionable transactions. If further advice is demanded, the costs of time would have to be passed on.

**Summary**

We have two clueless senators (and more importantly their staff) who have focused on a fiduciary standard with no idea of what is currently occurring in real life under the basic suitability requirements.

There are no retail brokers dealing directly with consumers. The B/D firms are purposely deceiving the public. Of course, RIAs may be deceiving the public as well since their background might have simply come from the industry. But the SEC will continue to avoid knowledge since Schapiro has generally paid lip service to any increase in a knowledge base. And she wants to help the public? See http://efmoody.com/nasd.html

The fundamentals of investing have never been taught save for some extra separate courses one might have attended. But since they were not 'approved' who is to say they were any good? (Though the state and federal governments have extremely little knowledge to judge a course. They are attorneys.)

Most of the planning organizations pursuing the fiduciary standards are active and knowing violators of state laws.

The Government Accountability Office (GAO) is to conduct a comprehensive six-month study of the need for regulation of financial planners. A fine study- they do good work overall. But I am concerned that they will be barraged/inundated by industry and planning propaganda and miss the fact that it is the consumer who is to be protected. FINRA and the SEC are incapable. The planning organizations should not be actively involved in the final process since they have told members to continue to violate the law but just keep quiet about it.

The bottom line is not the regulation, it is the real life review of product application. This cannot happen without wholesale changes in licensing instruction and mandatory selective continuing education. Or set up our country for more Enrons, Worldcoms and 2000 and 2008.

**ERROLD F. MOODY JR**

April 12, 2011

Public Hearing on Definition of Fiduciary

EBSA's Office of Regulations and Interpretations,

Attn: Public Hearing on Definition of Fiduciary

U.S. Department of Labor

Washington, DC, 20210

RE: U.S. DEPARTMENT OF LABOR

EMPLOYEE BENEFITS SECURITY DMINISTRATION

DEFINITION OF FIDUCIARY INVESTMENT ADVICE

Gentlemen,

I have reviewed all the comments on both days of the testimony, positions by the financial planning community, Schapiro's comments on the necessity of consumer education and just about everything else in regards to knowledge and competency for 'broker's, planners, arbitrators, attorneys et al for over two decades. There are lots of pros and cons regarding who should do what, are commissions the devil incarnate, are fee advisers absolved of ethical conflicts (not even close) but nary a word on whether the advisers identified can act under suitability rules never mind fiduciary. No they can't.

## Brokers?

Neither the DOL nor the industry understands the problem. In fact, the DOL panelists are validating deceit of the industry in their own testimony. And the bulk of testimony from participants could be an attempt to validate an egregious deception to the DOL, consumers and just about everyone else.

What is it? You are all using the term **'broker'** in the two days of testimony. That is almost a complete lack of understanding of what goes on in the real world. Here is a sample:

"Independent broker/dealers and their **representatives** are especially well suited to provide middle-class Americans with the investment products and services necessary to achieve their retirement security and other financial objectives and goals.

When I call my **broker** and say, "Bernie" "what should I buy?"

But if I ask my **broker** to send me his firm's research on Cisco, and that research contains a buy rating and a price target available to all the firm's clients, that advice is not individualized and arguably should not carry with it fiduciary responsibility, at least when it's provided to plan fiduciaries

If all **brokers** who provide market color or investment information are deemed to be fiduciaries regardless of the intentions of the parties, the vast majority of commission-based accounts may move towards fee-based asset arrangements.

The Department's proposals would deem a **broker** a fiduciary merely because it is complying with industry rules intended to set standards for **brokers** who are not **investment advisers**."

The DOL's expanded definition of fiduciary is expected to limit **brokers'** ability to recommend their firms' proprietary investment products to employers, and to prohibit them from collecting commissions from product sponsors.

**Brokers** can continue working with plan clients as recordkeepers without accepting the fiduciary standard of care, but some plan sponsors might want to bring in third-party plan advisors to help them make fund selections."

*End*

The point is that there are ***no*** retail brokers left in the U.S. They have been called various monikers for decades. First it was 'vice president' or 'senior vice president' depending on the amount of commissions generated. In the late 90s the titles expanded to include 'financial planners, advisers, consultants, wealth manager' and more all with the clear intent to show that the individual agent has an extended ability to apply far greater competency than just acting as a sales person.

Go into Wells Fargo, BofA, Chase, Merrill etc. all across America and one is inundated galore with supposed professionalism with all the signs pointing to 'financial whatevers'. But not a single card with the term broker or registered representative. You have to live in a tomb to miss this clear marketing attempt to sway the naive consumer to utilize one of a firm's unknowledgeable reps (lack of fundamentals).

otIn testimony last year in an arbitration I stated that if you are want to be called a financial 'whatever' you must be held accountable to that level of competency. The defense attorney asked if the use was illegal. It is not. But it absolutely is a breach of a fiduciary duty, suitability et al to attempt to state you are something other than what you are. To sway consumers with marketing may be OK with a Bud Light commercial, but the allowance in marketing for lifetime assets to 'brokers' who have had nothing more than a one week course in securities is patently absurd.

I repeat- there have not been any retail brokers for over a decade. It is a travesty to the public to allow this. Fix this now. It is an absolute breach.

## Knowledge

This is *the key* to suitability and fiduciary ability. I find the inherent lack of knowledge in the industry to be absolutely abhorrent. And no one steps up and wonders why so much goes wrong. This is noted about the rule- from 1975- "The advisor must (1) render advice as to the value of securities or other property, or make recommendations as to the advisability of investing in, purchasing or selling securities or other property and do so (2) on a regular basis (3) pursuant to a mutual agreement, arrangement or understanding, with the plan or a plan fiduciary that (4) the advice will serve as a primary basis for investment decisions with respect to plan assets, and that

(5) the advice will be individualized based on the particular needs of the plan." OK- how???

Thirty five years ago there may have been some assumption about the knowledge and ability of a securities licensee. Not anymore. Not even close. Specifically, "the adviser must render advice...." How? A series 7 is so sophomoric in its knowledge base since at least the mid/late 1980s, they are so far behind the times that they may never catch up.

There are two points to this- the first will invalidate most 'brokers' and broker/dealers from offering fiduciary advice to customers. (I am excluding appraisers and more that are outside my expertise and involvement.) I am directing my commentary to those that deal directly with the various plans covered by the DOL- for that matter, any organization or rule including ERISA, SEC, FINRA, state governmental entities and so on. And that is that a broker or registered representative, by definition those with a series 6, 7, 24, 63, etc., have never been taught the fundamentals of investing. It is disingenuous for any governmental organization to suggest competency (real life knowledge) in working with retirement plans, ERISA standards, providing education, etc. unless you know what the background of the agent is. I will repeat this statement again- the fundamentals of investing have never been taught to a broker, are not now, and may never will be unless and until the governmental entities have a clue to what a professional adviser must know. After all, if one does not know diversification by the numbers, under what scenario can any instruction, advice, education be passed on to the public? It is not just diversification that is missing in instruction for licensing- asset allocation, standard deviation, correlation, risk of loss, budgeting, efficient market theory, capital asset pricing, Sharpe ratio and on and on. No training in the use of a financial calculator. Why would anyone use an adviser who does not know how money works (though they try to indicate they have a computer at work. Not even close.).

There is nothing on 'suitability' in licensing since it effectively appears as a word only. *No real life application of product.* Of course one can say- and the industry does- that 20 or 30 years of experience is more than adequate time to address additional sophistication in the needed areas of investing. And one would therefore choose a witch doctor with 50 years of experience over that of a relatively new physician with a full medical degree and residency overseen by other professionals. A compliance officer or supervisor with none of the underlying fundamentals as a basis for a suitability determination is also a pretty useless decisionmaker save for the most mundane of issues (whatever those may be).

As for the attorneys at any of the firms- there is nothing in the education that offers the fundamentals of investing. Any subsequent position has to be based on a very limited opinion rather than the fundamentals of investing. Never meant one who understood the true meaning of diversification. Or an arbitrator. Admittedly there must be some- just never met any.

In fact, I doubt anyone that anyone at the DOL has bothered to learn diversification since my attempt in 1995 to suggest updated education to the fundamentals. No one knew what I was talking about. (*How many stocks must you have in a portfolio in order to insulate it due to unsystematic risk? If you do not know that, then you cannot get to risk. If you cannot get to risk, you cannot get to suitability.) Sure diversification is *mentioned* in the series 7 classroom material but that is the extent (generally don't put all your eggs in one basket. And that means??? If it cannot be defined with numbers, it is pretty useless.) The bottom line is that the sale of most individual securities is a breach of suitability- and obviously fiduciary responsibility- because there are not enough stocks in the portfolio to keep risk 'acceptable'. As a result of that gross ineptness across all levels of industry knowledge, we had Enron, Worldcom, Adelphia and devastation on thousands upon thousands of retirees that should not have happened. Some basic education- none of which has stayed up with the times over the last 35 years- could have tempered much of the financial ruin and saved many a retiree.

## Risk

Here is the second major problem. Whenever a portfolio is designed, where are the numbers for risk? Is there anything taught on risk of loss in a portfolio? No. So how is risk designed for the consumer? It starts with a complete hack job with client questionnaires. The *consumer* is required to indicate what their risk is. The consumer is going to the adviser to ask what they should do, not vice versa. The difficulty is that there are NO definitive standards for risk. What is conservative, moderate, aggressive, speculative? The answers would be totally variant for both consumers and advisers. And universally just as useless. There *must* be consistency in an explanation of risk.

That statement begs the issue- isn't risk known by standard deviation (SD)? No. How about volatility? No. Yet so many offerings to American consumers tend to include something about standard deviation as risk since so many 'brokers/advisors' use Morningstar reports. But there is nary a reader of these reports that has a clue to the annual standard deviation of the numbers mentioned therein (trick question which I doubt any reader will recognize. Hence the problem.)

It is true that SD goes down over time and that is what is presented- as though the *risk* goes down. It is a breach of duty to ever allow SD to be used even with some caveat or exculpatory disclaimer in the 'small print'. Why? It is the fact that the risk of LOSS goes up the longer you hold equities. How much you can lose is the key to deciding what one will do.

And where is risk of loss? Nowhere to be found. This lack of fiduciary focus is the reason we got into the mess in 2000 and further in 2008. An inability to teach what is necessary to consumers. If there had been some simple coursework identifying real life risk, a great number of Americans could have avoided the bulk of losses they have sustained. But the risk of loss is not generated in any of the computerized software by any firm dealing under DOL standards. Or ERISA. One cannot offer education regarding risk and reward without the necessity and ability to at least show the exposure to risk for effectively any allocation. It can be done. It must be done. If not, the Dodd Frank requirements are useless. (Most allocations will have at least a 50% possible loss over time-though that can be in as short as one year.) Every equities investor (401k in particular) needs a fiduciary to address that statistic (which can *only* be done by a personal financial calculator at present. Firms do not want to include it because it would open up difficult dialogue with the advisor and inherently reduce sales).

Further, any fiduciary viewing the economics before 2000 and 2008 should have identified the overriding economic risks. But where was the knowledge? Where was the real life element of the inverted yield curve. (It is a 100% indicator of a recession.) Unemployment. Real Estate. Dollar. Asia. Even if certain issues are touched upon, there are none of the potential implications in licensing preparation. In any case, what can one expect from a one week licensing course that does not include the fundamentals.

And while I am on the subject, where is correlation? No adviser, no software program can do an allocation without addressing the very difficult movement of one investment to another. A fiduciary must be able to do it. But it is not in the series 7, series 24, or any others, CFPs included. How can you even have suitability applied? You cannot. And one can sure not be a fiduciary. Since the subject is not addressed anyplace in any rule, I have to assume that the DOL, SEC, FINRA and more are clueless to what is necessary for fiduciary responsibility.

## Returns

Testimony noted representations to consumers about returns-and of course the education under 401ks et al include various groupings of performance coupled with some pretty Powerpoint graphs. Almost universally they are based on past history that starts in 1900 or maybe 1925, or 1960 or ????? If one backtests (also not taught) enough, it is possible to make certain scenarios appear better or worse. No matter, past results are an emotional and professional crutch for advisors unwilling to spend time in the present and look to the future. One does not really have to read or think- just let the computer dump out an allocation that is the same for just about anyone and then sit back with a buy and hold and reap the money from fee advisement. Just where has the broker/advisor added value?

Doing nothing can work- if one is lucky. It also is the reason we are in the financial devastation we are now in. Yes, there might be some sophomoric commentary about risk- returns are not guaranteed, etc. Not good enough when risk of loss can be calculated for each consumer's allocation. It can be taught- but again, one needs a personal financial calculator. And the use of a financial calculator is not required by a broker. Nor attorneys dealing in any securities matters. Nor compliance officers. Nor supervisors with a series 24, nor arbitrators. How is anyone going to be a fiduciary to a plan without knowing how money works? They cannot.

## Registered Investment Advisers

is the competency of Registered Investment Advisers per se. While the SEC regs demand a fiduciary duty to consumers, where is the knowledge to justify it? There are a few CFAs, PhDs, MBAs in the mix but the bulk of the RIAs came from the brokerage industry and used the series 7 as the background for the RIA (like myself in 1984). Hence the comment- the fundamentals are not there either. And recognize that there are NO continuing education requirements. So why is it not apparent that the lack of knowledge was one of the key reasons for the failure of so many allocations in 2000 and 2008?

## Annuities

There have been comments about the inclusion of annuities in the education and inclusion in 401ks. Where will this education come from? Certainly not from RIAs. There is nothing that covers indexed annuities, step ups or guaranteed income streams. Anyone doing this is going to have to have a insurance license and/or a mandatory fee insurance license from the 30+ states that require one. Otherwise how can they present the appropriate knowledge, experience or competency?

## Life Insurance

No education of retirement can be done without covering the policies that are already in existence. For the purposes of this short paper, I will exclude the issues about the necessity of having insurance when one is younger. It is the fact that many retirees already have insurance purchased decades ago. Perhaps there is an idle comment about the decision of whether one needs to keep old insurance that may no longer is needed or too expensive and that would be it. So just surrender the policy. And that would be wrong. Unneeded policies for the old or sick become an asset that can be sold for greater than the existing cash surrender value. A fiduciary has to know what a life settlement is and how they work. This asset could greatly assist many retirees.

## Long Term Care

No retirement education can exist without addressing the need to cover for the eventuality of assisted living and nursing home care. It is expensive and while not being an absolute statistic, it must be formally addressed in the retirement budget. An RIA has no background in annuities, life insurance, life settlements or long term care. A fiduciary explaining retirement is responsible for all of these sections and more.

### Summary

I have read most blogs, articles, reports, presentations, etc., on fiduciary duty for decades and nary a one has ever mentioned competency via knowledge. FINRA doesn't want to rock the boat; the SEC is... well the SEC and guided by a commissioner who refused to include the fundamentals of investing when at FINRA; state governmental entities - like the others- are underfunded and not all that competent either. All have been swayed, cajoled and marketed to maintain the status quo over the past 35 years. It is financially beneficial for the industry. Knowledge would certainly slow sales. When I went to the NASD in the mid 90s with a proposal to instruct arbitrators, I was told that the industry would never allow it since it would slow sales (true). In the mid 2000s with another 'suggestion' to increase education overall, I was met with Schapiro's office that FINRA was a procedural entity, not a substantiative one. The writing was on the wall- the industry pretty much controls what happens.

The exponential surge of technology from the mid 1990s has changed every facet of our lives. Increased volatility is now the norm, as is 24 hour trading, derivatives, lack of pensions, longer lives, instantaneous transfer of information (not necessarily knowledge), Alzheimers, terrorism and more. Old school financial education- actually the lack thereof - has left consumers and advisers living on past history as their guide to the future. It is obvious that the old homilies and inviolate theories that became dogma were and are not suited to this new world order. We need forward thinking fiduciaries who understand the past but are duty bound to do the heavy lifting to move into an entirely different economic arena. Thirty five year old licensing material with no true focus towards risk has left the entire nation in a financial mess. 'Brokers' do not exist and the advisors acting in almost any capacity- and certainly as a fiduciary- must increase their grasp and understanding of real life product application. The series 7 and 24 have never provided the fundamentals of investing.

You can hear all the testimony you want about the formal inclusion of fiduciary standards. But the key is mandatory education with absolute coverage of the fundamentals of investing and insurance/annuities.

## FINANCIAL PLANNING
## FIDUCIARY STANDARDS UNDER DODD FRANK

Dodd Frank has provided an opportunity to scale up an industry far different from a marketing system with very little substance. Fiduciary duty is where the adviser has the requisite skills to provide knowledge. Maybe 35 years ago but not for the last 15- 20 years.

Fix this.

**ERROLD F. MOODY JR**

March 29, 2010

FINRA XXXX

I, Errold F. Moody Jr provide the following expert report:

This report is based on my personal knowledge and experience as well as my investigation in this matter and reflects my expert opinions on certain issues to which I may testify.

This case, as in many others I have conducted, hinges on the competency of the agents and their adherence to the law- particularly the elements of suitability and fiduciary duty as addressed to the consumer.

Conclusions:

I am stating that the firm (MF) and its representatives sold Jones various investments that were not suitable for an individual 85 years of age. The investments were not diversified, contrary to MF's statements. The overall economic conditions were as grave as at any time in decades- where securities losses were historically above 40%; the high yield investments had projected returns far above an acceptable risk, the maturity dates were decades out and inconsistent with a 85 year old- further that the redemptions and guarantees were hedged in such a fashion that to invalidate reliance and more. While risk was identified as a word, MF failed to state- at any point in time- the potential risk of LOSS that could be computed for most allocations and identify the excessive exposure taken at that period. Yet given that, it was impossible to determine the risk of loss for the new allocations (preferreds) which clearly puts the exposure far higher.

Lastly, even as MF and its representatives suggest/indicate/infer that Jones wanted and demanded such exposure, there were at least two issues negating the sale. Statistically, about 10% of those over age 65 experience Alzheimers and senile dementia, 40% by age 75 and 50% over age 85. I am not in a position to conclusively address Jones's personal state of mind, but the statistical exposure cannot be overlooked- certainly when dealing with very involved investments. There are also the extensive notes by MF agents clearly indicating a confused and irrational persona. Someone in the supervisory position of MF had to know of such inherent problems and clearly told agents of the potential concern. Further, while the elderly have more experience, it is a simple fact that age significantly reduces the ability to comprehend demanding issues, contracts and situations. No matter, the contracts for the junior preferred are far beyond almost all people of any age.

Lastly, even if Jones 'demanded' high return, high risk investments, any MF agent should have recognized that the risk was far beyond his ability (risk of loss) to accept and therefore declined to make the sale. This is a standard element taught in the Series 7 license.

In short, no matter the position of MF in disagreement with Jones, a prudent, objective broker dealing with Jones's age, conduct and ability to comprehend the risks being taken (though not identified by MF) would have either suggested low/no risk investments for effectively all his exposure or, barring that, terminated the relationship in total.

Fundamentals of Investing/Financial Counselor/Consultant/ Adviser

While pundits may feel that the following is a diatribe against the industry or a direct rebuke of MF and its agents expertise, it is merely a factual statement as to the suspect knowledge base of the financial counselors in question. Brokers via the Series 7 or Series 24 licenses have never been taught the fundamentals of investing. Diversification, asset allocation, standard deviation, correlation, risk, risk of loss and more are not addressed in the licensing preparation since they are not tested. No matter, the offering of products must be suitable per laws established decades previous.

## FINANCIAL CALCULATOR

A critical issue regarding the use of money is the use of a financial calculator. While there are software programs that do basic calculations, it is imperative that an adviser do the variations that a canned program cannot consider.

A financial calculator is not a requirement with any securities license nor is the training a part any mandatory continuing education.

## FINANCIAL CONSULTANT

The issue arises that the term "Financial Consultant" is used as a pseudonym for the MF salespeople. My writings have definitively stated once the title of a broker is 'changed' from simply saying registered representative, there clearly intends to be a statement of capability far greater than a pure salesman of product.

From Elder Investments, a Critique of Professional and Consumer Mediocrity that I was asked to author for Marquette University Law School and published by them in 2008, "Individual licensing is not providing the fundamentals of investing that would allow sound advice at the time of sale. Industry designation- supposedly portraying knowledge and competence- abound but only a couple are warranted for consideration. Most are superfluous undertakings of one to a few days of "instruction" and are almost solely geared to marketing. Since the industry is effectively bereft of the fundamental knowledge base, the consumer, therefore, is almost completely unable to understand those products and their appropriate applications.

That said, most consumers undertake little effort at a reasonable review of their financial product purchases. More often, the primary focus for the selection of an adviser is based on what a good golf game, they seemed so nice, she is so pretty, what a nice car and other perceptions that have nothing to do with financial competency. They are particularly susceptible to anything 'free' or 'food' In fact, during the past few years one of the most highly successful marketing strategies was to offer "free food" seminars offered by, universally, 'a nice young man', extolling the virtues of indexed annuities (one of the most complicated of all products). As a result, thousands upon thousands of the elderly paid out millions upon millions of dollars primarily based upon thousands upon thousands of dead chickens. Absolutely tacky. Absolutely true.

The states and the federal government subsequently came down hard on these offerings due to, among other things, a surrender period of up to 15 years. But such effort is well after the fact. The financial damage has been done- more importantly, the psychological damage has been done when they recognize they have been duped. Given such real life emotion, perhaps neither government nor professional oversight can protect the investor from unknowledgeable or unscrupulous agents, or bad products.

Critics may initially feel that this commentary is controversial or off-base considering the millions of dollars spent by the Securities Exchange Commission (SEC), Financial Industry Regulatory Authority (FINRA), North American Securities Administrators Association (NASAA), and every state insurance department in supposed guidance in making sure that investments of any type are suitable. However, it is important to stress that element - an investment must be suitable given the facts on the investor. Therefore, general review is insufficient. Additionally, millions are spent in licensing training for thousands who enter the business each year. When the current system fails, millions more are spent in arbitrations, mediations and lawsuits to address the failed suitability of investments.

If all that were so valuable and valid, how can so many investors and 401k participants make so many errors in their investing decisions? How is it possible that over a trillion dollars was lost in the Dotcom debacle if adequate and appropriate information was available to investors – due at least in part to adequate and appropriate training for the securities agents leading to clear statements of what is suitable investment and why?

(Of course, we have somewhat the same scenario with the Housing and Credit debacle just recently with similar unsupported valuations; the idea that "times are different now"; the human emotion of greed all coupled with the refusal to do objective homework.)

This author has worked with (and against) the various state, governmental and private agencies and organizations to try to protect the public and to insure knowledge of all entities at acceptable levels. For the most part, I have been unsuccessful.

All in all, this article asserts that investor problems are caused primarily by one major issue- lack of knowledge. Knowledge is woefully nonexistent at all levels. This article examines the various systemic failures to create that knowledge, and the forces and incentives to continue that failure despite its grievous impact on individuals, especially the elderly who rely on their investments for income when they no longer can work. The first section reviews the knowledge required to qualify for various levels of individual licensing.

Licensing Of Individuals to Sell and Advise

With the following education, individuals can hold licenses to advise regarding investments and other products to the public and to advise other licensed persons.

The Series 7 General Securities License

This is licensing for the broker, including most stockbrokers. The Series 7 securities license concentrated study of various elements of stocks and bonds, leading to a six-hour qualifying exam. However, it represents less than one college course on money. The course material has never covered the fundamentals of investing- alpha, beta, correlation, standard deviation, Monte Carlo- even diversification (defined later). Instruction covers what is tested, not what is needed for real life application. Continuing education was mandated in the early 1990's, but none of it demands the fundamentals either.

For example, no instruction for the use of a financial calculator is mandated. If an advisor cannot use a financial calculator, it is impossible to discuss money or how it works. Further, no formal guidelines exist for suitability to match investment and investor. Diversification of investment also is neglected. An advisor who does not understand diversification cannot understand risk, and therefore cannot understand suitability"

Series 24 General Securities Principal License

This license is for those who supervise the activities of other agents, generally Series 7 brokers. Education includes

Supervision of Investment Banking

Trading Market Supervision

Sales Supervision

Primary and Secondary Markets

Investment Companies

Supervise Customer Accounts

Most licenses in the securities industry fall in the above two categories. In each case the dominant focus for consumer protection -- a complete understanding of suitability -- is noticeable by its absence.

Insurance Sales License

All states now require a license to sell life insurance. However, the coursework can vary from mandated formal instruction in a classroom (California- 32 hours including 12 hours on ethics; Alabama 20 hours) to those that have no formal classroom instruction such as Idaho and Arizona.

There is a very valid reason why the consumer has a negative commentary regarding insurance salespeople. Forgetting the incentives of commissions to sell regardless of suitability, the background instruction is abysmal. Even California with its 32-hour life only course -- more extensive than any other state at this time – fails to demand a review of a policy illustration. There is no mandatory instruction for the use of a financial calculator, as described above.

Beyond all that is the almost exponential increase in product types- variable annuities and life insurance Equity Indexed- and every type of variation one can imagine. There are the additional problems with Stranger Owned Life Insurance, Viatical settlement, etc. The list of such uniqueness probably encompasses over 400 different types of policies and state licensing instruction covers none of these. Or at least provides none of the insight to properly evaluate. Most agents are decidedly poorly trained to advise consumers since they have no clue to the products at all. The info is whatever they might receive from the life company or an insurance agency- and that is assuredly designed to sell the product.

Yet, if one is seeking insurance, the ONLY way an individual gets information on such products is being licensed. There is no service that provides critiques about policies- there is no service that even lets you know about company offerings. The only way is to be licensed and get the material via simply having your name on a mailing and Email list the companies maintain and can buy from the state insurance departments. CPAs, attorneys- including estate planning attorneys- do not have this material. They may want it, they may very well need it. But they can't get it unless licensed. Licensing is the only way to stay current on insurance. Of course my commentary does not indicate that the recipient can understand it. But a true professional will have all the material on which to initiate a formal investigation

Certified Financial Planner (CFP) License

This is the most highly marketed designation in the United States. It covers six courses that include

Financial Planning: Process and Environment,

Fundamentals of Insurance Planning

Income Taxation

Planning for Retirement Needs

Investments and

Fundamentals of Estate Planning.

The CFP license encompasses about one semester of college work. Some students will attend a formal classroom though it is not necessary to prepare for the exam. An applicant can take the courses via self-study.

Under guidelines staring in 2007, new licensees are required to pass a 10-hour exam. As of 2008, a new licensee is also required to have a college degree. However, the degree can be in any discipline. Three years of experience are required before beginning to provide financial planning.

This designation is highly marketed and coveted for the supposed ability to do comprehensive planning for the consumer. The consumer reasonably perceives that the designee will offer sophisticated planning, but basic licensing requirements do not provide the knowledge to make that possible. When I got my license in 1984, I found that the material did provide insight into many areas that would not have been identified through any other licensing curriculum. The caveat was that the material did not make one very astute at all. I said "I don't think I know very much" and I was right.

A review of the Dalton CFP Instructional Manual for 2002 (there are several others firms) shows some major flaws. The material does not adequately demonstrate risk. Statements from a CFP "graduate" in 2004 indicated diversification was not taught. The Brinson Beebower review offers asset allocation modeling but with the wrong focus. Further, none of the models are complete or applied to actual situations. There is no material regarding the odds of loss (addressed below). In other words without a definitive study of each area and a real life application by professionals, there is nothing to suggest competent and thorough planning expertise.

Lastly a critical area of study- insurance. It is well known in the industry that this section of CFP study is inherently weak. It does not cover the material as inclusive as the licensing exam for California (the only state that I can comment on directly) nor anything close to the Life and Disability Insurance Analyst exam. (I am the only CFP that has ever taken and passed the exam- and it had effectively nothing to do with the knowledge base provided by my CFP study). I would never suggest a CFP for insurance advice. Just not very strong at all.

On the limited positive side, the instruction requires the ability to use a financial calculator. This is a minimum level of competency.

## Chartered Financial Adviser (CFA) License

This is not a financial planning designation but one focused almost solely on investments. It is a highly disciplined and intense study of investing with major focus to stocks and bonds. While the public might be well advised to use these licensees, they almost always serve institutions rather than individuals. They are not educated in financial planning. That is not a derogatory comment- just further identifying their particular focus.

## Other Financial Advisor Designations

At least another 150+ designations are offered to the public with more being added each year. (Consider, for example, the Chartered Financial Consultant (ChFC) or the Certified Public Accountant Personal Financial Specialist (CPA PFS). They may have some focus on areas that might assist a consumer but due to their limited scope and generally limited instruction on formal risk and reward, I hesitate to suggest these entities as well without some personal research on all of an individual's background and knowledge. Generally, the elements missed by the CFP instruction are missing from instruction for these designations as well- though the ChFC is heavily grounded in insurance. (These are generally those that passed the Life and Disability Insurance Analyst exam in California.)

One designation of special (negative) interest is the Certified Senior Adviser, with instruction that takes a couple days to complete. The curriculum is so highly focused on marketing that a few broker dealer firms refuse to let their agents use the 'designation' in any advertising, on business cards, etc. The idea that a couple days of 'study' makes one able to grasp what is needed to address for the elderly (actually anyone) is ludicrous. The same with the Certified Financial Retirement Advisor that required three days of training. The organization is defunct- but it did impress thousands of senior to invest millions. They did no homework on the background of the adviser. They assume the government agencies would scrutinize a designation. Has not happened until recently where too many elderly lost monies.

In comparing the licenses, it is notable that while the CFP and ChFC are limited in depth, they are far better licenses for advising individuals than a securities broker license because the curriculum reviews various activities beyond the nature and scope of investments. The least useful element for CFPs is insurance advice for the reasons described above and because since the instruction in that area is way behind the times (and has been identified by CFP officers as needing a complete update).

With regard to continuing education, the securities industry instituted requirements starting in the early 1990's. Insurance continuing education is demanded by most states but the number of hours varies tremendously. Neither license requires additional study for a financial calculator, study of risk, or understanding of policy illustrations. The competent instructor may indeed provide critical information, but that is neither mandated nor universal. Additionally, there is no requirement of diverse education. One can keep taking the same focus- generally investments- each required reporting period (30 hours every two years for CFPs) The continuing education is valid to keep advisors sharp- but it all depends on what they are taking and whether it is simply to cover the mandatory hours. Lastly, 30 hours every two years is not much.

## Formal Education As Qualification For Financial Advisors

Post-secondary academic work generally provides bodies of knowledge that imperfectly serve the needs of individuals, including seniors, seeking financial planning advice."

The critical issue here is the duty to assure the client has been competently serviced is clearly apprised of the any of the risks of the investments (and more) chosen. Where is the MF competency that MF infers?

# FAILURE OF MF AND ITS AGENTS

I am aware of the absolving commentary from MF but find several critical issues were not presented to Mr. Jones.

First are the Hartford funds Mr. Jones held before this controversy existed. I know Mr. Jones sold out these accounts but my commentary is that his risk level was chosen as 'medium". And it was supposedly selected by Jones. Just what background did Jones have to select this 'risk'?. Just exactly what does it represent? I do not know- and in fact neither does anyone else. There are no standards that have ever- to my knowledge- been taught as an industry standard at any level to anyone in the industry- and that includes CFAs. And as an absolute fact, there are no consumers that have a clue to what conservative, medium, aggressive or speculative risk means. That said, I submit that almost any risk of loss per a chosen allocation can be statistically evaluated via Morningstar stats and basic investment education. MF does state in its commentary that Morningstar material was utilized by its agents and given to Jones. As such, the standard deviation for each fund chosen (Hartford for this evaluation) was known as well as the percentage of asset as a part of the total. Therefore, one takes one minus the standard deviation over the time utilized to the power of the number of years involved. But in order to further define the number, it is necessary to know the correlation matrix of each asset and how it corresponds with each other. But such correlations are not provided. Therefore absent that, one takes an estimate around the norm. In this case, the allocation of the Hartford funds shows that with a single standard deviation movement, a client would lose from 40% to 60% of the value of their entire investment. That is how one figures out the risk of loss (Investments by Bodie, Kane and Marcus). Admittedly the future is not necessarily like the past (Peter Bernstein) but unless there is extenuating circumstances, this is how it is done.

Note that I addressed the standard deviation for the investments. But how can it be determined when the products are new and untested? Essentially they cannot. That therefore makes the use of preferred junior subordinates et al so far beyond any viable current risk analysis that they could not/should not be presented to a client- save for very unique circumstances. And certainly never to a novice. I submit that nary a one could read the 100 page prospectus and even remotely grasp what the real life implications are. I further submit that neither Financial Consultant read the prospectuses.

The question (answer?) is therefore were the risk level exposures analyzed fully identified to Jones and what Jones was clearly willing to take? MF can contend the prospectuses showed the risk- but they only showed "A: risk, not "THE" risk. And wrong. The MF comment about diversification of the preferreds was absolutely wrong

It is easily possible to do a risk of loss- though it does require a personal financial calculator. That said, the lack of statistical data on the preferred securities forces anyone to avoid a new product with extensive caveats.

Additionally, irrespective of the internal risks, one must closely follow the current economics. A 100% probable loss due to extreme risk is not prudent, rational or objective.

Economic conditions and 2006, 2007, 2008, 2009 impact

There are several links below regarding a totally faltering economy (Fannie Mae and Freddie Mac) and the statement of conditions from the International Monetary Fund.

Yet there is one statistic known by all that tells of impending recessions- the inverted yield curve.

From No Nonsense Finance II- "The easiest way to understand this issue is simply to consider what you bank does with a CD. If you get a 3 month CD, I'll say it is for 3% (I am just picking numbers to make the point clear). If you take a 1 year CD, the rate is 4%. If you are willing to commit for a longer period of time- say 10 years- the rate is 5%. Nothing out of kilter here. The longer the time frame, the greater the risk and the higher the return they need to offer to get you to invest.

But economics does not always follow a normal path. There are times when long term rates will actually be LESS than short term rates. It is not necessary to explain all the reasons since politics and economics seldom have to make sense. But suffice to say, once that happens, the economy is in almost complete disarray and must come back to 'normal'. As part of that process is the 100% guaranteed recession. There you have it. Every time the yield curve inverts, a recession has occurred. It does not state when it will happen (an average of 12 months), nor how bad it will be nor for how long it will last. But it is 100% in the overall accuracy. (See http://www.ny.frb.org/research/current_issues/ci2-7.pdf) The average losses during such a period are 40%+."

In early 2000, the curve inverted and the subsequent recession was a 44% loss in equities. In 2006, the curve inverted again. A recession was statistically 100% preordained. It is true that the future does not have to mirror the past, but no matter the caveats to a guaranteed recession, long term rates cannot be lower than short term rates. It is an economy upside down. Huge risks are evident- or should be evident- to advisers and consultants. See the commentary below to the massive real estate defaults and disruption to our financial and banking system. It is not a time to expose an investor to these investments.

As time progressed the economy went further and further south. The total drop in equities was 57%.

Was there independent validation of a significant economic problem? One of the best analyses is the International Monetary Fund and their report of April 2008, Global Economic Environment,

http://www.i.org/external/pubs/ft/weo/2008/01/pdf/exesum.pdf,

(Remember this was written in April but reflects a system already in disarray).

"The global expansion is losing speed in the face of a major financial crisis. The slowdown has been greatest in the advanced economies, particularly in the United States, where the housing market correction continues to exacerbate financial stress. Among the other advanced economies, growth in western Europe has also decelerated, although activity in Japan has been more resilient. The emerging and developing economies have so far been less affected by financial market developments and have continued to grow at a rapid pace, led by China and India, although activity is beginning to slow in some countries.

At the same time, headline inflation has increased around the world, boosted by the continuing buoyancy of food and energy prices. In the advanced economies, core inflation has edged upward in recent months despite slowing growth. In the emerging markets, headline inflation has risen more markedly, reflecting both strong demand growth and the greater weight of energy and particularly food in consumption baskets.

The financial shock that erupted in August 2007, as the U.S. subprime mortgage market was derailed by the reversal of the housing boom, has spread quickly and unpredictably to inflict extensive damage on markets and institutions at the core of the financial system. The fallout has curtailed liquidity in the interbank market, weakened capital adequacy at major banks, and prompted the repricing of risk across a broad range of instruments, as discussed in more detail in the April 2008 Global Financial Stability Report. Liquidity remains seriously impaired despite aggressive responses by major central banks, while concern about credit risks has intensified and extended far beyond the subprime mortgage sector. Equity prices have also retreated as signs of economic weakness have intensified, and equity and currency markets have remained volatile.

These financial dislocations and associated deleveraging are affecting both bank and nonbank channels of credit in the advanced economies, and evidence is gathering of a broad credit squeeze—although not yet a full-blown credit crunch. Bank lending standards in the United States and western Europe are tightening, the issuance of structured securities has been curtailed, and spreads on corporate debt have risen sharply. The impact is most severe in the United States and is contributing to a further deepening of the housing market correction. In western Europe, the main spillovers have been through banks most directly exposed to U.S. subprime securities and disruptions in interbank and structured securities markets.

The U.S. economy will tip into a mild recession in 2008 as the result of mutually reinforcing cycles in the housing and financial markets, before starting a modest recovery in 2009 as balance sheet problems in financial institutions are slowly resolved (Chapter 2). Activity in western Europe is also projected to slow to well below potential, owing to trade spillovers, financial strains, and negative housing cycles in some countries. By contrast, growth in emerging and developing economies is expected to ease modestly but remain robust in both 2008 and 2009. The slowdown reflects efforts to prevent overheating in some countries as well as trade and financial spillovers and some moderation in commodity prices.

The overall balance of risks to the short-term global growth outlook remains tilted to the downside. The I staff now sees a 25 percent chance that global growth will drop to 3 percent or less in 2008 and 2009—equivalent to a global recession. The greatest risk comes from the still-unfolding events in financial markets, particularly the potential for deep losses on structured credits related to the U.S. subprime mortgage market and other sectors to seriously impair financial system balance sheets and cause the current credit squeeze to mutate into a full-blown credit crunch. Interaction between negative financial shocks and domestic demand, particularly through the housing market, remains a concern for the United States and to a lesser degree for western Europe and other advanced economies. There is some upside potential from projections for domestic demand in the emerging economies, but these economies remain vulnerable to trade and financial spillovers. At the same time, risks related to inflationary pressures have risen, reflecting the price surge in tight commodity markets and the upward drift of core inflation.

Monetary policymakers in the advanced economies face a delicate balancing act between alleviating the downside risks to growth and guarding against a buildup in inflation. In the United States, rising downside risks to output, amid considerable uncertainty about the extent, duration, and impact of financial turbulence and the deterioration in labor market conditions, justifies the Federal Reserve's recent deep interest rate cuts and a continuing bias toward monetary easing until the economy moves to a firmer footing. In the euro area, although current inflation is uncomfortably high, prospects point to its falling back below 2 percent during 2009, in the context of an increasingly negative outlook for activity. Accordingly, the European Central Bank can afford some easing of the policy stance. In Japan, there is merit in keeping interest rates on hold, although there would be some limited scope to reduce interest rates from already-low levels if there were a substantial deterioration in growth prospects.

Beyond these immediate concerns, recent financial developments have fueled the continuing debate about the degree to which central banks should take asset prices into account in setting monetary policy. In this context, Chapter 3 looks at connections between housing cycles and monetary policy. It concludes that recent experience seems to support giving greater weight to house price movements in monetary policy decisions, especially in economies with more developed mortgage markets where "financial accelerator" effects have become more pronounced. This could be achieved within a risk-management framework for monetary policy by "leaning against the wind" when house prices move rapidly or when prices have moved out of normal valuation ranges, although it would not be feasible or desirable for monetary policy to adopt specific house price objectives. Fiscal policy can play a useful stabilizing role in advanced economies in the event of a downturn in economic activity, although it should not jeopardize efforts aimed at consolidating fiscal positions over the medium term."

In October 2008, the I noted, http://www.i.org/external/pubs/ft/weo/2008/02/pdf/exesum.pdf

The world economy is entering a major downturn in the face of the most dangerous financial shock in mature financial markets since the 1930s. Global growth is projected to slow substantially in 2008, and a modest recovery would only begin later in 2009. Inflation is high, driven by a surge in commodity prices, but is expected to moderate. The situation is exceptionally uncertain and subject to considerable downside risks. The immediate policy challenge is to stabilize financial conditions, while nursing economies through a period of slow activity and keeping inflation under control.".

In view n view of all the above, why would one enter a high risk investment scenario? Investing during a recession can work- but one is generally attempting to short the market or use some element of a unique hedging strategy. The first is not for unsophisticated investors and most everyone else as well. The second is perhaps best addressed by Long Term Capital. In such regard for investments, does this seem also logical?

Both Freddie Mac and Fannie Mae were taken over in September 2008.

## BUDGET

While this element may seem out of context here, it is one of the most important items necessary to determine IF a type of investment is warranted and the type of risk that is suitable..

From No Nonsense Finance, "Of all the issues impacting retirement, the amount of money you project to spend during retirement has a significantly greater impact on the amount of funds needed than the projected inflation rate, return on investment or anything else. Further, using a rule of thumb- say 60% to 80% of current budget- is invariably a simplistic method designed for very superficial analysis and should never be used for any long term planning. If you are off "just a bit", the amount of funds you believe you will need may not remotely match the funds you will spend during retirement. You don't want to find out at 70 years of age that you are going to run out of money in the next five years because you didn't do the number properly when you were 50. It's too late at that point to make adequate adjustments.

(For the purists, I understand that there is a lot of "compromise" and "guesstimates" with some figures and that the projections of inflation and returns in the future are also based on unknown rates. That said, if the budget- which can be determined with some exactness- has no real life element, the whole process can be wasted. Further, if the retiree/investor refuses to so the necessary homework, the analysis will tend to be valued accordingly.)"

It is stated that Jones needed extra income to pay for building. But what was actually needed? I cannot state since, without a formal budget, it is impossible to determine. Was it truly necessary to try for such high income? Only a budget can determine but against that is even if Jones did want such income, could he bear the risk of loss? The issue is suitability. No consumer can be allowed to take a risk beyond what a prudent man would believe would be reasonable.

I point again to the basic Hartford funds. Would a prudent person be willing to accept a 40% to 60% loss as defined by a medium risk? And he is utilizing a huge amount of junior preferreds with 25 year maturities, and unknown subsequent redemption market, no history at all and a truly terrible economic scenario.

## CLIENT QUESTIONNAIRE

Equally important for an analysis of Jones's situation is a formal questionnaire of Jones and his wife and family. He is 85 years of age. I know his wife is younger, but are there issues regarding her security that needs to be addressed. I know she was concerned about the finances but I cannot estimate the exposure to her as well of his/her children. The full questionnaire may not need to be completed in full, but without knowing more of the situation, it is impossible to figure out what risk might be acceptable- if any. Of course, as stated above, the budget is still mandatory.

Without these, an analysis is effectively limited if not useless. Either way, I find no way that a risk level of with a

potential/probably loss of 40% or more fits in any category of suitability or fiduciary responsibility.
http://efmoody.com/planning/questionnaire.html

## DIVERSIFICATION

"The National Association of Securities Dealers' (NASD) Rule 2310 (formerly Article III, section 2 of the Rules of Fair Practice) provides, "[i]n recommending to a customer the purchase, sale or exchange of any security, a member shall have reasonable grounds for believing that the recommendation is suitable for such customer upon the basis of facts, if any, disclosed by such customer as to his other security holdings and as to his financial situation and needs." Reasonable grounds means you- or your agent- certainly must have an understanding of the fundamentals of investing. And NYSE Rule 405 (know thy client) requires that a firm use due diligence to learn the essential facts relative to every customer and every order.

But you cannot determine suitability without totally understanding risk. And you cannot understand risk without understanding diversification by the numbers. You cannot understand risk without understanding diversification by the numbers.

The MF agents spoke of diversification. I do know their initial training via the Series 7 in this area was nil no matter the time frame. Diversification of individual securities is" how many stocks must you have in a portfolio in order to insulate it due to unsystematic risk. Or more colloquially, how many stocks must you have in a portfolio in order for it to be properly diversified.

From No Nonsense Finance II, "In the "old days" before the computer and Internet, a portfolio of 15 to 20 stock was able to mirror quite closely, the risk of the entire market. Of course, that assumes that the correlations were random- they did not do the same thing at the same time for the same reason. For example, if you picked auto, steel, glass, rubber etc., they will do the same thing at the same time. In such instances, one would need at least 100 of these stocks to reduce the unsystematic risk.

(There are caveats to this making the "old" theory highly suspect. Ron Surz, CIMA, and Mitchell Price, Roxbury Capital Management state, "we now see that a 15-stock portfolio gets 76% of available diversification versus the Fisher & Lorie 93%; this improves somewhat to 82% if tracking error is used as the diversification measure, but note that the tracking error is still a formidable 8.1% per annum. Even at 60 stocks we still have less than 90% of the available diversification whereas Fisher & Lorie would suggest virtually full diversification at this level.)

No matter, once the computer age started in the mid 90s, along with the Internet, the volatility of individual stock increased dramatically and now it takes a minimum of 50 stocks to offer the lower limit of diversification. Other analyses suggest 350 stocks- and at the level one might as well use the entire market as a guide. Considering the newer studies on risk, investors would be well advised to focus on hundreds of stocks in order to diversify away excess risk for which there is little to no benefit. It is simply illogical for consumers to buy individual stocks to properly build a portfolio. Further, they simply do not have the expertise. PERIOD."

The MF agents talk about diversification in the use of the junior preferred securities (1060). That is wrong since it is completely out of context. A portfolio can have a section of the entire portfolio that may be 'diversified' within its own section but does little or nothing as to the overall risk.

It is easiest to explain this way. A gold fund may have 50+ different gold stocks in its portfolio and it can be said that the GOLD fund is diversified. But it is only at the level of a gold risk overall which is at a high level of risk (see pyramid of investing NNF). If you have a portfolio at such a level, you have not reduced the risk overall simply by saying that the unique fund is diversified.

Asset allocation is a separate reduction of risk in that it the attempt is to use different types of investments with various correlations (see pyramid of investing NNF).

## INVESTMENT CORRELATIONS (NNF II)

Correlation refers to how one investment moves when compared to another. The point being does it move in the same amount at the same time for the same reason in the same direction. If two assets move in tandem, they have a correlation of 1.0. If they move opposite each other, the correlation is -1.0. If they have no specific relationship, the correlation is 0.0.

When involved with the development of a portfolio, correlation becomes one of, if not the most important consideration of risk since the intent is to provide offsetting movements over periods of time. It does not mean that you are looking for -1.0 since a 50/50 allocation means that any gain on one side is being offset by the other. One tends to seek positive correlations that show slightly different movements. Not only are the correlations necessary when the market is moving up, but more important when the market goes down as one investment might offset another's losses. That is the theory anyway- and not a good theory overall as we have seen recently.

Correlations Rene Stulttz, When an institution has many positions or projects, the risk of the institution depends on how the risks of the different positions or projects are related. If the correlation between the positions or projects is high, it is more likely that all the firm's activities perform poorly at the same time, which leads to a higher probability of a large loss. These correlations can be difficult to assess and they change over time, at times abruptly. A partner of LTCM described the problem they faced in August and September 1998 as being one where correlations that they thought were extremely small suddenly became large. With this perspective, correlations would have been misestimated. It is well-known in finance that correlations increase in periods of crisis. Failure to assess correlations correctly would lead to the wrong assessment of the risk of a portfolio or of a firm. The problem of mismeasurement of correlations is more subtle, however, if correlations are random and sometimes turn out to be unexpectedly large ex post. In this case, risk managers could not be expected to know what correlations will be, but their assessment of the risk of a portfolio or of the firm would depend on their estimates of the distribution of the correlations..

It might be possible to figure out the correlations between two stocks. But then again, using just two stocks defies all elements of proper diversification and the associated risk. Therefore, if one attempts a diversified portfolio of, say 30 stocks, it is necessary to not only compare the correlations against one security, but also against all the other securities and then tie them all together in the portfolio. Per Benoit Mandelbrot, "to build efficient portfolios, you need good forecasts of earnings, share prices, and volatility for thousands of stock. Otherwise garbage in, garbage out. Finally, for each stock, you must laboriously calculate its covariance with, or how it fluctuates against, every other stock. For a thirty stock portfolio, about the minimum needed to make the numbers work well, that means 495 different calculations of mean variance and covariance. For the entire NY Stock Exchange, 3.9 million calculations. And because prices change, the exercise needs constant repetition."

## FALSE BELIEF

Hence the fallacy again in the selection of individual stocks for a portfolio. A consumer attempting singular securities has no understanding of such calculations for correlations and certainly does not have the computer program capable of the calculations in any case. And it is a moot attempt anyway since they would never select the necessary number of stocks (300+) for a diversified portfolio. So now what?

The consumer needs to select mutual funds (and possible some ETFs) to build a proper portfolio. However the correlations still play the critical role in the selection process since one still looks for the offsetting positions. Such selection can include the S&P 500, emerging countries, bonds, gold, small cap, value, real estate, and many more. Just what are the percentages for each product and why? Are there valuable/valid statistics to use as a guide- and why? How do these products relate to each other when the economy changes?"

The overall risk of the portfolio was extremely high given the economy (terrible), the bulk of the assets were in high risk securities (junior preferreds), and the MF agents and the investor were clueless to risk in any case. It is true that large dividends can offset equities losses, but the preferreds were used where the financial system was clearly exposed to risks that it had not seen in generations. The very high projected returns were identified by the MF consultants as reflecting high risk.

## RISK OF LOSS

So far I have identified the lack of a budget. It is generally irrelevant what the client wants to do or has done in the past. It is mandatory to figure out what he should be doing given the scenario presented. The investor rarely can do this analysis since, 1. They do not know of the significance of a formal budget nor can use a financial calculator, 2. They do not know what assets might provide such a income or growth and 3. They are completely clueless to what the risk is in attempting such a focus. As previously indicated, a medium risk says there can be a loss. Fine- what is the statistical exposure? The prospectus says there can be a loss. Fine- what is the statistical exposure?

### Hartford

Per MF Jones 0149, there was approximately $902,000 of Hartford funds identified. The breakdown was 73% in Floating Rate Class A with a Standard deviation of 15.80; 8.7% in

Advisers Class A with a standard deviation of 16.91; 8.7% in Dividend and Growth with a standard deviation of 18.77 and 9.3% in Capital appreciation with a standard deviation of 25.10%. By using a weighted average of the deviation over the time frame selected and the risk of loss per Investments by Bodie Kane and Marcus. Using a 3 year time frame and just a single standard deviation movement (68%), an investor would have just 60% of the assets projected. Or in other words, that is a 40% loss with just a simple economic 'hiccup'. I am not addressing a pure Black Swan even like 1987- the problem with this economy was the inverted yield curve of 2006 and the effectively 100% period of extreme risk. One does not know exactly when the recession will occur, how long nor how bad, but I repeat that an exposure to 40%+ losses is not conducive to an investment nor would a prudent agent suggest exposure to such a potentially devastating situation.

## Preferred Securities

As stated, there was no diversification in the preferred securities. There was a high risk solely due to the economy.

Bancorp prospectus. I understand the incentive of the almost 8% return- effectively twice that of a CD. But at what exposure to risk? The Board must declare a dividend first and foremost. Will it? Unknown. Would not the commentary and the difficulties with bank loans per the attached commentary on Freddie Mac not give a rise to a major concern? The dividend is not cumulative. Given the economics, does the loss of such a return seem possible? The preferred is NOT redeemable till 2013 and ONLY IF at the discretion of the Board.

It is important to note on page 20 of the prospectus that "we are a holding company that conducts substantially all of our operations through our banks and other subsidiaries. As a result, the ability to make dividend payments on the preferred will depend primarily upon the receipt of the dividends and other distributions form out subsidiaries."

I repeat from the I commentary above- "The financial shock that erupted in August 2007, as the U.S. subprime mortgage market was derailed by the reversal of the housing boom, has spread quickly and unpredictably to inflict extensive damage on markets and institutions at the core of the financial system. The fallout has curtailed liquidity in the interbank market, weakened capital adequacy at major banks, and prompted the repricing of risk across a broad range of instruments...................."

In addition per page 20, "The preferred D Stock in Equity is subordinate to our Existing and Future Indebtedness".

Per page 22 is the headline (addressed above) Dividends are Non Cumulative." and "Investors should Not expect to expect Us to redeem the Series D Preferred Stock on the Date It Becomes Redeemable or on any Particular Date after It Becomes Redeemable"

Page 23- "If we are deferring payments on our outstanding Junior Subordinated debt Securities or are ion Default under the Indebtedness covering those Securities, we will be prohibited in making distributions or redeeming the Series D Stock" and

"The Series D Preferred Stock and the Related Depository Shares may not have an active trading market."

There are 92 pages of material but the highlights above should have completely halted the use of such securities. Further, I fail to see how an 85 year old man with no experience in such detail could have ferreted out essentially any of these implications.

## MF Capital

In the second paragraph of the prospectus, it is stated that, "The junior subordinated debentures due on March 2068..............

My initial reaction is the maturity is so far beyond an 85 year old that it defies logic. It is the enticement of the almost 8% return, but what can remotely justify an exposure for an 85 year old with a standard actuarial lifetime of 5.3 years?

Page 6 of 116 notes that in addition to be subordinated preferred securities where the payments and be deferred up to 20 quarters and as far as 40 quarters without being subject to default.

As to a guarantee of payments, page 10 notes that :the guarantee only guarantees payments on the capital securities if the trust has cash available".....

Per page 11, Our obligations under the junior senior subordinated debentures and the guarantee are unsecured and rank junior in right of payment to all of our existing and future senior debt. Our senior debt includes approximately $2.7 billion of existing junior subordinated debt securities issued in connection with trust preferred securities issued by our capital trusts....... In addition, MF was obligated to date under letters of credit, guarantees, foreign exchange contracts and interest rates swap contracts to which the junior subordinated debentures will be subordinated pursuant to the terms of the indentures. The indenture does not limit the amount of senior date we may issue.

The dissertation goes on for 116 pages of a very detailed contract that I can essentially guarantee no consumer has ever read. The point is that an investor looking to guaranteed high rates may only get them by luck when an extremely bad economy would exist.

FREDDIE MAC AND FANNIE MAE
Just a terrible. Consider the following:

Freddie Mac Cuts Dividend in Half
By THE ASSOCIATED PRESS

Freddie Mac cut its quarterly dividend Tuesday and announced plans to sell $6 billion in preferred stock to bolster its finances in anticipation of more losses.

November 28, 2007
Bargain Hunting on Wall Street
By MICHAEL M. GRYNBAUM

Investors leapt into the ailing stock market, snapping up discounted shares of financial companies that had been battered by shake-ups and write-downs tied to subprime mortgages.
November 24, 2007
A Bad Loan by Any Other Name
By FLOYD NORRIS

Chalk up one more term from the credit debacle. Nina loans - an abbreviation that stands for "No income, no assets."
November 23, 2007
Loan Crisis Entangles Freddie Mac
By MICHAEL M. GRYNBAUM

Losses at the big mortgage finance company on Tuesday underscored the continuing turmoil in the housing industry.
November 21, 2007
Settlement Will Cost Freddie Mac $50 Million
By THE ASSOCIATED PRESS

http://query.nytimes.com/gst/fullpage.html?res=9A01E3DE143 1F93BA1575AC0A9619C8B63
The mortgage finance company Freddie Mac will pay $50 million to settle federal charges that it fraudulently misstated earnings over a four-year period.
September 28, 2007
When Markets Are Too Big to Fail
http://query.nytimes.com/gst/fullpage.html?res=9D00E5D91E3 AF931A1575AC0A9619C8B63
What is unacceptable is that neither Ben Bernanke nor Henry Paulson Jr. has called for new rules to constrain excessive risk-taking in the financial markets.
September 22, 2007
Freddie Mac Earnings Drop 45%
By THE ASSOCIATED PRESS
www.nytimes.com/2007/08/31/business/31freddie.html
The nation's number 2 buyer and backer of home mortgages saw a 45 percent drop in second-quarter profits after setting aside $300 million to account for bad loans.

Fannie Mae 2007 Annual Report

Last year marked the start of the worst housing market in a generation. The decline and fall of housing, normally a pillar of the U.S. economy, touched off a crisis that has spread from the rows of empty homes in Las Vegas, Detroit and other American cities to the balance sheets of many of the world's largest financial institutions.

Fannie Mae is not immune to the housing market crisis.

Providing stability, liquidity and affordability amidst the housing market turmoil has not been easy, and our $2.1 billion net loss in 2007 is a reflection of that.

Three key drivers affected our 2007 results:

We increased our provision for credit losses on our guaranty book of business by $2.8 billion to $3.2 billion.

The second half of 2007 drove the credit story for Fannie Mae. As home prices tipped and fell nationwide, mortgage delinquencies and defaults rose in the final months of the year, especially in major markets in Florida, Michigan, Indiana, Ohio, California, Nevada and Arizona. These states together generated more than half of our credit losses in 2007. The deteriorating conditions in the fourth quarter led us to increase our provision significantly.

Our loss reserves as of year end were $3.4 billion, or 12 basis points of our guaranty book. For reference, in 2007 our credit losses were 5.3 basis points of the average guaranty book, and ran 2.2 basis points in 2006.

## AGE AND INFIRMITY

This commentary is not offered as a professional in the field of aging. That said, I taught the 8 hour continuing education course in Long term Care for life insurance agents (among others) for over 6 years. I accumulated a wealth of data on all areas of aging and used it in the various classes. I have several friends and relatives die of Alzheimers- including recently my mother. I have read extensively in the area and use the information when dealing with all clients of any age- certainly as it impacts the elderly. A broker/registered representative per the Series 7 would not have been taught any of this. Yet the products must be suitable for a specific client. That an exam preparation did not cover the area does not dismiss what would be required of a prudent man in offering products to the elderly in particular.

On the other hand, a financial consultant/adviser/planner, via the extended knowledge and capability, to the retail client of all ages, is clearly holding themselves out as recognizing the implications of age.

The Age of Reason: Financial Decisions over the Life-Cycle with Implications for Regulation (http://ssrn.com/abstract=973790),

Sumit Agarwal, John C. Driscoll, Xavier Gabaix, and David Laibson.

October 19, 2009

Prepared for the Brookings Papers on Economic Activity

"Many consumers make poor financial choices and older adults are particularly vulnerable to such errors. About half of the population between ages 80 and 89 either has dementia or a medical diagnosis of "cognitive impairment without dementia." We study lifecycle patterns in financial mistakes using a proprietary database that measures ten different types of credit behavior. Financial mistakes include suboptimal use of credit card balance transfer offers, misestimation of the value of one's house, and excess interest rate and fee payments. In a cross-section of prime borrowers, middle-aged adults make fewer financial mistakes than younger and older adults. We conclude that financial mistakes follow a Ushaped pattern, with the cost-minimizing performance occurring around age 53.

Adults in their early 80's are on average about 1.0 standard deviation below the adult mean. This implies a decline of one percentile per year of age (after age 20)."

This paper covers describes in detail cognitive difficulties and is not suggested for the average reader. But it does cover the implications of the problem and the other material at my site is illuminating. Beyond that is common sense.

I have read and reviewed the various notes, letters, accusations, threats et al, and there simply is 'something wrong' with Jones and an attempt to continue to try to do or sell anything but the most simple of products would apt to be a breach of fiduciary duty to such individual. I do not believe Jones, at age 85 and experiencing major outbursts of temper and more, recognized the financial exposure he was taking. Any rational intelligent person in America has read of the baby boomer scenario and is aware of at least some implications of aging. Certainly Alzheimers and dementia has been mentioned in every major magazine and newspaper and has been the subject of many TV specials and plots.

Regarding MF and its agents, they had to be cognizant of the implications of aging. The rantings and ravings of Jones as identified throughout the material I have reviewed shows a man so emotional that a prudent adviser would have had to cease sophisticated dealings with him if not for that hour or day, but in toto if such inconsistencies in behavior continued on an ongoing basis.

Yet in any case, such comment may be moot since the consultants presented high risk non diversified investments in a faltering economic scenario clearly identified in every newspaper for months and months. They know- or should have known- of the past implications of a recession.

Worse yet, they knew or should have known how to present the risk of loss for Jones' portfolio- or for anyone else. They presented words describing risk- medium- or you can incur a loss- without ever doing the simple math of the risk of loss

The Hartford funds showed a 40% exposure for one standard deviation. The preferred securities- of which there were only nine all doing effectively the same thing- had no past history on which to evaluate a standard deviation. New untested products are put in a high risk position because there is so little data overall. Add in the economic conditions where extremely high rates were being thrown out to attract and losses well above the norm might be anticipated

## Summary

For all the reasons above, the investments utilized were improper and unsuitable for Jones's age and sophistication.

The use of the preferred stocks was NOT diversified- nor therefore the entire asset allocation.

Jones's alternatives were FDIC CDs. The CD returns in 2008 averaged around 4%- depending on maturity- which should probably not extend beyond 2 years- which would exclude laddered treasuries. I would have to know the budget for a more concise estimate.

If Jones did not like these rates and demanded something higher, MF should have simply indicated that such risky investments were not suitable and that he should choose another firm

MF and its agents violated basic competency levels for risk and acting as prudent responsible agents. They sold products unsuitable for Jones.

**ERROLD F. MOODY JR.**

September 26, 2008

RE: AIG and Premium Financing

Dear Dr Smith

I have reviewed extensive material from AIG, talked to their customer service reps, Director of Advanced Planning and one of the two attorneys that deal with estate issues. I have reviewed countless illustrations as well as ordered my own.

Additionally, as is obvious, I have had extensive conversations with Marc Johnson regarding same as well as having conversations with brokers. In short, not only do I not believe that the product will produce as projected, you could never have been presented this product in the beginning.

The brochure clearly states that you have to have a minimum of $15 million in order to use this product. Per Marc, you are around $10 million. Now, I am aware of the real world of this industry and if you were $14+ million, then perhaps not a problem. But this is too much of a discrepancy. Further, an agent has a duty to the company to submit only clients who fit the profile required by the company. Any deviation to this is considered a breach of the agent's fiduciary duty. Unless there is some documentation provided by you attesting to the $15 million requirement, they have committed a fraud.

But for the purposes of this report, and assuming some legitimate excuse for the processing of the application at the higher net income, I offer the following.

First, insurance illustrations are notorious for presenting numbers that are either fictitious, too great or some combination thereof.

The illustrations I received do have ***some*** acceptable numbers, but they are categorically deceptive and there is not a legitimate advisor who would allow them to be used. Please see the attached 5 year rolling summary of the S&P 500, the Hang Seng and the Stoxx. It is not necessary that you go through the numbers to do any calculations. Here is the point. Look at the returns in the 90s. I doubt that anyone would suggest that the over exuberance of that decade made sense nor that it would be repeated again. They are using an effective 17.53% return internationally. That will not be repeated. In any case, you multiply that by 60% participation rate for the 10.52% figure used in the illustration. Admittedly the subsequent 8 years are reflective of two recessions and the returns would be lower but the reliance on the previous decade distorts returns. They are simply unsustainable going forward. Some advisors indicate that one can only look at the past for any numbers at all. But the world has changed radically starting around the mid to late 90s. From my article, *Investment Malfeasance and Breach of Fiduciary Duty*, due to the proliferation of the computer and the launch of the Internet came the "ability" to view millions of pieces of information (not necessarily knowledge)". The industry and marketplace has been forever changed by the instantaneous ability to gather up all types of information and statistically validate computations by simply selecting a unique time frame, a special formula, a unique quote from some advisor in a sophomoric 'money' magazine (which have grown almost exponentially), whatever. It is possible to support almost any contention you want by enough selected marketing. But a wholesale reliance on past history cannot match astute analysis of current economics as a guide to the future. The analysis is this: after the decade of the illogical dotcom- Warren Buffet, along with other advisors- indicated that there might be a reversion to the mean- essentially that stocks must have lower returns to return to the average of the 9.4%. average of stocks for the past 50 years as of 1984. Many state that market returns will be in single digits for some time to come.

I also offer this additional commentary from one of the preeminent advisors, Peter Bernstein:

"For institutional investors, the policy portfolio [a rigid allocation like 60% stocks, 40% bonds] had become a way of passing the buck and avoiding decisions. **The problem was that institutions had settled on a [mostly stock] asset allocation because in the long run, they concluded, that's the only place to be. And I think the long run ain't what it used to be. Stocks don't have to do well in the future because they did well in the past. In fact, the opposite may be more likely.**

**As you know, I have my doubts about the certainty so many investors feel about the long-run attractions of investing in stocks. We do not know what is going to happen over the long run, never have, never will, and when [in 1999] the institutional funds were relaxed about [holding] equities, it was a moment when equities were far away from anything resembling real value.** Ben Graham said to invest with a margin of error, so you don't get killed when you are wrong. They invested with a margin so small or nonexistent that meant they had to be right or they would get killed -- and they were.

As such, I took the 10 years from 1998 to 2007. That is 8.00% return- but one must recognize that the number represents a 60% participation rate (you take the returns of two indexes at a 75/25 split and then multiply that number by 60%).

By dividing the 8% by 0.6, that is really an expected 13.33% overall return.

No. That is unacceptable. Still too high.

Considering that the last 8 years have been tumultuous (at best) has merely reinforced the general consensus for even lower returns going forward. Further, with the impact of oil on every day prices, the resurgence of inflation, and a potential bailout up to $1 trillion, it would appear difficult to use returns even at 13% overall still considering the use of international stocks. They too will bear the brunt of increasing oil prices; second tier countries are experiencing increasing inflation and the credit mess caused by the United States will impact them even longer than the U.S. I believe that a 10% return is adequate. If you therefore use the 60% participation rate, that leaves an overall 6% return for the index.

Nonetheless, I did request and review the 8% illustration. In this case, the value is $134,000,000 by age 100. But with a 13.33% true return internationally. However, as noted above, I don't think you will get it. And they 'want' $640,000 for ten years to do it (the implications of that number is addressed under estate planning below).

Marc also requested a 6% return. They provided a 6.35% midterm return and that was acceptable. The illustration shows it will last for 50 years- age 100- and should cover 99% of a real life lifetime. But while the death benefit would be $28,000,000, your loan would be about $25,000,000, so you have gained essentially nothing for coverage.

It also still costs $6,400,000. Admittedly you did not have to pay it yourself- but you didn't get anything in return anyway. And if you wanted/needed insurance within a trust, no company is going to give you more than the $11,500,000 already in your name.

Probably a participation rate of around 6.75% would allow you to have your full $11,500,000 insurance and still be able to pay off the loan. That is an overall 11.1% return. That might be possible but still beyond what professional advisors expect.

Can you use bonds in the AIG portfolio and eliminate part of this volatility? Yes- but the returns- as with stocks- are not guaranteed and, generally, are less than equities. Therefore, you will not have enough return at any point in order to pay off the loan

## Non Financed Insurance

In order to have a better idea of premium financing, one first looks at what a basic policy would cost. I asked for two AIG illustrations directly. One was for a 6.75% return for a 7 pay. It showed that if you paid $140,000 annually yourself for 7 years, the policy would last till age 82. That was not acceptable. So I asked for another—and another. The illustrations received were not what I requested and at this point I am not sure if I can get what I want. But by extrapolating the various illustrations, it appears that a payment by you of $175,000 for 7 years would provide coverage to age 100. Admittedly you are paying for it directly- there is no loan. (The only request at this point was with AIG. There are other companies that will have lower premiums costs and more guarantees but that is a separate study.) The comparison to premium financing and the risk is detailed below.

## Premium Loan

It has been presented to Marc that this is a guaranteed loan for your lifetime. It is not. These are annual callable loans- it is at the whim of Exavier if they wish to continue. The rational for a 'lifetime' loan is that they would call the loan due and payable 'only' if the returns in the policy are *insufficient* to cover the loan. The problem is the contract does not state that. Therefore the loan can be called at any point and if the cash value of the policy is insufficient to pay the loan (almost a certainty) then you will have to use any collateral you put up for security. Once again the rationale is that it is 'obvious' that they would never do such a thing. By the same token, it was obvious that the mortgage mess could never occur, that WaMu and many other banks would not default, Merrill Lynch would never be sold and that a bailout of close to $1 trillion by the U.S. was impossible.

Creditors are calling whatever loans possible because they are uncomfortable about foreclosures, bankruptcies and more. Could it happen to Exavier? Why not? As such you need to recognize a difficult financial scenario the loan is called and you have to use other collateral.

Of course the situation with Exavier may be more like this. They will review your policy each and every year to determine if the underlying returns cover their position. If they were to find that the returns were not sufficient, they will call the loan only then. You will have to cancel the policy and use whatever cash there is to offset the loan demand plus pother collateral as necessary.

The problem is that many years could pass before this happened (if at all, obviously). But if your health conditions had changed (and they assuredly will), then you may not be able to get another policy. Certainly it will cost more due to your age. You would have therefore accomplished nothing in terms of coverage and then actually diminished any chances of reducing any estate taxes.

And I will repeat- if the terms of a call are not listed in the contract, then any oral commentary is effectively useless and non binding.

## Loan interest

The loan interest is based on a very familiar LIBOR (London Interbank Offering Rate) plus 95 basis points (0.95%). They use a 6.14% charge based upon, one again, past history. I do not like this method and feel that one must allocate some risk element to looking out that far. I did use 6.25% in my loan calculations- though I still am uncomfortable being that low. (My past work has required estimations for inflation and I used 3.25% and 5% for years. You now note that inflation is 5.25% and growing. Even viable alternatives can have difficulties). Here is the point. The LIBOR short term rates was under 3% two days ago- then it shot up to 6.9% because of this credit mess. I admit the annual rate did not increase substantially, but it hopefully is clear that you have to add in some adjustments for what can go wrong. I am not sure that 7% is the 'magic number', but one MUST address risk and that past history is not necessarily any reflection to the future. If the economy straightens out and overall market volatility subsides, maybe you can make a lot of money in the trust. That is essentially how it has been explained to you. However, I think risk has gone up, volatility has gone up, and the world is not the same place as before. The Dotcom craze will not happen again for decades and real estate will suffer the same consequences. Future returns will be lower. So, the LIBOR rate could be higher than projected in the illustrations and make the scenario even more precarious.

## Gift Taxes

Here is another conundrum that has not been addressed. This policy is to go into an ILIT (Irrevocable Life Insurance Trust). You will be gifting monies to the trust since it is a loan. However you will only need to treat the **loan fee** as a gift and file a gift tax return. That, by itself, is not a big deal. But the whole premium package is a big deal in terms of the odds of working over the next 50 years.

I believe that you have about a 15% chance of getting an effective 17%+ return as identified for the 10.52% (60% participation) as shown in all your illustrations.

About another 15% probability of perhaps having about $11,500,000 in net life insurance in 50 years due to the lower returns and the requirement to pay off the loan.

So there is a 70% chance that it will not work as intended because returns will be less than 10.52% and interest rates will be higher. Therefore if the loan is called due to underperformance, what are the financial implications to you?

Assume 15 years from now and the loan is $15,000,000. Your cash value is $10,000,000 (all hypothetical). They call the loan. You will have to come up with the extra $5,000,000 from your collateral. But, according to AIG's attorney, the entire $15,000,000 will be treated as a gift. Here is what will occur. About 10,000,000 of that (estimated) will be subject to gift tax at 50%. So you will have to pay another $5,000,000 in tax to the IRS. Your total costs to pay off a $15,000,000 loan could be $20,000,000.

That is not an issue with the high projected returns since they can conceal any of the negative possibilities that might occur. But it is not real life. By the same token I am not saying the above would happen. Just that it could- and you should have been told that.

## Summary

Premium financing can work. Yours might.

But as I told Marc initially, whenever you have so many moving parts, if one goes wrong, the whole scenario can collapse. I think that their projected returns are far overstated for the future and the interest on the loan should be higher to account for a level of economic risk which has escalated substantially since 1999.

The GBFG group has a duty to explain the risks. They have not. I think it doubtful they could. Even if you wished to still consider premium financing, I would suggest you engage another firm who would provide a complete analysis of what the risks truly are. But this is also assuming that you can buy the product at all under the minimum guidelines.

All my work addresses risk first and foremost. This report is no different. I believe the approach looking forward is absolutely appropriate. The past can be a guideline and needs to be considered. But a wholesale reliance on such dismisses where the world currently is and potentially could or will go.

The risk scenarios identified above are appropriate for the amount invested, the manner of the indexing, the loan, your age and the anticipated needs.

In short, premium financing can work but the odds in this perceived economic environment is not very convincing. If I am right, the financial repercussions will be dire. No matter, look elsewhere for the necessary duty to provide the appropriate disclosures. You are being provided illustrations for a sale only.

**ERROLD F. MOODY**

May 3, 2010

Mr. Frank Smith

RE: National Farm Insurance Company and agent Mike James

Dear Mr. Smith,

Pursuant to your request and authorization, I have conducted a report on the activity and competency of agent Mike James (James) and National Farm regarding the policies sold to Frank Smith (Smith).

In short, Mr. James sold policies that were far in excess of need or not needed at all. There was an almost complete lack of assuring the correct placement of Smith's policies and the policies for his children and wife were wrong. Additionally and most specifically, he committed direct fraud by perpetrating forgery on all but the initial life application. That is five policies in total.

## Errold Moody background

A resume is attached but there are a few items that need elaboration, specifically as they address the insurance elements of this report. I have been a practicing financial planner for almost three decades and have held an insurance license since 1983. I have taught most courses in planning for the likes of the University of California at Irvine and Berkeley. I have a Masters in Financial Planning and have taught insurance continuing education for over 10 years. In 1998, I became one of about 30 Life and Disability Insurance Analysts in California. I have unilaterally pursued unethical and incompetent agents who have sold products primarily for the commissions.

I act as an expert witness on a variety of complicated economic and financial matters and have presented testimony in court and arbitrations.

## Overview

Frank Smith

Mr. Smith was born in the Honduras and his native language is Spanish. He worked as a laborer when younger but received an auto accident insurance claim in 1987 and started a business selling................ systems in Los Angeles. His formal education is limited with just a high school diploma. By his own admission, he is neither good with math or paperwork- it is simply his hard work and a lot of long hours that had made him successful in his trade. That said, he has made some glaring investment errors when trusting advisers and agents far too much. It tends to lead to poor investing habits and a reliance on individuals that is unjustified. But that is simply how the general public does business with investments and insurance and therefore must be addressed in that context. It is real life. Insurance, in particular, is a very difficult product to understand- save for most term policies- and an agent's and company's duty is to use reasonable competency to assure the products will work as intended.

Mr. Smith did recognize the need for insurance and had been referred to James/National Farm many years prior for his business insurance. In 1992, at age 32, married with four children, he contacted James/National Farm and requested $1,500,000 of life insurance. He was never asked about his net worth or annual income. His estate at that time was about $500,000. There is a problem right there. James/National Farm had to have known initially or by asking at that point if Smith had done any estate planning since the $2,000,000 total estate (including the $1,500,000 life proceeds) was going to be included potentially at his death or at the second to die. Even given the 1994 estate exemption of $600,000 ($192,800 tax), close to about $700,000 would still have gone to taxes. James/National Farm had a duty to Smith to inquire about any estate planning that he had done even as simple as a will- to validate the proper use of the policy. Smith was wasting money in the purchase of a product that would lose 50% at some point- and absolutely if both he and his wife died simultaneously. I am not suggesting that James/National Farm had to do the planning- that would have been referred to others. But anyone who has been licensed since 1979 and had taken hundreds of hours of continuing education over time and certainly by 1994- was fully aware of the implications of estate tax. If nothing else, National Farm would have certainly addressed the issue in material sent to its agents as education. There simply is no excuse for the sale of a policy that was far in excess of need and, in any case, was far less than what Smith anticipated due to a tax that he did not understand since he had not, nor could he, do any of the computations regarding said tax. He trusted James/National Farm to do the best for him. Admittedly the issue is trust once again. But the reality is that people have to trust an insurance agent since few consumers have a clue how to read and properly analyze a life or annuity contract. The suitability of a product has to include the requirement that the agent and company are competent to do the best for the client.

The problem was actually known by James/National Farm when the agent stated that Smith would actually lose too much of the policy due to taxes and thereafter sold a second to die policy for an additional $1,000,000 to supposedly cover the taxes due to the excess exposure of the first policy. But since neither policy was in a ILIT (Irrevocable Life Insurance Trust), it too would be included in the estate of the second to die for even more tax roughly 50%- for another loss to taxes of $500,000.. This compounded the scenario with extra costs for unnecessary policies where the James/National Farm actually took over the planning of Smith's estate.

It ends up that there is a $3,000,000 estate in 1994 impacted by about a 50% estate tax that was going to net Smith and/or his family far, far less that what he assumed- potentially $1,200,000 LESS. Needlessly. Since James/National Farm were aware of this fiasco, they had a duty to inform Smith that he should seek estate counsel before purchasing the policies. Admittedly it does cost money to implement and the annual gift strategies do require careful scrutiny, but had the estate been set up properly, with an ILIT, the exposure to tax would have been nil. This is a fact of the three year rule. If Smith purchased the policies, it would take three years after transfer into an ILIT in order to avoid the significant taxes if he died during that period.. Had the trust already been completed, no three year rule need apply. None of this information is new, so unique or difficult to address to a client. It is basic criteria established for the proper implementation and use of life insurance. However, it is within that context that there is a problem with the use of such a policy for estate purposes while at the same time looking for the internal retirement funds- as indicated by Smith. In the most simplistic terms, the ILIT is not to be touched by the grantor/Smith. If so, the proceeds of the policy can be included in his estate due to an incident of ownership. So the question then becomes, what was this policy intended to do? Was it for an estate? It appears to be the initial case. But James/National Farm made a presentation for universal life that accrued cash. So was it now a retirement vehicle that had to be kept out of an ILIT but that would lose 50% of its value when he died? These are two distinct- yet counterproductive- purposes that could not be obtained without one losing its value over the other.

## Children policies:

Smith purchased four $200,000 universal life policies on each of his children. The position in the life business is that one only needs insurance if one is financially dependent on another. That is relatively simplistic but a real life rule of thumb for the vast bulk of situations. Obviously one can buy insurance simply to reward others at death, etc. and there are business purposes (which are excluded here). As for children, it is acceptable to cover children for the contingencies of the expenses at death where the parents can effectively get reimbursed for funeral and associated costs. It can also be a method of insuring very young children in the event that they become uninsurable later on. Yet I see nothing to support either of these issues. In fact, it appears that James/National Farm simply asked if he wanted to insure his kids.. Smith said yes probably because he thought it was the correct thing to do. I am not stating that the purchase is categorically wrong- simply wondering on the reason and questioning the use of a universal policy in this case. Term insurance is generally more accepted in formal planning since coverage for the children would only be till they turned 18 or through college. Lastly, the amount of coverage was determined by what he could afford- hence the $200,000.

## Wife, Betty

Betty is covered with a 10 year level term insurance for $2,550,000 and annual premiums of $2,875 commencing in 2005. She started working to pick up the slack due to the reduction of Smith's income. She was 43 years of age at that point so coverage would only go to 53 without a huge increase in costs thereafter.. It appears that that is all he could afford at that time but the focus is backwards. The children essentially did not need insurance while that for Betty was mandatory since she was a part breadwinner. She continues to work and expects to do so until formal retirement. If the intent was to truly cover Betty for her income, the kids coverage should have been reduced. Or as an alternative, Betty should have gotten 20 or 30 year level term. As it is, the ability to get reasonable coverage for her at the expiration of the 10 years is debatable. She will be at a higher attained age and her health might be bad. A 10 year level term is poor and inadequate insurance planning by James/National Farm.

Additionally, if she should die in the time frame and Smith was alive, irrespective of his insurance, there is still the exposure to estate tax. And should they both die together, there is his $1,500,000, her $2,550,000 and the second to die of

$1,000,000 for a total of approximately $5,000,000 just for the insurance, not including any assets at all. Or approximately $2,500,000 of unnecessary taxes to be paid. That is not responsible insurance planning.

## 1994 forward

First forgery and the wrong forgery
On July 24, 1997, the policy was changed by $25,000 addition to the Universal Life policy. But there seems to be no reason why it was done except unilaterally by James/National Farm. While that is a concern, the greater issue is that Smith signature was forged on the document. Smith never received the document nor has any idea what the adjustment was for. But that is to be expected in that James/National Farm committed forgery.

## Adjusted Premium

Smith left the U.S. in 1998 for a business enterprise in Mexico selling textiles. He invested everything in this venture and lost it all. He returned to the U.S. and contacted James to reduce his insurance premiums since his income and assets had dropped so much. Smith asked that he did not want either the cash value or the death benefit to be reduced. James/National Farm indicated that they could reduce the premium from $10,686 to $3,540 annually. It is interesting to note that that is a 67% drop in premium and, to an insurance professional, reflects a price reduction at the extreme level that could also retain the current cash value while maintaining the $1,500,000 face amount. I do not believe an illustration was ordered by the agent since a formal in force illustration would have identified the that the policy would lapse in relatively short order at such a low premium.

The reduction in premium did take place but Smith was unaware of the implications. An illustration was never sent to Smith. It is true that National Farm did send annual statements but Smith has stated that he had about 25 other National Farm and he could not understand all the policies nor had he the time. No matter the comments from pundits, the bulk of the business in the life insurance industry is done by referrals and subsequent trust of the agent and company. Insurance contracts demand the competency of the agent and the company to assure proper coverage.

James/National Farm cannot put the onus on a Honduran immigrant with language difficulties who held menial jobs all his life to do the proper planning of his life, health and business coverage. I understand the significance of the need to read statements. But Smith neither had the legal skills nor the intellectual wherewithal to grasp the significance of the material sent. That Smith looked to James/National Farm exclusively to guide him (trust) may be considered a fault, it is absolutely real life and an element that the industry conveys as the key focus in the sale of such products.

In 2003, Smith thought he needed more insurance coverage for his family and suggested another $2,000,000. He still did not even have a will and the added coverage was going to be cut by at least 50% at his death, his wife's death if it was simply transferred by a marital transfer or if both died at the same time. James/National Farm had an obligation to tell Smith that this type of coverage was not going to serve the double purpose of providing a net estate as well as providing retirement assets. That was even a larger issue since Smith wanted the minimum payments that would not impact his death benefit or cash value. There was no illustration sent to Smith. An in the previous example, an illustration was mandatory to assure continuation of the policy.

And any of these illustrations should have addressed the fallacy of taking out cash for retirement. The cash would be needed simply to keep the policy in force longer.

In 2005, Smith once again thought he needed more insurance- $5,000,000 in total- still not recognizing the issues addressed above. No will, no trust, no ILIT and a very probable reduction of his estate by $2,500,000 for estate tax just for the insurance itself. Illogical in the extreme. He indicated that he wanted the premium stay as low as possible without impacting his cash value yet guaranteeing the coverage. The premium was $1,170 monthly or $14,400 annually. He received no illustration for this change- in any case, he was relying on James/National Farm to inform him of just what his options would be.

Admittedly in 2007, James indicated the premiums needed to be raised. Smith paid $1,470 monthly or an annual premium of $17,640 annually. For $5,000,000 in supposed benefit- That is simply not enough to sustain a policy of this size save for a huge existing cash value. However, Smith trusted his James/National Farm to guide him through the morass of these policies.

## More forgery

And finally we have the most important issue of more forgery. As addressed above, the 1997 forgery was even for the wrong person.

Then there is the $75,000 increase on 3/29/00 which has a forged Smith signature

A $100,000 increase on 5/28/02 with Smith's forged signature

An application on 5/29/03 which has Smith's forged signature. What is interesting is that the application was declined in writing the following day. How was that possible?

An application for an increase of $2,000,000. On 10/25/03 which has NO signature.

An illustration receipt on 10/25/03 for the above policy which has Smith's forged signature

An additional increase of $1.3,000,000 of insurance on 2/22/05 with Smith's forged signature.

### Summary

James/National Farm sold Smith policies that they knew would not work to pass assets to beneficiaries effectively. James/National Farm actually accepted the roll of planning his estate when they suggested the addition of a second to die policy of $1,000,000 to offset the taxes on the first policy. Yet never asked whether he even had a will. Certainly James/National Farm knew of the basics of an Irrevocable Life Insurance Trust and had a duty to be sure he contacted the appropriate experts to formulate a correct estate plan- not try to cover up taxes with even more sales of products and more taxes I question the coverage for the children both of the amount and type while Betty was left with insufficient coverage.

Lastly is the forgery of numerous documents, lack of signature or even the wrong person. This is indicative of an agent and company that is not only violating the rights of the client but also in violation of National and U.S. laws.

James and National Farm must change individual and corporate policies to terminate immediately such practices. And they will need to readdress all of Smith's policies to reflect professional standards.

December 26, 2011

Hilda L. Solis

U.S. Department of Labor
200 Constitution Ave., NW
Washington, DC 20210

RE: The 99% and Financial Planning Fiduciary Standards under Dodd Frank

Dear Ms. Solis,

As you are essentially responsible for the oversight of ERISA, I believe you will find the insight of my recent book the essence to redirect adviser responsibility to consumers.(This text is the hard copy complement to two video courses approved by the State Bar of California for Continuing Legal Education

Fiduciary Standards Dodd Frank: Investments

Fiduciary Standards Dodd Frank: Insurance and Annuities)

ERISA, as does Dodd Frank, reflects the necessity for fiduciary duty. Unfortunately, non of the simplistic demands/requests/laws will make it work. The debacles of 2000 and 2008 reflect a nil understanding of risk and left hundreds of thousands of retirees/pre retirees in a financial morass for which they will never recover. And given the current and projected economics, the simplistic positions of buy and hold, rebalancing et al will cause the same thing to happen to younger employees over and over again. The DOL may not cover all 99% of consumers, but it's failing grade with 401k employees and more does the same thing.

Per the DOL:

..... while a fiduciary may have relief from liability for the specific investment allocations made by participants or automatic investments, ***the fiduciary retains the responsibility for selecting and monitoring the investment alternatives*** that are made available under the plan.

Is it a valid assumption to say a 'fiduciary', in name only, has a clue to selecting and monitoring?

No.

Please see my chapter on Illiteracy and Aliteracy. As well as "How do Financial Literacy and Financial Behavior Vary by State?" at http://www.usfinancialcapability.org/download/FinLit_By_State_EBRI.pdf. A sample question for anyone from the financial literacy 'quiz' is "Buying a single company's stock usually provides a safer return than a stock mutual fund." All states failed the question. And while a 'fiduciary' can answer that question, the essence is irrelevant to the real world of diversification

The question and answer says nothing a to how many stocks are needed to have the same risk as the market (see diversification chapter). Fiduciaries are not taught this so where are they helping the employee (99%)? Failing the question and then failing the American public in teaching the reality of risk is a breach of fiduciary duty- right to the core of responsibility by the DOL. Diversification has never been taught to brokers. Nor is it even in the mandatory curriculum for CFPs. It must be presented to employees. And yet the rules say that a fiduciary has relief from liability made by participants. A fiduciary KNOWS that the public is so bereft of an understanding of the fundamentals of investing as to make massive errors in judgement. Don't they? A fiduciary must know diversification in order to have any claim to acting as a fiduciary. But they do not.

If you do not know diversification, you cannot get to risk. If you cannot get to risk, you cannot get to suitability. You sure have failed any type of fiduciary responsibility.

Look at this question- "If interest rates rise, what will typically happen to bond prices?" All states came in at 37% correct or less. A basic bond question that MUST be understood by any and ALL 401k employees. They are obviously clueless. But a named 'fiduciary' can escape liability since they are effectively removed from the participants selection. Totally absurd- unless, I suppose, the definition of a fiduciary is the word only that does not have to be backed up by reality. But the reality is that financial advisers, including RIAs who essentially use the Series 7 license to validate becoming a fee adviser, are not taught the fundamentals of investing nor, more importantly, the real life implications. No wonder the financial system for the 99% failed so miserably. The fiduciaries used for training were- and are- inept.

A fiduciary can also hire a service provider or providers to handle fiduciary functions, setting up the agreement so that the person or entity then assumes liability for those functions selected. If an employer appoints an investment manager that is a bank, insurance company, or registered investment adviser, ***the employer is responsible for the selection of the manager,*** but is not liable for the individual investment decisions of that manager. However, an employer is required to monitor the manager periodically to assure that it is ***handling the plan's investments*** prudently and in accordance with the appointment.

First of all, how does an employer select a manager. An employer has no criteria or which to base a valid decision. Is it solely returns? What about risk? Well it cannot be since risk is not taught to the industry. Is it MPT- well past its prime. Use of correlation? Standard Deviation? Just what? Is the handling of the investments merely providing quarterly statements? I am clueless in that if risk is not taught to employees there has to be improper handling. Yet never heard a word on this after 2000 or 2008. Why not? Every allocation has a numerical risk of loss that identifies just how bad things can get. But only returns are ever shown. Not simply illogical- a failure of those in knowledge and education.

Information about the quality of the firm's services: the identity, experience, and ***qualifications of professionals*** who will be handling the plan's account; any recent litigation or enforcement action that has been taken against the firm; and the firm's experience or performance record; A description of business practices: how plan assets will be invested if the firm will manage plan investments or how participant investment directions will be handled; the proposed fee structure; and whether the firm has fiduciary liability insurance

ERISA, the DOL, SEC et all talk about professionals as indicated above. And just what does that mean in real life? The term "professional" is essentially a moniker for those with extremely limited background in the financial area. Certainly there are a few, but the bulk of RIA advisers/professionals come from the securities side of investing where the bulk of the knowledge base is a ***one week*** course of the series 7 where the fundamentals of investing are not taught. There is no insight to asset allocation. There cannot be since there is nothing on correlation. Or the inverted yield curve, There is no mandatory continuing education for RIAs. And while the comments address litigation etc., where is the knowledge to really address performance record? Would it not be true that the losses sustained in 2000 and 2008 by, in particular, 401k employees was a major fault of the professional? Sure is. Pundits may say that there is no way a 'professional' was at fault- they did do their job(?) by their instruction of asset allocation.

No they did not. They had a duty to address risk. They had a mandatory obligation to state the exposure of employee allocations and what they would do- if anything- in limiting the losses due to a severe downturn. After all, the recessions WERE known beforehand (see inverted yield curve and year to year real GDP%). It was also known that the correlations would all move together when such occurred and that all equity positions would lose an average of 40%+. But if that is not taught- and it is not due to the sophomoric licensing and testing requirements- then you can have trillions of dollars lost and the professionals can simply say it was an ***aberration***.

Wrong. It is a statistical probability. Further, there is a 85%+ probability that we will have one recession over the next decade which will produce another 40% equity loss. And a 50% chance of two recessions.

The fault of such trivialization lays at the feet of the SEC and its continuing refusal to instruct. But it also lays at the DOL, NASAA, State regulators, and more with their inept staff that has- and remains- clueless to the real world of risk. It is also clear that the UPIA needs a revision to the real world as well- as I have identified as a chapter.

Obviously I do understand the need for long term investing. But the failure of current instruction is that they do not tell the employee they will lose about 50% of their investment once or twice a decade. This is a new world order where massive losses have been and will continue to be sustained. It is true that employees and the 99% will do the wrong thing at the wrong time- changing investments at the very lowest prices. But why are all the 'professionals' not even bothering to instruct them as to what to do and when?

Nothing will change without an absolute change in 'professional' competence which is not possible with the current legalese that refuses to address what background is mandatory before one can offer fiduciary services.

I am fully aware that my book treads on a lot of egos in a lot of departments in a lot of states in a lot of ......

But there comes a time when the regulatory entities have to stand up and formally recognize that what worked(?) in the past simply existed as long as one kicked the can long enough. When it could go no further, real life took over. Sure there was a breakdown by banks and other corporate entities. Maybe that will get better- at least the FED is trying.

But the 99% and all employees will continue to be victimized by an industry and regulatory entities that have, at least so far, addressed fiduciary only as a word.

Hopefully, you will find the validity of my statements in the book and a recognition that a wholesale revision of industry knowledge and competency is needed ***NOW***.

**Curriculum Vitae**

**Errold F. Moody Jr**

510 459 7797

Summary of Qualifications

Over 37 years of hands-on experience as a financial and real estate consultant to title companies, corporations, CPA's, attorneys, partnerships, credit unions, non-profit organizations and individuals. The major focus for the last 30 years has been in individual fee financial planning. Expertise has covered investment analysis and monitoring, estate and pension planning, living trusts, charitable gifting, sales and management (stocks, bonds, partnerships, insurance, REIT's and mutual funds), retirement planning, life and disability insurance review, security arbitrations, taxation and national and international economic analysis. Acted as NASD/PSE arbitrator. Offer expert testimony on brokerage and financial issues. Have written and taught extensively in the field since 1977.

## DEGREES, LICENSES AND DESIGNATIONS

BSCE, LLB, MBA, PhD (Real Estate)

Masters of Science in Financial Planning (Estate Planning Major)

Life and Disability Insurance Analyst 0626414 (One of about 30 in California)

Certified Financial Planner 1984- 2010

Registered Investment Adviser (California)

California Real Estate Broker

California B-1 General Contractor

Series 7, 24, 27 and 63 Securities Licenses- inactivated

Series 65 Securities License (Multi State Adviser)

California Life and Disability License 0626414

## ARTICLES and PUBLICATIONS

Author Financial Planning Fiduciary Standards under Dodd Frank 2011

Author No Nonsense Finance, McGraw Hill 2004, 2009

Author of ELDER INVESTMENTS: A Critique of Professional and Consumer Mediocrity, Marquette University Law School, 2009

Authored the only courses on investments accepted for continuing education by the State Bar of California (1995 and 2008)

*"Practical Investment Theory and Application"*

Author of "Practical Life Insurance and Annuities Analysis and Application"- the only course on life insurance and annuities ever approved for continuing education by the California State Bar (2009)

Authored two courses accepted for 4 and 16 hours of continuing education for Certified Public Accountants by the California Board of Accountancy. Previous course accepted for CPA credit in 10 states.

*"Advanced Business Continuation and Estate Planning"* *"Advanced Financial Planning and Investing"*

Authored two real estate courses granting 9 and 21 hours of continuing education by the California Department of Real Estate. Material was used in courses at several colleges including UC Irvine as part of Certificate program.

*"Current Concepts of Real Estate and Investing"*

*"Major Concepts of Real Estate and Investing"*

Authored courses accepted for securities continuing education in financial planning, estate planning, taxation and tax planning, investments and suitability, ethics, retirement planning and insurance and annuities. (1996) Authored additional courses in Long Term Health Care, College Funding, Business Continuation, Investments, Trustee Selection and Charitable Gifting.

Authored "Arbitrators Guide to Securities" for the Center for Investor Protection

Above material was compiled and offered as text for UC Certificate course in Survey in Financial Planning.

Author a monthly investment and financial planning newsletter- Moody's Review- 1987- 2010. Author the largest (5,000+ pages and 1,650+ links) and most comprehensive financial planning site on the Internet (www.efmoody.com) designed for consumer education and knowledge. The Web site is noted as a Top Retirement Site by Forbes, Business Week, USA Today, MoneySmartz and many more. Has also been linked by Ernst and Young for Financial Planning, Department of Aging for Long Term Care and other sites around the Internet for Real Estate, Retirement, Investments, Long Term Care, Estate Planning, etc. and was selected by AOL and Netscape as one of their top sites for stocks and financial planning advice, among others.

Have been published/quoted in numerous business magazines (San Francisco Chronicle, California Broker, Investment Adviser, Smart Money, Wall Street Journal, New York Times, Money Magazine, National Underwriter, Consumer Reports, Mutual Funds Magazine, Life Insurance Selling, Parenting Magazine, Realtor Digest, Corporate Finance, Numerous national newspapers, Registered Investment Adviser, Ticker magazine, Orange County Register, etc.) and have been interviewed frequently on local and national radio and TV.

## PROFESSIONAL EXPERIENCE/AFFILIATIONS

1981-1997: Dearborn Financial Institute & Securities Training Corporation. Instructor for the Series 6 (mutual funds, variable life and annuities); Series 7 exam (stocks, bonds, options, economics, security regulations); Series 22 (limited partnerships, personal and corporate taxation); Series 24 (General Securities Principal); Series 26 (Mutual Fund Principal); Series 63 (multi state license); Series 52 (Municipal Securities); Series 62 (Corporate securities) and insurance, special education programs and securities continuing education courses.

1977- 1999: Professor/instructor for University of California at Berkeley and Irvine, University of San Francisco, Orange Coast, Santa Ana, Coastline and Scottsdale Community Colleges. Includes MBA course in Real Estate Finance, courses for the UC certificate programs "Professional Designation in Financial Planning" and "Professional Designation in Investment Real Estate" and specialized seminars.

1987- 1998: Arbitrator with the National Association of Securities Dealers and Pacific Stock Exchange1995- 2004: A.D. Banker, Instructor in Insurance for continuing education courses in Estate Planning, Managed Health Care, Annuities, Long Term Care, Qualified Retirement Plans, Government Programs and Medicare Supplements, Disability Income, Ethics, Principles of Contract Law, Principles of Agency Law, Taxation of Life Insurance and Annuities, and Financial Products for Financial Planning.

**INDEX**

INDEX

www.ingramcontent.com/pod-product-compliance
Lightning Source LLC
LaVergne TN
LVHW052214200926
848481LV00001B/106